Recasting Race
AFTER WORLD WAR II

Recasting Race

AFTER WORLD WAR II

Germans and African Americans in American-Occupied Germany

Timothy L. Schroer

University Press of Colorado

© 2007 by the University Press of Colorado

Published by the University Press of Colorado
5589 Arapahoe Avenue, Suite 206C
Boulder, Colorado 80303

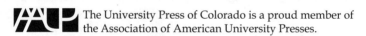 The University Press of Colorado is a proud member of
the Association of American University Presses.

The University Press of Colorado is a cooperative publishing enterprise supported,
in part, by Adams State College, Colorado State University, Fort Lewis College,
Mesa State College, Metropolitan State College of Denver, University of Colorado,
University of Northern Colorado, and Western State College of Colorado.

∞ The paper used in this publication meets the minimum requirements of the
American National Standard for Information Sciences—Permanence of Paper for
Printed Library Materials. ANSI Z39.48-1992

Library of Congress Cataloging-in-Publication Data

Schroer, Timothy L., 1966–
  Recasting race after World War II : Germans and African Americans in American-
occupied Germany / Timothy L. Schroer.
    p. cm.
  Includes bibliographical references and index.
  ISBN 978-0-87081-869-1 (hardcover : alk. paper) 1. Reconstruction (1939–1951)—
Germany. 2. African Americans—Relations with Germans. 3. African American
soldiers—Germany—History—20th century. 4. Germany—Race relations—History—
20th century. I. Title.
  D829.G3S316 2007
  940.53'14408996073043—dc22
                                                                    2007009968

Design by Daniel Pratt

16   15   14   13   12   11   10   09   08   07   10   9   8   7   6   5   4   3   2   1

To Kim

Contents

Illustrations

Acknowledgments

I received a great deal of help on this project. It grew out of my dissertation, for which I was fortunate to have the guidance of Alon Confino. I learned much from the other members of my committee—Lenard Berlanstein, Reginald Butler, and Richard Handler. I am also grateful for the valuable insights offered in the early stages of this study by Robert Geraci, Erik Midelfort, and Stephen Schuker. I cannot imagine a better environment in which to have trained than the Corcoran Department of History at the University of Virginia.

I benefited from generous financial support from the United States Department of Education Jacob K. Javits Fellowship, the University of Virginia Graduate School of Arts and Sciences Dissertation Year Fellowship, the German Historical Institute Dissertation Fellowship, a Norman Graebner Research Travel Grant from the Corcoran Department of History at the University of Virginia, a Dean Huskey Research Grant from the University of Virginia Graduate School of Arts and Sciences, and a University of West Georgia Faculty Research Grant.

The History Department at the University of West Georgia has provided a supportive environment in which to bring this work to completion. My colleagues have aided my growth as a teacher and historian. I thank Elmira Eidson and my research assistants, William Willey and Justin Arrington. My friend and colleague Michael de Nie read the entire manuscript and helped me to strengthen the work in many ways.

Many more friends helped during this project, commenting on drafts, answering questions, or offering a place to stay. I am pleased to acknowledge the help of Rusty Sullivan, Mike Ong, Jonathan Ablard, Stephanie Wright, Dan Williams, Keith Bohannon, Susan Fox and Jeff Markowitz, Jennifer and Charlie Hein, Pete Levitas, Brad and Theresa Wiegmann, Martin Siegel, David Harding, Brad Whitener, Bill and Sue Drury, the Schlatterers, and especially Frau Gunda Meiler. I thank my parents, stepparents, and parents-in-law for their encouragement and support along the way. To Kim I owe my greatest thanks, for everything.

A Note on Translation

This book deals with interactions between Germans and Americans across a language barrier. During the military occupation, Americans relied heavily on Germans to translate documents from German to English and from English to German. The archival files I used often contained both German and English versions of documents, one or the other of which represented a translation by a native German speaker. As the reader will see, opportunities for inelegant or sometimes inaccurate translation abounded. Throughout the book I have quoted the original translation where it was available in order to render what non-German-speaking Americans read. Documents in German are cited in the notes in German and documents in English are cited in English. Where peculiarities in the original translation merit it, I have offered my own translation or gloss on the text as well. In cases where no English translation of a German original from the archives existed, all translations are mine. In cases of published works translated from German to English, I have generally relied on the published translated version cited in the notes.

Recasting Race
AFTER WORLD WAR II

Introduction

This book examines the encounter between African Americans and Germans after 1945 and how it helped change thinking about race in both Germany and the United States. By the end of World War II, the idea that Germans belonged to a superior Aryan Master Race had been decisively discredited. Germans, however, did not give up on race as a concept for categorizing groups but recast its meaning and contours, exchanging an Aryan racial identity for membership in the white race. German whiteness became salient in contacts with African American soldiers serving in the American army of occupation. The race of Germans and African Americans mattered according to the public imagination in occupied Germany in two main areas. First, sexual relations between African American men and German women figured as an especially acute challenge to prevailing ideas about race. Second, African American culture, especially music, represented another important field in which Germans worked out the meanings of blackness, whiteness, and Germanness and the differences among them. Briefly stated, Germans understood their race in opposition to perceived amoral and uncultured African Americans. Postwar constructions of German whiteness operated not only to demarcate Germans from African Americans but simultaneously to serve as a bridge between the defeated Germans and the occupying white Allied nations.

With the unconditional surrender of the Third Reich to the Allies in May 1945, Germans in the American zone of occupation found themselves subject to an army officially committed to eliminating Nazi race hatred, as it was most commonly termed at the time. The subordination of Germans to African American soldiers in the occupation forces repudiated Nazism's claims of Aryan racial superiority in a particularly pointed fashion. African American soldiers, who made up roughly 10 percent of the American army in Germany throughout the four years of military occupation, enjoyed considerable wealth and power in comparison with the people of defeated and economically devastated Germany. Substantial numbers of black GIs entered into sexual relationships with German women and sometimes physically intervened against German civilian authorities who attempted to enforce German laws against their companions. Although some Germans eagerly welcomed black soldiers, as well as the American jazz music that came along with the victorious occupying army, the majority of Germans reacted with dismay. Statements of Nazi race hatred, however, were expressly prohibited, and so Germans necessarily treated the subject carefully. Complaints about the immorality of interracial relations could find sympathetic listeners among white officials in the U.S. military, which was racially segregated in Germany even after President Harry Truman's 1948 executive order calling for racial equality in the army. This book examines how Germans, as well as white and black Americans in Germany and the United States, struggled to define the practical implications of race in the aftermath of Nazism.

For a considerable period of time historians paid scant attention to whether the postwar encounter between Germans and African Americans affected German or American thinking about race. The subject, to the extent it was considered at all, generally was regarded as insignificant in the history of racism. George Mosse's history of European racism concluded that although racial anti-Semitism was widely discredited by 1945, racial prejudice against blacks survived the war against Nazi racism comparatively unscathed. Robert Moeller's 1997 survey of the historiography of postwar Germany similarly expressed the consensus among historians of postwar Germany that in 1945, Nazism's racist ideology was "not understood to include other forms of racial discrimination."[1]

A number of scholars focusing primarily on the 1950s lately have begun to devote sustained attention to the subject of African Americans in Germany.[2] They likewise have emphasized the continuity in thinking about race across 1945. Heide Fehrenbach's recent book asserts that "for the entire period of military occupation . . . postfascist German society was democratized by a country whose institutions, social relations, and dominant cultural values were organized around the category of race and a commitment to white supremacy." She further argues that "'race' barely figured in formal reeducation programs" of the Allies after early, fairly ineffective efforts to expose the evil of Nazism's genocidal racism. Fehrenbach locates the crucial developments in the emergence of a West German liberal school of thought on race during the 1950s as West Germans attempted to smooth the integration of Afro-German children into society.[3] Maria Höhn similarly describes persistent racial discrimination in examining the ostracism of German women who entered relationships with African American GIs in the 1950s Rhineland-Palatinate.[4] Likewise, Uta Poiger has attributed German opposition to jazz into the 1950s largely to fears of the blackness of jazz.[5]

The defeat of Nazism, however, marked an important change in the history of thinking about race, despite the fact that race was still regarded as a biologically meaningful category. From 1945 onward growing numbers of Germans and Americans were persuaded that the atrocities committed by the Nazi regime on the basis of its racist ideology had undermined white-supremacist thought and had relevance to discrimination against blacks. Germans, who by 1945 were adept at trimming their sails to the prevailing winds of political orthodoxy, prudently refrained from public condemnation of the black troops that might have been construed as demonstrating continued adherence to Nazism. African American civil rights advocates, on the other hand, insisted that segregation and racial discrimination against blacks within the U.S. Army smacked of Nazism. They therefore urged that the campaign to democratize the Germans necessitated a corresponding transformation of practices in the U.S. Army. These proponents of racial equality for black Americans, however, faced opposition from defenders of segregation and inequality, who indeed believed that the fight against Nazism had nothing to do with the relations between black and white people.

Close examination of interactions between Germans and black GIs and of postwar discussions of music reveals a complex landscape. Relations between African Americans and Germans in occupied Germany, which on the surface seemed remarkably amicable, were in reality more troubled than they appeared.[6] It is certainly true that no storm of objections to stationing African American soldiers in Germany arose after World War II comparable to that which occurred when France stationed colonial troops in the German Rhineland following World War I.[7] The comparative public calm owed more to American constraints, which made bald expressions of white-supremacist thought risky, than to German equanimity. In fact,

African Americans occasioned considerable, albeit guarded, complaint from Germans in the period, especially during 1946, when tensions concerning misconduct by African American (and indeed all American) troops peaked.

The United States, in fact, paid substantial attention to convincing Germans that the Aryan race was a myth and to trying to eliminate German race hatred. The guideposts indicating the general direction for developments in the 1950s were placed very early in the occupation period. In the immediate aftermath of the war Germans and Americans drastically recast the terms in which they discussed the subject of race. The end of military occupation offers a sensible endpoint for this study because by the conclusion of military occupation, American constraints on German discussions of race had mostly disappeared.

This work devotes sustained attention to both the German and the American sides of a transnational story, because revised thinking about race emerged as the result of an international dialogue. Here I would disagree with Maria Höhn, who discerns an "Americanization" of German attitudes about race in the 1950s, as Germans moved, in her account, from accepting African American GIs during the occupation period to discriminating against them along the lines of the American Jim Crow system.[8] I think viewing developments through the lens of "Americanization" obscures more than it clarifies. The term suggests a deep gulf between German and American ideas about race before 1945, homogeneity in each society's thinking, and a passive role for Germans. None of these suggestions seems apt. American constraints certainly changed the public discourse about race in the American zone, but German views were not simply Americanized. Furthermore, although the effect of developments in Germany on thinking about race relations in the United States was less dramatic, the inconsistency of democratizing the Germans with a Jim Crow army produced insistent calls for racial reform within the United States.

My work draws on the growing number of studies that have sought to historicize whiteness. American historians launched the study of whiteness as they effectively demolished the notion that whiteness was a natural category and showed how whiteness has been socially and historically constructed, most notably as immigrant groups qualified for status as whites by distinguishing themselves from black African Americans.[9] The insights of these historians have begun to be applied in the German context as well, as scholars have considered how whiteness was construed in Germany. Tina Campt and Erin Leigh Crawley have convincingly shown that the existence of Afro-Germans within Germany was treated through most of the twentieth century as an anomaly in white Germany. Uli Linke has emphasized in the German context that whiteness serves as a means of dominating the Other, defined as black.[10]

My study builds on the initial studies of German whiteness in two ways. First, it begins by questioning the perceived naturalness of German whiteness. The white race was a social construction, just as the Aryan race was. The notion of an Aryan race, which held sway during the Third Reich, was jettisoned quickly by most Germans at the onset of the occupation as they came to re-embrace membership in a broader white race that linked them to the victorious powers. Although the idea that Germans were white was not new in 1945, the characteristics of German whiteness were conceived and expressed differently in the postwar period than they had been before Nazism discredited the most naked expressions of white racial-supremacist thought. Germans after 1945 defined whiteness in terms of what they believed African Americans lacked.

Second, I explore the function of whiteness as implying a code of conduct that operated to police white Germans. Germans were subordinated to the African American soldiers of the victorious occupying force. They nevertheless thought in terms of whiteness because it defined not only alien blacks but also appropriate conduct for individuals within the white group. Whiteness played an important role as Germans came to regard women who engaged in sex with African Americans as beyond the pale of moral German whiteness. German officials, in cooperation with white Americans, applied those ideas about whiteness when prosecuting women who transgressed against the color line for spreading venereal disease or for other offenses.

I have attempted to heed the oft-repeated injunction to elucidate connections between categories of race and gender.[11] During the period examined in this book, people commonly insisted that race and sexual morality constituted distinct matters. In fact, however, the two were inextricably connected in rhetoric and action. Blackness became especially troublesome in the context of sex with white women, and whiteness gained meaning as defining appropriate sexual conduct. American occupiers' attitudes about women and sexual morality facilitated certain German objections to the conduct of African American troops.

In discussing race, geographic or spatial metaphors are often employed.[12] W.E.B. Du Bois, for example, famously identified the "color-line" as the problem of the twentieth century.[13] The fact that Du Bois's formulation has scarcely been improved on underscores the usefulness of such conceptualizations. Our understanding of race nevertheless might be deepened by shifting the metaphor. Here again, Du Bois offers a fruitful alternative. In his essay "The Superior Race" he suggested the impossibility of defining racial groups in strictly biological terms. Race had meaning as it found application in practice. "The black man," Du Bois wrote, "is a person who must ride 'Jim Crow' in Georgia." I propose to explore race as defining a code or set of rules instead of as a visibly demarcated territory that a person falls into or outside of.[14]

Race formed the basis for a social code of conduct in the sense that being black or being white involved expectations about how a person ought to act. According to Nazi racial dogma, as in the segregated American South in the 1940s, the racial code dictated that blacks defer to whites and that white females refrain from social intercourse with black males. In occupied Germany, the racial codes differed, as blacks were not expected to defer to Germans but, to the contrary, enjoyed greater power than Germans in many respects. On the other hand, white German women still were expected to refrain from sexual relations with blacks. Those women who contradicted such expectations were defined as disreputable, un-German, and un-white. Considering race as a code of conduct underscores the secondary role of physical characteristics in defining race and emphasizes its mutability. Moreover, understanding race as normative highlights the serious implications of violating the racial code of conduct. Finally, conceptualizing race as a code of conduct suggests that moral concerns and racial concerns were inextricably linked, as morality and race were understood in and through each other.

Chapter 1 quickly sketches important themes in thinking about race through 1945 and describes the postwar effort to redefine Aryan Germans as white. That reclassification marked an important new development in the decline of scientific racism and the growth of a consensus around new understandings of racial difference in the postwar world. It nevertheless represented a confirmation of the idea that race, when the category was properly understood, had a biological reality. Postwar understandings of German whiteness drew on ideas concerning race whose roots antedated Nazism, including the equation of whiteness with sexual morality, the belief in the inferiority and sexual license of blacks, the proscription of sexual relations between races, and a continuing tension between biology and culture in defining difference. The postwar insistence that morality, especially sexual propriety, was a quintessentially German quality represented, as a number of scholars have noted, a common convention in the history of European nationhood.[15]

Chapter 2 details the complications of the American assault on Nazi race hatred that at the same time sought to avoid alienating white Germans while subordinating them to black soldiers. Influential military officials believed that African American troops, by their sexual relations with German prostitutes and other acts of misconduct, threatened to alienate the German population. Accordingly, the military initially limited the role of African American soldiers in Germany. That policy, however, came under increasing pressure from American civil rights leaders, who argued that a Jim Crow army could not stamp out Nazi race hatred and democratize Germany.

Chapter 3 examines the ways in which Germans, in dialogue with white Americans, applied ideas concerning moral whiteness against

German women who contravened its tenets by engaging in sexual relations with African American soldiers. German authorities singled out the women involved in such relationships as the culpable parties and, with the cooperation of American officials, carried out punitive measures against those women. Germans justified their actions by a rhetorical exclusion of such women from the white German nation in a language that was explicitly moralistic and implicitly racial.

Chapter 4 investigates the interactions between African American soldiers and German women. Race retained meaning in such relationships at both the personal level and the public representational level, as actions that seemed fundamentally to subvert the category of race paradoxically served to reinforce it in certain ways. Whiteness figured as valuable property held by the women, which gave them greater power in their relations with African American soldiers than they otherwise had as female members of a defeated and economically devastated nation under military occupation. By the same token, such relations served to fetishize the blackness of the soldiers and their children. For African American GIs, the relationships helped bolster claims to power according to the terms of a masculine discourse in which sexual access to women without regard to their race stood for achievement of full civil rights. At the public level, the willingness of German women to accept African Americans framed a critique of American racism that charged that, incongruously enough, true democracy, as exemplified by interracial sexual relations, existed not in the United States but in the territory of the former Third Reich.

Chapter 5 examines how Germans and Americans rethought the relationship between race and music after 1945. The Nazi idea that music expressed the racial essence of its composer had been discredited, but Germans and Americans generally agreed that jazz, as well as spirituals, was in some sense "black music," just as other music seemed especially German. Indeed, Germans in the 1940s often disparagingly referred to jazz as *Negermusik* ("Negro music"). The relationship between black and German music became important as American authorities tried to persuade Germans of the greatness of American music and culture, an effort greeted with considerable skepticism by Germans. German audiences responded enthusiastically to African American spirituals as an authentic expression of black folk culture in terms that drew on the older vision in which biological race determined a group's cultural products. Jazz, on the other hand, tended to divide German opinion more sharply, with most Germans regarding jazz as a threat to German culture. A minority composed of jazz proponents, however, lauded jazz as a revitalizing influence for stagnant European culture. Both musical forms were regarded as black and therefore foreign to Germans, but jazz uniquely threatened to undermine cultural boundaries as performers "jazzed up" classical works and popular tunes. Jazz accordingly represented a greater peril to Germanness, conceived in terms of a pure cultural essence.

As an anonymous reviewer of this manuscript aptly observed, "[T]his is an oddly framed book about German racism." The category of the Aryan race had been drawn in opposition, of course, to the so-called Jewish race. The Holocaust represents the central event in the history of German racism, as was recognized during the postwar period. John J. McCloy, American High Commissioner in Germany, stated in 1949 that Germans' relations with Jews would be regarded as the "acid test of German democracy."[16] This book does not focus in detail on the subject of German postwar relations with Jews. Instead, it considers what race meant in the immediate aftermath of the Holocaust. In those years, at the same time that the notion of a Jewish race was being debunked, Germans and Americans recast race as a category marking the black/white divide.[17]

This book does not pretend to cover all of Germany. It focuses mainly on developments in the American zone of occupation, where most African Americans in Germany were located but which was only one part of what became two German states in 1949. The southern part of Germany occupied by the United States had its own peculiarities and was not representative of all of Germany. Nonetheless, events in that region were important for thinking about race beyond the region. Important aspects of what race meant after 1945 were rearticulated in the context of the meeting between African Americans and Germans. Suggestive, albeit limited, evidence from Berlin and the other three zones of occupied Germany suggests that the experience resonated beyond the limits of the American zone.

Scholars have repeatedly observed that race has been socially constructed.[18] Historians have historicized race, as they have shown how the notion emerged and has been transformed. Less attention, however, has been paid to historicizing racism, which too often has appeared as a transhistorical phenomenon operating everywhere and always as a means of defining and subjugating variously defined racial others.[19] I hope to contribute to the project of historicizing racism by illuminating the demise of a particular type of scientific racism and the increasing currency of a cultural-racial understanding.[20] I believe that the terms *racism* and *racist* are nearly as problematic as the notion of race.[21]

Historians have had somewhat better success in defining *racism* than *race*. Imanuel Geiss, in his short history of racism, essays a useful definition of *racism* as the belief in the existence of distinct races, each with particular characteristics, which are subject to change only through the biological process of race mixing.[22] That broad definition glosses over a variety of distinctions in thought and practice. It is, however, insufficiently capacious, since many statements or attitudes that today are regarded as racist do not fall within it. Given the breadth of the concept of racism, to locate and to label practices or ideas as "racist" represents a fairly modest achievement. Too frequently, use of the term *racist* ends inquiry where further questions could be posed productively.

Few readers will be surprised that I detect the persistence of what today would be regarded as racism throughout the American military occupation of Germany. Nevertheless, the emergence, through a dialogue between American and German participants, of a new understanding of race as marked by the black/white divide and of German whiteness as marked by a particular morality and culture amounted to a significant development following on the demise of the notion of the Master Race.

CHAPTER ONE

Germans, Blacks, and Race through 1945

Race emerged as a category for defining human groups during the modern era, and by the turn of the twentieth century it had become the preeminent conceptual tool for understanding differences between groups.[1] Race has always proved impossible to define, and its very slipperiness has contributed to its ability to serve a variety of ends.[2] One of its most important functions has been as a theoretical justification for subjugating nonwhite people, whether in slavery or in imperial regimes, especially in order to extract labor from them.[3] More fundamentally, race gained prominence as an intellectual category by which Europeans interpreted their relationship to peoples of the New World, Africa, and Asia with whom they had increasing contact from the fifteenth century onward. On the heels of the rise of nationalism, race further came to serve as a means of theorizing the asserted unity of members of a nation through a biological connection beyond accidents of common language, citizenship, and customs.[4] By the twentieth century, a recognizably racist system of thought asserted and justified European preeminence over peoples of different races on the basis of biological superiority.

In recent years, historians have illuminated how ideas about race have functioned as a justification for regulating sexual behavior, especially that of women. That is, race defined the people with whom women of one group could properly engage in sexual relations. The sexuality of white women has often been defined by marking sexual relations with blacks as improper and immoral. This prohibition on sex between the races applied primarily to women. White men enjoyed comparative freedom to engage in sexual relations with black women.[5]

Racial difference in the European imperial settings served both economic and sexual functions, as whites attempted to extract labor from Africans and limit sexual contact between white women and African men. Crudely schematized, each function carried with it images of the black that justified ends served by racist social practice. If blacks were lazy and stupid, their labor could be extracted only by slavery or physical coercion. If blacks were amoral and oversexed, white women needed to be protected from them.

American-occupied Germany presented an anomalous situation because economic competition between blacks and whites was virtually nonexistent. Racism thus served no discernible economic end for Germans. For that reason, one might expect racism to have withered. At the same time, and not purely coincidentally, sexual relations between black men and white women flourished, producing considerable concern. Race played an important role in efforts to police the sexuality of German women, and it provided a means of defining community and more generally served to cognitively order the world. Whiteness both excluded immoral German women and included proper Germans within a larger white international community that included the white American occupiers.

Themes in German Racial Thinking

Tracing the evolution of thinking about race in Germany up to 1945 is a difficult endeavor. Proof of the difficulty may be found in the remarkable disparities in the numbers of races identified by various people, from a relatively simple breakdown into three races up to a variegated classification discerning ten different races in Europe alone.[6] In addition, until Germany acquired African colonies late in the nineteenth century, Germans had little opportunity or reason to develop established practices for dealing with black people. Although Africans lived in Germany before that time, their numbers were so small that societal practices regarding them received little attention.[7] Even after the acquisition of colonies, Germans' thinking about what race was and how people of different races acted often lacked clarity and consistency. In their confusion, Germans differed little from other Europeans.[8]

There was little to distinguish a particularly German pattern of thought or practice about race through the nineteenth century. In some respects, Germans in the nineteenth century attributed less significance to race than other Europeans.[9] The entry on the "Negro" in the 1846 Brockhaus encyclopedia insisted that recent scholarly works had shown Africans to possess greater intellectual capacity than uninformed, prejudiced European travelers previously had reported.[10] The work of the leading French race theorist, Count Joseph-Arthur de Gobineau, received a cool reception in Germany initially, and German physical anthropologists in the main rejected theories that Africans were a wholly different species from Europeans. Gobineau's nationality, however, may have been the most significant reason that German scientists took a dim view of his work. In addition, racism could coexist comfortably with a belief in monogenesis.[11]

Despite the confusion in racial thought and practice and the important caveat concerning the distinctively German aspect of such thought, important themes in German thinking about race were so durable that they would prove significant for relations between African Americans and Germans and the reconceptualizing of race after 1945. First, racial theorists consistently linked racial differences to differences in sexual morality.[12] Whiteness was commonly associated with sexual propriety and blackness with sexual license. Johann Gottfried Herder's thought exemplified this tendency. Although he did not strictly delineate distinct races, he nevertheless attributed an important role to biology in determining the behavior of different groups, contending, for example, that Africa's hot climate made its inhabitants more sensual than Europeans. Applying the teachings of physiognomy, Herder asserted that the purportedly large lips, breasts, and sexual organs of Africans expressed in physical terms the sensuousness that stamped their character. He explained that it was natural that "in nations for whom the sensual appetite is the height of happiness in life, external marks of it should appear." At the same time, however, his work undercut the notion that firm racial boundaries existed, as he noted that "fullness of the lips, even among whites, is considered by physiognomy as the sign of a very sensuous disposition." Inner character expressed itself transparently in outward appearance across groups and individuals. Herder regarded Africans' sensuousness as a compensation for the fact that nature had deprived them of "nobler gifts."[13] In contrast, the climate of ancient Germany inclined its inhabitants to sexual virtue, as Herder linked whiteness and sexual propriety. Sexual mores thus from the first represented an important element of culture.[14]

Belief in Africans' amoral sensuality cropped up again in Georg Wilhelm Friedrich Hegel's philosophical works on history. He asserted that the African embodied natural man in his original state and that Africans had no conception of a higher being or morality. Blacks, according to Hegel, sold their wives and children into slavery or practiced cannibalism without compunction because they were governed by mere sensuality. Hegel did not expressly attribute such differences between Africans and Europeans to biology, but his work is important precisely for linking blackness and amorality but leaving the reasons for such a connection obscure.[15]

Scientific racism reemphasized the fundamentally sexual and amoral nature of blacks and claimed to have located the biological basis for such propensities.[16] Fritz Lenz, Germany's first professor of racial hygiene and coauthor of the authoritative genetics textbook of the interwar period, asserted that "the Negro" was in thrall to his "immediate sense impression." Lenz claimed that heightened sensitivity accounted for blacks' alleged disinclination to work, low intelligence, childlike quality, sexual prowess, and promiscuity.[17]

Racial theorists, besides agreeing that blacks were especially sexual, further reached consensus that Africans belonged at the bottom of any hierarchy of races.[18] Even Herder's generally pluralist acceptance, indeed celebration, of human diversity showed its limits in his beliefs about Africans.[19] For Darwinists, the Negro served as the primary foil for demonstrating the superiority of the white race.[20] The Social Democrat Eduard David gave testimony to the deeper taint of African blackness when, in debating the merits of legislation outlawing marriages between colonialists and colonized in German Samoa, he defended the beauty of Samoan women by insisting that they ought not to be "thrown into the same pot with negro women."[21]

A third consistent theme in German racial discourse (like European beliefs more generally) was the nearly universal condemnation of mixing among races. The habit persisted from the beginnings of discussions of race into the twentieth century, with warnings issued by thinkers ranging in quality from Immanuel Kant to Houston Stewart Chamberlain. German physical anthropologists generally held that race mixture produced pernicious results. Darwin's evidence of the negative effects of crossing different species appeared to provide an important further scientific basis for arguments against race mixing.[22]

The opponents of race mixing were not confined to the right wing but could be found across the whole political spectrum during the Kaiserreich. The Social Democrat Georg Ledebour in 1912 condemned the government's colonial policy for encouraging extramarital sexual relations, which ended up producing mixed-race children.[23] Although the primary danger of race mixing generally seemed to be the birth of inferior children,

sexual contact with black men was also worrisome because it was presumed to debase white women. Thus, one writer decrying the presence of
French colonial troops in the Rhineland in 1920 made the dire prediction
that if "mulatto-ization" were left unchecked, in a few years the "German
woman" would be reduced to "a black whore."[24]

Although race gained in importance as an explanatory mechanism
through the nineteenth century and into the twentieth, it could never
completely shake loose culture from a role in defining groups.[25] At the
inception of German nationalist thought in the synthesis by Herder, the
fundamental groups (*Völker*, or nations) into which humanity was "naturally" divided were defined in terms of homogenous cultural units.
The culture produced by a nation effectively defined it and expressed its
essence. Herder's role in the development of theories of race is the subject
of disagreement, but Isaiah Berlin seems correct in insisting that Herder
believed that the nation was defined by "'climate,' education, relations
with its neighbours, and other changeable and empirical factors, and not
by an impalpable inner essence or an unalterable factor such as race or
colour."[26] Herder indeed expressly rejected the idea of "races," in the
sense that humanity was divided into distinct biological groups having
separate origins. Nevertheless nature, which Herder believed produced
differences in complexion, played a critical role in forging national character.[27] It is noteworthy, too, that the perceived dangers of *cultural* intermixture were as grave as those stemming from *racial* intermixture. For
Herder, the idea that valuable music or other cultural products might be
created independent of their natural milieu was anathema.[28] The conception of national cultures as natural was inseparable from his condemnation of cultural mixing as inauthentic and pernicious.[29]

Since late in the nineteenth century, German thinking about race, like
that of many Europeans and Americans, involved competing racial typolo-
gies. A luxuriant variety of racial taxonomies coexisted along a spectrum
of differentiation. At one end, all of humanity was divided into three races:
white, black, and yellow. Other racial theorists regarded these groupings as
insufficiently precise and elaborated a more differentiated racial categoriza-
tion that closely mirrored the national boundaries of Europe, with a particular Germanic, Teutonic, Nordic, or Aryan race distinct from, but perhaps
closely linked to, an Anglo-Saxon race. Of course, this latter sort of racial
typology was less inclusive than the tripartite division, according to which
all Europeans formed a unified white group, and it thus often came to the
fore in struggles between European states. Nazism and its *völkisch* prede-
cessors infamously insisted on the primacy of the national/racial typology,
according to which Germans belonged to an Aryan "Master Race," although
the Nazis never dispensed with the notion of the white race or races.[30]

In the context of overseas empire, Germans conceived of the dividing
line separating them from the colonized peoples as a racial line between

white and black.[31] In the Reichstag debates regarding colonial policy in Africa, German politicians continually cast issues as a matter of relations between whites and blacks. The liberal Ernst Müller-Meiningen, for instance, expressed the conviction that "if the blacks are to be preserved alongside the whites, then it is indispensable to sharply separate the two races from one another." Similarly, the conservative Wilhelm Lattmann maintained that "the black race, even when it accepts Christianity, cannot from the standpoint of race be considered to be of equal worth to the white race."[32]

The German regulation of mixed-race marriage in the colonies in the first two decades of the twentieth century illustrates the complexity of whiteness.[33] Before 1900 it was not uncommon for German men in the German colony Southwest Africa to enter into sexual relationships with African women. Such relationships aroused comparatively little concern among colonists, and, according to established German citizenship law, those children of German fathers qualified as German citizens.[34] In 1905, however, in the wake of the genocidal campaigns against the indigenous Herero and Nama peoples, German officials in Southwest Africa prohibited marriages between Europeans and Africans. In 1906 officials in German East Africa followed suit. A year later, the Southwest African courts retroactively invalidated all such marriages that had occurred before the prohibition.[35]

A number of factors contributed to produce the marriage ban. The desire to limit the potential political power of the children of such marriages provided much of the motivation.[36] The fact that officials within Southwest Africa, not the Reichstag, instigated the ban testifies to the decisive importance of local circumstances in the colony, as does the tardiness of German East Africa and German Samoa in imitating the ban. Practices toward the indigenous African populations indeed varied among the German colonies, with Togo widely regarded at the time as a model for humane colonial administration.[37] Ideas about race, even if they did not monocausally determine the marriage ban, informed the debate about it. Colonial director Wilhelm Solf, who generally pursued a paternalist policy toward Africans, defended the marriage ban by raising the specter of German men returning home with black wives, and he warned that "worse still . . . white girls might return with Hereros, Hottentots, and Bastards as husbands."[38]

Debate provoked by the marriage ban between Germans and women in the colonies brought to the surface the important themes in German thinking about race. In Southwest Africa, for example, a German citizen named Becker wrote to Governor Schuckmann in 1909, protesting the invalidation of his marriage to his African wife. He complained, "If I go anywhere with my wife, who is almost white (a picture of my family is enclosed) and in moral and intellectual respects is the equal of any white woman in the Protectorate, I have to face unpleasantness."[39] The proffering of photographic evidence of near whiteness suggests the importance in the colonial period of biological facts. Biology, however, was followed closely by morality and intellect in defining race.

The relationship between biology and other attributes was even more complex outside German Southwest Africa. In German Samoa, colonial officials issued a prospective prohibition on mixed marriages only in 1912. Children of preexisting valid mixed marriages were, however, deemed legally "white." Any children born from subsequent illegal marriages would be deemed indigenous. Even those children could achieve the status of whiteness if they demonstrated fluency in German and the achievement of a requisite level of education, or *Bildung*.[40] Within Germany proper, some African inhabitants of German colonies were able to obtain German citizenship and marry German women.[41]

Race obviously represented a fairly malleable category, one that sometimes failed to trump education, legality, and the vagaries of political circumstances in individual colonies. Nonetheless, colonial officials' resort to a marriage ban confirms the central importance of interracial sex in German racial thought and practice. The connections among whiteness, sexuality, and ideas of the Master Race were neatly summarized by one conservative Reichstag representative who asserted that in order for "the white race to consider itself everywhere to be the master race . . . every sexual relation of blacks with whites in the colonies must be put under penalty of the law."[42]

Around the time of World War I, the German public imagination increasingly came to regard race as defining the nation.[43] Following Germany's defeat in World War I, blacks began to appear as especially threatening when France stationed colonial troops in the occupied Rhineland. Germans, shocked and outraged by their sudden and surprising defeat during the war, reacted bitterly to the presence of blacks among the victorious occupiers as a further humiliation. That reaction, whipped to a fever pitch by German propagandists who denounced the French action as "the Black Horror" (*die Schwarze Schmach*), produced lines of argument that would be reworked in the period after World War II. Assertions that the black troops posed a sexual danger to white German womanhood occupied a central place in the campaign. The episode also illustrated that racial arguments were fully compatible with arguments concerning cultural difference. Finally, the campaign particularly emphasized German whiteness as it appealed to the British and Americans to aid Germany in defending the white race against depredations by blacks brought by the French into the heart of white, cultured, moral Europe.[44]

The French action provoked outrage in the German press, as well as among British and American commentators.[45] In Munich, the German

Emergency League against the Black Horror formed to agitate for the withdrawal of the nonwhite troops.[46] Its message had many sympathizers across the political spectrum in Germany and internationally. The first president of the Weimar Republic, the socialist Friedrich Ebert, for example, denounced France's action as a "provocative injury to the laws of European civilization."[47] Agitation against the nonwhite troops continued sporadically until their departure.[48]

The campaign played unmistakably on the sexual theme. The propagandists feared the unleashing on German womanhood of black men, who were believed to be endowed with especially potent, primitive sexuality.[49] The opponents of the French action categorically rejected the possibility that any sexual relationship between the occupiers and white women might be voluntary, despite evidence to the contrary.[50] One particularly shrill denunciation of the desecration of the white woman by the bestial, syphilitic "Negro" appeared in the *Hamburger Nachrichten*. The 1921 piece inveighed, "Now the negro, who . . . generally stands on a lower rung of the evolutionary ladder, is not only being brought to Europe, not only being used in battle in a white country [*Lande des Weißen*]; he is also systematically being trained to desire that which was formerly unreachable for him — the white woman!"[51]

While the most rabid critics played up the sexual danger in such a vein, slightly less strident propagandists cast their arguments on a cultural basis. Thus, the *Leipziger Tageszeitung* asserted, "What offends European sensibility in the use of black troops, is not their blackness, but rather the fact that savages are being used to oversee a cultured people." The *Grenzland Korrespondent* of April 24, 1922, linked culture to whiteness, explaining that the French had debased not only Germany but had brought "the desecration of white culture in general . . . [which] means the beginning of the end of the predominance of the white man."[52]

Tina Campt and other scholars have persuasively interpreted the emphasis on whiteness in the German press as a calculated appeal to the sympathy of a white international audience. In fact, the threatened race could appear as both German and white, as the *Grenzland Korrespondent* claimed in an April 26, 1922, article stating that the threat of racial contagion affected "not only the German race, [but] the entire white race."[53] Whiteness could coexist with and even predominate over a putative German racial type where such a move had tactical advantages. Whiteness as a racial category thus had a useful malleability. Whiteness, rather than a particularistic German racial quality, would be mobilized in a far more guarded manner after World War II, when Germans pitched their appeal across national boundaries to potential sympathizers who might feel a shared racial bond.

Nazism

Nazism regarded race as the fundamental reality in human affairs and endeavored, albeit inconsistently and fitfully, to order German society according to racial principles. Nazi ideology was premised on the notion of the existence of an Aryan race, which was believed to be superior to all others and locked in a mortal struggle with a supposed Jewish race.[54] The incoherence that characterized much Nazi theory and practice could be found in questions of race as well. Some theorists were dissatisfied with the concept of the Aryan race because they thought it too imprecise. The Committee of Experts for Population and Racial Policy, formed by the Ministry of Interior in 1933, accordingly attempted to clarify the racial identity of German Aryans. Its members offered the following rather unsatisfactory definition as part of a draft citizenship law: "A person is German who is of German-Aryan descent. A person of German-Aryan descent is someone who is of German or predominantly German, and at least Aryan descent."[55] Needless to say, this definition clarified nothing. The commentary on the Reich Citizenship Law eventually issued at Nuremberg in 1935 explained that the German *Volk* comprised people belonging to several different races, which included the Nordic race but also, among others, the Dinaric, East Baltic, and other races, along with their intermixtures. This mishmash together supposedly constituted "German blood." The commentary further recognized a category of "kindred blood" (*artverwandtes Blut*), that is, blood of a *Volk* closely related to German blood. Although the commentary called for replacement of the term *Aryan* with *of German or kindred blood,* in practice *Aryan* continued as the most common term for the Germanic Master Race.[56]

Racial theorists in the Third Reich might differ on particular nuances of racial theory, but Nazism clearly rested on the premise that non-Jewish Germans represented a biologically defined group that was distinct from both Jews and other Europeans who would generally be classed as "Caucasian." Nazi racial theory insisted that the supposed biological unity of the "white race" was a fiction. Amateur musicologist and SS officer Richard Eichenauer, in the paradigmatic statement of Nazi music theory, thus asserted that musicians and lay music fans hitherto had failed to apply racial science to the study of European music because they had been "satisfied with the concept of the 'white race.'" Placing the term *white race* within quotation marks to indicate his skepticism, Eichenauer explained that the supposed "common European language" of music was really "a complete illusion." In fact, according to Eichenauer, the Nordic race had produced the majority of the great European musical works.[57] It is impossible to know the extent to which Germans embraced the Aryan racial identity celebrated by the Nazi Party, but it should be recalled that many Europeans (and Americans) thought in terms of the national/racial typology before the Nazis came to power. Eichenauer went further than most in regarding the Nordic race as more "real" than the white race, but his view had a considerable number of adherents.

The Nazis regarded Africans as belonging to a so-called Negro race, which occupied the lowest rung of the racial hierarchy. Indeed, the presumptive inferiority of blacks to Europeans served as a bedrock principle underpinning Nazism's argument that humanity was divided into biological races of different capabilities. Hitler in *Mein Kampf* thus supposed that the absurdity of racial egalitarianism was demonstrated by efforts to train African Americans as lawyers. Nazi race theorist Alfred Rosenberg similarly believed that he might expose the lunacy of the Christian principle of common humanity by citing "the Eucharistic Congress in Chicago in 1926, where nigger bishops celebrated the mass."[58] During World War II, he warned that by treating Ukrainians like "Negroes," the Third Reich unwisely alienated potential allies against Soviet Russia.[59]

Nazi ideology, consistent with its precursors, regarded the danger of race mixing to the Aryan race as twofold: sexual and cultural. In both the sexual and cultural realms, Nazi theory posited the existence of a threat to a pure Aryan race from foreign, corrupting elements, especially blackness. The Nazis thus harped on the French stationing of colonial troops in the Rhineland and the purported defilement of German womanhood that resulted.[60] Nothing, according to Rosenberg, illustrated French racial degeneracy more clearly than scenes in Paris, where "Negroes and mulattoes stroll[ed] about on the arms of white women."[61] The Nazi organ *Der Weltkampf* proclaimed that if the party came to power, blacks would be barred from coming to Germany.[62]

In addition to the direct biological threat of sexual relations between blacks and German women, the menace posed by African American culture, especially jazz, imported into Germany likewise occupied National Socialist propagandists. The Nazis decried the "Nigger-fication" (*Verniggerung*) of German music and culture more generally as symptomatic of the ills of Weimar Germany. Hitler warned that African American influences could produce a "negrified" German music. The Nazi *Völkischer Beobachter* likewise pointed out the danger posed to Germany by the importation of African American music and musicians. The twin cultural and sexual threats were linked in the association of jazz music with unrestrained sexuality, as that quintessentially black cultural product imperiled moral, cultural, and racial purity.[63]

In Nazi racial schemes, although blacks occupied the lowest position, Jews figured as the most dangerous race because they were supposedly more clever and they posed an insidious internal threat to the German nation. Nazi thought most often tied beliefs about blacks to anti-Semitic doctrine by depicting blacks as the pawns of Jews. Hitler, for example, claimed that a Jewish conspiracy had orchestrated the stationing of French colonial troops in the Rhineland.[64] The malevolent Jewish influence also played the animating role in the cultural threat to German purity in black jazz music, since Jews supposedly hoped to debase German culture through jazz.[65] With the Nazi seizure of power, racism became Germany's express policy, as the regime aimed to eliminate perceived threats to the purity of the Aryan race. The Nazis regarded the several hundred so-called Rhineland bastards, the children of French colonial soldiers and German women, as one such threat. The National Socialist regime thus applied the Nuremberg Laws to blacks as well as Jews. In 1937 the Gestapo sterilized more than 300 mixed-race children in the Rhineland.[66]

There nevertheless remained ambivalence in Nazi policies toward blacks.[67] In fact, one young man with an African father managed to join the Hitler Youth in 1933 and later serve in the Wehrmacht.[68] The Afro-German Hans Massaquoi survived the Third Reich and, though his position was certainly precarious, he lived in many respects as an "ordinary" German.[69] Several blacks, including both Germans and foreign nationals, were employed as film actors to play African parts.[70] An October 1935 document signed by Nazi Party official Martin Bormann even indicated that Hitler was concerned that "colonial negroes" from Germany's former colonies who had fought on Germany's behalf and who were living in Germany should not be prevented from finding work.[71] The Third Reich did not adopt an expressly discriminatory policy against captured black soldiers during the war, although some captured African American servicemen and French colonial troops appear to have been murdered on account of their race, and many probably suffered mistreatment for the same reason at the hands of German captors.[72]

Despite these examples, the public pronouncements of the regime made clear its disdain for people of African descent. Nazi propaganda during World War II drew on German fears of another Rhineland occupation by black troops. A wartime poster, for example, recalled the *Schwarze Schmach* as it depicted, against a backdrop of a German city consumed by flames, a slavering, black soldier grasping at the breasts of a German woman in a torn dress. The caption urged, "Germans! Don't Let This Happen Again!"[73] By May 1945, Germans had lived for years with official public discourse that depicted blacks, including specifically African Americans, as a danger to German racial purity.

Nazi racial ideology bore direct implications for the role of women in society. Nazism emphasized women's biological and moral function as mothers to the race. The Third Reich raised public celebrations of Mother's Day, observance of which had begun in the Weimar Republic, to new prominence and awarded the Cross of Honor of the German Mother to especially fecund women. Although the demands of war increasingly required women's participation in the economy, at the level of ideology Nazism always defined a woman's proper role as mother. German attitudes regarding women up to the time of the war thus emphasized that women owed a special responsibility to the nation in their sexual conduct, which was inseparable from their reproductive role as the mothers of the nation.[74]

Racisms: Nazi, German, and American

Nazi race hatred did not exhaust the varieties of racial prejudice, and it drew on assumptions and beliefs that were not specifically or exclusively National Socialist. In fact, even within the Nazi Party racial orthodoxy proved elusive, as racial speculations produced several Nazi variants. Dr. Edgar Schulz, for example, complicated the standard Nazi doctrine positing the existence of a "Jewish race" in theorizing that Jews did not belong to one race but rather represented a mixture of "Negro" and "Oriental" races. Nazism, indeed, made few innovations in race theory, and many of its racial policies, including calls for the sterilization of the so-called Rhineland bastards, dated from the 1920s. Nazism's originality lay chiefly in its unprecedented implementation of racist ideas in murderous practice.[75]

Before 1945, Germans were aware, in general terms, of the troubled history of American race relations.[76] Nazi propagandists not infrequently referred to American racial attitudes and practices, favoring the particularly virulent white supremacist habits of the South, not the ideas of American reformers who pushed for civil rights for African Americans.[77] At the Nuremberg war crimes trials, Hermann Göring taunted his American captors on the subject of American discrimination against African Americans, asking if black officers were permitted to ride in the same trolley cars as whites.[78] In October 1945 nearly one-third of Giessen's residents surveyed about African American soldiers believed that "white soldiers looked down on the Negroes as inferior."[79]

Nazis and non-Nazis shared many beliefs regarding race and blacks, and preexisting racial ideas retained currency among Germans during and after the Third Reich. For example, Friedrich Percyval Reck-Malleczewen, whose anti-Nazi commitment was demonstrated by his confinement and death in Dachau, betrayed a firm conviction in blacks' inferiority when he condemned Nazism in his diary for having produced the "complete Nigger-fication of the masses."[80] Some racial ideas had their origins in folk tradition. One physician, for instance, wrote soon after the war's end that a husband whose wife was pregnant with a child fathered by a black soldier had expressed the fear that the act of giving birth to the "foreign" child would permanently alter his wife's body so that any children he later fathered himself with her would also bear "racially-foreign characteristics."[81] The survival of such notions, whose origins predated the Third Reich, testified to the heterogeneity of ideas about race and their tenacious hold.

Attitudes about race among Germans and white Americans showed many similarities up to the war and, to a lesser degree, even through the war. In the first three decades of the twentieth century, American racial hygienists influenced colleagues in Germany in a variety of ways. German racial hygienists read work by American race theorists and followed with interest American measures combating immigration and miscegenation, as well as the American Medical Association's refusal to accept African American members. Although Germans and Americans figured most prominently in the eugenics movement, in fact, racial hygiene had supporters around the world, and its international conferences drew delegations from several countries.[82] A focus on Nazism could obscure deeply rooted traditional racial prejudices of most Germans according to which blacks were amoral, uncontrollable, and uncultured, prejudices widely shared by white Americans.

White Americans and Germans also shared attitudes concerning women's sexuality, which would influence the way that German and American authorities treated relations between African Americans and German women in the postwar period. During the occupation, the American military quickly devoted considerable attention to German women's sexual morality because of two interrelated problems: the general flouting of the ban on fraternization and the concomitant rise of venereal disease among American soldiers. The very term *fraternization* came to be synonymous with relations, generally sexual, with German women.[83] General Lucius Clay believed that the ban on fraternization "forced" American soldiers, "who could not be kept away from the opposite sex," to meet the "lowest type of girl, the tramp," in secret. Clay regarded venereal disease as the predictable result.[84] Such attitudes would inform officials' reactions after 1945 as the racial and the moral proved inseparable.

A War against Racism? Nazi Racism and the Race Question in the United States

Throughout World War II, Americans debated whether the war against Nazi Germany was inconsistent with domestic racial discrimination against African Americans, including especially segregation in the military. While continuing a policy of segregation, the government strove to improve the situation of African Americans in the military and in society at large. Policy makers bowed to pressure by civil rights advocates and adopted incremental ameliorative measures chiefly in order to minimize the friction in the operation of the American war machine. Although pragmatic considerations motivated administrators to grant such concessions, policy makers publicized such measures on the basis of principled justifications that emphasized African American citizenship and the inconsistency of racial discrimination with the war against Nazi racism. In time, the rhetoric of fighting racism would prove ever more potent as its logic seemed increasingly irrefutable.[85]

Many Americans saw no inconsistency between fighting Nazism and maintaining segregation. In 1942 Assistant Secretary of War John J. McCloy wrote, "Frankly, I do not think that the basic issues of this war are involved in the question of whether Colored troops serve in segregated units or in mixed units and I doubt whether you can convince the people of the United States that the basic issues of freedom are involved in such a question."[86] The army continued to practice segregation throughout the war, although late in the war it experimented with some success with integrating black and white platoons in the same companies. Segregation extended even to the blood supply. The Red Cross, which initially had declined to accept blood from African Americans, marked plasma from African Americans with the label "AA."[87] Perhaps the most strident public defense of segregation during the war came from the members of the South Carolina House of Representatives, who in 1944 adopted a resolution reaffirming their "belief in and . . . allegiance to established white supremacy" and pledging their lives and "sacred honor to maintaining it, whatever the cost, in war and in peace."[88]

The very defensiveness of the declaration testified to civil rights advocates' increasing attacks on racial segregation and discrimination more broadly during the war. Racial tensions mounted within both the army and society at large, as interracial violence became a real problem for the War Department. Racial violence in the military peaked in the summer of 1943 with outbreaks involving many soldiers at Camp Van Dorn, Mississippi, and Camp Stewart, Georgia, as well as at other posts. Trouble flared outside the military as well, with the most serious violence occurring in Detroit, where June riots produced 34 deaths, more than 700 injured, and millions of dollars in property damage.[89]

Faced with growing racial strife and a pressing need to utilize all available manpower, the War Department attempted to convince African Americans that it treated black soldiers fairly and that disagreements over civil rights should not be permitted to interfere with the war effort. The Bureau of Public Relations within the War Department established a Special Interest Section in 1942 to deal exclusively with the black press in hopes of obtaining favorable coverage.[90] The stories put out by the office highlighted the contributions of African Americans and at times expressly offered the black GIs' achievements to disprove Nazi claims to racial superiority. A War Department press release from January 1945 reported, "The myth of the great Nazi 'super' race is taking a beating every day from a company of Negro soldiers," who guarded captured Germans. The release concluded, "The 'Superman' claim is a shallow dream of the past and the Nazis have to swallow the bitter pill of serving under the very soldiers whom they tried to belittle to the citizens of French towns."[91] The Public Relations Section in the European Theater of Operations continued to send stories to what came to be called the "Negro Interest Section" following the end of hostilities in Europe.[92] The most striking product of the War Department's effort to mobilize African Americans and calm racial tensions was the film *The Negro Soldier,* which in May 1944 the War Department ordered to be shown to all soldiers, white and black.[93] The film, which received the praise of the National Association for the Advancement of Colored People (NAACP), portrayed an African American minister reading from *Mein Kampf* to an all-black congregation Hitler's statement deriding the education of African Americans as lawyers.[94]

The army also attempted to improve relations between African Americans and their predominantly white officers through distribution in 1944 of a pamphlet titled "Command of Negro Troops." The pamphlet cast the American race relations problem in the context of the fight against Nazism, warning officers against trying to run their units on the basis of "racial theories," which could not form the basis of effective command. "The Germans have a theory that they are a race of supermen born to conquer all peoples of inferior blood," the pamphlet noted. "This is nonsense, the like of which has no place in the Army of the United States — the Army of a Nation which has become great through the common effort of all peoples." The pamphlet's writers, who also worked on the script of *The Negro Soldier,* insisted that "no scientific evidence" existed to support the notion that the Negro race, or any other race, lacked "soldierly skills." Indeed, "[i]n all the vast number of studies by psychologists and other scientists during the past two or three decades," the writers explained, "not one piece of research . . . proves that Negroes are, as a group, mentally or emotionally defective by heredity."[95]

The army admitted that its disavowal of the doctrine of white superiority might "seem inconsistent" with segregation, but it justified that policy as "a matter of practical military expediency, and not an endorsement of beliefs in racial distinction."[96] The army's public statement during the war that it rejected the idea that African Americans were racially inferior marked it as one of the more progressive institutions in American society. Nevertheless, the army's effort to square the circle of racial egalitarianism and its commitment to segregation proved increasingly unsatisfactory to racial progressives over time.

A larger instruction manual, used in training officers in the Army Service Forces, in which many of the army's African Americans served, amplified the thrust of the pamphlet's argument. It stated, "The Army accepts no theories of racial inferiority or superiority for American troops." It went to considerable lengths to explain that African Americans scored lower on average in army tests than whites not because blacks were racially inferior but because they enjoyed more limited educational opportunities than whites. Like the other programmatic statements on race prepared by the army during the war, the manual opposed American racial egalitarianism to the "doctrine of 'Aryan' superiority," which, according to its authors, had "become one of the dominant factors in the present world struggle."[97]

Government officials could draw on the work of leading social scientists in portraying the war against Nazi Germany as an ideological battle against racism. Franz Boas, the German-born head of Columbia University's Anthropology Department, stood at the forefront of the important group of intellectuals who, even before the United States entered the war, believed in the necessity of educating the American public concerning the fallacies of Nazi (and much American) thinking concerning race. Ruth Benedict, who was one of his students and, although she did not have the credentials of a specialist on the subject of race, could trace her ancestry back to the *Mayflower,* authored a book pitched to the general public in which she summarized established expert opinion debunking Nazism's racial dogma. Social scientists praised the work as an effective means of moving public opinion.[98]

The War Department availed itself of such academic resources in its efforts to educate its soldiers on the subject of race. In 1943 it widely distributed to GIs a manual titled "Psychology for the Fighting Man," which appeared in a second edition in 1944. The manual instructed that "skin color in itself means nothing about the intelligence, wisdom, honesty, bravery or kindliness of man."[99] The army, however, risked offending substantial elements of white opinion if it insisted too strongly on African Americans' racial equality. A public outcry arose in 1944 concerning plans by the Orientation Branch within the Army Service Forces' Morale Services Division to distribute copies of "The Races of Mankind," a pamphlet by anthropologists Ruth Benedict and Gene Weltfish written in a more accessible manner than Benedict's 1940 book. The USO refused to stock the pamphlet in its centers, and the army had decided not to distribute the pamphlet even before an investigative subcommittee of the House Committee on Military Affairs issued a report opposing the plan.[100]

Early in the war the American military resolved that African Americans would serve overseas in Europe and elsewhere, despite the danger that their presence would irritate the racial sensitivities of allied white nations. Wartime relations between African Americans and the British, French, and Italian citizenry raised some of the same issues that would recur in somewhat different form during the occupation of Germany. Neither the British nor the French had developed established practices of racial segregation in the metropoles, and, as a result, the color line was largely absent in Europe, much to the surprise of black and white Americans. That absence of segregationist practice in Europe met with general approval by African Americans and disapproval by white Americans. As large numbers of GIs were stationed in Britain in preparation for D-Day, relations between African American soldiers and local white women, however, produced friction among black GIs, white American soldiers, and British civilians.[101]

Planning for the military occupation of Germany seems never to have seriously questioned the inclusion of African American soldiers in the occupying forces. In September 1944 a member of John McCloy's staff asked whether a program ought to be developed "to prepare the German population for the possible use of Negro troops." McCloy suggested in a note to the Operations Division the need to address the question whether African Americans should be included in the occupation force once the fighting ceased. The Operations Division responded that "operational needs" alone should determine what role would be played by black troops in Germany, not only during combat but also in the occupation. By the same token, the division opposed any program to prepare Germans for the arrival of African Americans on their soil. It therefore rejected the notion that "the German population merits special consideration in this regard," observing that any such propaganda campaign "would in all likelihood lead to unfortunate publicity in the United States."[102]

Disquiet about sending African Americans to Germany nevertheless evidenced itself, as the staff suggested that "the friendly nature of the Negro" would necessitate instructing black troops on the need "to treat the German population as a conquered nation." McCloy's staff further recommended limiting the number of African Americans stationed in Germany because of the dangerous ramifications that such indoctrination might have once the soldiers returned to the United States.[103] Thus, while the fighting continued, American policy made no allowances for Germans' whiteness in its use of black troops, but Americans nevertheless recognized the potential difficulties involved in placing African Americans in a position of authority over a defeated white nation.

African Americans' disappointments with American society and the army did not mean that they harbored illusions regarding Nazism's insistence on the inferiority of blacks.[104] African Americans declined, though, to place the struggle for civil rights on hold during the war but sought instead a "double victory" over fascism abroad and over racism at home, a program captured in the popular "Double V" slogan.[105] In the end, World War II produced Nazism's defeat, but the victory over American racism remained to be won. Nevertheless, the war focused the attention of racial progressives on the situation of African Americans in the military and situated that issue in the context of the struggle against Nazi racial doctrines.[106] In addition, growing numbers of Americans came to believe that something would have to be done about the race question after the war.[107] The postwar period would witness the military's continuing effort to address African American demands while eliminating Nazi race hatred.

First Meetings

Nazi propaganda in the last phase of the war had tried to instill in Germans fanatical commitment to the cause by raising the specter of rampaging African American soldiers in the event of Allied victory. For a state that claimed to have waged war in order to establish the preeminence of the German race against its enemies, the prospect of occupation by alleged racial inferiors epitomized its defeat. As the fighting in Europe drew to its conclusion, Germans awaited the impending arrival of African Americans with trepidation.[108] Those fears proved largely groundless, as the German population received generally good treatment from African Americans. Oral histories are replete with testimonies to remarkably good relations in the first contacts, typically involving the distribution of chocolate or other food by the soldiers to grateful recipients.[109]

German civilians anticipated the arrival of French colonial troops with similar dread. Those "colored" Moroccan and other colonial soldiers, like African Americans and unlike white French troops, seemed racially foreign, but Germans' relations with French colonial troops tended to differ from their dealings with African Americans. German fears of French colonial soldiers did not disappear with the first contacts. Instead, French colonial troops are remembered as having committed large numbers of crimes against the civilian population, ranging from rape, to theft, to general "swinishness." French colonial troops seem to have been second only to the Russian soldiers in the incidence of cases of mistreatment of defeated Germans. In general, Germans regarded the American forces as more disciplined and orderly than French troops, especially the colonial forces.[110]

Part of the disparity between reports of crimes by French colonial troops and by African American soldiers probably was due to the different ways in which those troops were employed. Reports suggest that rapes and other crimes occurred most often in the hours or days immediately after troops entered a locality where they had encountered resistance. Colonial soldiers often served as combat soldiers, who were more likely to commit crimes against the population than soldiers in service and supply units that generally operated at a distance from battle.[111] African Americans were heavily overrepresented in such noncombat units. Moreover, the French carried fresh memories of atrocities committed by German troops on French soil. The general of the French army responded to the Archbishop of Freiburg's complaints concerning crimes by French troops in Germany by reminding him of the "German terror" practiced in France, while noting that his soldiers nevertheless endeavored to control their justifiable anger.[112]

In addition, colonial soldiers at times appear to have been held by their commanders to a lower standard of orderliness than were European or African American soldiers. Two different members of the German clergy reported in 1945 that complaints of misconduct, including widespread rape of German women, by colonial troops in the town of Bruchsal had been met by the response that such excesses simply amounted to the application of the "African law of war" following the town's sharp defense against the French forces. The differences in the German population's relations with French colonial troops and with African Americans testify to the multiplicity of factors involved in relations between Germans and "blacks." Race never existed in isolation from other aspects of social existence, such as customary mores, nationality, status, and education.[113]

The wave of rapes by African American soldiers predicted by Nazi propaganda failed to materialize, although some cases did occur. The number of rape allegations involving U.S. troops in the European Theater peaked at 501 in the month of April 1945. Germans brought most of those allegations, and many of them alleged that the perpetrator was African American. The salience of the specter of the black rapist in the German imagination at war's end had less to do with people's experiences than the expectations attached to the first contacts with blacks in Germany.[114] Prompted in part by the recommendation of physicians who urged that women who suffered rape by black soldiers should have access to abortions, the Bavarian Council of Ministers decided at its July 26, 1945, meeting to legalize abortion. German women who sought approval for abortions sometimes identified the father as a black rapist and based their petition on the Nazi-era "eugenic indication."[115]

White American officials were likely predisposed to credit German allegations of rape leveled against African Americans to a greater degree than charges against white troops and to respond with harsher measures against black perpetrators. Between June 9, 1942, and January 19, 1946, ninety-nine African American soldiers in the European Theater were convicted of rape, compared with fifty-eight white soldiers. African Americans were overrepresented in those cases, since they made up only about 10 percent of the soldiers in the army. In the same period, four white soldiers were executed for rape, compared with twenty-five black soldiers.[116] The decision by an army court-martial in April 1945 to sentence two black GIs to death and a third to a life in prison for raping two German women provoked heated criticism in the black press. The *Chicago Defender* asserted that the evidence from the trial showed that the women had consented and that the soldiers were convicted only because "German women are Aryans, are white."[117] Despite the persistence of racial prejudice in courts-martial in Europe, it appears that African American men stood a better chance of successfully defending themselves against a rape charge brought by a white woman in occupied Germany than they did in the American South.[118]

Among the German population the image of women as victims of black marauders rapidly dissipated as Germans focused increasingly on the larger numbers of German women who engaged in voluntary sexual contacts with African Americans.[119] A priest in Mannheim-Wallstadt, for example, reported that African American soldiers had committed two rapes in the parish, but, on balance, most people took the crimes and lesser offenses committed by the occupiers as "unavoidable consequences of a lost war." The priest seemed at least as concerned by German women's willingness to engage in consensual sexual relations during the following weeks, reporting that "some black soldiers . . . had carried on in an immoral manner with German girls . . . even within the cemetery walls."[120] Events in Jöhlingen illustrate the rapidity and sharpness of the turn against German women. The local priest began his report by describing a wave of rapes perpetrated by French Moroccan combat troops upon the taking of the town. Soon, however, the front advanced and the combat units moved on. The minister complained that in the ensuing days "all of the terror of the past weeks" had seemingly disappeared, and women now ran after the occupying soldiers, from whom previously "they could not hide themselves well enough."[121]

Defeated Germany

When the Third Reich offered its unconditional surrender to the Allies in May 1945, Germans faced a desperate situation and an uncertain future. The closing years of the war brought home to the Germans the mass death and privation previously visited on others. German military losses amounted to roughly 5.3 million dead.[122] Millions more soldiers were prisoners of war in the hands of the Allies on V-E day. During and immediately after the war, approximately 14 million Germans were displaced from their homes in the east, in many cases forcibly expelled by Soviets, Poles, Czechs, or others. The refugees had enormous difficulty finding shelter within a shrunken Germany, which had suffered increasingly destructive aerial bombing. Indeed, in some cities the majority of the housing had been destroyed. In all of defeated Germany's cities, people crowded into existing buildings or improvised primitive dwellings in cellars, bomb shelters, or garden huts as they faced the prospect of hunger. Food was in short supply. In summer 1945, Allied food rations distributed to the occupied population amounted to only about 950 calories per day.[123]

Germans in 1945 expected a harsh peace from the Allies, who had suffered unprecedented losses caused by Nazi aggression. The Allies had agreed among themselves to administer Germany jointly, marking out four separate zones of occupation where the armed forces of the United States, the Soviet Union, Great Britain, and France would be stationed to oversee the denazification and democratization of the Germans. The victors had offered no assurances upon accepting the surrender, and they contemplated various plans to reform and to extract reparations from the Germans. The vanquished rightly feared for the German nation-state's continuing viability under this four-power control.

The occupied population quickly recognized the reality of their defeat and continuing subordination. As Berlin fell in 1945, Soviet soldiers perpetrated mass rapes of civilian women in retribution for the war of annihilation that the Wehrmacht had waged against the Soviet population. Nothing like the scale of that sexual violence occurred in the western part of Germany. The Americans, however, aimed to demonstrate to Germans their new pariah status by implementing a policy of non-fraternization, according to which American GIs were prohibited from exchanging pleasantries or even shaking hands with Germans. From the beginning, American soldiers consistently flouted the ban, such that the military relaxed it in successive stages and finally abolished it on October 1, 1945, but it pointedly demonstrated that the Germans lived under an occupying force that considered itself militarily, economically, and morally superior.[124]

As the months passed, Germany's economic problems persisted. Wartime disruption could not be overcome. Four-power cooperation in the administration of Germany proved elusive, and each of the occupiers quickly began to administer their separate zones of occupation in divergent ways. As a result, the previously integrated German national economy faced new, seemingly insurmountable obstacles to recovery. The Germans in the American- and British-occupied regions, which had been net importers of food, could not feed themselves. The Americans and the British thus found themselves in the position of paying for the privilege of occupying Germany, as they funded imports of food to supply the population. Food, coal, and other necessities for the Germans were rationed and remained scarce. As late as April 1947, civilian rations in the merged American and British "bizone" still amounted to only 1,040 calories per day on average. In the flourishing black market that grew up alongside the rationing regime, cigarettes served as a medium of exchange in the absence of a reliable currency. Almost three years after the war's end, many Germans survived only by selling possessions and scrounging or stealing what food could be obtained in foraging expeditions.[125]

By the spring of 1947 the wartime cooperation between the United States and the Soviet Union had given way to the confrontation of the Cold War. Occupied Germany represented a crucial point of tension between the Americans and the Soviets, where the differing policies carried out in the neighboring occupation zones cast into sharp relief the two nations' competing ideologies. Although neither power had a detailed blueprint for reshaping Germany, each fitfully moved toward building a society in its own image. The Soviet state socialist model differed fundamentally from the liberal capitalist system that the United States envisioned for

Louis E. Martin, editor and publisher of the Michigan Chronicle, *during a European tour by members of the African American press in 1948. Testifying to the comparative wealth of African Americans in occupied Germany, the original caption ironically explained that Martin, in a "mood of reckless extravagance," was pictured contributing one cigarette to a "Berlin one-man band." Courtesy* New Journal and Guide, *Norfolk, Virginia.*

reformed Germany. By spring 1947, American policy makers had given up on cooperating with the Soviet Union and, with influential Germans, had embarked on a course that would create a separate West German entity linked to other countries in Western Europe and oriented toward the United States.[126]

As Cold War tensions escalated, American priorities in occupied Germany shifted from punishing and reforming the Germans to reviving the West German economy and winning Germans over to the American side. An essential step in that direction occurred in June 1948, when the Americans introduced a new currency in the three western zones of occupation. The measure, designed to revive the western German economy by providing a stable medium of exchange, effectively split west Germany from the Soviet zone, revealing the fault lines that would form the borders of two separate German states in 1949. The currency reform, which was accompanied by the elimination of price controls, proved a remarkable success in the western zones. Literally overnight, businesses filled their shop windows with goods for sale, as the reform established a stable basis for economic recovery.[127]

Eliminating Race Hatred

In the wake of the Third Reich's fall, American occupiers, as well as influential Germans, believed that Nazi race hatred, as it was most commonly described, needed to be eliminated from Germany if the country were to be democratized. Of course, Nazism's principal victims had been Jewish, and the effort accordingly focused primarily on the evils of anti-Semitism. Contrary to conventional historical wisdom, though, Nazi racial ideology, in fact, was commonly understood in 1945 to include more than simply racial anti-Semitism. It certainly included the belief that Germans belonged to a Master Race and less prominently, but importantly, included belief in the racial inferiority of blacks.

To a significant degree, the American assault on Nazi racism constituted an effort to replace the national/racial typology with the tripartite racial schema, demoting the Aryan race to German ethnicity. Ruth Benedict neatly summarized the critique in "The Races of Mankind," rejecting Nazi racial doctrine in favor of a tripartite division of races identified as Caucasian, Mongoloid, and Negroid. "Aryans, Jews, Italians," Benedict insisted, were "*not* races."[128] The German Committee of the Office of War Information (OWI), which bore responsibility for planning the postwar democratization of Germany, included Benedict's book on race among works approved for distribution in occupied Germany.[129] American field press control officers likewise chastised the author of an article in the newspaper *Der Allgauer* for exhibiting "a racist strain of thought" in attributing the sympathy shown by a departing American officer for the local population to "the German blood that flow[ed] through his veins."[130] Although the national/racial typology retained some currency in the United States, American policy makers consistently sought to persuade the Germans that they were not Aryans; they were white.[131]

The effort to convince Germans that they were white, not Aryan, served to bridge the purported racial division between Germans and other whites while simultaneously reinforcing the division between Germans and blacks. Individual Germans felt that dynamic in operation in postwar Germany. That dual function of whiteness is manifested in one German woman's recollection of an episode of "reconciliation" between the French and Germans that occurred in the early days of the occupation. The

woman recalled that two Frenchmen, "educated whites," were searching
a building when they noticed a Tour de France poster on the wall of the
room of one of the tenants, an elderly member of the Nazi Party. Upon
learning that he had ridden in the Tour de France, they fell to exchanging
recollections of cycling races. The wartime divisions between the soldiers
and civilians were quickly smoothed over as the soldiers assured the man
that the building would not be requisitioned. The woman's description of
the two Frenchmen as "whites" provided an appropriate means of framing the reconciliation between French and Germans.[132] Whiteness played
a similar role in a Bremen woman's memory of the occupation, as she
recounted an incident when a white American soldier, accompanied by a
black soldier, offered her a ride in a jeep. The young woman put aside her
initial reservations as she thought to herself, "If the white is there, then
nothing can happen to you," and hopped in. She received a scare when
the white soldier got out after a short time and left her "alone with the
black," but the "comical" ride passed without incident.[133]

Public appeals based on whiteness, like those issued during the French
occupation of the Rhineland, did not appear in postwar Germany. In private, though, individual Germans nursed such sentiments. The American
anthropologist David Rodnick, who authored a postwar study of German
national character, quoted an anonymous German informant:

> We were deeply hurt when you Americans sent Negroes to Germany
> in soldiers' uniforms. How can America do this to us, a white people?
> We are not used to Negroes here; you in America are, because you have
> mongrels of all kinds; but here in Germany we are a pure white race.
> To see a Negro shocks us, as we would be shocked to see a poisonous
> snake while walking through the woods.[134]

The speaker eschewed the ideology of a German Master Race and instead
appealed to common whiteness between Germans and white Americans.
Germans, according to that appeal, differed from white Americans not
in any Aryan racial superiority but only in their "purity" and concomitant lack of familiarity with blacks and "mongrels," differences that white
Americans, the informant asserted, should have respected.

Shared whiteness could assume a menacing cast when directed against
nonwhites. One American officer involved in the re-education of German
prisoners of war proposed in February 1945 recruiting German POWs to
fight against the Japanese, who were engaged in a war not only against
the "Anglo-Saxon powers but also *against the white race.*" The scheme had
the advantage of saving American lives, but its advocate urged that fighting against the common racial foe would further "lead slowly towards an
ideological reorientation of the German prisoners of war into the ideological world of the western and civilized powers."[135] That sort of racial war
would have found a willing recruit in one German POW who returned

from captivity to find that his wife had borne the child of a black soldier. The German man's reaction was described in a letter from a doctor
who advocated permitting abortion in such cases. The doctor wrote that
the man wished to leave his wife and volunteer for the war against the
Japanese in hopes of finding death on the battlefield.[136] Race, according
to such logic, produced a peculiar reconfiguration of wartime alliances,
with African Americans and Japanese ranged against white Germans and
Americans.

Critical observers perceived the formation of a postwar alliance
among whites against blacks in Germany as evidence that "Allies and the
Germans agreed on something: discriminating against blacks."[137] That
critique received its fullest statement in the postwar period in Wolfgang
Koeppen's novel *Tauben im Gras* (*Pigeons on the Grass*). The novel, with its
unusual openness on the subject of race and its avowedly antiracist stance,
was intended and received as radical. It was thus in many ways unrepre-
sentative of German public opinion, and its popular and critical success
was modest at best.[138] It bears examination, though, as an effort to expose
and critique a transnational alliance of whites against blacks and Jews.
The novel was premised on a belief that Germans shared whiteness with
white Americans, a "[s]olidarity of the white race" prized by one character
who represents unreconstructed Nazi racism.[139]

A wide gulf divided whites and blacks in the novel. African American
soldier Washington Price in Germany is stranded in the "white world, the
hostile world."[140] The division between blacks and whites represented not
merely social distance but real danger. In an important scene, a crowd of
pimps and other lowlifes unite in a melee against the black GI Odysseus
Cotton. The "pack leapt up, the herd won out, camaraderie was victorious," as the Germans attack Odysseus, "the gorilla, King Kong, fucker, . . .
fucking nigger." Odysseus is "back in the old war White against Black. The
war was being fought here, too."[141]

At the novel's climax, a false rumor that a black GI has murdered a
German child whips a white German and American crowd gathered in
a beer hall into a frenzy. After only a moment of hesitation for lack of
a "Führer," the crowd, resembling a lynch mob in the American South
or Nazi thugs on the Night of Broken Glass (*Kristallnacht*), bursts out of
the beer hall and makes for a black soldiers' club. The "nigger music"
audible outside the club provokes the crowd to throw stones through its
windows. While "the tinkling glass" reminds the mob's older members of
"another blindness, of an earlier street action, of other splinters," the black
soldiers inside the club are paralyzed by the "fate that pursued them, the
lifelong persecution that wouldn't let them free, even in Germany." White
racism assumes its most grotesque form in the person of Frau Behrend,
who incites the crowd to stone her daughter for defiling herself with the
unborn child of a black man.[142]

Koeppen's critique of international white racism, in which he equated Nazi racial anti-Semitism with postwar white discrimination against African Americans, was unusual in Germany. Nevertheless, Americans and Germans alike shared a sense after 1945 that white racial discrimination against blacks would be coming under increased scrutiny. Nazism had given racism a bad name. The assault on Nazi race hatred in fact extended to critiquing racism more broadly.

The effort had several dimensions. Planning for the occupation specifically targeted the Master Race doctrine for eradication, but military officials believed that the task would prove difficult, fearing that "[t]he German conception of themselves as a 'Master Race' [had] been too deeply implanted to be eradicated outright."[143] The army instructed the individual soldier participating in the occupation of Germany on the racial issue in the Civil Affairs Division's "Pocket Guide to Germany," which warned that Germans believed in their own racial superiority. The guide advised soldiers that their "very presence on German soil [would] serve as a constant demonstration to the German people, that the master race theory that sent them forth to bathe the world in blood, was just so much tragic nonsense." One of the nonfraternization radio announcements urged American soldiers, "The German civilian's complete acceptance of the Nazi doctrine means that he supports and encourages Hitler's theories of the Masterrace [sic]. Have nothing to do with those who *think* they are superior to you."[144]

American officials recognized, however, that Americans themselves often harbored racist prejudices as well and therefore guarded against American racism to the extent possible. The "Pocket Guide to Germany" admonished each soldier to guard against the likely German effort to "plant seeds of . . . racial intolerance . . . in *your* mind."[145] In early planning for the occupation, G-1 officials specifically warned of the danger of German "appeals to racial and cultural similarities between Germans and Anglo-Saxons" directed at American soldiers.[146] Such fears suggested a belief in the continuing hold of the national/racial typology on the American mind, as well as a vision of the American soldier as an Anglo-Saxon, which obviously overlooked the presence of people of different ethnicities, Jews, and African Americans in the occupation force. The army also targeted German racism in the film shown to occupation troops titled *Your Job in Germany,* which informed soldiers that Germans needed to be cured of the belief that they were a super race.[147]

The primary focus of the American effort to reform Germans' racial beliefs rested, of course, on the German population. At the most basic level, the well-publicized American policy dictated the repeal of all "racial laws" in Germany. Immediately upon the U.S. Army's entry into the territory of the Third Reich, General Dwight Eisenhower decreed the abrogation of such laws.[148] Incongruously enough, many American states at the time still had anti-miscegenation laws on the books. The effort to excise Nazi race hatred from the law found its formal expression in Control Council Law No. 1, which repealed Nazi racial laws and prohibited discrimination by Germans on the grounds of "race, nationality, religious beliefs, or opposition to" Nazism or its doctrines.[149] More ambitiously, the Americans aspired to purge racism from public discourse in occupied Germany. The Civil Censorship Division banned the circulation of any existing works in Germany that spread "racial theories or race hatred."[150] As part of the general censorship of German media in the American zone, military government prohibited Germans from publishing newspapers or books, or staging plays without a license. Military government granted licenses after screening applicants, subject to restrictions designed to prevent the spread of Nazi propaganda through the media. The restrictions on licensees included a prohibition on "the propagation of National Socialist or related 'voelkisch' ideas, such as racism and race hatred [wie Religions- und Rassenhaß], any Facist [sic] or anti-democratic ideas."[151] In November 1945, the Office of Military Government for Bavaria (OMGBY) informed the Bavarian Ministry of Justice that it had received reports that the Munich public prosecutor's office continued to designate the race of prisoners with the term Aryan on Nazi-era forms. OMGBY instructed Bavarian officials that the use of such racial classifications violated occupation policy.[152]

Following American military government's decision in spring 1946 to permit Germans in the zone to receive international communications, censorship policy mandated intercepting any such communications that included "[e]xpressions of sympathy or agreement with the principles of National Socialism, including its racial theories." American censorship officials thus found themselves in the curious position of protecting Germans from racist letters sent by Americans.[153] Despite such occasionally embarrassing contradictions, American military government further endeavored to implement a re-education program to persuade Germans of racism's evils.

As part of that effort, the occupiers also tried to convince Germans of the dignity of African Americans and to suggest that the United States offered a model for equitable treatment of racial minorities. American officials staged numerous public events on the subjects of African Americans and American race relations, including lectures by African Americans and presentations of African American music.[154] The head of the America House cultural exchange program in Bavaria delivered a radio address in December 1948 in which he addressed prejudice against blacks. He condemned racial hatred as undemocratic and asked rhetorically, "Why would it be unbearable to think . . . that a colored man should be a lawyer or a doctor?"[155] In May 1946 the Information Control Division (ICD) proposed producing a film to correct German "misconceptions" about

African Americans by "showing how intergrated [sic] the Negro is in American life." ICD acknowledged that the subject was a "touchy" one and suggested that any such film would need to deal in part with "the seamier side of Negro treatment." Other American officials believed that the "Negro question" was too sensitive to merit a film devoted to it alone and suggested that African Americans needed to be included in a general treatment of minorities in the United States. That approach won out, as the Office of Military Government for Germany, United States, ultimately sponsored the production of a documentary film completed in April 1948 that provided "a history of the races of mankind, tracing man's cultural and physical development in the light of modern scientific discoveries."[156]

Americans soon found themselves hoisted on their own petard, as discussions of African Americans inevitably provoked questions about the extent of racial discrimination against African Americans in the United States.[157] Germans on occasion sought to expose American hypocrisy regarding Nazi race hatred by pointing to the persistence of racial prejudice in the United States. As the fighting in Europe drew to its conclusion, Joseph Dunner, a member of OWI's London office, prepared a summary of German POWs' attitudes toward the United States to guide American democratization efforts in occupied Germany. According to Dunner's May 1, 1945, memorandum, the prevailing sentiment among captured Germans held that "Americans had better be quiet about Nazi Germany's treatment of the Jews," since anti-Semitism existed in the United States and "the main racial problem in America, the Negro problem, is treated with the same ruthlessness and sense of discrimination as the Jewish problem in Germany."[158] Cardinal Graf Clemens August von Galen observed in a March 1946 address delivered in Rome that Germany had no monopoly on "race hatred." In the United States, "the land of unlimited democracy," American Indians had been "exterminated" (ausgerottet). Moreover, Americans made no secret of their "aversion toward the yellow race," and the Ku Klux Klan continued to commit "the wildest excesses against the Negro."[159]

With the onset of the Cold War, Soviet (and to a lesser degree German) criticisms of American racism grew more troublesome for American claims to practice true democracy.[160] Indeed, occupied Germany witnessed the first moves by American policy makers as they began to wrestle with the connection between civil rights for African Americans at home and the Cold War struggle for American leadership abroad.[161] As the African American journalist Roi Ottley wrote in 1946, "It is a rather melancholy fact that the American race problem came into dramatic focus on German soil."[162] Military government addressed the question of American race relations directly in a series of talks delivered in German to German audiences by Lieutenant Colonel Marcus Ray, the African American Adviser on Negro Affairs to General Lucius Clay. Ray spoke on the subject of "the

American Negro" at most of the America Houses in Germany.[163] The text of Ray's speech acknowledged that African Americans continued to suffer discrimination in the United States, but, in an echo of Gunnar Myrdal's work, Ray argued that growing numbers of Americans were working to realize the ideals spelled out in the Declaration of Independence and the Bill of Rights. The speech included no mention of Nazism or German racism. It likewise avoided mentioning the Soviet Union directly, but Ray clearly had Soviet allegations of hypocrisy in mind. He opened by observing that, whatever its faults, at least the United States permitted free inquiry and public debate, even on vexed questions like race relations. He implicitly presented the Cold War as a battle of ideas and closed by optimistically looking forward to the time when American ideals might be realized by "all of humanity."[164]

Germans, especially members of the political elite and the press, participated in the critique of racism. In the new atmosphere, political and religious leaders inveighed against Nazi racism, as the founding statements of the new postwar parties condemned "race hatred."[165] Antiracist concerns especially motivated Jews and other returning German émigrés.[166] The critique of Nazi race hatred was not limited to such individuals, however. In September 1945 the *Frankfurter Rundschau* printed a lengthy essay identifying racism as the "source" (*Ursprung*) of the Nazi system and all of its crimes.[167] The Christian Democratic Union (CDU) publicly professed its intention to fight against race hatred in its *Kölner Leitsätze*. In a December 1946 programmatic statement, the Bavarian Christian Social Union (CSU) included as the second of its thirty points a rejection of "every form of race hatred," as contrary to the Christian recognition of the dignity of the individual.[168] The minister-president of Bavaria, Dr. Wilhelm Hoegner, speaking before a meeting of fellow Social Democrats in November 1945, asserted that the crimes of Nazism showed that if the necessary "inner purification" was to be carried out, it was important to assert the fundamental common humanity of all people above and beyond divisions of "religion, race, nation, and class."[169] Nazi race hatred clearly had suffered a loss of legitimacy in the eyes of Germans by 1945.

German diagnoses of the root causes of Nazism, however, often highlighted other aspects of the regime. Religious leaders in the Catholic and Protestant churches focused especially on secularism and materialism as the more fundamental developments that had prepared the ground for Nazism, which represented simply a particularly malignant manifestation of these modern ills. Conservatives discerned in Hitler's charismatic hold over the German people evidence of the dangers of mass democracy, whereas communists saw Nazism as the logical outgrowth of monopoly capitalism.[170] In each of these competing assessments, Nazism's racial doctrine could be considered of secondary importance. All of them, however, were consistent with the official antiracist line.

The double-pronged assault on anti-Semitism and prejudice against African Americans targeted two important aspects of Nazism's racial worldview, which regarded Jews and blacks as allied members of inferior races. Eligibility for membership in the party had depended on the applicant's ability to certify the absence of any "Jewish or colored taint." In this respect, Nazism had drawn on a deeper linkage in German thought between the two groups that regarded blacks and Jews as radically different from Germans.[171] Maggi Morehouse has interviewed one African American GI who had a "Jewish girlfriend" in occupied Germany. He recalled that among Germans he encountered, "None . . . wanted to be Nazis then." Although Germans may have refrained from openly registering objections to that relationship, older attitudes persisted in places. An anonymous poster appeared in the Schwabing suburb of Munich in 1947, proclaiming that Germany "had been reduced to a playground for Jews and Niggers."[172]

The dispelling of the myth of the Aryan race made the notion of a Jewish *race* untenable. The persistence of religious and cultural anti-Semitism in Germany among both Germans and American occupiers after 1945, however, must not be underestimated. Polls measuring German public opinion carried out by American military government in the postwar period demonstrated that many Germans continued to hold anti-Semitic beliefs. However, *racial* anti-Semitism suffered a decisive defeat.[173] As Jews grew less important to the postwar German racial imagination, blacks gained importance as a foil for racial self-definition. One observer voiced fears that African Americans threatened to replace Jews in the German racist worldview, reporting that "[c]onversation among civilians in this area indicates that anti-Negroism has replaced anti-Semitism as an expression of German race superiority."[174] Such a change matched an exchange of an Aryan racial identity for whiteness.

American policy had a dramatic, immediate effect on the public language of race in the American zone. Public statements of Nazi racial dogma, including expressions of anti-Semitism or a belief in the racial inferiority of blacks, disappeared. Objections to the presence of African American soldiers in the territory of the defeated Third Reich did not appear in the German press, a dramatic change from the Nazi propaganda campaign at the close of the war. There was no counterpart in post–World War II Germany to the propaganda campaign against the "Black Horror" on the Rhine that followed World War I. Germans understood that overtly racist statements attacking African Americans were no longer publicly acceptable. Indeed, Germans after 1945 sought to avoid even using the word *race*.[175]

Of course, racism did not simply vanish with the defeat of the Third Reich. Although no longer acceptable in public pronouncements, racism doubtless found frequent expression in private. Ideas about race could also appear after 1945 clothed in a new language of morality. In Hans Fischer's comparison of the 1935 and 1955 editions of Robert Pfaff-Giesberg's historical-ethnographic study of slavery, for example, Fischer effectively shows how Pfaff-Giesberg adapted to conditions before and after 1945. The 1935 edition attributed a role to slavery in the fall of the Roman Empire, as the aristocratic Romans took mistresses from slaves "of every race." The 1935 edition explained that the fall of the empire was promoted by "this corruption of racial morality" (*diese Zersetzung der Rassenmoral*). In 1955, Pfaff-Giesberg prudently cut the reference to race. He revised the text to attribute the problems to "the corruption of notions of morality" (*die Zersetzung sittlicher Begriffe*).[176] As will be discussed in Chapter 3, the use of the language of morality in place of expressly racial language exemplified here occurred on the everyday level in occupied Germany very shortly after the war's end.

There is ample evidence that many Germans privately continued to regard African Americans as inferior to whites, among whom Germans numbered themselves. And many Germans regarded the presence of black troops in the occupying American forces as a particularly pointed insult to German dignity. David Rodnick cited the views of two conservative leaders of the Christian Democratic Union party in Eschwege for evidence of the continuing hold of racist ideology in Germany. One asserted that a "Negro" could "never be the equal of a German." This informant, who had insisted on anonymity, was undoubtedly among the most extreme found by Rodnick, as such views served as representative of the political Right in Germany, but an appreciable number of Germans must have held similar opinions.[177]

In 1945 the unseating of the "Master Race" in Germany was only beginning. In that process, African Americans would serve as a foil to Germans' self-definition as white. Whiteness from the first suggested the existence of a bond to Germany's American conquerors, one that could facilitate the embryonic project of integrating Germany into the white, Christian West.

CHAPTER TWO

Blackness and German Whiteness through American Eyes

African American troops in occupied Germany posed a fundamental problem in the eyes of most American officials at the time. How could African Americans be used in the democratization of Germany without alienating the Germans? The conceptualizing of the problem in such terms rested on a particular set of beliefs. First, in the eyes of the officials who determined American policy, Germans were members of the white race, who objected sharply to being subordinated to black soldiers. Second, the army regarded African American GIs as generally inferior and troublesome, especially as sexual relations between them and German women produced a train of difficulties for officials tasked with maintaining order. Misbehavior by African Americans might well strengthen latent German resistance to the occupation and belie American pretensions to be a model for Germany. Accordingly, the military sought initially to limit the presence, visibility, and role of African American soldiers in Germany in order to avoid arousing Germans' racial antipathy.

U.S. policy on the use of African American soldiers in Germany, and in the military more generally, however, came under increasing pressure by civil rights leaders, who argued that a Jim Crow army could not stamp out Nazi race hatred. The reformers based their arguments on one or both of two inconsistent bases. On the one hand, they claimed that Nazism would only be strengthened if the War Department bowed to German racial sensitivities by restricting African American servicemen to an inconspicuous presence in occupied Germany. Alternatively, advocates pressing for greater civil rights in the United States pointed to the willingness of considerable numbers of German women to carry on relations with African Americans as evidence that white American prejudice constituted the real source of racially discriminatory policies pursued by the War Department.

Throughout the period of the military occupation of Germany, the prevailing view in the military regarded African Americans as poor soldiers, whom the army nevertheless needed to use. The army command in Europe (from July 1945 organized as the United States Forces, European Theater [USFET], and then reorganized as the European Command [EUCOM]) accordingly resolved to use African American soldiers with caution in order to minimize friction with the German population. Initially, the military opted for heavily restricting the role of African Americans in Germany, while some commanders wished that they might be banished from Europe altogether. From 1945 to 1949, slowly and haltingly, reformers increased African American soldiers' role in the occupation. Their success corresponded with improved measures of control over soldiers in Germany, which helped to reduce trouble between GIs and local civilians.

The Army's View of Germans

Military officials running the occupation of Germany regarded Germans as members of the white race. As such, Germans might be expected to object to occupying a position subservient to black soldiers serving in the army. At the same time, occupation authorities generally held that substantial numbers of Germans adhered to Nazism's race dogma, which insisted upon Germans' racial superiority over all other races, including and especially the "Negro" race. Policy makers generally saw Germans as espousing an illegitimate doctrine of racial superiority but also, as whites, feeling an understandable and, in some measure, legitimate distaste for being subjected to black soldiers.

Occupation authorities amassed considerable evidence attesting to the powerful hold of racist beliefs on German public opinion. Army commanders in Europe reported to the War Department in response to a May 1945 questionnaire on the utilization of African American soldiers that relations between blacks and Germans were "not as amicable" as those with other Europeans.[1] One report opined that relations between African Americans and German civilians "will never be amicable, because of the Nazi propaganda directed against the American Negro."[2] The author of another report was more inclined to believe African Americans than the Germans who brought allegations of rape against them. He noted that though several instances of rape committed by African Americans had been reported, many of the reports were false. The author speculated that "[p]rior German propaganda to the German people directed against Negro troops may well have been a large factor in causing the German women to always report instances of difficulties with Negro troops."[3] Military intelligence analysts believed Germans' attitudes toward African Americans could cause resistance to the American occupation. One intelligence officer wrote: "Racial friction was reported from numerous areas where Negro troops are stationed, and unless the situation is watched carefully, more serious incidents are likely to occur. The display of racial intolerance is music to the ears of the many Germans who have not forgotten the teaching of the Nazis."[4]

German thinking about African Americans and race more generally became the subject of two systematic studies early in the occupation. The first of those studies was carried out in October 1945 in Giessen, where 8,000 of the 10,000 troops in the area were African Americans. The survey concluded, "[U]nfavorable reactions on the part of the Germans were fewer than expected; in fact, a considerable proportion of the GIESSEN population has a better opinion of the Negro since they have had contact with him." Although respondents generally had a "favorable impression of the American Negro," nevertheless they were "definitely opposed to 'relations' between German girls and Negro soldiers."[5]

The Office of Military Government for Germany, United States (OMGUS), conducted a similar study in October 1946 in Mannheim following reports of serious disturbances in the city where large numbers of white and black troops were stationed. Misconduct by African American troops in that city had been the subject of an inspector general investigation in August 1946. A further report of trouble surfaced in September 1946, as the Information Control Division (ICD) for Württemberg-Baden raised concerns that crimes by African American troops, including "rapes said to be occurring almost daily," had aroused considerable antipathy among the local populace.[6] In order to better discern the reactions of Mannheim citizens to the black troops quartered in the area, ICD carried out its October survey. ICD found that "a large proportion of the Mannheim population" was "concerned about the behavior of the [black] troops stationed in their city"; 15 percent of respondents were "much afraid" of the African American troops. The report noted that the study had found among the population of Mannheim "some effect of prejudice" and fear stemming from the "appearance and strangeness" of African Americans. The real root of the problem, however, was not preexisting German racial doctrines but "rumored extra-legal actions in which the troops are alleged to indulge."[7] The survey's conclusion, though, fit imperfectly with the finding that 38 percent of the respondents agreed that "Negroes, compared with the white race, are a lower race." At the same time, about 70 percent of respondents with an opinion on the question believed African Americans to be "friendlier" than white troops.[8]

Other surveys addressed Germans' ideas on the subject of race more generally. In an August 1946 survey, 30 percent of respondents agreed that "Negroes are members of an unworthy (lower) race." Four surveys over the period from December 1946 to January 1948 asked, "Do you think that some races of people are more fit to rule than others?" In all of the surveys more than 40 percent of Germans answered yes. The American social scientists divided Germans into five rather wooden categories (assuming, apparently, no overlap) according to their predominant attitude, "little bias" (20 percent), "nationalists" (19 percent), "racists" (22 percent), "anti-Semites" (21 percent), and "intense anti-Semites" (18 percent).[9]

None of these surveys offered policy prescriptions for the use of African American troops, nor could they provide a clear picture of Germans' attitudes toward African American soldiers. The influence of the surveys on USFET policy is thus difficult to judge precisely. It is apparent, though, that they did nothing to dissuade policy makers from seeking to limit contacts between African American troops and the German population to the extent possible, a goal upon which the American military settled fairly early in the occupation. In addition, the surveys testified to the conviction held by influential elements in the occupation forces that many Germans resented the presence of African Americans on their soil. The army further understood that Germans were attentive observers of its policies toward African Americans.

American officials insisted that pragmatism should determine the army's use of African Americans in Germany. In opposing formation of a black constabulary unit, for example, Major General Willard S. Paul, the head of the War Department's Personnel and Administration Division, argued that even if a sufficient number of competent African American soldiers could be found to form such a unit (which he doubted), the racial prejudices of the Germans would make the tasks insuperable for African Americans: "[T]he obvious fact must be recognized that effective supervision by Negro troops over German Nationals would be difficult, even for highly qualified individuals, because of prejudices and beliefs held by the Germans generally. The fact that we decry such prejudices and beliefs should not cause us to overlook the problems and difficulties which they raise in the discharge of occupation tasks."[10] Once the fighting ended, U.S. military officials in Germany generally declined to use black troops to confront and dispel Germans' perceived racial prejudices where such use might interfere with what were regarded as more important issues. Instead, USFET sought in its use of African Americans to appease the German populace on the issue without publicly repudiating the United States' avowed commitment to fighting Nazi race hatred.

The Black Soldier in the Eyes of the White Military

A dismal view of African American soldiers proved at least as important in determining army policy on their use in Germany as the desire to avoid irritating Germans' racial sensitivities. At the conclusion of World War II, most (but not all) military officials believed that African Americans made bad soldiers. The low quality of black soldiers was believed to express itself in three interrelated ways: poor performance, low intelligence, and high rates of misconduct, including especially infection with venereal diseases. The explanations for African Americans' perceived failures varied. Some advanced biological reasons and others pointed to environmental factors. More common was a confused amalgam of the two.

On May 23, 1945, at the recommendation of Assistant Secretary of War McCloy, the War Department circulated a questionnaire to all thirty-five of its major commands regarding "Participation of Negro Troops in the Post-War Military Establishment." The information collected was intended to provide planners with a comprehensive assessment of the army's experience with black troops and its current practices as it formulated its postwar plans. The army's responses reflected widespread disappointment with African American soldiers.[11]

USFET reported that the overall performance of African American troops was below average. Brigadier General R. B. Lovett summarized, "The average Negro soldier lacks initiative, aggressiveness, dependability, personal pride, sense of responsibility, and the ability to make decisions." USFET asserted that instances where African American units had contributed outstanding work resulted from "the leadership of capable white officers." The failures of African American units thus were attributed to the African Americans, and in the cases where black units achieved successes, credit went to the white officers leading them. European commanders recommended that the War Department continue its policy of segregation.[12]

USFET's assessment fit into the general pattern of army views of African American troops' performance and its support for maintaining segregation. The responses to the survey further indicated a consensus that large all-black units like the 92nd Infantry Division had been a failure.[13] The commanders most directly responsible for formulating American policy in Germany shared the widespread belief that African Americans had performed inadequately. Both General Joseph T. McNarney, the commander of USFET, and General Lucius Clay, who served as deputy military governor until March 1947 and head of American forces throughout Europe in his capacity as commander of the reorganized and renamed European Command (EUCOM) from March 1947 until May 1949, held a dim view of their effectiveness.[14]

White commanders up and down the chain of command believed that one of the main reasons that African American soldiers, as a group, had performed poorly was that they were less intelligent than white soldiers. That belief rested in large measure on the fact that black soldiers generally scored lower on the Army's General Classification Test (AGCT). The army administered the test to its recruits after March 1941 in order to determine soldiers' assignments. Scores on the test were divided into five grades, with most people scoring in Grade III and a target average score of 100. People scoring in the two highest grades were expected to form the army's leadership cadre. African Americans generally scored lower on the test than did whites, although the scores of African Americans and whites with similar backgrounds were comparable. Since the army segregated African Americans, black units tended to include disproportionate numbers of low-scoring soldiers. Indeed, about half of the average black unit was composed of men scoring in the lowest test grade, in marked contrast to the average white unit, which drew around 9 percent of its personnel from the lowest grade.[15]

In the 1940s, army leadership focused intensively on AGCT scores. Many people believed, despite denials by army psychologists, that the test measured intelligence. Even if sophisticated people recognized that African Americans' generally lower scores did not reflect differences attributable to biology, convinced racists could misuse the disparity as support for their belief that the "black race" was less intellectually gifted than the "white race." More seriously for army policy on African Americans, however, the test scores suggested to army leadership convinced of the utility of such tests that blacks were poor soldiers. Officers tended to assume that a unit with disproportionately high numbers of personnel in the lowest AGCT grades was doomed to fail.[16]

The preoccupation with AGCT scores was not the sole province of whites. Marcus Ray, who served as Civilian Aide to the Secretary of War from 1946 to 1947, and after August 26, 1947, as adviser to General Clay on Negro Affairs in EUCOM, equated AGCT scores with IQ and thought men with low scores would be poor soldiers.[17] Based on a correlation between misconduct and low AGCT scores, Ray urged the War Department in April 1946 to discharge all personnel, white or black, who had AGCT scores in the lowest category. The men discharged would be replaced by recruiting new personnel with higher test scores. Although the War Department in April 1946 was unwilling to do without the extra manpower of its lowest-scoring personnel, by August the department instructed commanders to discharge unsatisfactory soldiers.[18]

Whereas most African American soldiers were criticized as too dull to be useful, African Americans who scored highly on the AGCT were labeled as troublemakers. One response to the War Department's May 1945 questionnaire, for example, stated, "Claims of discrimination almost invariably originate from men with high AGCT scores." That report iconoclastically found "little or no relation" between AGCT score and performance.[19] USFET's report similarly faulted African American officers, who generally had higher AGCT scores, for having in many cases "displayed a high degree of racial sensitivity."[20]

In addition to problems of perceived poor job performance and low intelligence, African American soldiers, according to army statistics, were guilty of misconduct to an unacceptably high degree. Venereal disease infection received special attention as a particularly troubling type of misconduct. Misconduct was generally expressed in terms of a unit's "serious incident rate," which was calculated by dividing the number of disciplinary infractions that occurred during a month by the number of soldiers, expressed in thousands. The problem seemed especially grave in Europe, where misconduct by both white and black soldiers rose dramatically following the end of hostilities. Army statistics showed a disproportionately high rate of misconduct by African Americans. On July 1, 1946, the serious incident rate among African American soldiers in USFET was more than three times as high as among white soldiers in the command. It was estimated that 70 percent of the serious incidents were committed against Germans.[21] The overrepresentation of African Americans in the crime statistics in Germany was consistent with the general pattern in the army. In 1946 when African Americans comprised only 9.35 percent of army personnel, they made up 25.9 percent of all soldiers sent to correctional facilities.[22]

Crime by African Americans in Europe came to public view when a report by the Judge Advocate General's Department in the European Theater, including a breakdown by race of the charges, convictions, and sentences for crimes committed in Europe, fell into civilian hands. Civilian Aide Marcus Ray urged that as a matter of general policy, such racially segregated surveys should not be made or, at a minimum, should remain classified. The Army Ground Forces, Army Air Forces, Army Service Forces, and Operations Division of the War Department General Staff, however, insisted that racially separated statistical data were vital for planning and operations. On June 26, 1946, in Circular No. 188, the War Department adopted the compromise proposal of General Paul, directing, "[a]ll racially separated statistical data which is prejudicial to the Negro race will be classified as 'restricted' and necessary steps will be taken to prevent its release to nonmilitary sources."[23]

Contemporaries, like subsequent historians, sought to explain the over-representation of African Americans in misconduct statistics. The African American press, which devoted attention to the issue of military justice in occupied Germany, laid much of the blame for the problem on white racism in the military.[24] White officers commonly complained that African Americans were unconcerned with being charged with misconduct or contracting venereal disease. In the view of one officer, African Americans failed to show that they were properly "morally concerned" even about trial by court-martial. The average black soldier similarly did not care that he had "disgraced his race, his unit, or his country by contracting Venereal Disease."[25] The artillery officer for the Third Army was unusual in evaluating "race pride" as a positive factor contributing to better performance by black soldiers, at least for enlisted men and noncommissioned officers. "Race pride and personal pride," the officer wrote, "are pronounced in the better men; conversely the men with most race and personal pride make the best soldiers."[26] That view did not find its way into the USFET report, although in other respects the USFET report borrowed heavily from the artillery officer's report.[27]

Other factors apart from a suspected lack or excess of "race pride" were more important in accounting for the disparity. The venereal disease infection rate among white soldiers, for example, certainly failed to include some cases, since the army did little in the postwar period to improve the reliability of its venereal disease statistics, which were recognized as underreporting the problem during the war.[28] As for misconduct, racial injustice perpetrated against African Americans may have provoked some soldiers to violate army norms. The leading historian of the desegregation of the military has attributed at least some of the disparity to the greater proportion of "disadvantaged individuals, soldiers more likely to get into trouble," in segregated African American units, especially "given the characteristically weak leadership in these units." In addition, selective reporting and enforcement could account for some of the disparity in white and black misconduct rates. Moreover, officers, the vast majority of whom were white, had great discretion in disciplining soldiers. A favorably disposed officer could decline to bring charges for a minor offense, or a martinet could punish even the most minimal infractions. The system thus permitted white officers to act more leniently toward white offenders than black offenders at a time when racial prejudice within society was omnipresent.[29]

Relations between white officers, who generally disliked commanding African Americans, and black troops were often tense in the postwar period. The Seventeenth Armored Group stated categorically that "white officers would in every case prefer duty with white troops."[30] One commander believed that black troops' "natural emotional instability" produced an enormous strain on their white officers, which at times was "about all that they [could] stand."[31] White officers often evidenced irritation at African Americans' sensitivity to racial issues and a lack of understanding of their complaints. Some officers confessed to being mystified by African Americans' objection to segregation. One military police commander observed, "Negro troops resent segregation even though they are given equal or more favorable consideration than white troops." He cited an incident where one section of a theater had been designated for African Americans. The black soldiers had walked out, even though the black section was "as good or better than" the section for whites. Despite the sensitivities of African Americans, the officer favored segregation because there would be "deep resentment by the majority of white personnel" were it abolished.[32]

Black units, composed of troops alert to every slight (intended and unintended) from their white officers, could rapidly develop a poisoned atmosphere. One officer recognized, "Colored troops are quick to identify officers who are prejudiced against them, and such officers can not successfully serve with them."[33] The testimony of another white officer in November 1945 revealed the anxiety, discomfort, and confusion that could follow:

> The Negroes . . . are so terribly sensitive. For example, they resent officers referring to them at a formation as "You people," which is, of course, a common expression with most all of us. Another thing that makes these men frightfully difficult, is that they watch everything you do and repeat everything you say. And, of course, it is difficult when you must continually salve over things that are said. Officers cannot, to my way of thinking, be as free in their habits as when on duty with white troops.[34]

The gulf of misunderstanding between white officers and black troops was manifested, too, in the admonition found in the wartime pamphlet distributed to officers commanding African American units to avoid "[s]uch words as 'boy,' 'Negress,' 'darky,' 'uncle,' 'mammy,' 'aunty,' and 'nigger'" in addressing their troops, because the terms were "generally disliked by Negroes."[35] White officers who needed to be educated regarding the offensiveness of such terms obviously lacked the means to calm tensions before trouble erupted.

White officers commanding black units undoubtedly tended to resort to the comparatively blunter instruments of formal disciplinary measures more quickly than officers commanding white troops. An investigative team headed by Brigadier General Elliott D. Cooke performing a detailed study of one subordinate command in 1946 found, for example, that African Americans were court-martialed at a proportionately higher rate than white soldiers.[36] Officers' discretion could also, however, lead to underreporting of offenses committed, as matters were handled off the books. Black noncommissioned officers appear to have customarily dealt with minor disciplinary infractions by chastising or sometimes physically beating the offending soldier. A commander of a black company stationed in Munich resorted to similarly harsh unofficial measures, giving men accused of misconduct the choice of standing trial for the offense or being confined for one week in a locked room in the barracks basement. The army sought to correct such informal arrangements when they came to official attention, but many infractions by African Americans doubtless met with responses that were never expressed in statistical measures of troop misconduct.[37]

If white commanders rarely understood or sympathized with their black troops, the friction was even greater between white military police and black troops. In May 1945 there were no independent African American military police units stationed in Europe. Individual black soldiers, however, did serve as military police. USFET made use of joint patrols by one black and one white MP in locales where both white and black troops were present and regarded the practice as a successful means of minimizing trouble. USFET, however, believed that the use of African American MPs among white troops was "highly undesirable."[38] Subordinate MP commands emphatically insisted that African Americans should not serve as MPs among white soldiers, and some believed that black troops had "no value" as military police, even among African American troops.[39] In April 1946 USFET headquarters formally recommended that its subordinate commands use military police patrols composed of both black and white MPs in areas where both black and white troops were stationed. USFET emphasized, however, that it understood that decisions regarding the employment of military police were ultimately the responsibility of each commander and therefore stated that its proposal was meant as "a suggestion only."[40] A few months later in November 1946, USFET began moving to designate African Americans formally as military police.[41] EUCOM reported to the War Department in April 1947 that two African American military police units had recently been organized.[42]

African Americans often complained that the military police treated black soldiers unfairly. Although white military police officials generally denied it, white military police in fact often selectively enforced laws against African Americans. One official defended the police against the charge, explaining that when his unit was required to police areas frequented by African Americans, he made it a "policy to hand-pick the police to perform this duty and to employ no men from the southern states if possible." The officer saw no need to elaborate on why employment of southerners was to be avoided if possible, nor did he say how often he was forced to employ southerners in policing African Americans.[43] Another USFET official in September 1946 forthrightly admitted that white military police made a practice of discouraging German women from associating with African Americans, but he defended such practices as necessary.[44]

Some of the higher incidence of crimes committed by African Americans in Germany also may be attributed to the power that African American men enjoyed in confronting the local white population from a position of unusual strength. Of course, white American men too were in a unique situation vis-à-vis the German police, which accounted in part for their higher crime rate in Germany than in the United States. African American men, though, faced considerably greater danger from the police in the United States than white men, and their sense of empowerment accordingly was all the greater in Germany.[45] The end of hostilities in Europe also brought comparatively greater freedom to African Americans, who during the fighting had received fewer pass privileges than white personnel.[46]

In addition, misconduct among black troops likely increased as their morale suffered from remaining in Germany while other soldiers returned home to be released from the service. Few black soldiers qualified for rapid redeployment after the war under the army's system because few of them had seen combat. Even those black units that qualified, however, included troops with a lower priority because they had been in Europe a shorter time. Those men were not redeployed with their units but instead were transferred to holding units. Such holding units often appeared to be dumping grounds, and morale generally sank as individuals from units who had been shipped home were assigned to units waiting for their turn to return to the United States. In Offenbach and Kunzelsau such units witnessed very high rates of misconduct.[47]

The environment of the American zone in Germany, especially through the end of 1946, included another unique factor in the dynamics of defining and prosecuting misconduct by African Americans. As the next chapter will explore in greater detail, certain kinds of misconduct by African Americans in fact were *under*reported, and African Americans at times could intervene against, or even assault, the German police and escape punishment. Misconduct by white soldiers of course also was likely underreported. If German authorities had been granted jurisdiction over African Americans, or if white American officials had been inclined to take stronger action against African Americans, the reported misconduct rate of African Americans in Germany could have risen to even greater levels. A racial and sexual logic that justified excusing misconduct by African American GIs but that mandated punishing the German women who associated with them provided yet another grievance for black soldiers, who resented actions taken against their companions. German and American authorities were more inclined to intervene in sexual relationships between African American soldiers and German women than in ones involving white soldiers. German women who associated with black soldiers were more likely to be charged with spreading venereal disease or other offenses than women who associated with white soldiers. One

African American soldier, for example, complained that military police only gave trouble to his black unit. He claimed that the police stopped him and his "fraulein" and apprehended her, ostensibly for a venereal disease check but actually to take her to the other side of town and tell her not to associate with black soldiers.[48] A July 1946 report of the Negro Newspaper Publishers Association to the secretary of war noted that the journalists had heard numerous complaints from black soldiers about persistent efforts by white American military police to discourage associations between black troops and German women. The report stated, "Strong-arm methods are employed at the mere sight of a Negro soldier and a white girl, regardless of her character."[49]

African American soldiers, who enjoyed a position of comparative strength in occupied Germany against the local police, could respond by aiding the women against the police. Such actions, even though underreported, at times found their way into misconduct reports, but they had had little counterpart among white soldiers. A March 1947 intelligence report illustrates the racial double standard in its differing explanations for the misconduct of black and white soldiers: "Colored soldiers, in particular, resented any steps taken to separate them from their girl friends. White soldiers, under the stimulus of alcohol, recalled that the Germans were once their enemies and they endeavored to prove that the real representative of the master race was the American soldier."[50] The report gave no reason to suspect that white soldiers (the group curiously enough credited with acting on the basis of race) would accept meekly any steps to separate them from their girlfriends. The implication, rather, was that neither German nor American officials made an effort to do so. Had they done so, no doubt the white soldiers would have intervened to prevent it, resulting in misconduct offenses.

Most commanders in Europe saw the origins of African American misconduct in simpler terms. They tended to believe unreflectively that blacks had propensities to crime and to venereal disease that could only complicate the work of the American military in Germany. Many viewed African Americans as racially inferior in ways that drew on long traditions of biological racism. The responses to the War Department's May 1945 questionnaire often committed the very error that Truman K. Gibson Jr., Civilian Aide to the Secretary of War, had warned against in August 1945. They were apt to ascribe "failures of Negroes to racial characteristics" rather than environmental factors, including "defects in Army policy."[51]

Officials inclined to view African Americans as inferior soldiers often emphasized their purported lack of self-control. One report complained that it was particularly difficult to persuade the average African American soldier to comply with the ban on fraternization with the Germans "because of his irresponsible nature and his inclination to disregard any but natural impulses."[52] Similarly, the XII Corps suggested that although the black soldier generally got along well with the civilian population of Europe, trouble could arise because "he is naturally more uninhibited than the white soldier and tends to follow his natural impulses to a greater degree. Negroes do, however, get along extremely well with children."[53] The Office of the Chaplain in XII Corps Headquarters noted that African American soldiers outnumbered whites in interviews with chaplains, welfare cases, and disciplinary cases, and he deduced that blacks had "less self-reliance, stability, responsibility and purposefulness" than whites.[54]

The Army Ground Forces' response to the War Department's May 1945 questionnaire stood out among the major commands' reports for its argument that African Americans' racial characteristics made them poor soldiers. The report declared that because of "inherent characteristics of the Negro, special methods of instruction had to be adopted involving detailed explanation, demonstration, and repetition, which necessitated an increase in the normally allotted training time." The Army Ground Forces also detected "an inherent tendency among Negro troops to neglect maintenance and care of equipment, particularly automotive vehicles," but noted also that "Negroes were more cheerful in their work than whites and responded more readily to praise." The report damned the Negro: "Compared to the white man, he is admittedly of inferior mentality. He is inherently weak in character."[55]

It seems unlikely that the author of the Army Ground Forces report puzzled long over the word *inherent* in describing the characteristics of African Americans. If pressed, the author might not have attributed the perceived tendency of black troops to neglect automotive maintenance to immutable biological facts. At one point the report cautioned: "In the process of social evolution, the American Negro has not progressed as far as the white man. As a race, he has not developed leadership qualities. His mental inferiority and the inherent weaknesses of his character are factors that must be considered with great care in the preparation of any plan for his employment of [sic] war."[56] The report nevertheless recommended that the "Negro" soldier "should be given every opportunity to demonstrate, as a race, his competency for combat duty." The author deemed it probable that "his capabilities will increase with his evolution."[57] The racial evolutionary idea was not unique to that author but found other adherents (if unreflective ones). The Army Ground Forces' subsequent 1946 study on African American soldiers, for example, referred to "the retarded development of the colored race."[58] War Department Circular No. 124, the army's official policy statement after April 1946 on African American troops, likewise described a recent "rise in the technical and cultural level of the Negro," which, according to the circular, had given African Americans a more articulate voice in government.[59]

According to such a vision, individual soldiers' experiences could improve the black race. Of course, the author of the Army Ground Forces report was probably not a careful student of Jean-Baptiste de Monet de Lamarck, the most famous advocate for the inheritability of acquired traits, and he evidently viewed the relevant entity as the race as a whole. The view did not rest on a belief that the black race was bound to an inferior position forever—only for the foreseeable future. With time, implicitly measured in generations, blacks, according to such a social evolutionary vision, could potentially be improved to the point that segregation could be gradually modified. The vision drew from a liberal faith in progress but included a large admixture of white supremacist conviction.[60]

Such beliefs were not universally held in the army. Many commands may have agreed with the views of the Army Ground Forces and phrased their responses more tactfully, but other commands certainly disagreed. One commander wrote, "When actually under fire I believe the Negro, if properly led, is just as brave and performs his job just about as well as comparable white troops."[61] Another observer expressed skepticism regarding his ability to generalize about African Americans. The report opined that "not a great deal of difference exists between white and Negro troops," and the author therefore found it "unfair and unwise to deal in generalities." The report did observe that since "the average Negro has probably had fewer educational and environmental advantages" than his white counterpart, a comparison "would perhaps reveal him at a slight disadvantage in such matters as care of equipment," but beyond such matters, the reporting command had observed "no essential difference" between white and black soldiers.[62]

Racial beliefs in the postwar military thus reflected division, confusion, and fluidity, as officials came increasingly to believe that biology did not irrevocably determine differences between blacks and whites but struggled to articulate such differences in otherwise comprehensible terms. Few white officers openly expressed a belief that blacks were eternally doomed by their biology to inferiority, but most insisted that for the foreseeable future, African Americans would need to occupy a carefully circumscribed position in the American military. Central to the need for and the nature of those limitations, even within the military, was the problem of sex.

The Army and Interracial Sex

Sexual relations between African American soldiers and white women aroused nearly universal disquiet among white American military officials. White uneasiness about interracial sex, indeed, formed a central support for the entire system of segregation. It may seem doubtful that a need to regulate the sexuality of black soldiers should influence the entire structure of the army. Defenders of segregation, though, insisted that separation of the races was necessary in social life above all and absolutely essential whenever white women were involved. General Eisenhower later recalled that during the time that he served as chief of staff after the war, objections to desegregation "involved primarily the social side of the soldier's life," because desegregation raised the specter of integrated soldiers' dances.[63] Similarly, during hearings conducted by the committee of experts formed to oversee desegregation in the military, the chairman expressed frustration to Omar Bradley that the army continually advanced objections to integrated social functions as a justification for segregation, asking, "General, are you running an Army or a dance?" Even in the army, anxieties about sexual relations between black men and white women proved central to racial policies.[64]

White dread of the threat of relations between black men and white women, the sociologist Gunnar Myrdal explained, was so great that it dictated the separation of the races in virtually every part of life. "Sex becomes in this popular theory the principle around which the whole structure of segregation of the Negroes—down to disfranchisement and denial of equal opportunities on the labor market—is organized."[65] The same proved true within the military, as the danger that black and white soldiers would compete for the same women dictated separating them.

The vision of strict wartime segregation in which contacts between blacks and whites were reduced to only the most formal and minimal in fact represented something of a myth. During the war in Europe black and white soldiers often shared facilities, despite serving in segregated units. USFET summarized practices in the theater: "In general, segregation was not maintained beyond the actual unit level." In some cases, white and black soldiers "shared the same mess, sanitary facilities, recreational areas and camp sites without any serious instances of friction." USFET added the qualification, however, that "where the number of Negro troops more nearly approaches that of white troops, it would be well to designate certain places for amusement and recreation for exclusive use of Negro troops."[66]

Some subordinate commands in USFET more emphatically denied practicing segregation, although such denials added a caveat regarding social functions. One quartermaster group headquarters asserted that no units attached to it or in its chain of command had practiced segregation.[67] Another unit stated that the headquarters "had no cause to maintain segregation" beyond the organizational unit level. The report further opined that "a policy of gradually decreasing segregation in the Army" would reduce prejudice among the troops.[68] The XII Corps wrote, "Without exception units of this command having Negro troops under their control practiced no segregation whatever." The report further stated, "It is felt that complete equality of treatment between the two races, where Negroes unavoidably serve with white troops, will result in eventual raising of the standards of Negro troop performance." Even this unit, however, wrote elsewhere that "non-segregation in the use of recreational and athletic facilities is not only appropriate but desirable, except for dances, which should be held separately for Negro and white troops."[69] White soldiers could stand working, eating, sleeping, and even showering with black soldiers, but they would not tolerate being required to watch black soldiers drink and dance with white women.

Social functions were the real bastions of segregation. USFET admitted, "Segregation has been the policy as regards social functions in almost all cases."[70] African Americans generally had separate social clubs from whites in occupied Germany. African Americans were unofficially barred from dances at those Red Cross clubs that were staffed exclusively by white workers.[71] In December 1946 USFET issued a reminder to all unit commanders, especially personnel in charge of clubs, services, and recreational activities, that War Department and theater policy prohibited discriminatory practices based on race.[72] In an April 1947 report on the implementation of War Department Circular 124, EUCOM reported, somewhat evasively, "Separate clubs for Negro units have been established where warranted for the purpose of increasing recreational facilities for their personnel."[73] By the end of the occupation, the army had developed a policy on social clubs that served to promote segregation without expressly mentioning race. The army prohibited designation of facilities as reserved for whites or blacks only. Facilities, however, could be reserved for the use of certain areas or organizations, which, in light of the segregated organization of units in the military, in practice amounted to racial segregation.[74]

If white women mixed with black and white soldiers, prevailing wisdom in the army held that trouble was sure to result. USFET noted that "[l]iquor and women" caused most of the trouble between white and black soldiers.[75] The Office of the Surgeon reported that segregation was not advisable for recreation activities "unless trouble is anticipated over white and colored soldiers mixing with white girls. This is usually the only condition necessitating segregation." The same report noted that the only instances of trouble between white and black soldiers had arisen when white soldiers objected to seeing African American soldiers with white women. One quartermaster battalion likewise used the presence of women as the test for when segregation was necessary. Theaters could be used jointly, so long as the "opposite sex is absent." Of course, the report stated, "[S]eparate dances must be held for white and Negro troops." Another report explained that separate recreational facilities were provided for whites and blacks "where women were available." Where women were not involved in recreational activities, "Negro and white troops have competed against each other in good spirit and without friction."[76]

A few units may have integrated even social functions. An artillery officer reported that the Third Army Intelligence Center maintained no segregation in recreation facilities since the end of the war in Europe. "Joint movies, athletics, swimming, and a joint enlisted man's club with beer, music, and entertainment, have been conducted . . . without incident." The absence of mention of dancing or women at the social club, however, suggests the limits of integration even at that location.[77]

The Use of African American Troops in Germany

The problem of African American troops in Germany received attention from European commanders and the army at large throughout the occupation period. Some officers would have preferred to exclude African American troops from Germany. Chief of Staff Brigadier General Bryan L. Milburn wrote to General McNarney in May 1946 that "[f]rom the point of view of a long-term occupation policy, it would be desirable if Negro troops could be eliminated altogether from our Occupation Forces." That view was shared in the lower echelons of command as well. One officer who surveyed the situation in Mannheim recognized that the War Department could not exclude African Americans from the army, but he nevertheless feared that stationing black troops in Germany would undermine the democratization effort. "It may be politically necessary for 10% of our Army to be colored, but it is just as politically necessary that we not bring colored troops into Germany. We are building up a terrific head of hatred by our present policy, and this hatred will come to light as soon as we leave."[78]

Necessity, however, dictated that African Americans would serve in Germany. The military's foremost concern after the war was to utilize all available soldiers, including African Americans, to the fullest potential. World War II had stretched the nation's resources to the limit, and military planners recognized that the approximately 10 percent of the American population of African descent formed an indispensable manpower pool. The military leadership favored instituting universal military training, and high-ranking officials were convinced that in the future the army's utilization of African Americans needed to improve, a conviction that grew stronger as the Cold War intensified.[79]

African American soldiers in the army continued to serve in segregated units after the war. Although it came under increasing attack, segregation in fact remained the rule in Europe into the 1950s, even after President Truman's Executive Order of 1948 appeared to order desegregation. Through most of the military occupation, the army's policy on African American soldiers was governed by War Department Circular No. 124, "Utilization of Negro Manpower in the Postwar Army," which was issued as official army policy on April 27, 1946. That policy distinguished between the "ultimate objective," which was utilization of manpower in the event of another major war "without regard to antecedents or race," and the immediate need to continue segregation.[80] The ultimate objective was progressive, but the acceptance of continued segregation permitted military decision makers to resist change.[81] How then could the army at once preserve its effectiveness as a fighting force, maintain control over African Americans, utilize them effectively, avoid antagonizing white soldiers, and democratize (without alienating) the Germans? It was a tall order.

USFET's Office of Inspector General performed a survey early in 1946 of the utilization of African Americans in the European Theater in an effort to answer that question. Although a completed version of the study does not exist in the inspector general's files, those files do contain the materials used to prepare the study. The complexity of the army's dilemma was revealed in a six-page assessment of the advantages and disadvantages of three different possible approaches to the utilization of African American troops. The first option was to increase the strength of existing black units. "Plan B" contemplated concentrating African Americans in one division, along the lines of the 92nd Infantry Division experiment during the war. The final possibility was to increase black personnel in other, non-divisional units, which would have involved dispersing African Americans throughout the zone of occupation. Each of the three plans had significant disadvantages, and none of them stood out as clearly the best option.[82]

"Plan A," which would have increased the strength of black units, would have relegated most African Americans to service units. In the judgment of the study's author, this option had the advantage of providing "employment for which the negro soldier is more adapted," while freeing up more white troops for "profitable employment" performing "the mission of the Occupation Forces." The most important drawback of such a plan, however, was that it would make it more difficult to maintain discipline. The option had the additional disadvantage that it would present an opportunity "for the increase of anti-racial feelings by the Germans and thus reflect dicredit [sic] against the entire Occupational Forces." Apparently, the author felt that Germans' belief in the inferiority of blacks, and by extension the army employing them, would be reinforced by seeing them relegated to subservient roles.[83]

The advantages of the alternative "Plan B," the creation of a black division, were modest. The problem would be localized, and esprit de corps in a black division might develop. Opportunities for friction between white and black troops would be minimized. Segregation further would "permit negro troops to associate more freely with their own people." This advantage would be increased if African American women were allowed into the theater, which would improve the troops' morale and reduce their inclination to associate with German women. These perceived advantages, however, were counterbalanced by considerable disadvantages. Concentrating African Americans in a single division would intensify the problem in the area in which they were stationed. A black division could "dominate and control a complete German area . . . with probable adverse effect upon the local inhabitants, thus impeding the . . . accomplishment of the Theater mission." Germans would receive "the wrong impression of the 'American way of life' incident to the concentration of such a force of negro troops in the area occupied." Whatever "the American way of life" was, the author evidently believed that it did not include large bodies of armed African Americans in positions of authority. The author further presumed that the army would not be able to rely on a black division in the event of combat. Finally, bringing African Americans together in one large unit "would offer a golden opportunity for agitation against authority" by stirring up unrest or bringing complaints against "segregation and discrimination etc."[84]

The final option, increasing African American personnel in smaller units, again had problems for every advantage. This program's most important benefit was that by distributing black troops evenly, they would everywhere be outnumbered by white troops. Disciplinary control would be simplified in the absence of a "concentration of a large force of armed negroes." Troublemakers would not have a sense of strength in numbers, thereby reducing the possibilities of serious revolt against authority. The author further believed that this option decreased the chances of "giving the Germans an erroneous impression of the 'American way of life.'" On the other hand, if African Americans were spread throughout the American zone, they could "by their conduct . . . cause anti-racial feeling throughout Germany and thus retard the accomplishment of the Theater mission." Such objectionable conduct included carrying on relations with German women, since the author numbered among the disadvantages the fact that the average black soldier would have "[l]imited opportunities to mix and associate with his own people." Furthermore, distributing African Americans throughout the zone would also increase the probability of trouble with white American soldiers.[85]

Every option thus could create its own problems with German civilians. Segregation of African Americans in a single division, although it could minimize the number of interracial sexual relationships, could deeply alienate Germans in the area where the division was stationed. Spreading African Americans throughout the occupation zone, on the other hand, would inflame German racial prejudice everywhere. Using African Americans primarily in service units would reinforce Germans' white supremacist ideas. The materials from the draft study contained no recommendation on which of the three options was believed to be the best. The all-black division option, however, seemed a poor choice, and no such division was formed in Europe after 1945. The army never defined a consistent policy on the use of African American troops, but it ultimately adopted something like a modified "Plan A."

In the earliest phase of the occupation, African American soldiers, like white GIs, were located throughout the American zone of occupation. Small African American units were often stationed in isolated areas, living closely among the civilian population, where higher-echelon commanders and the military police could not supervise them effectively.[86] The nature of the work assigned to African Americans, especially transportation, required them to be widely scattered around the zone and provided them with the means to travel easily, which further increased the difficulties of controlling them or reducing their contact with the civilian population.[87] In addition, few secure military-style encampments were available to house white or black units in the immediate postwar period because displaced persons used many such compounds.[88] Over time, USFET concentrated the bulk of its black troops in a small number of locations, although some black units continued to be stationed throughout the American zone.

USFET initially placed considerable limits on the role of its African American troops. There was a policy against stationing African Americans in Berlin, Frankfurt, or Austria.[89] The commander of the Berlin District "urgently requested" in September 1945 that no African Americans be stationed in Berlin because of a lack of housing and recreation facilities and in light of the "general nature of [the] mission."[90] OMGUS included no African American soldiers, although it did employ four African American civilians as of October 1946.[91] USFET, like the army at large, generally reserved African Americans for unskilled work in service units. African Americans likewise were foreclosed from serving in a "prestige guard" capacity.[92] In addition, African Americans in the European Theater were not to be used as supervisors of white civilian labor.[93]

When the U.S. Constabulary began operation in July 1946 as the principal police force in Germany, African Americans were excluded. Most officials remained firmly set against civil rights leaders' proposals to use African Americans in the constabulary in the fall of 1946. According to a Counter-Intelligence Corps (CIC) study, the German civilian population reacted unfavorably to the prospect of being policed by African Americans.[94] General Paul hoped that a public expression of the War Department's intent to bring African American troops into the constabulary at some point in the future might satisfy African Americans and their white liberal allies.[95] The constabulary indeed proved highly resistant to integration. Although black units were attached to it in 1948, the constabulary remained essentially for whites only, even after Truman's executive order.[96]

The commander of USFET through March 1947, General Joseph McNarney, had a low opinion of the abilities of African American combat soldiers and would have preferred excluding them from Europe. He strove to reduce the number of African Americans in Europe to the 10 percent quota.[97] Lucius Clay's attitude toward the African Americans under his command was characterized by patrician southern paternalism. Clay, who initially served as deputy military governor and then succeeded McNarney as commander of American forces in Europe, could take aesthetic pleasure in seeing martial or musical performances by African Americans. Clay's memoir of his service in Germany recounts a luncheon in 1945 hosted by Eisenhower in Frankfurt for the victorious Allied commanding generals. Entertainment for the august gathering was provided by a touring group of African Americans. The musical performance helped foster international harmony as Eisenhower, together with Soviet Marshal Georgy Zhukov and other attendees (including presumably Clay), joined "with the Negro performers . . . in singing, humming, or trying to sing, in whatever language one could use, 'Old Man River' and other old favorites."[98] Clay's recounting of the anecdote suggested that he could be comfortable with a fairly visible, if carefully circumscribed, role for African Americans in occupied Germany.

Clay believed in the power of a positive example of spit-and-polish military display. In fall 1946 he voiced his opinion that African Americans could best be utilized in Germany as parade troops. His response to a German complaint about the misconduct of African American troops in 1947 was to establish an honor platoon of African American troops. Clay explained, "We are going to dress them up, and if it works out as I think it will, we will send them around to other colored troops in the [German states] as an example of how colored troops could look and act." On July 20, 1947, the 7800th Infantry Platoon was organized and assigned to Berlin as an honor guard to Clay.[99]

Apart from their fears of German reactions to African American occupiers, American commanders also restricted African Americans to limited roles because they believed that black troops were incapable of performing more demanding duties satisfactorily. Commanders asserted, for example, that African Americans were unsuitable for supervising German laborers because they required supervision themselves.[100]

USFET officials became convinced that the best way to lower the venereal disease rate and improve discipline among black troops was to concentrate them in military enclosures separated from the German population. A May 1946 supervision survey of African American troops performed by a team of three officers recommended regrouping black units to central locations where higher-echelon commanders could better supervise them and quartering them in secure military encampments. Existing arrangements, which permitted easy intercourse between black troops and the local populace, had been "a source of constant trouble." Appropriate quarters for black troops were specified as a " 'Caserne' where the buildings are enclosed in a wall or well constructed fence that has not more than two easily guarded gates." The physical enclosure's prisonlike protections should be supplemented by a nightly bed check and a system of punishment for offenders. In addition, the survey recommended locating clubs for enlisted men inside such enclosures.[101] As USFET's operations staff expressed in November 1946, the high rate of crime and venereal disease among African Americans made it desirable "to minimize contact" between them and the Germans.[102] By the end of 1946 the army had succeeded in concentrating black units geographically and improving control over their barracks. EUCOM, in accordance with army policy, sought to locate black units "where civilian attitudes [were] most favorable."[103] The concentration of soldiers (both black and white) in secure encampments probably proved most effective in reducing the number of misconduct incidents in succeeding years.

The effort to bring black troops in Germany under tighter central control was accompanied by a successful effort to reduce their proportion in the occupation army. African Americans made up slightly more than 8 percent of the American armed forces in the European Theater of Operations in May 1945, but for three reasons that percentage quickly increased in the months after V-E day. First, because black troops had rarely seen combat, disproportionately large numbers of them waited in Europe while white combat troops with higher priority in the army's redeployment scheme returned home. Second, despite its shortcomings, the army was a more attractive employer to many African Americans than the alternatives in the U.S. economy, which typically relegated blacks to the least desirable jobs. Black GIs therefore reenlisted in greater percentages than white soldiers. Finally, many African Americans preferred service in Europe to service in other theaters, including the United States. Under War Department regulations, they could choose which theater they would serve in so long as they enlisted for a three-year term. As a result, the percentage of African American troops in Europe was expected to reach 15 percent by July 1946.[104]

The War Department and USFET officials regarded the growing percentages of African American soldiers in Europe with consternation, because the situation violated the army's 10 percent quota for black troops, which had been adopted before the United States became involved in World War II. The War Department expended considerable effort in the immediate postwar period, negotiating with its subordinate commands on how to allocate the excess numbers of African American servicemen and how to reduce the oversupply. Since the army was short on manpower, the War Department at first preferred to exceed the 10 percent quota rather than do without the additional soldiers.[105] On February 4, 1946, the War Department notified overseas commands that it anticipated that by July 1, 1946, African Americans would make up about 15 percent of the army, and overseas commanders would need to absorb their share of the additional black troops.[106] USFET officials urged the War Department to reconsider its policy and limit blacks in the European Theater to around 8 percent of the command.[107] On March 9, 1946, the War Department informed theater commanders that in light of objections by some commands, it would reconsider its prior directive and asked the commands how many black enlisted personnel each command could absorb "without endangering [its] mission."[108]

The army meanwhile attempted to lower its number of African Americans by using two policies that were on their face color-blind.[109] First, reenlistment in the regular army was to be denied anyone with a score below seventy on the AGCT (except for soldiers decorated for valor and those scoring above sixty-five who were recommended by their commanders). In addition, the army ceased accepting men who suffered from active venereal disease.[110] These measures, in fact, aimed to reduce the number of African Americans. It is unclear the extent to which the measures were responsible, but on April 16, 1946, the War Department rescinded its mandatory 15 percent quota for major commands.[111]

USFET continued its efforts to reduce the numbers of African Americans in Germany. On June 6, 1946, General McNarney made a personal request to Eisenhower that the War Department stop sending African Americans to Germany. When a head count of personnel revealed that USFET would have an "overage" of 14,466 African American personnel as of July 15, 1946, the War Department agreed to cease transport of African Americans to the European Theater.[112] The War Department further eased USFET's race problem on July 4, 1946, by authorizing it to accelerate its return of African American personnel to the United States. On July 17 the War Department suspended new enlistments of African Americans in the regular army, with the exception of individuals qualified for a few specialties.[113] A week later, the War Department adopted the recommendation by the NAACP that eligible African Americans who had been denied assignment to their preferred theater be honorably discharged from the military.[114] In September 1946 USFET adopted a program to discharge undesirable personnel under which a board of officers visited units throughout the theater and examined personnel to determine if they should be discharged as unfit.[115]

The effort to maintain the quota continued to occupy commanders in the European Theater and Washington through 1949. The move to reduce the number of African Americans in Europe had been so effective that when the Berlin Airlift began in 1948, the European Theater faced a shortage of African Americans, who manned many of the transportation service units needed to support the airlift. A special recruiting campaign was launched in October 1948 to enlist 1,500 African American veterans for service in Europe, as the army reversed course to meet the exigencies of the Cold War.[116]

The Problem Receives National Attention

The role of African Americans in the occupation of Germany assumed national prominence in 1946 as part of the investigation into military government in Germany conducted by the U.S. Senate's Special Committee Investigating the National Defense Program. Military government in Germany came to the committee's attention in August 1946 when Colonel Francis Pickens Miller, who had been a member of the Office of Director of Intelligence within OMGUS, testified before the committee that rampant misconduct plagued military government. Just before the committee chairman dismissed him at the conclusion of his testimony, Colonel Miller noted that "something else" had occurred to him that the committee should investigate. He stated that the conduct of African American troops in Germany was "one of the most disgraceful episodes in American history." He admitted that he felt some reserve in raising the issue, since he knew that as a southerner, his views would necessarily be "taken with a grain of salt" because of the prejudices that southerners tried "at times to live down." He broached the issue, however, because he feared that "for generations to come, the German people will remember what undisciplined, uncontrolled Negro troops have done to them."[117]

In specifying the misconduct of African Americans, Miller focused on interracial sex and its consequences. He stated, "It was the common habit of a Negro company to have 20 or 30 whores, prostitutes living off in the woods somewhere, clothed in American uniforms and eating American Army rations." He described an incident in which African American troops reportedly had stormed a jail where military government had imprisoned some women and, in freeing the women, killed four German policemen. Miller asserted that such incidents occurred "not too infrequently," in part because white officers feared to impose discipline on black troops. "The junior officer feels that he cannot crack down on a Negro outfit publicly," Miller stated, "because of the repercussions here unless he is going to be backed by his superior, and if his superior is scared to touch the thing, then he is afraid to do anything."[118]

In response to an inquiry from Republican senator Homer Ferguson of Michigan about the conduct of white soldiers, Miller stated that the white troops were better than black troops but that white soldiers also often misbehaved in Germany. Miller provided to the committee a draft of a report prepared by his office on depredations of American military personnel on the German civilian population. In fact that report had not singled out African Americans as committing assaults on Germans but instead showed that white soldiers too were responsible for many of the problems.[119]

African American soldiers also stood out as a problem in the testimony before the committee by Assistant Secretary of War Howard C. Petersen. He volunteered that the "terribly high" venereal disease infection rate in Germany was a matter of considerable concern to the War Department.

Petersen endeavored to explain away the high infection rate by racializing it. He explained that "the rate is as high as it is largely because the vene-real-disease rate among the colored troops is so high," between ten and twenty times the rate among white troops. Petersen evidently felt no need to explain to the senators why the venereal disease rate should be higher among African American soldiers.[120]

The committee tasked its chief counsel, George Meader, with investigating Miller's allegations. Meader, accompanied by other investigators, traveled through Germany from October 13 to November 3, apart from four days in Austria, interviewing McNarney, Clay, and other top USFET and OMGUS officials, including military government officials at the state (*Land*) level in Wiesbaden, Stuttgart, and Munich, as well as inspecting some liaison and security detachments at the lowest level of military government. African Americans figured prominently among the issues Meader studied during his trip to Europe. According to a report to the assistant secretary of war submitted by Brigadier General Theodore M. Osborne, special assistant to the undersecretary of war, "General McNarney and General Clay and . . . practically every officer who was questioned on the matter and who had had any experience with colored troops" voiced concern over the troubles caused by African American soldiers. Osborne, who had accompanied Meader on most of his trip and heard virtually all of the interviews conducted, asserted that black soldiers were "definitely giving the Germans a very poor impression of the American soldier." Osborne, however, expressed the opinion that the committee would "never make a recommendation to the Senate on this matter because of its political implications."[121]

Meader, in fact, did address the conduct of African Americans in Europe in his report, informing the committee that the proportionately large number of African American soldiers in the occupation force presented a "major difficulty" for the army. Meader questioned whether "Negro troops should have been utilized at all for occupational service, because the race question was bound to be encountered, since no Negro population is to be found in Germany." He reported that General McNarney thought that the War Department should withdraw all African Americans from Germany. General Clay was reported to favor retaining some African Americans in Germany but restricting their use to "parade troops." Meader believed that the War Department was reluctant to take any action because it feared "political repercussions from negro groups." In light of the misconduct by black troops, which was "no credit to the negro race," Meader opined that the "proper action to solve the problem should not result in any unfavorable reaction from any intelligent negro leaders." Meader shared with many USFET officials the opinion that much of the problem stemmed from the inability to effectively quarantine African Americans from the Germans. African American soldiers with access to army supplies made a habit of sharing them with German women. "In view of food shortages," Meader wrote, "some German women have been unusually receptive to the generosity of the Negro troops."[122]

The specific aspects of misconduct by African Americans described in Meader's report tracked the standard litany of USFET complaints about black soldiers' high venereal disease and crime rates. He explained that the problems, as well as attacks on German civilian authorities who tried (or were suspected of trying) to intervene, were interrelated. According to Meader, military government officials in the town of Wertinger, where black troops were consorting with German women, conducted a raid arresting fifty-four women, twenty-three of whom were infected with venereal disease. The black troops responded by beating up the mayor (*Bürgermeister*), who they believed had reported the women to military government. The terrorized *Bürgermeister* declined to identify the soldiers who had attacked him for fear of further reprisals.[123]

Misconduct by African American soldiers was by no means the only sensational criticism contained in Meader's report. Meader's acid pen did not spare the lower echelons of white military government. He noted that one in ten men in a shipment of 236 replacements for liaison and security detachments in Bavaria had scored so low on the AGCT that they did not qualify as "even high-grade morons." The report's treatment of Jews in Germany was more politically explosive. Meader's views on Jews fleeing from Poland reflected at least a breathtaking insensitivity to their plight and, in raising the specter that American policy was being manipulated by a sinister Zionist plot, suggested an underlying anti-Semitism. He characterized Jewish displaced persons as indolent and blamed them for many of the violent crimes committed in the American zone. He called for an investigation to determine whether prejudice against Jews in fact existed in Poland, from which most of the displaced persons were arriving, and whether "these mass migrations are spontaneous or are encouraged . . . for the purpose of building up a pressure in the United States Zone in Germany to further Zionist objectives."[124]

If much of the substance of the report was sensational, Meader's recommendations were comparatively moderate. None expressly addressed the subject of African Americans. The issue was dealt with under a general recommendation that "steps be taken immediately to improve the quality of military personnel assigned to occupational duties."[125] Meader's final recommendation—that the committee undertake further investigation of military government activities in Germany—appears to have been the most objectionable element to the War and State Departments, who had no desire for Congress to meddle further in foreign affairs or to bring disrepute to military government.[126]

The committee met on November 13, 1946, in executive session after Meader's return to the United States to discuss its investigation with Secretary of State James F. Byrnes, Senator Arthur H. Vandenberg of Michigan, Senator Tom Connally of Texas, and Brigadier General Osborne. Byrnes and the others urged the committee to exercise caution so that its investigation did not embarrass the United States or encroach on the executive branch's foreign policy prerogatives. Turning to the subject of African American troops in Germany, Byrnes stated that an investigation could "furnish more ammunition to the Soviet press." Byrnes, an ardent segregationist, stated that utilization of African Americans in Germany was a matter for the War Department, and he anticipated difficulties could arise for the United States if the committee made a sensation "out of the conduct of some few colored boys." Senator Vandenberg likewise warned the committee that the successful conclusion of the nation's negotiations with foreign powers was "far more important than catching porch-climbers, even though they ought to be caught."[127]

Senator Owen Brewster of Maine, a Republican, maintained that the problem was considerably more serious. He pointed to the high rate of venereal disease among black troops and warned that "white troops are getting the discredit of the situation, and what is the effect upon the German population of an infiltration of that character?" Brewster reminded Byrnes of the "bitter criticism" in the United States of the French colonial troops stationed in the Rhineland after World War I and suggested that the committee should be concerned about "whether it is necessary for us to have this group over there where the effect upon our American policy is so obviously unfortunate." Brewster turned back Byrnes's warning that probing the matter could "do great harm abroad" with the assertion that Germans and people in other countries already knew the facts. Brewster further urged that the administration should trust the committee to exercise discretion in preventing sensitive matters from becoming public.[128]

The committee subsequently met and voted six to four along party lines, with the lame-duck Democratic members making up the majority, to reject Meader's recommendation for further investigation of the matters raised in his report. The Democratic chairman of the committee, Senator Harley M. Kilgore of West Virginia, told the *New York Times* that the investigation would have taken the committee outside of its jurisdiction and into questions of foreign affairs. Kilgore further criticized the report's characterization of African Americans, complaining that Meader's views were "obviously . . . based upon hearsay, since there is nothing in the report to indicate that the investigator had any personal contact with those troops or personal knowledge of them."[129]

After the November 27 story in the *New York Times*, the four Republican members of the committee sought to have the entire draft report released publicly. The six Democrats voted against the request. More information on the report, however, appeared in the *New York Times* in a December 2, 1946, story. In that story the race question predominated, as the article bore the subtitle, "Meader Findings Are Said to Disclose a High Social Disease Rate — Conduct of Negro Troops Especially Assailed." Besides the widespread misconduct and high venereal disease rate among African American troops, the article stated that Meader reported the existence in Germany of "[f]lagrant miscegenation." The article quoted at length from the report's discussion of Negro troops' misconduct, although the language differed somewhat from the version of the report subsequently released by the committee.[130] The next day, yet another article on the Meader report appeared in the *New York Times,* this one dedicated to the report's discussion of the problem of displaced persons.[131]

By this time, the subject had clearly become a political issue, with President Truman, who had originally approved Meader's investigative trip to Germany, and congressional Democrats opposing the Republicans, who had recently won control of the Senate in the November 1946 elections. The Republicans directed Meader to release the entire draft report to the press and stated that the committee would press ahead with its investigation once the new Congress, with a Republican majority, met in January. A prefatory statement by the Republican members in the published committee hearings emphasized that Meader's report was a draft of a report on an initial inquiry and disclaimed any approval by the committee of the contents of the report.[132]

The Meader report controversy publicly aired conflicting positions on the presence of African Americans in Germany. The episode revealed that the spectacle of African Americans engaging in sexual relations with German women, depicted as diseased prostitutes, appalled influential officials in the military and in Congress. Those officials would have preferred to eliminate or, at least, quarantine African Americans to avoid discrediting the United States in the eyes of the German people.

Vocal and increasingly influential advocates, however, defended African Americans against the Meader report's charges of misconduct. In response, the NAACP issued a statement insisting that "the overwhelming majority of Negro troops" in Germany in fact "behaved themselves far better than whites."[133] Walter White, executive secretary of the NAACP, sent telegrams to President Truman and senators on the committee, denouncing the report and calling for the formation of a commission to rebut the report's allegations about African Americans in Germany.[134] The black press generally rejected Meader's account and insisted that the occupying force endeavoring to democratize the people of the defeated Third Reich needed to include African Americans.[135]

The Reformers' Arguments

The postwar military could not afford to ignore increasingly influential civil rights advocates in the United States. African American civil rights leaders' campaign for a "double victory" against fascism abroad and racism at home had attracted growing numbers of allies across the color line. The federal courts in the 1940s showed increasing sympathy toward arguments by NAACP lawyers fighting segregated schools and housing. During the war, pollsters at the National Opinion Research Center for the first time turned their attention to examining American popular attitudes concerning racial prejudice. In May 1946, for the first time a majority of white Americans polled agreed that "Negroes are as intelligent as white people." The war against Nazism had helped to weaken the hold of white supremacy on Americans.[136]

Demands for increased opportunities for African Americans in the military did not cease with the war's conclusion. Critics of the military insisted that segregation was inherently discriminatory and inconsistent with democracy. Indeed, no question loomed larger for African Americans during the 1940s than segregation in the military, which seemed especially intolerable to African American citizens on whom the nation had called in its defense.[137] A diverse collection of individuals and groups within the United States pushed between 1945 and 1949 for greater opportunities for African Americans in the military. They included the NAACP, the black press, church leaders, and prominent individuals like A. Philip Randolph. Within the army, the interests of African Americans were represented in the office of the Civilian Aide to the Secretary of War for Negro Affairs, whose occupants devoted sustained attention to the situation of African Americans in occupied Germany. These voices had influence at the highest level, producing a signal, although incomplete, triumph in President Truman's Executive Order 9981 of July 1948, which called for equal treatment of African Americans in the military and looked forward to desegregation.[138]

Although civil rights leaders and army leadership devoted considerable attention to the question of African Americans in the postwar army, the broader resonance of the question with the white public at large was limited. Beyond general apathy, civil rights advocates also faced determined opposition from some ardent racists who opposed any moves that appeared designed to end segregation. The military habitually had tended to defer to whites who insisted on segregation and rejected African American objections. General Paul, the War Department's director of personnel and administration, for example, believed that racial prejudice held by some army personnel was simply "too deep-seated" to be ignored.[139]

Civil rights activists consistently attacked the army's restrictions on African Americans in Germany on the ground that they undermined the effort to democratize the Germans. African Americans, especially the black press, generally insisted that black troops in fact performed well. Informed critics of the army pointed out that African Americans scored as well on the AGCT as whites with comparable educational opportunities. Civil rights leaders also maintained that the higher rates of misconduct by African Americans were mainly attributable to discriminatory treatment by the military. With respect to the situation in Germany specifically, African Americans generally claimed that Germans actually had few racial prejudices and that the real source of the problem was the attitude of white American soldiers and officers.

Truman Gibson, a former Civilian Aide to the Secretary of War for Negro Affairs, pointedly equated American racial discrimination with Nazism in June 1946. He accused General McNarney of harboring prejudice against African Americans in an article that appeared in the *Pittsburgh Courier* under the sensational headline "Nazis in Army: American Officers Abroad Propagating Race Hatred." Gibson recalled statements about African American soldiers that McNarney had made a year earlier during Gibson's trip to Europe in his former official capacity. McNarney reportedly had said that the "Negro" was a failure as a soldier and would require 100 years to reach parity with white Americans. Gibson asked, "How much can a man like McNarney be expected to do to combat the slowly rising tide of intolerance in Europe?" Although McNarney "could not be accused of sympathy for all or even in any Nazi doctrines," nevertheless Gibson asserted that his "racial attitudes" permitted "some of these doctrines to take root."[140]

McNarney defended himself at a September 21 press conference, denying the accuracy of Gibson's account and explaining that he had only suggested that "since the Negro, through no fault of his own, had been unable to find in America during the last 100 years completely equal opportunities to develop his full social and economic potential, it would appear profitable if, for the next hundred years, American Negroes could be afforded the opportunities which Mr. Gibson claimed they had been denied."[141] McNarney clearly recognized that such a blanket condemnation of the abilities of African American troops was inconsistent with the effort to root out traces of Nazism in Germany. His press release closed by noting, "Finally, all of us realize that our victory in the war included the overthrow of dangerous Nazi doctrines of racism, while our efforts here are to promote democratic doctrines."[142] He voiced his confidence that American soldiers, by their conduct, would succeed in winning the peace as they had won the war.

McNarney's comments quieted the issue, but the exchange is important for showing how Nazism had eroded the public acceptability of racial prejudice in the United States. Gibson, especially in the headline, had tarred McNarney as a Nazi, using a familiar rhetorical strategy of American civil rights activists in attacking racial discrimination.[143] In the body of the article, however, Gibson more carefully asserted that, although McNarney himself was not a Nazi, his racial views facilitated Nazi attitudes. McNarney denied harboring racial prejudice but insisted that misconduct by American soldiers could undermine the American campaign to democratize the Germans.

Representatives of the Negro Newspaper Publishers Association, who spent nearly a month in Europe visiting Germany, Austria, Italy, France, and England in 1946, similarly critiqued USFET's treatment of African American soldiers. "The very people whom the Army of occupation seeks to democratize are aware of the Army's policy of separation of Negro and white, and they . . . question us strongly for seeking to teach what we fail to practice." This hypocrisy appeared especially egregious, since the three journalists claimed to have found "practically no discrimination of Negro soldiers by the civilians in any of the countries visited."[144] The representatives of the black press insisted that the conduct of African American troops in Europe was "no better or worse than that of the white soldier." The journalists observed that little progress had been made toward the army's avowed ultimate objective of desegregation and criticized the military's effort to limit the visibility of African Americans in Germany, objecting to the absence of African Americans at General McNarney's headquarters in Frankfurt and in OMGUS. The journalists found particularly galling the military's use of German prisoners of war instead of African Americans in "positions of trust and confidence." The journalists suggested that African Americans should play a visible role at the Nuremberg trials of the major Nazi war criminals, which the delegation regarded as an opportunity for driving home the error of Nazi racial dogma. The report recommended that African Americans serve in an integrated unit guarding the accused, "if this thing called Democracy [is] to take real root" in Germany.[145]

The report's recommendations for change to the secretary of war were far-reaching. First, the report called for an end to segregation. In addition, the journalists urged that African American troops be used in prominent locations, such as Frankfurt, Berlin, Nuremberg, and Munich. They also recommended instituting an orientation campaign to instruct officers and enlisted men on "proper racial attitudes." The journalists expressed the opinion that the venereal disease rate could be brought down by locating troops in "governable conditions," requiring examinations of civilians, and banning excessive drinking.[146]

USFET officials sharply disagreed with the publishers' report. The staff in the Personnel Division pointed to the higher venereal disease and crime rates among African American soldiers for support in rejecting the assertion that the conduct of African American soldiers was no worse than that of whites. They pleaded ignorance, however, on the question whether white military police discouraged white women from associating with African American soldiers.[147] Roderick Allen of the Operations Division rejected the report more sharply. He defended the command's maintenance of segregated units as wholly consistent with War Department policy and rejected the assertion that African Americans were excluded from USFET headquarters, pointing to the assignment of an African American band unit to the headquarters and to African American civilians who worked in the office. Allen was particularly emphatic in rejecting the report's conclusion that Germans had no objection to the presence of African Americans in Germany. In fact, he wrote, compared with whites, blacks were "most unpopular and have created a most undesirable condition in practically every locality in which they are stationed." Allen asserted, without further explanation, that African Americans could not be utilized in Austria or Berlin, and experience showed, in Allen's view, that POWs and civilians did not cooperate with African American supervisors as well as they did with white supervisors. Allen admitted that white military police might have been discouraging German women from associating with African Americans, but he believed such measures were required to limit trouble.[148]

Criticisms of army policy came even from individual officers. A Lieutenant Green in the Quartermaster Corps of the Third Army suggested to General McNarney that black enlisted men could serve more effectively in headquarters units than whites. African Americans who had been placed in responsible positions were motivated to "demonstrate that a member of his race is capable of filling an important position as well as a white soldier." If blacks were excluded, the effects on morale would be negative. Moreover, the author noted the "purely hypothetical consideration" that the army was in Europe to "foster the development of democracy and to insure equal opportunities for all peoples." The author asserted that placing white enlisted men in a headquarters commanding mainly black soldiers "would appear not only un-democratic but also would stand out as a living example of the ideology that the Armies of Occupation are sworn to stamp out."[149]

Third Army Headquarters forwarded Green's letter to McNarney with the note recommending that suitable personnel be transferred from the United States to serve in headquarters units.[150] The Operations Division staff expressed disagreement with the proposal, arguing that past experience had proven that African Americans were unsatisfactory in administrative and supervisory positions. In addition, sufficient black units to sustain a headquarters unit composed of black personnel, they stated, could not be concentrated in one area. Since African Americans should definitely not supervise a white unit, the proposal was impossible.[151]

One of the more important critiques of the European Theater's policies came from within the War Department from Marcus Ray, the Civilian Aide to the Secretary of War. In November 1946, just as the Meader report directed national attention to the issue, Secretary of War Patterson dispatched Ray to Europe to investigate the situation of African American troops in Europe.[152] Ray toured Europe from November 16 to December 17, 1946. At a November 23 press conference in Frankfurt, he stated that

Marcus Ray, Civilian Aide to the Secretary of War, addresses an audience in Munich during his November 1946 tour. The nationality of the woman in the foreground is unknown. Courtesy National Archives, U.S. Army Signal Corps, photo no. SC267332.

he was engaged on a "routine tour" of the European Theater, and he reported that his initial reactions based on a visit to Berlin were favorable. By the time he returned to Washington, though, he viewed his report as a rebuttal to the Meader report. The *New York Times* reported that Ray had found "no situation in Germany that would support allegations of misconduct by Negro troops" made in the Meader report. The black press in the United States trumpeted Ray's findings, sometimes with banner headlines, as a vindication of African American troops in Germany against the "slanders" in the Meader report.[153]

Ray's report criticized USFET's policies on African Americans. He noted that African Americans were relegated to service units or to one of four army bands. He attacked the exclusion of African Americans from the constabulary and reported that the decision to limit the constabulary to whites only had been based on the belief that it would be "inexpedient" to place blacks in the position of exercising supervision or police control over Germans in light of "the racial ideologies of the German people." Ray criticized the policy as undermining the re-education program. "To accept the racial prejudices of the German people as a reason for the

Marcus Ray and Brigadier General Leroy Watson investigate conditions at the Talley Ho service club for African American soldiers in Nuremberg during Ray's November 1946 tour. Courtesy National Archives, U.S. Army Signal Corps, photo no. SC273934.

non-utilization of the American soldier who happens to be non-white is to negate the very ideals we have made a part of our re-education program in Germany."[154]

Ray further asserted that, in fact, the fear of alienating Germans was groundless. He claimed that in conversations with "representative German nationals, such as the burgomeisters [*sic*] and police representatives," he had found "no carry over of Nazi racial ideologies directed against the American Negro soldier." He stated that "expected ideological difficulties in the use of Negro troops in Germany [had] not materialized." Indeed, Ray stated that African Americans were smoothly running the German youth program in Grafenwöhr. Ray contrasted the situation in USFET to that in the Mediterranean Theater, which he stated used black soldiers according to their capabilities, including at theater headquarters and on the staff of war crimes prosecutors. That policy had not harmed the theater's morale, discipline, or training, which Ray stated were at high levels. Ray made six recommendations, most notably urging formation of an African American combat unit to be a part of the constabulary. In addition, he recommended implementation of an education program for all soldiers stationed in Europe, as well as calling for the assignment of qualified individual African Americans to positions in headquarters.[155]

Signs of Change

Starting in 1947 General Clay and his staff moved beyond stubborn opposition to the European command's critics and sought to improve the training and morale of African American soldiers in Europe. The most important of these measures in the eyes of European commanders was the establishment of a training center for African American troops in Germany. In May 1947 Lieutenant General Clarence R. Huebner, in consultation with Marcus Ray, established a center at Grafenwöhr, Germany, to train black soldiers in two newly formed infantry units over a twelve-week period in both academic and military subjects. The army's initial experience with the center, and its interim successor at Käfertal near Mannheim, satisfied General Huebner that such a "system of rigid basic training with carefully controlled conditions" could develop pride in the African American soldier. Huebner therefore expanded the program by establishing a training center for African Americans at Kitzingen Air Base. The course included six hours per day of basic military training and two hours of academic instruction at the secondary school level. Nearly all African American soldiers in Europe rotated through the center. Policy makers credited the program with producing higher scores on the AGCT and a general decline in incidents of misconduct by African Americans in Germany. The army's experience with the Kitzingen training center offered further support for those who argued that the performance of African Americans could be improved through better training.[156]

In February 1947 Lucius Clay addressed the question raised by the black press delegation's recommendation whether African American attorneys ought to participate in the Nuremberg trials. He explained that the members of the Nuremberg staff wanted to comply with War Department policy, but they expressed concerns that black attorneys might lead "a relatively solitary existence" in the absence of a "substantial Negro population." Clay himself recognized "the desirability of having some colored lawyers participate in this work," but he could not "promise an environment . . . satisfactory to these employees." Although the war crimes trials in Nuremberg did not feature African American attorneys, a black honor guard unit did stand watch over the prisoners in the dock in 1948.[157]

The military further attempted to improve the situation of black troops by appointing Marcus Ray as Advisor on Negro Affairs in EUCOM in August 1947. In addition, it adopted new materials for an expanded education program designed to improve race relations in the army. "Army Talk 170," published in April 1947, sought to educate the troops about the army's racial policy. The pamphlet noted that discussions "of 'race' [were] likely to touch off sparks from individuals who have deep-seated beliefs, convictions, or prejudices in one direction or another." The army stated that the education program must respect "differences in personal

Otto Ohlendorf, dwarfed by African American guards, stands to hear the death sentence imposed on him at Nuremberg for crimes committed during World War II. Courtesy National Archives, U.S. Army Signal Corps, photo no. SC299799.

opinion" on the subject and that it hoped only to inform the troops and to develop understanding through discussion.[158]

Movement, if at a glacial pace, occurred too in the War Department. In 1948 Secretary of the Army Kenneth Royall invited members of the African American press to Europe to survey improvements in the situation of African American servicemen. Seven African American journalists traveled for three weeks through France, Germany, and Austria, receiving the VIP treatment, including a ride in the limousine formerly used by Heinrich Himmler.[159] Their report, submitted to Secretary Royall on April 21, 1948, described a calmer situation in Europe than that witnessed by the black journalists nearly two years earlier. Misconduct and venereal disease rates were lower among black troops and the command as a whole. In addition, by 1948 the Cold War was an incontestable fact of which the journalists were acutely aware.[160] Much, however, remained the same in Europe. Segregation remained the rule, and it once again came in for criticism from members of the delegation, who traced all of the deficiencies in the army's handling of African American troops to the "one wrong basic concept" that "a segregated army can be an efficient army." The journalists, however, did not confine their arguments to matters of efficiency. They, like others before them, asserted that they had seen "at first hand the inconsistency of the democracy we preach and the hypocrisy we practice." The report evidenced the growing importance of such inconsistency in the context of the Cold War struggle for the allegiance of the Germans. "Leaders of both the Army and Military Governments in Germany and Austria admitted," the report stated, "that the most embarrassing question they were asked and the question which they could not satisfactorily answer was that pertaining to the treatment of Negroes in [the] democratic United States."[161]

The journalists' report met with predictable results. The army would not depart from its policy of segregation, although its justifications were advanced with less conviction. In meeting with civil rights leaders after the report's submission, Secretary Royall clumsily defended the army's policy:

> It is not the intention of the Army that there be any discrimination other than such as you may think is inherent in segregation itself, and I would not be other than frank if I didn't say that there is some element of, at least from a mental standpoint, discrimination inherent in segregation, but, with that exception, there is no intention of permitting any segregation—I mean discrimination—in the Army.[162]

Royall, tripping over a triple negative and misspeaking, expressed perfectly the army's discomfiture and confusion over the role of blacks in the postwar military. Still, in Europe, the constabulary remained a white preserve, with the exception of some black units attached to it. General Paul rehearsed the same arguments that he had made in 1946 against including blacks in the constabulary in rejecting the recommendations of the journalists.[163]

Nevertheless, by 1948 arguments against segregation in the military began to tell. In spring 1948 A. Philip Randolph testified before Congress that if a draft law were passed that provided for segregation, he and his Committee Against Jim Crow would urge blacks not to report.[164] Few civil rights leaders were willing to adopt civil disobedience, but they continually argued that the democratization of Germany could only be successful if Germans could see that African Americans were being treated fairly. President Truman, although he opposed social equality for African Americans, recognized both the injustice of segregation in the military and the political gains to be reaped by taking a public stand against it in the context of the 1948 presidential election in which he faced a challenge on the left by the Progressive Party led by Henry Wallace. In order to obtain the support of African Americans to defeat that political threat, Truman chose to demonstrate his support for civil rights.[165] On July 26, 1948, Truman issued Executive Order 9981, which had been under consideration for at least six months, declaring that "equality of treatment and opportunity for all persons in the armed services without regard to race, color, religion or national origin" was the policy of the president. The order also established the President's Committee on Equality of Treatment and Opportunity in the Armed Services to oversee implementation of the order. Truman clarified the executive order's omission of the words *segregation* and *integration* a few days later in a press conference when he answered with an unqualified affirmative when asked whether the order envisioned the eventual end of segregation.[166]

Segregation in the military, however, was not to be ended with a single dramatic stroke. Only the exigencies of the Korean War ended segregation in the army. In the meantime, the committee established by President Truman, chaired by former solicitor general Charles Fahy, waged a drawn-out campaign in favor of integration against committed segregationists in the army.[167] Indeed, even the army's favorable experience with integration in Korea did not immediately translate into changes in Europe. African Americans in Europe served in segregated units as late as 1954. European commanders believed that whereas integration might work in Asia and in the United States, it was impractical in their theater, where the civilian population was white. The momentum behind integration ultimately proved decisive, though, and in November 1954 the last black unit in Europe was finally deactivated.[168]

Conclusion

The United States faced a problem in attempting to democratize Germany with a Jim Crow army. Both civil rights leaders and their opponents used the racial attitudes of the Germans in pressing their own arguments for and against expanding the role and improving the treatment of African Americans in postwar Germany. African Americans and their white allies tended to portray Germans as remarkably lacking in racial prejudice. They pointed to widespread relations between African Americans and German women as evidence that Germans accepted blacks. American racial discrimination figured as monumental hypocrisy, recognized as such by Germans, which threatened to undermine American efforts at democratization.

On the other hand, the military commanders who sought to limit the visibility of African Americans in Germany advanced evidence of Germans' racial prejudice as an argument in favor of such limitations. Germans in this account would only be alienated by the granting of a high profile to African Americans in the occupation. Such arguments found support in stories of black soldiers intimidating local officials and assaulting German police. It was these Germans, not the few women of dubious morals who associated with black soldiers, who mattered and who needed to be accommodated according to the prevailing views of military commanders.

The arguments of American reformers and defenders of the status quo provided a double alibi for Germans after the war. Critics of American racism, who celebrated Germans' supposed willingness to treat African Americans with respect, suggested that Nazi race hatred had been an aberration. That rhetoric served the interests of Germans who insisted that Germany had no race problem after 1945. At the same time, particular instances of discriminatory treatment of African Americans in the Federal Republic could be blamed on Germans' unfortunate imitation of the U.S. Army. Germans might look to both sides of the American debate for justification in asserting that they did not engage in racial discrimination, and, to the extent they did, white Americans bore responsibility.

CHAPTER THREE

"Bad Girls" and "Boys Who Never Had It So Good"

Sex and Race in American-Occupied Germany

Sexual relations between German women and African American soldiers in the army occupying the territory of the defeated Third Reich represented an acute challenge not only to Nazi racial ideology but also to notions about race more generally shared by Germans and white Americans alike. German officials, who lacked jurisdiction over Allied personnel, had no independent power to control the behavior of African American soldiers engaged in relations with German women. Moreover, officials' efforts to police women associating with African Americans could be frustrated in cases where the soldiers blocked the civilian authorities. In such instances, German officials depended on persuading white American officials to intervene on their behalf.[1]

German officials found it impossible to openly condemn interracial sexual relations per se. They could, however, object to unlawful or immoral conduct that appeared to result from such relations, such as spreading venereal disease, prostitution, and attacks by African Americans on German police officials who tried to enforce laws against German women. German officials phrased objections on these issues in terms of morality. They typically argued to American officials that they required assistance in enforcing the law against immoral women, who were manipulating black soldiers to serve their own ends. German officials accordingly called for punitive measures against those women, actions for which white American officials' cooperation was generally essential. The women involved were rhetorically excluded from the white German nation as officials policed whiteness in the postwar period.[2] Such arguments often proved persuasive to white American officials, who nevertheless felt freer to recognize openly the agency of the soldiers involved. German officials, in making such arguments, aimed to enforce the law, to discourage interracial sex, to promote moral conduct, and to strengthen their own authority, goals that were inextricably bound up with thinking about race.

Since statements that could be construed as promoting race hatred were prohibited in the press and could bring rebukes or even criminal prosecution, prudent German officials crafted their objections to the conduct of African Americans and German women in terms likely to be acceptable to American military officials serving in a segregated military. They translated protests based on the soldiers' race into a language that condemned the women's immorality. Anxieties about black soldiers were directed against the women involved with those soldiers. The tendency to single out the women derived not only from a desire to avoid appearing as an adherent of Nazi racial ideology but also from ideas of betrayal and the traditional sexual double standard.[3] Regardless of its motivations, such rhetoric produced action against the women involved to a far greater extent than measures against the soldiers. German women accordingly bore the brunt of measures to police the bounds of moral whiteness in postwar Germany.

Condemnations of immoral conduct rested on beliefs regarding gender and race that generally went unstated explicitly. Although the Nazi regime's insistence on German women's role as mothers of the Aryan race did not survive the war's end, women, according to conventional thinking, bore a special responsibility to act as the moral guardians of the nation.[4] When women fornicated with the enemy, they betrayed the nation. When such liaisons crossed not only national boundaries but also the color line, they came in for special condemnation. Sexual relations with African Americans seemed more immoral than sex with white Americans. Indeed, morality and sexual propriety signified intrinsically white qualities. Women who engaged in sexual relations across the color line were by definition immoral and could even run the risk of somehow ceasing to be fully white.

On the other hand, the African American soldiers were cast as the women's amoral pawns. Europeans had long harbored the belief that people of African descent were somehow more sexual than they. In the age of scientific racism, biologists had attempted to ground this notion in theories about the greater sensitivity of members of the Negro race to external stimuli, but the currency of the idea predated and outlasted the period of biological racism's vogue. The presumed overwhelming sexuality of blacks supposedly rendered them unable to control their sexual desires. Europeans furthermore commonly believed that white women were especially attractive to black men. These ideas prepared them to believe that black men were easy prey for any unscrupulous white woman who favored them with sexual intercourse. Hoary notions of black sexuality and lack of self-control received a new twist in a postwar discourse that cloaked race in the language of women's immorality.

Gender Trouble in Postwar Germany

The war and the collapse of the Third Reich produced an earthquake that violently shook traditional German gender relations. The postwar years witnessed a "crisis of masculinity," in which the men of the defeated German nation, shattered by the experiences of the war, subjected to foreign occupiers, and outnumbered by German women, faced a sharp challenge to their authority as men. Simply in numerical terms, German women held the upper hand, as expressed at the time in worries about a "surplus of women." Owing to war deaths and the continuing imprisonment of soldiers, women made up more than 54 percent of the population in the American occupation zone in October 1946.[5] Beyond the sheer decimation of Germany's male population, the national indignity of Germany's defeat contributed to a sense of crisis in gender roles. The wave of rapes that began with the entry of Soviet troops into East Prussia in 1944 and reached a peak in the wake of Berlin's fall in May 1945 only intensified such anxieties, as Germans typically perceived the rapes as yet another humiliation for German men who had failed to live up to the masculine ideal of defending womanhood.[6]

Whereas German men seemed either absent or emasculated in 1945, German women appeared to be in danger of becoming unsexed as they assumed conventionally male roles of worker and provider. The traditional pattern, in which women's roles were primarily restricted to the domestic sphere and their sexuality expected to express itself within the confines of marriage, had evidently broken down in the immediate postwar period. Germans responded by seeking to reestablish patriarchal gender roles and family structures as a means of reining in newly assertive women and reviving the nation.[7]

In this charged atmosphere, sexual relations between German women and white American men were profoundly objectionable to many

Germans.[8] German women's voluntary sexual contacts with occupying troops humiliated German men. Women who associated with Americans were branded as immoral and, more seriously, their actions were deemed to have larger consequences for the nation. German women's failure to "maintain the morally necessary distance" from Allied troops, as one man put it, constituted an assault on "the dignity of the defeated."[9]

Interracial Sex

A minority of Germans who retained a belief in the superiority of "Aryan" Germans may have regarded many white Americans as "inferior racial types," but generally interracial sex in postwar Germany meant sex between black men and white women.[10] Those sexual relations between African American soldiers and German women pressed the attack on German dignity to its limit. As one American official phrased it in 1946, "German civilians resent [f]raternization between American Military personnel and German women, [but] [t]heir attitude is even more pronounced concerning the fraternization of their women with American Negro soldiers."[11] Sexual relations between white German women and black American soldiers lay at the root of complaints about vice and assaults on German authority. A white American investigating officer in the town of Offenbach, for example, charged that African American soldiers had beaten and threatened German civilians and policemen, and even engaged in a gun battle with members of the military police who had attempted to restore order. Although such actions were grave, the officer noted, "Perhaps the worst aspect of the present situation, and the one that causes the most unrest amongst the civilian population, is to be found in intercourse between Negro soldiers and immoral teen-age girls."[12] If the specter of the fraternizing woman referred to by epithets like "American-lover" (*Amiliebchen*) and "Ami-whore" haunted Germans' imagination in the postwar years, the "Negro-lover" (*Negerliebchen*) represented German officials' ultimate nightmare as they endeavored to reestablish their authority. Race thus supercharged German discourses and practices aimed at controlling immoral German women in the postwar period.[13]

A Third Army intelligence report from the period summarized effectively the breadth and nature of the problem of interracial sexual relations as perceived by Germans.

> Negro troops are deeply resented in practically all localities where they are stationed, and most, if not all, this resentment is due to the association of these troops with frauleins of questionable character who flock to the towns where negroes are billetted [*sic*]. Promiscuous intercourse in public places, often in the presence of children, is viewed with anxiety by the local population. Efforts by local authorities to control the influx of undesirable females, and to subject them to VD tests frequently result

in forceful "liberation" of the suspects out of jails and hospitals by their negro friends.[14]

In order to better understand how German officials responded in rhetoric and in practice to the sort of ultimate challenge to German male authority posed by German women carrying on with African Americans, this chapter turns now to particular events, especially in the Bavarian towns of Wirsberg and Weißenburg, like those described in general terms in the intelligence report.[15]

The Rhetoric of Race and Gender

On July 13, 1946, two officers of the Bavarian Rural Police (Landpolizei) went to the small town of Wirsberg in *Landkreis* (or county) Kulmbach, in Upper Franconia, to investigate a report of stolen property in the possession of a woman at the Hotel Hubertus. When the officers arrived at the woman's room, they found a suitcase containing thirty packs of American cigarettes, as well as chocolates and other sweets. The woman said that the items belonged to her boyfriend, a black GI in the second platoon of the African American 596th Laundry Company, which was quartered in the town. The soldier was sent for and he verified that the items were his. The police accepted that statement and headed down the stairs of the hotel to leave.[16]

They were stopped, however, by another African American soldier who asked what they had been doing. Other soldiers soon appeared, and the mood turned ugly. Some of the soldiers drew weapons and threatened one policeman that if he set foot in Wirsberg again, he would be a dead man. The soldiers laid one of the men over the banister of the hotel stairs and beat him. As he made his way back to the police station, a truck full of black soldiers overtook him. One of the soldiers jumped out of the truck and grabbed him by the throat, threatening him with a pistol. The German police reported that only the arrival of an American officer at that moment prevented further harm. The military government public safety officer subsequently directed the transfer of the two German policemen in order to protect them from further attacks.[17]

Four days after the trouble in Wirsberg, the head of the German police for the region, Hugo Freiherr von Imhoff, sent a three-page memorandum to American military government regarding "[e]xcesses of coloured members of the occupation army," in which he described the incident and called for corrective measures to be taken. The memorandum described eight incidents in which members of the German police had been beaten or intimidated by African American troops for threatening prosecution of German women for prostitution or other offenses, or for simply making remarks that the soldiers interpreted as derogatory. The first five cases discussed in the memorandum occurred in Feucht near Nuremberg beginning in early March 1946. The last of the incidents, and plainly the one that provided the impetus to compose the memorandum, was the one in Wirsberg.[18]

The memorandum painted a vivid picture of African American soldiers running roughshod over the German police. It may initially appear to be a fairly bold condemnation of the behavior of African Americans. Imhoff, though, composed his argument with care and crafted a departure from rhetorics of race that had been prevalent in Germany during the Third Reich. In Imhoff's memorandum, the need to control immoral, manipulative women worked hand in hand with a belief in the gullibility of African Americans to frame an argument that proved persuasive to white American officials.

Imhoff pinpointed precisely the cause of the excesses committed by the African American troops. "The reasons for such excesses are the prostitutes, who dwelling with the units, are fed by the soldiers and incite them to acts of violence, to be protected against the intervantion [sic] of the police." Imhoff claimed that the incidents recounted in the memorandum "prove, how these prostitutes[,] helped by their lovers, violate law and order and try to assert themselves succesfully [sic]." The memorandum closed by stating that improvement could only be attained "if there will be acted with all means and all severity *against the girls*, who believe [themselves] to be protected against law by their coloured soldiers, and if they will be heavily and severily [sic] punished."[19] Imhoff notably did not request that the Americans act to restrain the soldiers. Instead, he maintained that if the "girls" were punished, the problem would be remedied.

The memorandum placed ideas about race at the center of its analysis but in a way that evidently was still believed to be permissible (and, indeed, was acceptable), even under an American occupation ostensibly committed to eliminating German race hatred. Imhoff clearly believed that racial distinctions mattered. The excesses of *African American* soldiers, apart from actions of American soldiers in general, were appropriate for in-depth comment. The abuse of German police by African American soldiers stood out as especially humiliating, representing "the greatest disgrace" for the police.[20]

In the weeks leading up to the time that Imhoff wrote his memorandum, African Americans were by no means the only perpetrators of attacks on the German police. On March 15, 1946, for instance, a white "American deserter" had killed a member of the Nuremberg police.[21] In addition, on May 22, 1946, the German police reported that a white American soldier had assaulted two German policemen in Nuremberg.[22] In April, Poles attacked German policemen in Upper and Middle Franconia on two occasions.[23] In Frankfurt, a highly publicized melee erupted between American soldiers and German police during a sweep for prostitutes of the area around the Frankfurt train station, a notorious red-light district, which, although outside of Upper and Middle Franconia, might have been mentioned because of its prominence.[24] Imhoff, however, excluded discussion of those attacks from his account. The principal reason for limiting his discussion to attacks by African Americans seems to have been that the racial and sexual logic of Imhoff's memorandum, according to which German women incited pliable blacks to attack German authorities, would have been inapplicable to cases involving white soldiers.

The victims in at least two of those assaults by whites, though, were members of the Nuremberg City Police, not the Landpolizei, and therefore outside Imhoff's jurisdiction. A concern to limit discussion to matters strictly within his official purview, however, did not trouble Imhoff, as shown by his inclusion of a discussion of threats made by African American soldiers to a forester. Foresters were not members of the Landpolizei and accordingly were not within Imhoff's responsibility. Imhoff's concern with protecting the authority of government officials was expansive where African Americans were involved.[25]

The events of July 13 in Wirsberg prompted Imhoff to complain to military government, but he was not content to raise only the single incident. He sought rather to show that the events in Wirsberg were part of a pattern of misbehavior by African American troops. For that he needed additional evidence. He turned to a May 6, 1946, report from Inspector Geißler of the Rural Police concerning the activities of prostitutes and African American soldiers in the town of Feucht.[26] Imhoff's assessment that the women were the root of the problem was his own notable innovation and had not appeared in Geißler's report. Imhoff, however, borrowed extensively (but not uncritically) from Geißler's report, cribbing several sentences and phrases verbatim.[27] Imhoff's use of Geißler's report further illuminates the central role of race in Imhoff's argument, a role, however, masked by expressed moral concerns. The inclusion of a discussion of events of more than two months earlier in a different town in Imhoff's account of the events in Wirsberg made sense because all of the incidents involved black soldiers and German women.

Inspector Geißler's May 6 letter had reported that between thirty and forty prostitutes and their African American "lovers" (*Liebhaber*) in Feucht were undermining order and public morals. Geißler stated that the women had come from outside the community and were living by prostitution. Because they refused to submit to police examination or medical control, they threatened to spread venereal disease. Moreover, they openly practiced prostitution, meeting with African American soldiers in the train station. Railway officials had been powerless to stop the immoral behavior in the face of soldiers' threats. Geißler sought the assistance of American military police in controlling the women.[28]

Imhoff's adaptation of Geißler's letter reveals careful authorial attention to the logic of race and gender. Imhoff included Geißler's account of five incidents virtually verbatim in his own memorandum, but he omitted material that would have undercut his assertion that arresting the women would end the attacks on the Rural Police. Most significantly, Geißler had luridly described suspected violence against a girl by a black soldier, writing that at night in Lohweg zu Feucht a sixteen-year-old girl, who was known to associate with African Americans, could be heard crying out in pain. Geißler presumed that the girl was being mistreated by a sadist.[29]

Imhoff chose to omit mention of that incident in his memorandum. He may have had a number of reasons for doing so. First, the girl's case did not represent a direct attack on the authority of the Landpolizei, which was Imhoff's principal concern. In addition, Imhoff may have found the matter too indelicate or too speculative to include. Alternatively, Imhoff may have chosen not to mention the attack on the girl because it undercut his theory about the cause of the attacks on the Landpolizei. The injuries inflicted on the girl in Lohweg zu Feucht demonstrated that German women associating with African American soldiers risked victimization. The incident thus suggested that the soldiers held the upper hand, contradicting Imhoff's interpretation that the women, not the soldiers, caused the problem. It would seem unlikely that arresting the girl in Lohweg zu Feucht would end the danger posed by a sadistic soldier. It is impossible to determine exactly why Imhoff excluded mention of the incident. Regardless of his intent, however, Imhoff's editorial decisions in composing his memorandum obscured the power of African Americans and the vulnerability of German women.

The problem described by Geißler, as well as relations between African American soldiers and German women more generally, had occasioned concern among the German civil authorities in the Upper and Middle Franconia district before the events of July 13 in Wirsberg. Georg Lowig, the prefect (*Landrat*) of Landkreis Nuremberg, the rural district surrounding the city of Nuremberg in which Feucht was located, had passed on to the district administrator Hans Schregle a report on the events Geißler had described in Feucht. The Landrat asserted that in locations where black troops were stationed, prostitution was becoming a "plague."[30]

Schregle in turn complained to the military government office for Upper and Middle Franconia that German authorities required military police assistance to take action against the prostitutes who refused to register with the police and threatened to spread venereal disease. Schregle's request, like Imhoff's later memorandum, called for action against the women. Schregle's letter lacked the picturesque details of Imhoff's account, however, and failed to move beyond generalities. He also skirted the issue of race more widely than did Imhoff. His letter of June 14 had as its subject "[p]rostitution" rather than "excesses of coloured soldiers." Schregle dealt with black soldiers only to say that women were carrying on pros-titution in locations where "colored members of the US-Forces have been quartered" and that the German police hesitated to intervene without American aid, because experience had shown that "the colored soldier lovers of such whores would either prevent, by use of force, [or] threat of arms, German civilian policemen from taking measures or enforce release of such prostitutes as were arrested." Schregle included a translation of a letter he proposed to send to the local German authorities in the district instructing them to carry out raids in cooperation with the local American military police against the "[h]omeless prostitutes [in]fected by VD and other infectious diseases" who were "menacing [the] moral[s] and health of both, German civilians and US Forces."[31]

Schregle's request met with a polite but noncommittal response from Major James Tillinghast, the head of military government for the district. He responded that Schregle's letters were "very interesting and your action is commendable," but Tillinghast declined to take the requested action, despite the fact that he could have approved the letter on his own authority had he wished to do so. Instead, he passed responsibility to Bavarian state officials, recommending that Schregle seek their approval. It is unclear why Tillinghast declined to support Schregle effectively in his proposed course of action, but the letter's comparative lack of narrative force may have accounted for its cool reception. Alternatively, Tillinghast may have been less concerned about the question than other military gov-ernment officials who later passed Imhoff's letter up the chain of com-mand. Whether because of its less effective argument or simply because it found a less receptive audience, Schregle's letter failed to produce the sort of measures that he had requested. Imhoff, though, was to prove more successful in prodding American officials to act.[32]

Imhoff wrote at a time when American controls powerfully restricted public discussion of racially charged subjects. In summer 1946, German newspapers did not dare to discuss the subject of misconduct by African Americans or, indeed, by white American soldiers. There was no public outrage expressed by Germans at the time over the events in Upper and Middle Franconia or similar ones elsewhere. The newspapers in the dis-trict published no stories in 1946 about misconduct by African American troops. The quiescence of German newspapers about racial problems in summer 1946 reflected more prudence than equanimity.[33]

Imhoff accordingly chose his words carefully. Throughout the German original of Imhoff's memorandum, he referred to African American sol-diers consistently as "coloured" (*farbige*) soldiers or members of the occu-pation army. The word Negro (*Neger*) appeared at only one point in his account. That usage occurred in his description of an incident on May 27, 1946, in which an African American soldier accused a police officer of having insulted soldiers by calling them "Negroes" (*Neger*). The perceived slur had been compounded when the officer had supposedly instructed German women not to "walk with" blacks, as the English version of the memorandum translated "*mit ihnen zu verkehren.*" The soldier threatened to kill the police officer if he did not stop such behavior. Imhoff rose to the officer's defense, stating that the officer had "never asked girls not to take a walk with coloured soldiers."[34] Evidently, both the policeman and Imhoff understood that German officials could not flatly forbid German women to associate with African Americans. Any objections to interracial sex required a more tactful phrasing.

The incident highlights the troublesome nature of the word *Neger* during the American occupation. The term *Neger* could be translated as corresponding to the American word *Negro*, which, outside of the German context, was generally considered an inoffensive term by white and black Americans alike. *Neger* thus could be distinguished from the American slur *nigger*, which was known to most Germans and used by some. On the other hand, *Neger* sounded to Americans very much like the odious *nigger*, and indeed could carry at times the same valence, and African Americans often found the term *Neger* offensive.[35] For that reason, white Americans could be sensitive to Germans' use of the English term *Negro* as well. An American military government officer in Landkreis Kulmbach tried to raise German consciousness along these lines in August 1946. The Kulmbach resident liaison and security office files contain an English translation and the German original of a report for the month of July, which dealt with the Wirsberg "encounter of negroes with County-Policemen" and which referred to the African American soldiers throughout as "negroes." The German original used the word *Neger*. An American military government official circled the word *negroes* in the English translation and made a marginal note: "Call Landrat. Colored Soldiers and not negroes."[36]

Imhoff understood the American sensitivity to the term *Neger*, as evidenced by his adaptation of Inspector Geißler's less sophisticated report. Geißler had used the term *Neger* eight times to refer to African Americans. Imhoff, in his adaptation, substituted *farbige* for *Neger* in each of the four instances where he otherwise borrowed Geißler's wording. Imhoff obviously was acutely aware of the sensitivity of the term in particular and the subject of race more generally.[37]

Imhoff's racial ideas were not those of an ardent Nazi. He came from an aristocratic family in Franconia and had entered the police service long before the Nazis came to power. In 1942 he was dismissed from his position because he refused to part from his Jewish wife. He returned to the police after the collapse of the Third Reich.[38] On the other hand, Inspector Geißler had been a Nazi Party member since May 1937. In October 1946 he retired from the police, ostensibly on grounds of health. In reality, the police leadership in Upper and Middle Franconia was under pressure to denazify the Rural Police, twenty of whose thirty-four inspectors were for-

mer party members. Geißler was one of the first to be forced out.[39] Upper
and Middle Franconia had been a bastion of support for the Nazi Party
during its rise to power, as signaled most prominently by the staging of
Nazi Party rallies in Nuremberg in Middle Franconia.[40]

Whereas the subject of race presented a minefield to be navigated gin-
gerly by Germans, the sexual immorality of women could be discussed
freely. Imhoff was far less careful and precise in his descriptions of the
women involved than he had been in writing about the African American
soldiers. He insisted that the women were prostitutes (*Dirnen*), although
it is unclear whether they received payment. Even within Imhoff's memorandum, however, his borrowing in one place of Geißler's term *lovers*
(*Liebhaber*) to refer to the soldiers struck a dissonant note in his theme that
the women were prostitutes. In fact, the boundaries defining prostitution
were blurrier than ever in the desperate situation of postwar Germany.
Since many German women were destitute, homeless, and hungry,
American men had enormous relative power and resources to attract or to
coerce them into sexual relationships.[41]

Imhoff had little sympathy. His terminology in discussing the women
indicated that he felt no compunction against expressing his views
regarding them, in marked contrast to his caution regarding the language
of race. He referred to the women variously as *Dirnen, Mädchen, Frauen,
Frauensperson, zweifelhafte Personen, geschlechtskranke Frauen,* or *ein fremdes
Mädchen.* Imhoff's editing of Geißler's report highlights the freedom he
felt to vent his spleen. Imhoff sharpened the terminology into an attack on
the women. Geißler's legalistic reference to *Prostituierten* was changed to
a somewhat more moralistic *Dirnen.* Imhoff also omitted the fact, noted by
Geißler, that one of the women was from the East ("*Ostländerin*").[42]

More striking than the free use of gender-related terms in the memorandum was the thrust of Imhoff's argument. His anger at the women,
whom the English translation mincingly referred to as "bad girls" (*Dirnen*),
emerged powerfully. The women humiliated the police by consorting
with the African American troops, sheltering under their protection,
and inciting them to attack the German authorities. There is no evidence
that Imhoff felt any need to be circumspect in calling for punishment of
German women who attempted to evade the law.

Imhoff ultimately presented the issue as one of morality rather than
race. He laid the blame on the "bad girls" and called for the mobilization of the combined power of the American occupiers and the German
police to control them. Whereas the women were immoral, the black soldiers appeared as amoral, pliable instruments in their hands. This view of
African Americans drew on long-standing beliefs about blacks and was
congenial to a white American audience.[43] Imhoff's ability to persuade
American officials to adopt his remedy may well have turned on American
officials' acceptance of his rhetorical move of phrasing the problem in

moral terms. Military government's ministerial handling of the document exemplified the currency of that distinction and showed that Imhoff won that crucial point. The adjutant general's office filed Imhoff's memorandum in its decimal subject file under the subject of morals and conduct (decimal 250.1) instead of the subject of race (decimal 291.2). The prosaic details of the army's filing system thus suggested that objections to interracial sex could be acceptable so long as they could be categorized as a matter of morals.

Race and Morality

Imhoff's memorandum has received detailed consideration because his argument is revelatory of the internal logic of race and gender in American-occupied Germany, not because Imhoff, a fairly high-placed Bavarian official with an aristocratic background, was a "typical German." Imhoff was not alone in blaming African Americans' actions on their immoral German lovers. The Germans who articulated their concerns about relations between black GIs and German women came from across a broad spectrum. They included not only a member of an aristocratic Franconian family who was married to a Jewish woman but also Nazi party members and the Catholic Archbishop of Freiburg. Josef Braun, the *Oberbürgermeister* of Mannheim who advocated placing such women in labor camps, was a member of the conservative CDU.[44] As the views of one female member of the Bremen Social Democratic Party (SPD) showed, condemnations of such relationships were not monopolized by the political right in Germany.[45]

Imhoff was an expert rhetorician, though, whose argument skillfully stated a case for action while skirting the highly charged issue of race. He likely would have protested that he had no objection to sexual relations between German women and black men in general, and he was certainly not so indiscreet to express such objections in writing to American military government officials. Other German officials using arguments similar to those made by Imhoff failed to negotiate successfully the boundaries of acceptable racial discourse. For example, the Munich police reported in August 1946, "At several robbery attacks committed by coloured American soldiers one has the impression that the perpetrators committed them only so that they can give gifts to girl friends or other acquaintances." The American public safety officer receiving the report responded with a rebuke: "Such comment is absolutely worthless and destroys the value of the report. If there are facts known to the Munich Police indicating that such a condition does exist, these facts should be stated and leave 'impressions' to others."[46] In that instance, the connection between the thefts and interracial relations was more attenuated than in the incidents described by Imhoff, where police officials directly confronted soldiers and their companions. Perhaps that difference, rather than greater skepticism about the malevolent influence of German women on African Americans, explains the different receptions that greeted the similar diagnoses.[47] Although Imhoff articulated his argument more carefully than most, his description of the situation, his condemnation of women involved, the American reception of his argument, and the results that flowed from his complaint exemplified rhetorics and practices concerning interracial sexual relations in the American zone.[48]

German church officials often issued condemnations of relations between German women and American soldiers in similar terms. It is perhaps unsurprising that religious leaders turned to a language of morality in addressing the issue. Nevertheless several aspects of that discourse are noteworthy. First, religious leaders targeted women more severely than the soldiers with whom they associated and attributed the decisive, pernicious influence to the women. Second, interracial sex clearly seemed worse than sexual relations with white Americans. Third, the discourse portrayed sexual propriety as an essentially German quality. The language of morality conveniently obscured racial objections. Fourth, the same clergy had often leveled criticism against the Nazis for having substituted race for religion as the guide for ordering society, without recognizing the racial basis of their own pronouncements. Finally, such objections were based on a moral calculus that regarded the postwar period as more depraved than the Third Reich.

In May 1946, for example, church officials in Württemberg-Baden complained vociferously about activities of German women and African American soldiers in the small town of Waghäusel in terms similar to Imhoff's memorandum. Once again, officials objected on grounds of protecting public morals. The Archbishop of Freiburg, Conrad Gröber, wrote that the women carrying on sexual relations with the soldiers represented "an open contradiction to every civilization, to every morality and decency." The archbishop, like the lower church officials on whose reports he relied, maintained that Nazism could be purged from the German nation "[o]nly if our youth are of modest and decent morals." Like Imhoff, he appealed for help in ending "the shameless doings of these bad German women." An earlier letter by a Father Sales likewise had asked military government to take action against the women.[49] The *Bürgermeister* of the neighboring city of Bruchsal referred to the women in a report to military government as "prostitutes" (*Dirnen*) or "women of doubtful character" (*zweifelhaften Frauenspersonen*), which was translated into English as "suspicious women." He was particularly incensed at their claims to respectability. He mocked the women's attempt to qualify as "ladies," complaining that the "soldiers, having been i[n]stigated by their 'Ladies[,]' take action against everybody who shows disagreement with their [shameless] behaviour." The black soldiers had made matters worse by according the women that status and even arresting Germans on charges of "insulting Ladies of the Club."[50]

In Waghäusel, as elsewhere, the German officials focused once again on the German women's pernicious influence on African American soldiers, who were assigned a subordinate role in aiding the women to flout the dictates of German authorities. The Bürgermeister of Bruchsal asked for American assistance to take action against immoral women brazenly carrying on sexual relations with black soldiers in his town. The appeal for help was necessary because, as the English translation of a letter by a Father Weiskopf expressed it, the soldiers, "instigated by their fast creatures," beat anyone who voiced displeasure at the spectacle.[51]

German moral authorities emphasized both the women's shamelessness and their slothfulness. The Archbishop of Freiburg, for example, asserted that the openness with which sexual relations occurred—in ditches and in fields, "under the very eyes of the children, who are in the streets"—threatened to corrupt the youth. In addition, the women, supported by the soldiers, did not work. "Whereas the other honorable Germans must have their papers to prove that they are working anywhere in order to get their food-cards, those disgraceful creatures who demoralise [sic] the young and spoil the good reputation of the parish get them without doing any work." He asked that "these streetwalkers" be put to work clearing rubble.[52]

Condemnations of women's sexual immorality, especially women who had sex with black soldiers, came not only from men. Many women likewise disdained a perceived general moral degradation among young women. Else Feldbinder, for example, authored articles in the woman's magazine *Sie* describing selfish, pleasure-seeking women who spent their time indulging their vices and spreading venereal disease.[53] Even women whom moral authorities condemned for engaging in relations with white soldiers could exhibit scorn for prostitutes who serviced black customers. One woman, who admitted that she was a prostitute working in a Munich brothel, for example, wrote to American authorities complaining that an American member of the military police had threatened to kill her for practicing prostitution. She buttressed her appeal for protection with the assertion that she had refused to cross the color line. "I want to state expressly that I only have intercourse with *white* American soldiers."[54] The file does not disclose what response her letter met.

Further evidence that immorality often served as a euphemism for interracial intercourse in German officials' pronouncements is found in the fact that African American soldiers and their German girlfriends understood such terms as code for referring to their relationships, even where race went unmentioned. In October 1945, for example, the mayor of Kunzelsau was prompted by some women's "immorality and impudence" to issue a proclamation noting that some women who had come from outside the town had stooped to "soil the German woman's dignity, bring[ing] shame to themselves" and giving a bad example to German youth. His proclamation called on "decent girls and women . . . to keep clean the highest [good] a woman can possess, her woman's dignity."[55] The mayor declined to specify exactly how the women were bringing shame to Kunzelsau. Indeed, the proclamation did not mention African Americans at all. Nevertheless, according to the mayor, it earned him the enmity of African American soldiers stationed in the area, who understood that the message referred to the women in town who associated with them.[56]

Race and Law

Such euphemisms for race were necessary because American sensitivities regarding race prevented the express criminalization of interracial sexual relations in occupied Germany like that which had prevailed during the Third Reich. German officials nevertheless could and did apply facially race-neutral laws to target women who associated with African Americans. The clearest evidence of such tactics comes from the files of Weißenburg city officials. In January 1946, local authorities discussed with the local military government official, Captain Carr, the growing number of women (some local but most apparently transients) carrying on relationships with black soldiers stationed in town. They asked whether something could be done to prevent the relations between the women in town and the soldiers. Carr explained that interracial relations alone were not punishable, but he suggested that city officials could find grounds under German law to take action against women engaged in relations with African Americans. The city officials' notes from the meeting reflected Carr's advice on applying the laws selectively to eliminate the problem.

> Punishment on account of intercourse [*Verkehr*] with colored Americans cannot be carried out unless a crime can be established. In other cases there may have been an offense detrimental to American forces. Immoral German women may be acted against in accordance with German law. Military administration and troops are already undertaking appropriate steps.[57]

Carr thus coached local officials on the regulation of interracial relations. He further attempted rather lamely to assuage their racial concerns by noting that "most of the colored soldiers already had more of the blood of the white than of the black race" in their veins.[58] That bit of armchair racial science seems to have left the officials unsatisfied, but they nevertheless understood that in the wake of Nazism's defeat, punishment of interracial sex alone was impolitic.

A variety of German and American laws remained at their disposal that could be applied to the same purpose. Of these laws, the German law for combating venereal disease proved most popular in the postwar period. That statute, enacted in 1927, subjected women suffering from venereal disease to mandatory treatment by public health authorities. Under the statute, anyone who knew or should have known that she (or he) was infected with venereal disease and who engaged in sexual relations was subject to imprisonment for as long as three years.[59] American authorities encouraged German civilian authorities to examine women who associated with soldiers for venereal disease and prosecute them under that law if they spread the disease.[60]

Besides targeting the spread of venereal disease, German law regulated, but did not absolutely prohibit, prostitution. Prostitution was permissible so long as it was practiced with appropriate discretion. The German Criminal Code subjected to criminal prosecution those individuals who practiced prostitution "publicly and in a conspicuous manner" and those who, "in a manner offensive to individuals or the public, incite[d] immorality." The statute specifically prohibited prostitution in the vicinity of churches, schools, or homes or other localities frequented by children. In addition, prostitution could be outlawed in communities of less than 20,000 inhabitants, if prohibited by an order for the protection of young people or by an order from state authorities.[61] That last provision left considerable room for debate among American and German officials on the question of what acts were punishable, because its prohibition of prostitution in towns with populations of less than 20,000 was not self-executing. Prostitution in the many small towns was illegal under that provision only if state officials issued an order to that effect for purposes of protecting the youth or preserving public decency. Bavarian officials, in fact, issued no such order after the war. Indeed, the Landrat of Landkreis Kulmbach, in which Wirsberg was located, believed in May 1946 that prostitution in towns with less than 20,000 inhabitants was not illegal, since he was unaware of any regulation to that effect issued by Bavarian authorities.[62]

The regulation of the sexual behavior of Bavarian women reached a high point in April 1946 with Ordinance No. 74 for the Confinement of Immoral Women and Girls.[63] The Bavarian state ordinance provided that women over eighteen years of age who contributed to the spread of venereal disease, or who were "otherwise morally corrupt," could be confined to a public institution for a period of three months to two years in order that they might be provided with "regulated work, an orderly life, and a general, reformatory influence."[64] The law clearly gave officials extensive discretion to determine who was "corrupt" (*Verwahrlost*), a profoundly ambiguous term that afforded great opportunity for selective application.[65]

In addition to those German legal provisions, American officials brought charges against German women, especially those engaged in relations with African Americans, under military government law. Military Government Ordinance No. 1 provided that Germans could be punished for any action prejudicial to the interests of the Allied occupation forces. That sweeping law was often used, especially in 1946 as unrest peaked, as a basis for charges against women who had sex with American soldiers while knowingly infected with venereal disease.[66] OMGBY's Legal Division came to recognize the possibility of abuse inherent in this provision's grant of considerable discretion to military government officials. "Indiscriminate use of this section by the Court is dangerous practice," the Legal Division explained in its 1947 manual for summary court officers, "because it creates the possibility of prosecution for alleged offenses or misconduct not contemplated as occupation crimes but which reflect only the opinion of the person preferring the charges."[67] American and German officials had considerable autonomy to select from a variety of means for targeting German women in relationships with African Americans if they so chose. Individuals applied particular laws as they best fit the circumstances. At times women were tried by U.S. military government courts, although German courts were often used as the preferred forum for trying German civilians.

Race and Disease

Sexual relations between African American soldiers and German women were inextricably linked to the subject of venereal disease. After the war, venereal disease rates in Germany increased dramatically among the civilian population and the occupation forces.[68] The German press devoted considerable attention to the spread of venereal disease.[69] The problem was regarded as a racial one in large part because the reported rate of infection among black soldiers ran at three or four times the rate among white soldiers.[70] The connection between venereal disease and blacks ran deeper than the often-cited statistical imbalance in postwar Germany, however. White Americans had often regarded African Americans as especially susceptible to venereal disease.[71] This belief drew both from notions about African Americans' purported immoderate sexuality and their believed racial predisposition to disease generally. High black venereal disease rates only strengthened the tendency to regard venereal disease as a black disease. Indeed, the extent to which venereal disease was marked as a black problem is testified to in the military's injunction that during venereal disease education programs for black soldiers, "[o]nly one thing is *mandatory*, namely, no reference to race should be made."[72] The military clearly viewed venereal disease as a race problem, but it could not say so openly to black soldiers without alienating them.

The association between venereal disease and blacks seems to have had a shorter history in the German mind than in the white American perception, although a connection with racial Others frequently appeared in German discussions of venereal disease before 1945. Syphilis had been known in Germany initially as the "Indian disease," owing to the belief that it had been brought to Europe by sailors returning from the New World. Members of the ultra-right *Freikorps,* on the other hand, referred to venereal disease after World War I as "the Jewish plague." German propagandists in the same period warned that the French colonial troops occupying the Rhineland spread syphilis, as well as a host of other diseases, among the local population. Venereal disease figured as a racial threat in Nazi ideology, and the marriage laws of 1935 included a prohibition on marriage by infected individuals among its measures designed to protect the Aryan race. Venereal disease thus carried shifting racial undertones in Germany before it assumed a distinctly African American cast after 1945. Bremen social welfare officials, for example, regarded the African American soldiers stationed there as the cause of the city's skyrocketing postwar venereal disease rates.[73]

The racial aspect of venereal disease was often submerged in the postwar period in the more explicit moral rhetoric that surrounded the problem. Since the turn of the twentieth century venereal disease had functioned in Germany as a potent metaphor for articulating both moral and racial dangers to the health of the *Volk.* No social or political group had monopolized use of venereal disease in discussing the national ills before the war's end. Weimar-era liberals, conservatives, and radicals alike had raised the specter of the apparently rapid spread of venereal disease to criticize perceived ailments of the body politic.[74] In a similar vein, the Oberbürgermeister of Mannheim in 1946 decried the decline in morals, which manifested itself in the large number of minor girls who "shamelessly" associated with "colored occupation troops." Such "moral squalor" found its chief expression in the high rate of venereal disease.[75] According to the terms of a familiar conceptual framework, the spread of venereal disease after 1945 embodied the hydra-headed moral and racial threats to the health of the German nation. The widespread condemnations of the problem effectively served as a code for condemning interracial sexual relations, which could not be openly discussed in racial terms.

The rising rates of venereal disease in the German population and the U.S. Army caused profound concern among American officials, who made increasingly strenuous efforts to halt the trend.[76] The army continually instructed soldiers about the dangers of venereal disease and the means of guarding against infection. Officials declined initially to adopt a policy of punishing soldiers who became infected out of fear that soldiers might attempt to conceal their infection and avoid treatment. By June 1946 General McNarney instructed all commanders to take stronger measures to control the spread of venereal disease, including declaring that soldiers who willfully concealed infection with venereal disease and who were absent from duty for more than a day as a result were subject to punishment. Penalties appear to have been mild and meted out infrequently, however, and in general the military eschewed punitive measures against the soldiers as counterproductive.[77]

Similar logic did not apply to the women with whom the soldiers had sexual contact. American and German control efforts focused mainly on these women.[78] Officials in Mannheim, for example, reasoned that "a certain class of girls and women [bore] principal responsibility for" the high rate of venereal disease in the city, and it was those women who, "as a consequence, [brought] the male sex" into the pool of infection.[79] In September 1946 Lucius Clay reported that the venereal disease control program for the German civil population was being "concentrated on the specific elements of the population which constitute the main source of infection for occupation forces."[80] Although Clay did not say so, it seems that those "elements" targeted by the American and German authorities included especially women who associated with African Americans.

The American military and German civil authorities adopted a distinctly penal approach against the women believed to spread infection. Chief of Staff Brigadier General J. D. Barker recommended to General Eisenhower the "formation of Labor Battalions of women who had been picked up as carriers of venereal disease," believing that physical labor would contribute to "the betterment of their mental outlook on life."[81] Barker's specific proposal was not generally adopted, but it reflected the powerful impetus from the highest levels of military government to control the spread of venereal disease by disciplining women infected with the disease.[82] Indeed, following revelations of trouble in the city of Mannheim in September 1946, General McNarney directed city officials to establish "a work farm for women" prisoners in the area. The idea had originated with Mannheim officials, and the inspector general's office endorsed their requests for such an institution where women would "serve their sentence at hard labor."[83] The camp was less draconian once established, with women convicts granted the choice of working in the camp in exchange for shortening their sentence by four days for every thirty days of work. Few women availed themselves of the option.[84]

Precisely who would serve time in such a camp was ambiguous initially. The inspector general indicated that it would house "all prostitutes and other women in the Mannheim area not possessing proper credentials." Josef Braun, the Oberbürgermeister of Mannheim, however, in a less reflective moment captured in the transcript of his testimony before the inspector general, had suggested, "It is the opinion of the Burgermeister that the women who are contacted by the Negro soldiers must be collected in labor camps and put at hard labor for about 4 weeks at least [which] would have a deterring effect on those in town and those who want to come to Mannheim."[85] Even allowing for a fair degree of imprecision in light of Braun's imperfect (but quite good) English, he clearly swept up virtually all women "contacted by the Negro soldiers" in the labor camp dragnet. His broad definition and its subsequent refinement by the inspector general testify to the general tendency to categorize all women carrying on relations with black soldiers as prostitutes or criminals but to omit race from the express public delineation of such categories.

Race and Authority

German civil and religious authorities seemed threatened in the postwar period not only in gendered terms but also in generational and political terms. Youth seemed particularly rebellious in the dislocation of the closing months of the war and the postwar period. The clergy, government officials, teachers, and parents often decried youth's challenges to their traditional authority.[86] The effrontery of youth became especially incendiary when aided and abetted by African American soldiers, as one minister complained that African American soldiers running the local recreation program for German youth had assured the children that the soldiers would have the minister replaced if he continued discouraging the children from attending. The minister wrote that such efforts by the soldiers to undermine his authority amounted to a continuation of the Nazis' efforts to impair the church's moral instruction of youth.[87]

American military government narrowly limited the power of German authorities in the period immediately following the war, and the desire of police and church officials to reestablish their positions influenced their view of German women and their African American partners. The enforcement of laws against German civilians lay within the responsibility of the German police, who suffered considerable dislocation in the immediate postwar period as American military government endeavored to denazify and democratize German government and administration. The United States broke up the centralized police organizations established during the Third Reich and gave control over the police to state and local authorities. City police forces were established in towns with populations of greater than 5,000. Outside of such cities, responsibility lay with the Landpolizei. The Landpolizei was initially subordinate to the presidents of the local government districts, but on January 21, 1946, the rural police forces of the three states (*Länder*) in the American zone were centralized at the state level, with the head of each state's Landpolizei reporting to the minister of interior.[88]

German officials' efforts to enforce laws against German women were hamstrung by their lack of jurisdiction over Allied personnel. The German police were powerless to prevent violation of the law by American soldiers. More seriously, American soldiers could prevent German police from enforcing German law against German women under the American soldiers' protection. Although in the disordered days of 1946 some officials proposed granting German police the authority to arrest American military personnel, the proposal was refused.[89] American soldiers, including African Americans, continued to be exempt from control by German police, and they often intervened against them on behalf of German women, as they did in Wirsberg and Feucht.[90]

The German police thus occupied a precarious position in the face of armed American soldiers, both white and black. Attacks on the German police by American soldiers became such a problem in 1946 that OMGUS felt compelled to clarify the circumstances in which members of the German police could defend themselves against attack by American soldiers. OMGUS explained that although military government law provided that a German policeman who used force against an American soldier could be punished by death, in any prosecution for such an offense the German defendant could assert the defense of self-defense, which excused actions taken to defend his own life or that of another person.[91] This interpretation offered scant assistance to German police who faced possible assault by American soldiers if they arrested the soldiers' companions.

American Responses

Many American military government officers sympathized with German officials in their efforts to enforce the law in the face of unrest produced by the tactical troops, whether white or black. Military government (OMGUS) was organizationally distinct from the tactical combat and support units under the command of USFET and later EUCOM. The numerous African American soldiers in Germany were all under the command of USFET or EUCOM. OMGUS initially included no African American military personnel and by October 1946 employed only four African American civilians. OMGUS personnel had responsibility for establishing and overseeing effective government over the German population, while at the same time carrying out denazification and democratization. The larger number of tactical and support troops remaining in Germany following the conclusion of hostilities quickly shrank with postwar redeployment, but they still far outnumbered the small military government cadre. At the time they had formulated their plans for military government, American planners believed that military government officials would continue to require the support of large numbers of combat and support troops to prevent or to respond to German resistance. As the threat of such resistance soon proved nonexistent, so did the role of many of the tactical troops.[92]

The tactical soldiers increasingly seemed to hinder rather than help military government's efforts to democratize the Germans. Misconduct included attacks on Germans perpetrated by white American soldiers, who themselves sometimes intervened on behalf of German women against civilian authorities.[93] In April 1946 the Third Army, which commanded the tactical troops in Bavaria, noted that "on many occasions military police and tactical troops have not given the German civilian police the moral and physical reinforcement which is vitally necessary to the performance of their duties." Tactical soldiers, who were immune from interference from the German police, represented a "priviliged [sic] class" in Germany, and they had been abusing that privilege. The Third Army required the assignment of a member of a military police unit to each German police precinct at all times, but the military police often proved unable to quell misconduct among American soldiers, both white and black, in spring 1946.[94]

The actions of U.S. soldiers often produced friction between members of military government and the tactical troops.[95] Military government officials often sided with German officials against tactical soldiers guilty of misconduct against German officials and civilians. In one town, for example, black tactical soldiers threatened at gunpoint a German policeman believed to be the "finger man" for the local military government officer.[96] OMGUS officials feared that the all-too-common attacks by unruly American soldiers, both white and black, on Germans threatened to create resentment in the population against the American occupiers.[97]

The situation in the town of Weißenburg in Middle Franconia, where soldiers of the black 351st Field Artillery Battalion were stationed after October 1945, exemplified the complicated array of competing forces in postwar Germany. The town of Weißenburg, about 50 kilometers south of Nuremberg, was surrounded by a predominantly agricultural region. The population included both Protestants and Catholics. Large numbers of displaced persons were present in the community at the conclusion of the fighting, and the population grew further with the arrival of German expellees from the Sudetenland. The U.S. military appointed as mayor of the town Fritz Traber, a druggist and Catholic member of the conservative CSU. Ludwig Thumshirn, a member of the SPD and of the Weißenburg Antifascist League, was selected as Landrat for the surrounding county.[98]

German officials in the town aligned with sympathetic American military government officials against the women and the soldiers. In January 1946 the local military government official, Captain Carr, had made modest efforts to allay town officials' concerns, explaining that interracial sex alone was not a crime but laws governing prostitution and the spread of venereal disease could be applied against the women involved. Weißenburg officials found a more sympathetic audience in Captain Carr's successors, Lieutenant Woodburn Williams and Lieutenant Glen Bowser. Lieutenant Williams informed German civilian authorities in April 1946 that he was determined to remedy the problems with the black troops and their companions.[99] A native of Texas, Williams had been a teacher in civilian life and flown bombers during the war. He was in his late twenties when the war ended and he was assigned to military government. Williams had shown little interest in his duties as a trade and industry officer in Landkreis Kronach in 1945, and he likely would have preferred flying to dealing with the pedestrian details of military government.[100]

Williams and Bowser supported local officials against the women and black troops. On one occasion, two women reported to military government that a German civilian in town, one Max Schober, had made derogatory remarks about African Americans. According to one witness, Schober had stated, "It is a vulgarity that Negros [sic] enter the house." The sixty-five-year-old Schober, who had been a member of the Nazi stormtroopers, was brought before a summary military government court on charges of making statements injurious to military government. He stated in his defense that he "[w]as indignant at [the] loose morals of [his] sub-tenant" and that his "[r]emarks were directed against immorality of [the] girl concerned and would have been as derogatory if boy-friends had been German civilians instead of coloured American soldiers." The court nevertheless found Schober guilty and sentenced him to a suspended jail sentence of three months.[101]

A subsequent inspector general investigation of events in Weißenburg shed additional light on the circumstances surrounding the Schober case. The German civilian interpreter who worked for military government, Ilse Matthisson, explained, "It appears that the goings on at the house were outrageous and Mr [Schober] said it is a fine thing and a shame the way the soldiers go in and out." Schober "had not said anything" derogatory, with the possible exception of using the word "Negro." Military government officials believed Schober's comments did not merit punishment. The summary court officer, Lieutenant Glen Bowser, nevertheless "thought it advisable to please the troops and he did not acquit the man."[102]

Letting Schober off with a slap on the wrist, Lieutenant Bowser then charged the two women who had informed on Schober with "inciting troops against the civilians." The women "readily admitted they obtained special favors by calling in the soldiers." They pled guilty and were sentenced to a year in prison, the maximum penalty that the summary court could impose. When Second Lieutenant Thomas J. Carney, the highest-ranking officer of the battery stationed in town, learned of the conviction of the women, he became "indignant" and sought clemency for them.[103] The incident illustrates the complexity of matters at the local level. The action by the women to silence their German critics within the town obviously boomeranged on them, as they received sentences of a year in jail, and the man they accused received only a three-month suspended sentence. There were definite limits to military government's efforts to stamp out race hatred in Weißenburg where immoral women were involved.

Trouble between the soldiers and the town's populace seems to have increased in spring 1946.[104] Whereas military government officials backed the town officials, officers of the artillery battalion—especially Major Linton S. Boatwright, at first the executive officer and later the commander of the unit, and Lieutenant Carney—tended to support the soldiers under their command. Major Boatwright in particular lacked confidence in Williams or the local police and believed that people in Weißenburg were engaged in "a concerted program . . . against the troops." Boatwright testified to the inspector general that Williams had admitted that the Bürgermeister had called the soldiers "Niggers" and that "there was a definite campaign in the town to cause trouble" by taking "advantage of the racial question."[105] In the subsequent inspector general investigation, the race of Boatwright and Carney was never specified, which suggests that they were white. They seem to have been mostly untroubled by the relations between the men and German women and had a fairly good relationship with the soldiers under their command.

In an effort to reduce the unit's venereal disease rate and to avoid problems with the local police, Boatwright instructed Carney to provide the police with a list naming about forty-three transient women whom he authorized to remain in Weißenburg. The women received passes permitting them to stay in town, but the passes were not licenses to "go out and tell the police . . . to go to hell or something like that." The women were to obey the law and, if possible, obtain employment. Carney further explained, "No woman could come in and stay just by saying she wanted to go with a soldier."[106] On June 24, Carney provided to the German police another list, which contained the names of fifty women and the fifty soldiers who promised to be responsible for them. Although similar systems were used in other locales where white units were quartered, the plan did not end trouble with the local police, and everyone but Carney seems to have understood the pass system as providing the women virtual carte blanche to disregard the German police.[107]

Williams objected to the plan and indeed to relations between the women and the soldiers in general. On June 5, 1946, he wrote to the public safety officer for Bavarian Military Government, complaining that the black troops in Weißenburg were causing difficulties. He insisted that German racial prejudice was not the problem. Indeed, he was rueful that the Germans were not more prejudiced.

> Contrary to expectations the core of the problem did not consist in educating the racially prejudiced German to refrain from display of a hostile or disrespectful attitude towards the negro soldier, but rather in supervising the springtide of fraternization in a manner to prevent too much Allied property such as rations and clothing items to disappear in German homes on the one hand, and to keep the alarming rise of VD rate from undermining the health of the occupational forces.[108]

Williams rejected the notion that his objections to the relations between German women and African American soldiers reflected racial discrimination.[109] He maintained that he sought merely to apply settled standards of morality, which any effort to democratize the Germans could not ignore.

> Similar girls loitering around barracks in the States are subject to apprehension for vagrancy and prostitution. American Military Government, however, is expected in all earnest to harbor and foster them over here, merely to avoid an impression of so-called racial prejudice. The question arises whether re-education of Germany to comprehend the principles of democracy can be done by disregarding what is held right and justified in the States and acting along lines which in actual fact constitute the official promotion of vice.[110]

Williams asserted that "the generosity of the negro soldier where frauleins are concerned" had attracted an "influx of notorious female characters." The women violated rules governing travel, identity papers, access to military installations, and venereal disease. Williams was pained that when local authorities tried to perform venereal disease examinations on the women, "[i]nstead of appreciating the precautions taken to prevent their exploitation and contamination, the colored soldiers resented Military Government actions to that effect and adopted a protective attitude towards their mistresses which was carried to the extent of liberating female prisoners from places of confinement." He complained that "the tactical officers concerned did practically nothing to discipline" the soldiers involved.[111]

Williams shared Imhoff's view that the problem originated with the women. "Every harlot in town," he wrote, "is aware of the fact that she need but give a hint to a colored boy, and anybody reprimanding her for flagrantly immoral conduct may be prepared for some kind of physical castigation by a negro soldier or being arrested for irreverance [sic] to the occupational forces in combination with racial misconceptions."[112] Whereas it is uncertain whether Imhoff really believed the women were the root of the problem or simply thought it best to avoid placing blame too directly on the black troops, Williams seems to have been firmly convinced of the women's primary role. City officials recorded a confidential statement of his that the problems were "above all usually a matter of the girls, who go with the Negroes and influence them." Williams also suggested that other, unnamed troublemakers could have been spreading word of the problem with the soldiers among the populace. It is impossible to determine to whom Williams was referring when he stated that "it is strongly suspected that behind it all there are still other people who are attempting to spread unrest."[113] That hidden malevolent influence went unmentioned in the annual historical report on the Weißenburg area covering the time period from April 1945 to June 1946, which was likely authored by Williams's successor, Glen Bowser. The report explained that most of the trouble between African American troops and German civilians was "caused by loose women exerting their pernicious influence on boys 'who never had it so good.'"[114]

Williams, however, included material in his June 5 letter that undercut such an interpretation. He explained that Carney had provided him with a list of women who were to be permitted to stay in Weißenburg as the "soldiers' mistresses." Transient women who were not on the list would not be permitted to remain in town. Williams interpreted this to mean "[a]ny other women happening to enter Weissenburg without the intention of putting herself at the soldiers' disposal will be expelled from the city."[115] The women clearly depended on the soldiers for permission even to remain in town. Williams, like Imhoff, nevertheless believed that measures ought to be taken against the women.

Troubles like those in Weißenburg caused by its own soldiers prompted USFET to establish an independent constabulary to function as a robust police force. This constabulary, which began operations on July 1, 1946, was responsible for maintaining order throughout the American zone. It was vested with jurisdiction over American tactical soldiers, as well as displaced persons and the German population. The constabulary often took measures at the behest of American military government officials when tactical troops threatened to interfere with the German police. Within less than a month after the constabulary began its operations, the Public Safety Branch of OMGBY expressed its gratification that the force had provided excellent assistance to German police officials.[116]

Immediately upon commencing operation, the constabulary devoted considerable effort to rounding up German women associating with African American soldiers against whom the German police had been unable to act. Indeed, the day after the constabulary began functioning, it conducted a raid in Weißenburg against German women. Similarly, the constabulary arrested a large number of women in Meitingen on grounds that they were improperly registered after local military government officials had reported that "German Police were powerless to deal with them." The constabulary performed the raid without the assistance of the German police owing to a concern that "colored troops would retaliate by misusing the German Police if they were actually connected with the raid."[117] The constabulary was ostensibly to arrest German civilians only at the request of military government and only in the case of "emergency," but cases where black soldiers might pose a problem normally qualified as such an emergency.[118]

The commander of the all-white constabulary, General Ernest N. Harmon, was a former tank commander who prided himself on his toughness. He took a dim view of the African American soldiers in Europe and favored firm measures to bring them into line.[119] In his unpublished memoirs he wildly overestimated that African American soldiers in Europe committed 90 percent of the crimes in the theater. On one occasion, he instructed one of his men in dealing with a troublesome African American unit not to hesitate "to shoot between the eyes the first person who spoke out of turn." When the subordinate did just that, Harmon instituted a court-martial that cleared him of wrongdoing.[120] Harmon assigned significant importance to problems caused by African Americans and their girlfriends, directing his staff that "special incidents," such as the trouble in Weißenburg, should be "brought to his attention directly."[121]

Misconduct in White and Black

The constabulary, intended to be an elite unit, had its own disciplinary problems. It should not be surprising, of course, that misconduct occurred in a sizable military unit like the constabulary, but it is noteworthy that the crime rate among the constabulary's personnel narrowly exceeded the theater-wide rate.[122] A high rate of venereal disease likewise continually plagued the constabulary, although its rate of infection was somewhat lower than the average rate in the theater.[123] The constabulary unit that moved into Weißenburg following the transfer out of a black unit suffered from high venereal disease infection rates. One white constabulary trooper contracted venereal disease in July 1946 from a woman in Bruchsal after picking her up and having sex in a park. The vigorous complaints from the German clergy made two months earlier about similar activities of black troops in that same district had failed to eliminate out-of-doors sexual relations between American soldiers and German women.[124] The soldiers of the constabulary thus engaged in the same sorts of conduct as the African American soldiers that they often policed.

Even when white troops engaged in violence against German civilians, German officials often excused them on grounds of drunkenness or newness to their station or duties. The Bürgermeister of Philippsburg, for instance, complained in January 1947 to military government officials in Bruchsal that American soldiers, members of the 1st Constabulary Squadron, had gone on a New Year's Eve rampage, beating anyone who crossed their path. The Bürgermeister explained that the "cause of the excesses may be traced to the excessive use of alcohol." He noted that the population had enjoyed a good understanding with another unit that had previously been stationed in town, and he hoped for similarly good relations in the future.[125]

When trouble involved black troops, Germans tended to slight the importance of drunkenness in favor of narratives of more pernicious female influences on African Americans. In Kreis Bruchsal, for example, three letters from German church officials and the one letter from the Bürgermeister attributed the trouble to the women of doubtful character who allegedly incited the soldiers to threaten or to attack anyone who criticized the women. The American Counter-Intelligence Corps agent who investigated found that the Germans in the district had "a strong feeling against the colored soldiers" and often "shout[ed] remarks at these girls about going with the colored troops." The agent, however, found that trouble occurred both when the troops were "incited by the girls, and at times the troops, when drunk, [took] action against the Germans on their own." German officials, focused on the immorality of German women and intent on avoiding express condemnation of blacks that might bring counter-charges of racism by white officials, declined to assert that African American troops independently engaged in violence against the population.[126]

American military officials, like the agent in Bruchsal, often believed that for both white and black soldiers "[i]ntoxication continues to be the root of the trouble."[127] Drunkenness could be linked, however, in American discussions of misconduct by black troops to their perceived racial proclivities. The commander of one ordinance battalion, for example, blamed instances of trouble between black troops and civilians on alcohol in racial terms. "Negroes are unable to drink any appreciable amount of intoxicants and still control their senses and faculties. The majority of Negro soldiers feel that they must have sexual intercourse, and too often resort to bodily force to satisfy this desire."[128]

Instances of misconduct among white soldiers appeared as something requiring explanation. Innumerable individual Germans complained about crimes committed against them by white Americans, but they did not risk sweeping condemnations of white soldiers comparable to the complaints about black soldiers. To question comprehensively the conduct of white American soldiers would have been to question the essence of the American occupation of Germany, a subject that was closed to discussion. In contrast, cases of black misconduct seemed more appropriate for guarded complaint. Commentators thus exhibited a willingness to move from a discussion of particular events to general (albeit carefully phrased) conclusions about African Americans.

Such characterizations of black troops rarely marshaled evidence sufficient to generalize fairly. Imhoff exercised more care than most officials in actually citing incidents from Geißler's report regarding other African American soldiers to buttress his argument that the problem in Wirsberg was symptomatic of the larger problem posed by African American soldiers and the women who associated with them. Dr. Heinrich Köhler, president of Landesbezirk Baden, made a similar move but with less supporting evidence. He passed on Father Sales's sensational account of the situation in Waghäusel, which described, among other details, children picking up used prophylactics from the ground and blowing them up like balloons. Köhler, without advancing supporting evidence, informed American military government officials in Stuttgart that such troubles in Waghäusel were "equal with those" everywhere colored troops were stationed.[129] The prevailing racial logic justified inferring general truths about

African Americans based on spectacular individual examples of misconduct, whereas cases of misconduct by white American soldiers necessitated particular explanations, such as drunkenness.

Moral Whiteness in Practice

The rhetoric mobilized by Imhoff, Williams, and others produced punitive actions against the women involved. On August 29, 1946, the constabulary conducted a raid in Wirsberg that netted twenty-two women, who were referred for trial to a German court on charges of prostitution.[130] In fact, any woman in Wirsberg found in the company of African American soldiers was caught in the dragnet. Five of the twenty-two women had been found in bed with soldiers, whereas seventeen of them had merely been "attending a soldiers['] dance."[131] Fewer than half of the women arrested in Wirsberg were infected with venereal disease.[132] With the aid of four African American soldiers, three of the infected women escaped twelve days later from the city hospital where they were being held for treatment. The soldiers had come to the hospital, removed bars from a window, and urged the women to escape at night. The women, however, returned to the hospital the same day because they became afraid.[133] The incident tends to undercut Imhoff's picture of German women manipulating the hapless soldiers.

Similarly, in Weißenburg the constabulary moved against the women involved. On June 28, at the direction of the commanding officer of the field artillery battalion, the women on the lists were instructed to leave town by Sunday, June 30. On Monday, July 1, the head of the public safety branch for Bavaria, acting on instructions from General Walter Muller, the head of military government in Bavaria, then ordered the local liaison and security officer to "have all the girls on the list arrested immediately, have their papers examined and a physical examination given to each of them, and to try in Military Government Court all those who were not clear of wrong-doing."[134] At 3:50 in the morning of July 2, the day after the constabulary began operating, twenty-five of its members, with the assistance of eighteen German police, began rounding up women in town. Within two hours, they had arrested forty-nine women, thirty-four of whom were named on Lieutenant Carney's list. Seven of the women were not German; six were displaced persons of unnamed nationality and one was Italian.[135]

The women were tried before a military government summary court in assembly-line fashion. The charge sheets in the cases were evidently mass-produced, with virtually identical language for almost every defendant's charge: "In that accused had sexual intercourse with members of the US Army despite suffering from venereal disease, thus endangering the physical health of the Allied Forces in or about May and June 1946; in city of Weissenburg." The charge sheets were completed after the defendants had been confined for at least two weeks.[136] All but two defendants were convicted of some offense.[137] It appears that even the "guilty" verdict was typed onto the form in the appropriate blank before the case was decided. In one case where the defendant was acquitted, the word *not* was squeezed in, handwritten in ink just before the typed word *guilty*.[138] That acquittal may have been because the defendant was employed in the battalion's mess hall or because she was Italian.[139] One other woman was acquitted on the ground that she was not infected with venereal disease.

The criminal convictions generally led to confinement in the local venereal disease hospital for a period ranging from five days to eight months, with most women receiving a one-month sentence.[140] The hospital came to resemble a prison, with bars covering the windows and the inmates dressed in "a kind of pajamas," so that they could be easily recognized as inmates of the venereal disease hospital in the event of their escape. Food was meager. In August, the military government summary court in Weißenburg convicted eight women for escape from the facility but suspended their sentences because they had escaped in order to obtain food, which was in short supply at the hospital.[141] The hospital was decidedly a disciplinary institution.

Although complaints concerning interracial relations produced punitive actions against the women involved, African American soldiers who intervened against German officials on behalf of the women often escaped punishment.[142] In Weißenburg, no legal action was taken against the soldiers, with the exception of one soldier who had killed a German man after the victim had asked the soldier's companion what she was "doing out with this 'Nigger son of a bitch?'"[143] In fact, on the day after the raid, soldiers of the 351st Field Artillery Battalion, with the authorization of Lieutenant Carney, visited the venereal disease hospital where the women were confined and brought them candy and cigarettes.[144] Military government officials informed town authorities that henceforth women suspected of prostitution should be arrested, regardless of whether they associated with American soldiers, but suggested that German police refrain from action in the presence of the soldiers, who remained immune from action by German officials.[145] The battalion had already been slated for transfer back to the United States as part of the general reduction in the strength of African American units in Europe during 1946 before these events came to a head in Weißenburg.[146] The constabulary's raid did not derail that plan, and the unit returned to the United States in late July and was finally deactivated on August 10, 1946, without any punitive measures having been taken against any of the soldiers. The next month, military government officials informed Weißenburg city officials that a constabulary unit would be stationed in town to preserve order. City officials' anxieties about more trouble with American soldiers were assuaged with the guarantee that stationing the white constabulary unit in town meant "colored troops would not be coming."[147]

In Wirsberg, no soldiers were arrested in the August 29 raid. The constabulary limited its measures against the troops in Wirsberg to "making every effort to keep close watch" on their activities.[148] American officials took no action against the soldiers despite the fact that knowledgeable officers believed, contrary to Imhoff's contention, that the African American soldiers were in control and represented the cause of the trouble.[149] Major Frank Meszar, the public safety officer for Stadt- und Landkreis Kulmbach, in which Wirsberg was located, reported that the soldiers of the second platoon of the African American 596th Laundry Company had "imported various and sundry prostitutes into the town of Wirsberg and had forced the Buergermeister to give these women accomodations [sic] in the town." He believed that the action against the women was "merely a temporary solution, because the soldiers . . . will recruit other women and continue to force the local German authorities to do their bidding."[150] Similarly, Major H. C. Kauffman, the director of the Kulmbach liaison and security office, doubted that the raid had eliminated the root of the problem. He opined that "serious trouble" would arise if the unit were permitted to remain in the area.[151]

In Feucht, as well, Geißler's report had produced the arrest of the women but had done little to restrain the soldiers.[152] On June 10, Inspector Geißler's office reported that three city officials in Feucht had been attacked by two "colored soldiers." The soldiers evidently "intended to revenge themselves, as all wenches of Feucht have been arrested and . . . they thought the Burgermeisters would be the responsible person for it." The report's author feared that "doubtful women persuade the colored soldiers to prevent that officials can further execute their duties for maintaining discipline."[153] Remarkably, the women thus evidently continued to exercise their malevolent influence even after their arrest whereas the soldiers again escaped punitive action. Even the June attack on the town officials provoked no action against the soldiers involved. USFET headquarters inquired on July 22 of the commanding general of the Third Army regarding the status of the matter and asked for weekly updates.[154] Such reports apparently were not made. As late as October 7, four months after the attack, the chief of personnel services within USFET complained that a thorough investigation of the situation in Feucht had not been made. That complaint was similarly ineffectual.[155]

African American soldiers in Germany, of course, did not always escape punishment for misconduct. In one instance, for example, the commander of an African American unit responded to a large number of disciplinary problems by imposing a curfew and court-martialing fourteen offenders.[156] Nevertheless, the weight of punitive measures generally fell on the women involved, who were regarded as more blameworthy.

Doubtless bureaucratic inertia and the press of more urgent business accounted partly for the lack of action against the soldiers. The files of both the tactical military units stationed in Germany under the command of USFET and of military government are replete with unheeded injunctions to comply with reporting requirements or requests for information of all kinds. In addition, some tactical officers like Boatwright were inclined to support their troops against officials in military government and civilian administration. Some of the reticence of American officials to take action against African Americans may also have stemmed from a concern to avoid the appearance of racial discrimination during a period when the army was increasingly under pressure from American civil rights advocates.[157]

Another factor in the disinclination to punish the soldiers was an acceptance that soldiers would seek sexual relations with women and occasionally misbehave. Indeed, the soldiers in Wirsberg had carried on relations with German women for some time. According to the Landrat, the situation had become less permissive only when a new officer assumed command of the unit in early May.[158] When the director of the Office of Military Government for Bavaria, Brigadier General Walter J. Muller, forwarded Imhoff's memorandum to Clay, it met with little reaction. General Clay reviewed the materials but found that the incidents were part of the "old . . . story" of typical army conduct and did not amount to a worrisome trend.[159] African American troops in Germany who slept with German women were simply viewed by many white American officials as "boys 'who never had it so good.' "[160]

Race and German Whiteness

Germans felt no inclination to excuse women involved in sexual relations with African Americans. Such women were continually branded as morally depraved traitors to the nation. In a meeting of the Bremen Woman's Committee, one female Social Democrat compared the situation in 1946 negatively with that after World War I, when the French had stationed colonial troops in the Rhineland. The current situation was even worse than the "Black Horror," she complained, because after World War I the women had to be forced into bordellos for the black soldiers, whereas in 1946 they entered them willingly. In her opinion, rape would have been preferable to German women's voluntary degradation.[161]

Denunciations of immoral women often equated morality and true Germanness. Church officials who opposed Nazism on moral grounds were not infrequently themselves committed German nationalists, and nationalist sentiments, fortified by racial ideas, lay at the base of objections to sexual relations with occupying soldiers.[162] The Catholic Bishop of Passau's first pastoral letter after the defeat of the Third Reich denounced

German women who shamelessly threw themselves at the occupying soldiers. In doing so, they "degraded not only themselves, but the whole nation [*Volk*] itself."[163] Germans who defined white Germanness in terms of sexual propriety were prepared to exclude such women from the fold. As one woman wrote to the editors of *Stern* magazine in 1948, women who engaged in sexual relations with African Americans were "not really German."[164]

Both Germans and white Americans understood sexual propriety as a white virtue.[165] In 1946 the liberal American intelligence officer Saul Padover described German women as "perhaps the easiest white women in the world."[166] That description associated whiteness with sexual propriety and blackness with promiscuity. It implied that no group of white women was as promiscuous as women of color. Padover probably did not believe that biological race straightforwardly determined the sexual propensities of women. Race nevertheless stood as a convenient shorthand explanation for differences in sexual morality. Other Americans continued to hold to a belief in the primacy of biological race. Sexual promiscuity was, as the surgeon of one black unit expressed in November 1945, "a racial characteristic among colored people." The problem in that surgeon's view had become especially grave in postwar Germany, where "the colored men for the first time are granted the social privileges of associating with white women."[167]

Promiscuous German women, especially those engaged in relations with African Americans, could approach the boundary of whiteness. The women's behavior made them practically black already. The case of one family in Wiesental illustrates how carrying on sexual relations with African Americans could bring exclusion from white German society. A Frau M. filed a report with the German police on May 17, 1946, against her sixteen-year-old daughter, Anna. She reported that Anna had been associating with black soldiers stationed in Waghäusel, on one occasion staying away from home for three days. Moreover, Anna no longer did any work around the house and refused to mind her mother. Frau M. concluded that her daughter was "totally morally corrupt" and had become "a hopeless victim of the black soldiers." Herr M. had given Anna a beating and confined her to the house, but the next day she disappeared from home. She was believed to be in Mannheim, infected with venereal disease, and still associating with black American soldiers. Frau M. recommended that her daughter be apprehended and placed in a reformatory.[168]

The police description of Anna that concluded the report suggests the power of the taint of blackness. Anna was described, in addition to being big and well-developed, as having "black hair, brown-ish skincolor, [and] somewhat thrust-out lips" (*schwarze Haare, bräunliche Hautfarbe, etwas aufgeworfene Lippen*). That description was translated into English for American military government as "Hight [*sic*] 165, well developed, black hair, brwnish [*sic*] skin, big lips."[169] The match between those physical traits picked out in the description of Anna with those habitually ascribed to African Americans seems too exact to have been purely coincidental. Anna's features suggested a distant echo of the assertion by Johann Gottfried Herder that "fullness of the lips [*aufgeworfne Lippe*], even among whites, is considered by physiognomy as the sign of a very sensuous disposition."[170] The police official completing the description was unlikely to have referred to a passing remark from Herder, nor did Herder's ideas descend directly to the postwar period. Nevertheless, the manner in which the authorities seized on physical correspondences with blackness in describing a woman whose actions had effectively disqualified her from moral whiteness suggests that moral and biological traits were translatable.

The notion that women marked as immoral and diseased seemed somehow almost black depended not only on fortuitous phenotypic similarities. Such women were described as psychological deviants from a German norm in terms similar to those that racial theorists had long used regarding blacks. One German expert on venereal disease noted that scientific studies of prostitutes and promiscuous individuals found a high percentage of women in both groups who had "a hereditary problem of a defective moral system in the sense of a lack of restraint in the sexual field." One study found that 18 percent of sexually promiscuous women (*HWG-Personen*) were mentally deficient (*schwachsinnige*) "from a psychological point of view." The women lacked "a certain long-range perspective and a goal-oriented direction of activity." They lacked any sense of responsibility and were "extremely libidinal" (*äußerst triebhaft*). African Americans were nowhere mentioned in the article, but it was perhaps unsurprising that such women would engage in relations with black soldiers, who purportedly suffered from the same lack of restraint, were similarly impulsive, and also were marked as sources of infection with venereal disease.[171]

Race and Democracy

German officials sometimes argued that the brazen immorality of interracial sex threatened to undo the American effort to democratize Germany, because it disgusted the "honorable Germans" who were forced to witness it. If, however, American officials took the necessary steps to carry out the "moral purification of . . . public life," they would win the gratitude of those Germans who "welcomed [the] victorious armies as liberators" from National Socialism.[172] This rhetorical strategy of condemning interracial sexual immorality under the occupation as worse than anything done by the Nazis found widespread application in postwar Germany.[173] A minister in Ermershausen-Birkenfeld complained about white constabulary soldiers to his superiors (but not to the Americans): "The established population, who keep their distance from these goings-on, say: they need not say anything to us about democracy, humanity, Christianity, and so forth, since not even the Nazis carried on worse."[174] The statement implicitly separated the upstanding German population from both the Americans and the Nazis. In the peculiar logic that equated immoral Americans with the Nazis, African Americans figured as the most vicious. In Meitingen, where African American soldiers were stationed, the saying among the local populace was "American negro troops are exactly the same as SS men under the Nazis."[175] In the same vein, another German official stated that citizens in his jurisdiction were "terrified" by African American soldiers stationed there. The people feared what would happen if the army truly "let these colored soldiers get out of control." He further argued that the African American troops' conduct produced negative consequences for the democratization campaign, as people asked whether "this is American culture and Democratic living," and some even claimed that "the Fuhrer was right when he predicted what would happen if we lost the war."[176]

American officials found themselves caught on the horns of a dilemma. On the one hand, the immoral activities of soldiers, especially black soldiers, threatened to undermine American claims to be a democratic and law-abiding people. Most German pronouncements failed to recognize any possible racial double standard. Archbishop Conrad Gröber of Freiburg, for example, castigated women engaged in relations with African Americans while also publicly condemning Nazism's cult of blood and race.[177] The immorality of interracial sex was manifestly undemocratic to German officials. On the other hand, African Americans maintained that actions against their girlfriends constituted racial discrimination, suggesting that American democracy was not free of the same sort of racism practiced by the Nazis.

Conclusion

American control over public discussion of race in the American zone changed what could be said openly about the subject. Strident public denunciations of the purportedly unrestrained nature of African Americans and calls for their control did not appear in the immediate postwar years and would likely have proven unpersuasive to American officials sensitive to the persistence of Nazi racial dogma. The new orthodoxy concerning women's sexuality broke with the prior ideology, which had defined women as the propagators of the German race but nevertheless continued to insist that women's sexuality should be regulated according to the needs of the nation. Morality rather than racial biology was advanced as the express basis for that need, pushing race into the background. German officials defined and prosecuted as prostitutes the women who associated with African Americans, even if they were merely attending a dance together and despite some confusion about whether the soldiers were the women's "lovers" or their customers. Such definitions derived their meaning from the logic of moral whiteness that excluded the possibility of respectable romantic relationships across the color line.

White Americans generally represented a receptive audience for German concerns about the immorality of German women engaged in relations with African American men. Out of the public eye, German and American officials could occasionally work out, as in Weißenburg, the selective enforcement of facially race-neutral laws to end interracial sex. More often, race remained the unspoken subtext to an express moral rhetoric. That language could prove effective because white Americans and Germans generally shared a belief that proper white women should not and would not engage in sexual relations with black men.

CHAPTER FOUR

Fräuleins and Black GIs

Race, Sex, and Power

This chapter examines more closely relations between African American soldiers and German women. Although such relationships were conventionally viewed as challenging racial orthodoxy, few actually represented resistance to prevailing beliefs in black inferiority, the danger of race mixing, or the importance of race in human interaction. In fact, sexual relations between German women and African American men were often motivated by, and reinforced, the fetishization by both African American men and German women of the exotic racial difference of their sexual partner. That tendency found further expression in the fascination with the physical qualities of the biracial offspring of such unions.

Relations between African Americans and Germans shared much in common with relations between Germans and white Americans. The same "twoness" that W.E.B. Du Bois described within black consciousness marked Germans' perceptions of African American soldiers. Germans certainly regarded them as a special sort of black people, very different, for example, from French colonial troops, even if they could at times be lumped together as black. Race, in German consciousness or practice, could never be extricated from other coexisting aspects of social reality, such as nationality, gender, and status or class. Germans often perceived African Americans as the most American of Americans. Black GIs seemed to embody, if in an exaggerated or even pathological form, the qualities of youthfulness, openness, generosity, and naiveté generally ascribed to Americans. Color-blindness, however, was notably absent from the maladies circulating in the American zone, and the blackness of black Americans was neither erased nor ignored.[1]

Sorting out the particularities of relations between black GIs and German women appears especially treacherous in the context of this chapter's attempt to decipher the complexities of attraction and power in sexual relationships, a daunting task in any historical setting. The job may seem even more difficult in the apparently abnormal setting of postwar Germany. American-occupied Germany certainly presented a unique landscape. Nevertheless, in many respects, men's and women's responses to the particular exigencies of American-occupied Germany in their relationships represented the pursuit of rather ordinary goals through the application of rather ordinary practices under extraordinary conditions.

A number of circumstances in the period conspired to derail German women from a path toward the social ideal of finding a suitable marriage partner. They included crushing military defeat and occupation by foreign powers, which threatened the existence of the German national state. In addition, the war produced tremendous social dislocation, tearing women from their homes and families at the same time that it reduced the number of suitable German partners available. Finally, tremendous economic desperation characterized the postwar years.[2] Those unique circumstances produced unusual complexity in the power relations between sexual partners. Power relations between black GIs and German women were complex because the balance of power was remarkably equal. The soldiers had money. They were immune from the jurisdiction of German authorities, and, as men in a military occupation force, they enjoyed a specifically martial, male power over women.

On the other hand, German women had their whiteness, which they could use to avail themselves of the protection of American authorities. Once women engaged in relations with African Americans, however, whiteness proved to be a wasting asset.[3] Wolfgang Koeppen's postwar novel, *Tauben im Gras*, illustrates the perceived value of a woman's whiteness in the character Carla, a young German woman who, in entering a relationship with an African American soldier, has forfeited it. Examining her body, she conceives of whiteness in terms of a valuable sexual commodity inseparable from her other bodily attributes. "I could have had a white man instead, a white man [*ein Weißer*], too, would have been satisfied, do these breasts sag? they do not, they're firm and round, what did the guy call them? milkapples, they're still milkapples, my body is white [*der Leib ist weiß*]. . . . I could have had a white man instead."[4] Carla's musings suggest that crossing the color line in postwar Germany could cost a woman a great deal. Indeed, women in relationships with black GIs could rarely obtain assistance from white American authorities, who regularly treated such women as having forfeited a claim to protection. Within the relationships, though, whiteness retained its benefits, as it, or its sacrifice for a black partner, could be carried indefinitely on the books of the parties' accounts.

Not all relations between African American soldiers and German women involved sexual relations. A widow from Wirsberg, who was in her late sixties when the war ended, for example, claimed to have become acquainted with several African American soldiers, who often visited her because she could speak English well. She had a son living in Pittsburgh, which likely contributed to her inclination and ability to befriend Americans in Germany.[5] Such relationships rarely caught the attention of German or American officials concerned with preserving law and order.

On the other hand, nonsexual relations between black GIs and German children did occupy an important place in the public imagination. In the paradigmatic account, a friendly black GI generously shared candy with German children. The public perception of those contacts between African Americans and German children drew on the common perception of supposedly simple, playful blacks as essentially "good-natured children" themselves. Such relationships generally appeared unproblematic, as German children and "childlike" African Americans interacted as unthreatening playmates, but they were clearly viewed through a lens of long-standing racial beliefs about blacks.[6]

Sexual relations between black men and German women represented the real problem. Such relationships often extended outward from the couple to encompass family members, landladies or landlords, black-market fixers, and friends in local communities. Such people, through their ties to a woman engaged in relations with a black soldier, could be brought into contact with, and sometimes affinity for, African Americans. Economic interest and personal ties could mitigate prejudices that brought no economic advantage in postwar Germany.

Allegiances within the local Wirsberg population, for example, were divided between the African American soldiers and white officials in military government. The African American soldiers had befriended one woman whose son "worked for" the soldiers. (He had been the only man arrested in the constabulary raid.) They told her that they had written to Washington complaining about the local military government official and assured her that he would soon be removed from Wirsberg and jailed. The woman, who formerly had served as an interpreter for the military government, passed the information on to her friend, who forwarded the information to the military government officer with a request for anonymity and on the condition that the information was to be kept confidential.[7]

As in the case of women who entered into sexual relationships with African Americans, Germans' willingness to enter into economic dealings with black GIs did not necessarily equate with a rejection of racism or Nazism. In Weißenburg, for example, simple economic incentives moved one woman to let rooms to women engaged in relations with African Americans. She explained frankly that she "[h]ad to make a living" and that both the "soldiers and girls paid her well for nightly visits."[8] Even former Nazis at times proved willing to facilitate sexual relations between German women and black troops of the occupying force where there was money to be made. Witnesses testifying in one 1948 denazification proceeding claimed that the defendant, a former Nazi block warden, made his apartment available for meetings between African American soldiers and their girlfriends. The neighbors seem to have been more irate about the defendant's postwar activities than his actions during the Third Reich. One witness charged that the defendant's family set "their sail to every wind" and endeavored to profit no matter what the prevailing circumstances.[9] The interplay of race and denazification in that case thus produced a peculiar twist in the American democratization effort, as a former Nazi's neighbors denounced him for pimping white German women to African American soldiers.

Placing the Women in German Society

Germans and white Americans continually asserted that the women who engaged in liaisons with African American soldiers represented the lowest elements in society.[10] An officer investigating racial tensions in the town of Offenbach explained that "only girls belonging to the worst elements of the population" engaged in intercourse with black soldiers.[11] By the same token, American venereal disease lectures were premised on the idea that black soldiers had sex almost exclusively with the dregs of society. "Only that element of a population which is down and out, or which does not care, or which stands in open disregard of local opinion or any other opinion—in plain words, the riff raff—is the element to which the masses of our [Negro] soldiers are exposed."[12] White Americans typically saw no need to prove such assertions, since the very act of engaging in sex with a black man conferred low status on any white woman. A respectable white woman engaged in relations with a black man was an oxymoron.[13]

In reality, the women who entered into sexual relationships with African Americans came from all social classes in Germany.[14] Upon reviewing the results of a 1949 survey of 600 German mothers of children by African American fathers, the American sociologist Vernon Stone found that although women from "the lower class, using that term in the socio-logical sense," accounted for a large number of the mothers, "134 of the mothers were classified as upper class and 180 middle class."[15] The rep-resentativeness of Stone's sample cannot be gauged, since he offered no explanation for how he identified the 600 women among the estimated 2,100 mothers of such children. In addition, Stone did not precisely define his terms, but they appear to have been rather rough categories based on American conceptions. Finally, Stone's general argument must be read with care, since he highlighted aspects of the relationships that supported a critique of American racism. Despite those caveats, Stone's figures indi-cate that appreciable numbers of women from middle- and upper-class backgrounds engaged in relations with African Americans.

Of course, the enormous dislocations brought about by the war and occupation meant that many women had suffered dramatic loss of posi-tion by 1945. Class origins often seemed irrelevant for women whose fam-ily members and patrimony had disappeared in the maelstrom of war and defeat. Doubtless, few of the upper-class women who responded to Stone's questionnaire were living upper-class lives at the time that they entered into relations with the African American fathers of their children.[16] Through race, however, status relations were reconstructed in postwar Germany, as the color line provided a bright line for demarcating high-class and low-class women. Those women who crossed it fell in status. Their middle- or upper-class origins became irrelevant once they entered relations with African Americans. Status in postwar Germany depended not only on economic resources or educational background but also on conformity with norms of whiteness. Eschewing relations with African Americans was a condition of retaining high status. The category of high-class "Negerliebchen" was an impossible contradiction.[17]

The disruption of comparatively stable family and work lives pro-vided a decisive impetus leading many women to become involved with American soldiers, including African American soldiers. The story of one woman can serve to illustrate that dynamic. Gertrud W., born in 1926, was the daughter of a factory worker in Ludwigshafen. Despite a number of moves during the war, her family survived the war intact. After its conclu-sion, she was living in Mannheim with her family and working in a shop, earning twenty-two marks per week. The critical event that unmoored her from her surroundings was her father's death in February 1946. Relations with her stepmother rapidly deteriorated, and her stepmother eventually ordered her out of the house. She moved to a rented room in Durlach. She claimed that she attempted to register with the police but "was not accepted" and thus obtained no ration card and had no regular employ-ment. She paid her rent in cigarettes.[18]

Gertrud spent most nights in the African American soldiers' club in Bruchsal, where she entered into a sexual relationship with a black GI. She explained that she typically stayed until 10:00 P.M. and then rode back to Durlach in a jeep that made a regular run carrying her and perhaps other women. She told the police that the soldier had given her no money but had given her cigarettes, chocolate, and oranges, as well as purchasing beer and Coca-Cola for her at the club. The cigarettes she received evidently sufficed to pay her rent and buy her meals in taverns. One rainy evening, her soldier boyfriend gave her a blanket and raincoat for the trip home, but she missed her ride and had to stay the night in a garden shed near the American barracks. There she was picked up for questioning by German police on suspicion of illegal possession of American goods, prostitution, and carrying venereal disease. She denied having venereal disease or practicing prostitution. She explained, though, that if her father had not died, she would have been living with him still.[19]

German expellees from the East and other displaced women were especially vulnerable to such vagaries, since they generally had few material resources or ties in the communities they entered. Germans in the West, who faced their own shortages of food and housing, often showed little sympathy for the new arrivals. Antipathy toward newcomers could be particularly sharp in traditionally insular rural Bavarian communities, where outsiders who entered into relationships with American soldiers, especially African American soldiers, faced virulent resentment from the local residents. The archives are full of complaints against such women.[20] These outsiders could be singled out for harsher treatment than women who had family, friends, or other allies in the local community. In Weißenburg, for example, the local military government officer instructed the local German officials in confidential discussions that no punitive measures should be taken against local women associating with soldiers of the African American unit stationed in town. "Since for the most part it is not a matter of local girls, but rather girls who have moved into the area," he said, "nothing is to be undertaken against the few local girls." In fact, however, local women were not spared when the constabulary raided the town.[21]

Germans commonly insisted that the ranks of women carrying on relations with African Americans were filled exclusively by camp followers. The evidence, however, belies that account. Besides the local women in Weißenburg, for example, five or six of the women involved in Wirsberg came from the small town itself. Approximately twenty more women came from neighboring towns in the Upper Franconia region, such as Bamberg and Hof.[22] It was not only outsiders but also locals who engaged in sex with African Americans. Why then did some German women from all classes and a variety of circumstances associate with men marked by prevailing racial notions as inferior?

Motivations

Contemporaries, as well as many historians, sought an explanation for why so many German women chose to carry on relations with African American soldiers during the occupation. The need to account for the existence of such relations was predicated on specific social, gender, and racial ideas. First, it was commonly believed that women's sexual desire was less powerful than men's. Accordingly, men generally needed to persuade women to date and to engage in sex with them, except in the case of women who had become sexually depraved.[23] Second, the racially based belief that white women would be disinclined to associate with black men lay behind the perceived need to explain the actions of the minority of German women who engaged in liaisons with African American men.

Observers in the 1940s perceived no comparable need to explain black soldiers' participation in relations with German women, despite the fact that African Americans might have been inclined to reject such relationships in light of Nazism's insistence on black inferiority or their relatives' disapproval of a white German girlfriend.[24] According to the mirror image of the assumptions regarding German women, African Americans, as men, and especially as soldiers, naturally sought out sexual relations with any available women. Beyond the gender and social bases of the presumption of soldiers' willingness to engage in relations with women of the defeated enemy nation, racial attitudes operated as well. According to notions that prevailed at the time, for black men white women were presumed to be at least not unattractive and more likely especially desirable. Those assumptions were neither universally applicable nor natural but amounted to social expectations.[25] Indeed, some of the motivation for the women in such liaisons can be explained by the relative scarcity of German men immediately after the war. In 1946 (the year in which births of children of African Americans in Germany peaked) there were 167 women between the ages of twenty and thirty for every 100 men in the three western zones.[26]

In fact, since at least the beginning of the twentieth century, a few German women had not scrupled to engage in sexual relations with men who were deemed racially inferior. To the consternation of commentators in the press, African performers in colonial shows that toured Germany before World War I at times attracted admiring German women.[27] Contrary to the international propaganda campaign against the *Schwarze Schmach* on the Rhine, which branded all sexual contacts between German women and French colonial troops as rapes, some women voluntarily pursued relations with African and Asian soldiers.[28] German women continued to act on sexual attraction for racial others under the Nazi regime. In 1939 an official observed that a surprisingly large number of German women entered into sexual relations with the black performers in the German Africa Show, which toured the *Reich* to promote colonialism.[29] Similarly, the Security Service (SD) indicated that it was receiving increasing reports of German girls engaging in "shameful conduct" with students from Turkey, Afghanistan, and China, among other nations.[30]

As Elizabeth Heineman has shown, less exotic, but still racially proscribed, foreign workers attracted German women during World War II. The prohibition against relations between German women and Polish workers in the Reich failed to put an end to them. Reports that a considerable number of women engaged in sexual relations with forced laborers or prisoners of war continually troubled Nazi officials. The Gestapo expressed increasing frustration over the population's unwillingness to expose women engaged in relationships with Polish laborers. The SD anxiously observed that numerous reports from all parts of the Reich indicated a continual increase in sexual relations between German women and foreign workers and attributed the problem to the absence among the German populace of a sense of the necessity for "a clean separation between members of different peoples."[31]

After 1945 the economic misery of the German population tended to foster relations between German women and occupying soldiers, regardless of their race. Some commentators attributed decisive importance to the material straits of German women and elaborated a typology of postwar prostitution under the headings of "survival prostitution," "occupation prostitution," and "professional prostitution."[32] At the time, Germans certainly stigmatized sexual relationships between black soldiers and women as prostitution.[33] African American men at times unquestionably exchanged money for sex, as in one case where a woman received twenty marks as payment for sex.[34]

More often, and more usefully in Germany before the currency reform of 1948, soldiers provided their sexual partners with material items. It was sometimes difficult to establish whether men provided material items in direct exchange for sexual relations. In the 1940s, American servicemen frequently gave women items such as food, often in far greater quantities than a box of candy traditionally presented at the start of a date. One British wife, for example, recalled how one evening her white American soldier friend surprised her with a gift of "tinned goods, butter, sugar, sweets, coffee, sheer nylons and makeup—not forgetting cartons of cigarettes . . . [and] two bucketfuls of coal." A few weeks later the soldier kissed her good night for the first time, and eventually they "made love." The woman's account contains not the slightest indication that she believed that she had prostituted herself, despite her acceptance of coal deliveries from her suitor, a rather untraditional sign of romantic affection.[35]

The material needs of women in postwar Germany were far greater than those of women in the British Isles with Yank boyfriends. Like those British women, they could meet those needs through their own paid work or the support of men. In the rationed scarcity of postwar Germany, many goods were practically unavailable to all but the most successful black marketers, unless, of course, they could be obtained from the Americans. Observers noted that American men who could "provide things for their women [were] simply basically more attractive" than German men, who in the wake of defeat and economic collapse could "offer little security to a woman." The willingness of many women to enter into relationships with American soldiers, including African American soldiers, was due in part to the material rewards that such relationships could bring.[36]

In that respect, however, German women's actions during the occupation differed little from many other women elsewhere. Emotional attachment could never be separated from the material advantages that a partner might be able to offer. The responses of women in postwar Germany to their unusual situation evidenced remarkable similarities to "normal" gender relations in Germany. The expectation for German (and American) women, which originated in the middle classes and achieved normative status during the nineteenth century, had been that most women would work only when required by economic or national necessity. The work of single women before marriage was generally motivated by necessity. Of course, a minority pursued employment as a matter of choice, so long as the work was appropriately fulfilling, like social work. Such work had always been in limited supply, and the number of women who could afford to pursue it was even lower in postwar Germany. The practical choice for the vast majority of German women was between physical labor and being supported by men.[37]

The postwar period certainly qualified as a national emergency, which seemed to require the mobilization of all available hands for the work of clearing rubble and the many other menial tasks necessary to restart the economy. Both the occupation authorities and German officials therefore moved in 1946 to mobilize all Germans, including women, to work. On January 17, 1946, the Allied Control Council issued Order No. 3, which required everyone within a specified age range (fourteen to sixty-five for men; fifteen to fifty for women) who was capable of work to register at local labor offices. The occupation authorities sought to compel compliance with the registration requirement by denying food ration cards to anyone lacking evidence of registration with the labor office. The law thus provided German officials with a means of coercing women into taking on work that, on its own merits, had little attraction for women who might obtain support elsewhere, such as from American soldiers. The law was not a perfect solution, however, because if women could somehow live without a ration card, they could forgo registering with the local labor office. Although substantial numbers of women (celebrated as "women of the rubble") reported for work, the control council's order did not result in the mobilization of all female labor in the American zone, as many women successfully avoided undesired employment.[38]

The system afforded local officials considerable discretion in determining which women would be excused from labor and which would be compelled to work. Married women in stable circumstances likely benefited from the exercise of that discretion.[39] On the other hand, German officials typically looked with disfavor on women who avoided work in favor of hanging around with American soldiers, especially African American soldiers. Army intelligence officers reported that the German police had provided the labor office in Selb with a list of women who had attended the local soldiers' club, and labor officials had assigned all of them to manual labor in the local clay pits.[40] Although implementation of such crude methods was exceptional, Germans certainly cried out in overwhelming numbers for measures to be taken to force immoral, indolent women to work. In a January 1946 meeting of the provisional advisory committee for Upper and Middle Franconia, for example, the committee recommended asking American military government officials to act against vagabond women who were consorting with American soldiers without registering with the police. The committee urged that it was necessary to bring the women into camps where they would be forced to work. Such demands were commonplace in postwar Germany.[41] Women who lived off the generosity of African American soldiers seemed especially parasitic, and local officials likely more often compelled such women to work than more respectable women.

In the American zone, women who carried on relationships with African American soldiers likely depended more on them for support than women who carried on relations with white soldiers. As noted, no German could obtain a ration card without registering with the local authorities. Local authorities generally regarded any woman who associated with African American soldiers as a prostitute potentially infected with venereal disease and thus might well refer her to the police or health office for a venereal disease examination, at least, and perhaps punishment for prostitution.[42] Moreover, the local labor office would certainly insist that such women work rather than spend their time entertaining black soldiers. Thus, African American men needed to supply their companions with food if they wanted to prevent them from being confined or required to perform hard work. The presumption that all women engaged in relations with black soldiers prostituted themselves in order to be fed thus in many cases obliged the soldiers to feed their companions.

In fact, most women who carried on relationships with African American soldiers appear to have avoided registering. In Wirsberg, for example, the *Landrat* explained that "women of doubtful character did not register in their place of residence with the police, thereby evading medical control." The women could survive without ration cards, "because the colored soldiers supply them with sufficient provisions."[43] One woman arrested in Weißenburg on charges of endangering the health of her sex partner and failing to register with the labor office explained that she did not like the work offered to her by the local office. Unsurprisingly, her testimony failed to persuade the court to acquit.[44] Another woman, a nineteen-year-old refugee from Silesia, was charged with failure to report to the local labor office and engaging in illegitimate work, that is, prostitution. She pled not guilty and explained frankly that "she did not like to work as she had savings." The labor office's offer of housework was less attractive than the alternative, and she therefore "spent most time with soldiers." She was convicted but escaped with only a three-month suspended sentence, provided that she took up "legitimate work" in Weißenburg.[45]

Beyond the material incentives, desire for companionship and diversion motivated many women to enter into relationships with soldiers, including African Americans.[46] Some relationships produced strong affective bonds and even, in rare instances, marriage. By the war's end, German women had long suffered under the fear and deprivation that reigned in Germany as the war brought increasing numbers of air attacks and economic difficulties before it ground to its conclusion with Germany's defeat. Peace brought no end to homelessness, disease, and hunger.

Some women responded by rejecting the continual demands to adhere to traditional values, to sacrifice, and to work hard. Contemporaries discerned in some young women an "ungovernable urge for freedom" that accompanied a release from previously overbearing social pressures.[47] Spending time with American GIs, many of whom were bent on enjoying themselves, seemed an attractive alternative to clearing rubble. The GIs might have appeared as attractive companions to lonely, bored, and poor women for whom a night of drinking, dancing, and sex seemed long overdue. The trial records of the women arrested in Weißenburg testify to such motives. Affection and the seeking of pleasure predominated over more pecuniary motivations in the testimonies. One woman stated that she "was in love and did not see any harm in going around with soldiers." Another "[t]hought she was not sick. Had gone with one and same soldier for 5 months. Th[i]nks doctor in VD Hospital does not know his business." Anneliese K. stated that she "[w]as born in small village. Came to town to have good time." A thirty-year-old housewife testified that she "[h]ad only one soldier friend. Husband in British captivity. Felt terribly lonesome." Another woman explained that she "[w]as lonely and disillusioned." Although the defendants in those assembly-line trials had good reason to downplay evidence of prostitution, they seem to have been remarkably candid. One stated artlessly that she had "[h]oped she would not be discovered" and that she "[e]njoyed having fun in Weissenburg."[48]

A variety of reasons induced German women to turn to American soldiers rather than German men in the postwar period. Besides their sheer numerical scarcity, German men lacked resources to entertain German women. As one intelligence report noted, "For the German girl the GI is the

only male in Germany who can provide her with not only food, but entertainment. The average German man cannot take a girl dancing or drinking
as can the GI."[49] At a very elemental level, the well-fed, healthy American
soldiers, whether white or black, appeared to offer better sexual partners
than most German men. The *Oberbürgermeister* of Heidelberg explained,
beyond the "chocolate, cigarettes, food and revelry" that American soldiers could offer, "It is a question of sex power because the American boys
are better fed than the German men."[50]

Part of the attraction of African American soldiers for some German
women must be attributed to their American-ness. African Americans
thus had greater appeal than other blacks. An episode from the remarkable life of Hans Massaquoi testifies to the importance of black GIs' status as Americans. One evening he took a German woman out on a date,
masquerading in an American uniform as a GI. His ruse worked perfectly
until an old friend from Hamburg recognized him on the tram and called
out to him "in unadulterated Hamburger Platt," spoken only by natives of
Hamburg. Massaquoi's insistence that he had no idea who the man was or
what he was saying left his irate date unconvinced. Although Massaquoi
met with failure in that attempt, he recognized the advantages of being an
African American rather than an Afro-German.[51]

Sexual gratification was an important motivation for entering into
relations with African American men. Sexual contacts between African
American soldiers and German women not infrequently amounted to a
single sexual act, with little prelude or postlude. Venereal disease contact sheets completed by soldiers described instances where an African
American soldier and a German woman unknown to each other met on
the street and proceeded quickly to sexual relations, sometimes out of
doors. Such encounters did not constitute prostitution, since the women
neither requested nor received money or food. Such sexual contacts,
though, ought not to be romanticized as based on love or even particular
affection.[52]

Relationships between white or black American soldiers and German
women were often initiated on the streets, and readiness to engage in
sex seems to have been undeniably high among both men and women.
According to Vernon Stone's study of the mothers of biracial children,
"one night stands" accounted for at least 120 of the 600 offspring. An
additional 210 children were the product of relationships that lasted less
than six months. None of the relationships studied lasted more than eighteen months, a fairly long time considering the soldiers' short stays in
Germany.[53]

If many women were attracted to African Americans owing to their
status as Americans with the advantages that American soldiers enjoyed
in occupied Germany, in some cases the blackness of African Americans
proved decisive. Some young women may have chosen African American

partners as a means of rebelling against social and familial expectations. Hans Massaquoi recognized that as he came of age under the Nazi regime, he signified "forbidden fruit" to the women with whom he engaged in romantic relationships. The dangers occasioned by enjoying such risky pleasures were sufficient to deter many women during the Nazi era. In the postwar years, however, Massaquoi enjoyed "the new, ego-bolstering experience of being pursued openly and unabashedly because, as far as the fräuleins of the immediate postwar period were concerned, black was definitely in." At least some of the attraction of blackness likely stemmed from its earlier proscribed status.[54] The transgressing of that racial boundary, however, did not equate to a rejection of race as a meaningful category. Indeed, race's importance could be paradoxically reinforced by its purported rejection. One woman (who one imagines probably had not had a black lover) insisted in a 1948 letter to the editors of *Stern* that she refused to abide by the pronouncements of any purported superior authority when it came to choosing a lover, even if she chose a "Zulu kaffir" (*Zulukaffer*). Blackness, implicitly still despicable, functioned as a means of rebelling against established authority.[55]

Even if women did not intend their actions as rebellion, their families could certainly read them in that manner, as did the father and stepsister of seventeen-year-old Else D. They appealed to military government to arrest her because she had run away from home to spend her time with African American soldiers in Bruchsal. Else had started going to Bruchsal when her African American boyfriend had been transferred there. Her father had urged her against going, but he did not prevent her because she promised that when her boyfriend was transferred back to the United States, she would settle down and wait for his promised return. Only two days after her boyfriend's transfer, however, she resumed her daily trips to the American club in Bruchsal. Her family pleaded with American officials that they could do nothing, and the German police had likewise explained that they were powerless to intervene. Else's stepsister stated, "Our family has a good reputation and never such a thing did happen before. Especially my father, who is 65 years of age, bears very much on this burden." Her appeal persuaded the American public safety officer in Bruchsal, and Else was arrested on suspicion of prostitution and carrying venereal disease. Although the medical examination found her free of venereal disease, the public safety officer nevertheless wrote to the German district court and the local youth office, recommending that Else be placed in a correctional institution.[56]

Some women viewed African American men as better companions than Germans or white Americans. According to Vernon Stone's 1949 survey, 125 respondents out of the sample of 600 mothers of biracial children stated that they hoped to marry an African American other than the father of their child. No doubt a desire to find a willing stepfather to their biracial child accounted partly for those responses, but the attractiveness of a black partner also seemingly played a role.[57] Contemporaries commonly asserted that African Americans were more "courteous" or "unaffected" than white Americans.[58] One Giessen resident responded to the survey of attitudes toward black GIs stationed in the area that "Negroes act less like victors and forgive more easily."[59] Many commentators also maintained that African Americans' greater generosity to the Germans fostered good relations.[60] German women may also have been attracted to the style of African American men, many of whom evidently paid greater attention to looking sharp while off duty than the average white GI. One military police battalion reported, "Off duty and on pass most Negro troops dressed neatly, usually even more neatly than white troops." That white officer, like others, also noted (with disapproval) black GIs' penchant for making stylish additions of "unauthorized articles" to the uniform. The sartorial innovations that white officers decried as betraying an excessive "fondness for display and a flair for the unusual" may have met with a more favorable reception from German women living amid the shabbiness of the American zone.[61]

Finally, African American men held a special sexual attraction for some women, as folk knowledge held that African Americans were "talented lovers."[62] The physical vitality of African American soldiers at times made a strong impression on young German women, as in the case of one sixteen-year-old who recalled that her first sight of the "fantastic, elegant bodies" of African American soldiers caused her to question the dogmatic racism under which she had been raised. She claimed that "the face of a black is at first quite foreign," but she nevertheless doubted that such "gorgeous bodies" could really belong to "subhumans."[63] Although this woman came to question the Nazi-era racial hierarchy, her thinking about race remained bound up with a fascination with the bodies of exotic black men.

"This One All-Important Phase of Democracy": German Women and the Fight against American Racism

For African Americans, the presence of black soldiers in the defeated Third Reich and their pursuit of sexual relations with German women stood as a singular occurrence in the struggle for racial equality. Nazism's insistence on the purported racial inferiority of blacks had been common knowledge among African Americans. Civil rights leaders' persistent critique since the 1930s of American racism as no better than Nazism had proven to be an increasingly effective rhetorical strategy. African Americans and white officials seeking to mobilize their support for the war effort celebrated black successes during the war against members of the putative "Master

Race" as demonstrating the falsity of Nazi racial ideology. The presence of African Americans in the force occupying the defeated Third Reich represented a further object lesson in establishing that blacks were not racially inferior to Aryans or other whites. After the war's conclusion, civil rights advocates continued to delegitimize American racism by associating it with Nazism. Thus, the noted white cartoonist Bill Mauldin urged soon after V-E day that the war against fascism had not ended with the defeat of Hitler but needed to be pressed home against racists in the United States, like Mississippi senator Theodore Bilbo, an ardent white supremacist.[64]

The critique assumed a new aspect during the military occupation, as sexual relations between German women and African Americans came to be used as a rhetorical weapon against American racism. Racial progressives asserted that surprisingly large numbers of women who had grown up in an atmosphere poisoned by Nazi racism had overcome that race hatred and entered into healthy, normal relations with black men. How, these critics asked, could the objections of white Americans to such relations be justified? Acceptance of relations between black men and white women became the acid test of racial liberalism, one that few Americans passed. Their failure was all the more remarkable in light of the purported ability of Germans, formerly the most virulent of racists, to pass it.[65]

The reality of Germans' reactions to African Americans' relations with German women was far more complex than most critics of American racism acknowledged. Many African American soldiers might have agreed with the small number of black GIs questioned by intelligence officers as part of the Giessen study who said that they "thought they were better treated as social equals by Germans than they would be by white people at home." Nevertheless, most soldiers likely also were aware of widespread German opposition to their sexual relations with German women.[66]

William Gardner Smith's 1948 social protest novel, *Last of the Conquerors*, argued that true democracy existed not in the United States but in the former Third Reich. The book, whose African American author spent about eight months as a soldier in occupied Germany during 1946, told the story of a romance between a black GI, Hayes Dawkins, and a German woman, Ilse. Throughout the novel, the Germans, with the notable exception of the German police, appear as paragons of racial tolerance, whereas the white Americans are universally racist and often anti-Semitic. Early in their relationship, Hayes and Ilse go to the Wannsee, a lake outside Berlin. Lying on the beach with his white girlfriend, Hayes has an epiphany as he realizes that he has been to the beach innumerable times, "but never before with a white girl. A white girl." In Germany, though, no one stared at them, since racial difference "had lost importance." Hayes reflects, "Odd, it seemed to me, that here, in the land of hate, I should find this one all-important phase of democracy. And suddenly I felt bitter." Later in the novel, another character, nicknamed "Professor," observes that he

Photograph of an African American GI and a German woman from the Baltimore Afro-American, *November 9, 1946. The caption to the photograph read, in part, "NO NAZIS HERE: An American GI and German fraulein relax at Wansee Lake." Courtesy* AFRO-American, *Newspapers Archives and Research Center.*

too would "always remember the irony of my going away to Germany to find democracy." German women's willingness to enter into sexual relations with black GIs and the acceptance of such relationships by the larger society demonstrated conclusively, advocates of racial equality urged, the comparative failings of the United States. Black men's sexual access to white women signified, in Smith's inelegant phrase, an "all-important phase of democracy."[67]

If the rhetorical attack on American racism were to be successful, however, two crucially important facts needed to be established. First, the women involved needed to be respectable, ideally including even middle- and upper-class women. Equally important, it was essential that affection for the soldiers, not mercenary aims, motivated the women to participate in the relationships. The willingness of starving, low-class women to prostitute themselves to black men in American-occupied Germany would have had no value in efforts to persuade white Americans that their prejudices against African Americans were unfounded and illegitimate.

African American discussions of black GIs in Germany and their relations with German women buttressed the critique of white American racism for the most part. After the war's conclusion, stories in the black press consistently maintained that African Americans received better treatment in the home of Nazism than they did in the United States, the supposed home of democracy.[68] As an October 1946 *Ebony* article stated, "Strangely enough, here where once Aryanism ruled supreme, Negroes are finding more friendship, more respect and more equality than they would back home—either in Dixie or on Broadway." As Berliners engaged in personal contacts with blacks for the first time, "[r]ace hate" gave way to "interracialism."[69]

The black press, when writing about blacks in Germany, focused on romantic relations, which were depicted as healthy and fulfilling, even if necessarily temporary. The reports insisted that the women attracted to black men came from respectable backgrounds. According to the *Ebony* article, the women came from all social classes, "from Junkers to 'farmers' daughters.'" Moreover, the article informed its black readership, "Many German girls between 18 and 26 have a steady Negro boy friend." The relationships' character as "steady" was, of course, essential for a critique of American racism. *Ebony* excluded from its account one-night stands, prostitution, and relationships between African American GIs and women outside of the appropriate age range for romance, such as minors or older women. The piece acknowledged that most of the women initially "become friendly with soldiers out of self-interest," in order to obtain cigarettes, coffee, soap, or other items. Such mercenary concerns, according to *Ebony*, however, "before long" faded in importance as "many find their colored GI friends good companions and sometimes fall in love."[70]

The journalist Ollie Stewart painted a picture of black soldiers' life in the occupation army that resembled respectable domesticity. With black service units "permanently settled" around Germany, he wrote, the GIs would generally "look around until they find a nice girl for companionship, rather than 'shack up' with the first one that comes along."[71] A December 1945 *Pittsburgh Courier* article by Roi Ottley similarly insisted that the reasons for German women's attraction to black soldiers were "normal and natural." The article maintained that African Americans in Germany had been "kind, considerate, and friendly" to the local populace, in contrast to many white Americans, who had been "running roughshod" over the Germans and had the habit of brusquely approaching women with a " 'Will you, or won't you?' attitude." German women were attracted to black soldiers, who "moved easily and with patience, allowing a relationship to develop naturally." The single most important factor, however, was the willingness of African American soldiers to share their rations with German women. The well-fed German female companions of the soldiers were, in Ottley's view, "emotionally balanced, content, and happy."[72] The black press typically emphasized that such liaisons were, however, temporary. The soldiers and the women knew that the soldiers would eventually leave for the United States, and the article asserted that army regulations prohibited soldiers from marrying German women.[73] Circumstances beyond the control of the individual soldiers and women thus absolved them from any potential moral stigma for engaging in frivolous relationships.

The black press insisted that white Americans posed the real problem in Germany. According to *Ebony*, friction arose between white and black troops over German women as white GIs resented the "competition in the 'romance' department."[74] Another article sounded the alarm in particularly harsh terms under the headline "U.S. White Supremacy Invades Germany." The story's author, Alfred Duckett, noted that resentment of the relationships was shared by many Germans as well, but the story laid blame chiefly on white Americans. He cited an unnamed black soldier as reporting that "scores" of African Americans in Germany were "being waylaid, beaten and killed, mainly because the blond, buxom girls prefer the company of tan GIs." The condemnation of white behavior thus constituted a two-pronged critique, as white objections had their roots in racism and a well-founded fear that blacks could compete on relatively equal terms for the affections of German women.[75]

Vernon Stone, whose article on the children of African American soldiers and German women appeared in *The Survey*, made similar arguments. Stone critiqued American racism by contrasting it with German acceptance of African Americans. "Despite Hitler's racial dogmas, most of the Germans, like other Europeans, attempted to treat the Negroes as equals. As a result, many of the Negro American servicemen tasted for the first time what hitherto had been for them only a theoretical aspect of democracy." Stone admitted the possibility that Germans suppressed their prejudices for the sake of obtaining "cigarettes, chocolate, and food" from African American GIs, but he nevertheless believed that many Germans, including "even former Party members," had come to reject "the gross fallacy of racial intolerance." He further suggested that such relationships were often exclusive, writing, "When a military unit is stationed in a given area, many German girls promptly acquire a 'steady' from the Negro ranks."[76]

Smith's novel similarly represents a sustained refutation of the possibility that the women involved in relations with African Americans were prostitutes, low-class, or even unfaithful. Hayes's girlfriend, Ilse, like every other German female character in the novel, remains true to her boyfriend. At considerable risk to herself, she follows him when he is transferred from Berlin to southern Germany.[77] Even while in prison after being picked up for a venereal disease examination by racist American white MPs, who object to her associating with an African American, she refuses to forsake Hayes, despite the fact that she could win her release by simply promising never to date black soldiers again. Ilse thus stands as irrefragable proof that, as another German female character explains to

Hayes, "When a German girl tells you, 'I love you,' then she means that. With all her heart." Ilse instructs Hayes before his return to the United States that he may sleep with other women so long as he does not fall in love with them. Ilse, of course, will wait chastely for his return.[78] The novel's exaggerated picture of the ideally faithful woman testified to the need for extraordinary efforts to buttress the respectability of white women engaged in relations with African Americans for a skeptical American readership.

Smith clearly intended his readers to regard *Last of the Conquerors* as a mirror of reality. In places, the novel closely follows Smith's news reporting for the *Pittsburgh Courier*.[79] Its devices to achieve verisimilitude included use of a first-person narrator, as well as reprinting texts of orders and newspaper articles from the period.[80] Given the novel's polemical purpose, its account of amicable relations between African Americans and Germans cannot be accepted uncritically.[81] In the novel and the journalistic pieces, German racial tolerance casts American racism in sharp relief.

Individual African Americans in Germany may have been less concerned with the implications of their relationships for battles for racial equality in the United States. The iconoclastic African American columnist George S. Schuyler professed to be unimpressed by the controversy over interracial liaisons whipped up by the Meader report. In a February 1947 column, Schuyler noted the charge that "the Negro troops in Germany, like their white comrades, were shacking up with German girls and swiping Government rations to aid their play" but asserted that similar activities occurred in any military occupation.[82] The race question was irrelevant to such relationships.

Certainly the personal meanings of a white companion for African American men cannot be reduced to a single experience. Considerable obstacles stood in the way of relationships between African American soldiers and German women. The relationships could only be formed under the shadow of, and in spite of, the long-standing white fantasy that held that all black men lusted after white women. In fact, many black GIs and their relatives at home viewed a white European lover or bride as undesirable.[83] Following a visit in fall 1947 to American-occupied Germany, Bishop William J. Walls of the African Methodist Episcopal Church asserted that stories of black GIs consorting with German women were exaggerated. He opined that "the Negroes do not want to marry the German girls, as a whole."[84] For the vast majority of African American soldiers, marriage to a white European woman was out of the question given the obstacles imposed by the American military and American anti-miscegenation laws.[85]

Relations with white German women nevertheless appear to have had particular significance for some African Americans. The novelty of the experience for young African American males can scarcely be overestimated, since relations with white women were a rarity, one often accompanied by considerable risk to African American men, even in the North.[86] According to an unscientific poll of African American GIs in the 761st Tank Battalion carried out in 1946 by Trezzvant W. Anderson, a member of the unit and contributor to the *Pittsburgh Courier,* reenlistment in the unit was high mainly because of "the 'frauleins.' "[87] A number of African Americans sought to memorialize their romances, or at least their associations, with German women in photographs. Hans Massaquoi recounts one such incident involving a black merchant marine sailor, Smitty, he met in a club. After talking for a time, the sailor asked whether Massaquoi knew the blonde lead chorus girl and if she would consent to being photographed with him. Massaquoi recalls that the sailor "was happy as a lark when Gerda consented not only to pose with him, but to do so cheek-to-cheek and with both arms wrapped around him. Within minutes, the roving camera girl had captured this touching scene for posterity — as well as, no doubt, for Smitty's envious homeboys back in Jim Crow Alabama." The sailor expressed his gratitude with gifts of cigarettes for both Massaquoi and the woman.[88]

The sailor was not alone among African Americans in his desire to obtain a trophy of his association with white women in Germany. During the war, black GIs mailed numbers of photographs of themselves with white European women back to the United States. After a photograph of a black soldier with a British woman appeared in 1943, the War Department had issued regulations providing for the censorship of photographs "showing negro soldiers in poses of intimacy with white women or conveying 'boy friend–girl friend' implication." The policy was based on the belief that such photographs might be calculated "to unduly inflame racial prejudice." In March 1945 General Eisenhower requested a revision of censorship policy to permit photographs of African American soldiers and white women to be sent back to the United States after being stamped by army censors "for personal use only — not for publication." Eisenhower favored continuing the restriction on publication of any such photographs, but after receiving a forceful protest from an officer in an African American unit, he recommended that censors permit amateur photographs to be mailed home by soldiers to their family and friends. It is uncertain when the censorship rule changed, but the matter was discussed by Eisenhower's staff and Colonel Curtis Mitchell of the War Department during his visit to Europe in March 1945.[89]

What is to be made of African American soldiers sending photographs of themselves and women to the United States? To a considerable extent, the practice likely continued an unremarkable tradition of sending back snapshots of oneself and a companion. To better understand the meaning of such photographs, it is useful to consider who the recipients of such photographs were. Family members surely received only a few of them. Given the exigencies of the war, with units moving frequently, the relationships struck up by GIs with local women before V-E day were for the most part necessarily temporary. The number of African American servicemen sending pictures home to their families (not inconsiderable numbers of which would have viewed a white bride as undesirable) to show them potential new in-laws accordingly must have been quite low. Correspondingly few young men were likely to send their parents photographs of themselves embracing a woman with whom they shared a one-night stand or a relationship of a few weeks.

The most likely recipients of such photographs thus were male friends, and the letters that accompanied such photographs presumably included accounts of the GIs' exploits overseas. The photographs served as trophies of soldiers' conquests, and, for that reason, the best ones to send home showed not the woman alone (as such photographs proved nothing to skeptics) but rather depicted the woman and the GI together. Such photos, of course, needed to convey, as the army phrased it, a clear " 'boy friend–girl friend' implication." Many of these photographs, therefore, may be attributed to the penchant of young males, black or white, especially those with limited sexual experience, to share accounts of their sexual activities with their peers. For African American men, however, the whiteness of European women depicted in their embrace likely gave them value as "flash" to be exhibited to their friends. Access to white European women meant an increase in status, measured in terms of sexual experience, for the soldiers sending such pictures to their friends at home.[90]

Power Relations

What were the power dynamics in relationships between black soldiers and women whose white bodies afforded them particular cultural and sexual capital? As discussed in Chapter 3, Germans and, to a lesser extent, white Americans often painted a picture of white women manipulating hapless African American men to do their bidding. That assessment by Imhoff and others, besides avoiding discussion of particular incidents where soldiers had victimized women, ignored the obvious disparities in resources between the women and soldiers. The African Americans in Wirsberg likely would have disagreed with Imhoff's characterization of them. One indication of the assertiveness and self-confidence they felt may be gleaned from the nickname assumed by one of them, who was known as "the Bürgermeister."[91]

The soldiers' comparatively strong position in Wirsberg was further supported by the possibility of seeking outside assistance. Following the American military's raid on the women in town, the soldiers informed their German friends in the town that they would complain to Washington about the racial discrimination.[92] They objected to the roundup of women, which Imhoff's memorandum had prompted, as discrimination against *them,* not against the women actually arrested. The soldiers believed that objections to racism could potentially find sympathetic listeners in Washington. Complaints of unfair treatment of women went unvoiced, if even conceived. Such complaints would have met only incomprehension within the War Department.

The possibility that African American men, despite their privileged position as members of a conquering army, their greater economic resources, and their male prerogatives, nevertheless might be under the thumb of their white lovers sometimes lurked in African American discussions of romantic relations with German women. Indeed, in Smith's *Last of the Conquerors,* the prospect that the African American soldiers in Germany are being "played" by their German girlfriends drives the narrative of the novel. The relationship between Hayes and Ilse can develop only once she has proven her commitment by following him after his transfer from Berlin to southern Germany. The novel reads as a narrative of the anxious fulfillment of African American manhood through the affirmation of the genuine love of a white German woman.

In one of the novel's important scenes, black soldiers in Berlin debate the question whether the German women are taking advantage of them. The soldier Murdock, who is scheduled to return to the United States, says he would rather stay in Germany and denies the possibility that his desire to stay is a product of his relationships with German women. Another soldier, Randy, who professes to hate all Germans after the wartime murder of his friend by a German soldier, disagrees. He insists that the "damn white chicks" in Germany have the black GIs wrapped around their fingers. He informs his fellow soldiers that the women "play you for all they can get while you're here and then as soon as you go they just get another soldier and play him the same way."[93] Another soldier, nicknamed Homo, counters that several local German women formerly dated black soldiers who were transferred home before Randy's arrival. The men told their girlfriends that they would return, but they never did. Still, according to Homo, the German women remained true to their absent black lovers. One girl even killed her black boyfriend and herself before he left, because she could not bear to live without him. These proofs of German women's constancy convince Hayes and Randy.[94]

Throughout the novel, the German women are, without exception, forever loving and faithful to the African American soldiers, but the fear of being manipulated or duped nevertheless dogs the soldiers. When Hayes goes to the military police station to search for Ilse after the racist police have brought her in for a venereal disease examination, the MPs taunt him. "First time you ever had a white chick and it drives you crazy. Let these chicks make a fool out of you." The remark provokes Hayes to rush toward Ilse's cell, but the MPs grab him and take him outside to rough him up.[95]

The question of how revealing the novel is about the psychology of African American men in occupied Germany obviously requires caution. It would be a mistake to read *Last of the Conquerors* unproblematically as, in the words of one critic, "an honest record of what Negro soldiers did and said and felt in occupied Germany."[96] The novel clearly was constructed as a piece of social protest intended to expose and to critique American racial prejudice. Smith manifestly focused consciously on the question whether the German women were playing the soldiers. It further seems probable that the principal audience to be addressed on the subject (as for the novel as a whole) was a white one. That is, Smith intended the dialogues between the soldiers concerning the German women's motives for entering into relations with black soldiers to anticipate and to rebut the suspicions of white readers that the women involved were merely desperate or depraved women who used the gullible soldiers. The effort to disarm potential objections by white readers rather than an effort to portray accurately the psychology of African American men seems to have animated the structure of the dialogue concerning the balance of power between black GIs and their German lovers.

Nevertheless, the same logic that underpinned Smith's anticipation of the white readership's skepticism could also influence Smith's less sophisticated fellow soldiers in Germany. The dialogue has a convincing ring to it, even if the actions of the German women that serve as evidence to dispel the soldiers' suspicions seem less believable. Moreover, the fear that German women were duping naive Americans applied to whites as well as African Americans, but African Americans were especially susceptible to this fear.[97] Finally, the same question can arise in any romantic relationship.

Questions of power and exploitation were especially complex in postwar Germany because relationships were forged across a deep, if perhaps unusual and temporary, economic divide, as well as national and racial boundaries.[98] It could be very difficult to determine who was in control. The balance of power in such relations eluded precise definition and was always shifting. The power dynamics between black soldiers and white women may be illustrated by consideration of one unusual triangular relationship that developed in Nuremberg in 1945 and that was described in the records of a trial for procuring.

In summer 1945 Martin W. and his wife, who was never named in the court record, began frequenting the American military compound outside Nuremberg where African American soldiers were quartered. In their visits to the camp, the couple presented themselves as brother and sister. In August, they made the acquaintance of one Sergeant A., who soon began visiting the couple's apartment regularly. He came with gifts of fabric, jewelry, and other items for the woman and cigarettes and food for Martin. According to the trial record, the husband tolerated the "exchange of kisses and caresses" between the soldier and his wife in his presence, but at other times he busied himself in the kitchen to allow the couple time alone together. Sergeant A. increasingly pressed the wife for sexual relations. According to records from the German court that heard the case, both Martin and his wife came to regret that things had progressed so far, and they hoped that Sergeant A. would soon be transferred to another base. The court found that the couple feared "violence" from the "disappointed lover" if they broke off the affair. They did not want to forgo the material benefits that the relationship brought with it or, worse yet, be asked to return some of the gifts they had received. Eventually, Sergeant A. and the wife of the accused had sexual relations a number of times, including instances in the couple's apartment while Martin was in the apartment.[99]

Who was in control in this relationship? German authorities placed the blame principally on Martin, who was pronounced guilty of procuring and sentenced to ten months in prison for having promoted sexual relations between his wife and Sergeant A. in order to receive material benefit. Martin's wife testified that he had forced her to go along with the scheme. Martin, on the other hand, testified that his wife was the real culpable party. The authorities apparently prosecuted only the husband, whereas the wife seems to have escaped punishment altogether. The court nevertheless found that the wife's behavior, which was "not at all impeccable," constituted a mitigating factor to be considered in determining the husband's punishment.

The court believed both the husband and wife had wrongly cooperated in duping the hapless Sergeant A. "The exploitation of [Sergeant A] was for both the reason for the initiation and the continuation of the relationship with him, as both of their conduct establishes without a doubt." Neither Martin nor his wife wished to part with the advantages that they had received from their "shameless game," even after it took an undesirable turn.[100] The court's characterization of the couple's actions toward Sergeant A. as "exploitation" cast Sergeant A. as the victim and the couple as the perpetrators. That script accorded with the purposes of a criminal conviction of Martin for procuring. It gained credibility from an unstated image of blacks as gullible simpletons, easily misled, but threatening to violently lash out at their exploiters if provoked.

Sergeant A.'s naiveté may be doubted, however. After he learned in late December beyond question that the couple were actually husband and wife, "the good personal relations between [Sergeant A.] and Frau W. were not adversely affected." Indeed, at the time of the trial, Frau W. continued to carry on "at least a lively, friendly association" with Sergeant A. The record is not completely clear, but he apparently continued sexual relations with Frau W. after Martin's arrest in January 1946. The soldier may have had his suspicions for some time that the sister-and-brother relationship was a ruse. At any rate, his success in persuading the wife to engage in sexual relations occurred, according to the court records, in the context of a potential threat of violence or, at least, the cessation of economic benefits. He had an arsenal of coercive measures at his disposal to use in his pursuit of the wife, which may have proved decisive in her decision to engage in sex with him.

The motivations of Frau W. are similarly complex. The continuation of her relationship with Sergeant A. after he learned that she was Martin's wife suggests that the implicit risk of violence had not led her to engage in sexual relations with him. In the end, affection may have proven decisive. One mystery is how the authorities learned of the matter and brought the charge against Martin. Martin may have been denounced by scandalized neighbors or reported by his wife. Regardless of whether Martin's wife reported him, she testified against him at his trial and continued some relationship with Sergeant A. after Martin went to prison. Sergeant A. probably continued his sexual relationship with her and continued to provide material support after the husband was in prison.

It is impossible to fully reconstruct the relationship between Sergeant A. and Frau W., and not every sexual relationship between soldiers and women was as tangled as this one. However, the court records offer a glimpse into a set of relationships where the parties were motivated by a mixture of considerations that included material advantage and sexual desire. Resistance to prevailing notions about race is notable for its absence from any of the actors' calculations. The case suggests the inadequacy of binary oppositions between love and prostitution or racism and sex across the color line.

The case also further highlights the intricacy of power relations in the unique circumstances where men marked as undesirable by their race but possessing distinct coercive advantages entered into sexual relationships with women among the politically subordinate and economically desperate occupied population. The strength and longevity of the image of a white woman manipulating a naive black soldier testify to the ability that whiteness had to counterbalance prerogatives of masculinity, political power, and economic resources to create, in the minds of many observers and participants, something like a level playing field for white women and black men engaged in sexual relationships.[101]

Reworking the Meaning of Race

The defining of sexual relations between African American men and German women as a form of rejecting and resisting American racism had consequences for the campaign for racial justice. Most importantly, such a definition equated the fight for racial equality with the struggle for manhood.[102] In that context, masculinity was premised on the act of heterosexual relations and equality was defined as the right to engage in relations with the woman of one's choice. Racial discrimination's victims in such a narrative were narrowly defined as men who were deprived of their "right" to engage in relations with any woman, black or white. By that logic, when German and American authorities arrested women in Wirsberg, African American soldiers complained of racial discrimination against themselves.

The situation of the women involved proved largely irrelevant to the debate over racial equality. Indeed, the soldiers' objections to the arrest of the women in Wirsberg sidestepped the women's situation nearly as neatly as Imhoff had skipped over the matter in his complaints to American military government. The German women involved in such relationships had little opportunity or rhetorical leverage to articulate independent demands. By the same token, African American women were elided from demands for equal rights in such a narrative.[103] African American women implicitly embodied the inferior pool of women to which black men in the United States were limited and from which they could escape in Germany, thereby experiencing full manhood for the first time.

In the military context, the assertion of racial equality in the 1940s frequently appeared as a call to accord African Americans the attributes of manliness. Even before the United States entered World War II, civilian aide William H. Hastie wrote, "In the Army the Negro is taught to be a man, a fighting man." Discriminatory treatment of black soldiers, Hastie argued, emasculated them, thereby rendering them ineffective soldiers.[104] Similarly, in the postwar context, *Last of the Conquerors* dwelt on the struggle for manhood. In a central scene in the novel, the African American soldier Murdock, who is scheduled to return to the United States, explains why he would prefer to stay in Germany. He denies that he wants to stay because of the "goddamn chicks." He likes Germany, he insists, because "[i]t's the first place I was ever treated like a goddamn man."[105] Murdock's denial that the experience of relations with white women had anything to do with his newfound status as a man in Germany rings hollow. Likewise, when the character suggests that he could walk into any bar in Germany and be served or buy a home anywhere he chose in Germany, these points seem unpersuasive. The possibility that soldiers stationed temporarily in Germany might purchase a house amounted to pure fantasy (although it had a basis in the greater economic resources that African Americans enjoyed in Germany compared with the United States). Moreover, white American clubs in Germany in fact could exclude blacks. The real basis of the claim to the rights of manhood was the access to white German women.

The rhetoric of masculinity had its limits as a critique of racism, as the same discussion in *Last of the Conquerors* further illustrates. Later in the debate, another black soldier rejects the idea that Murdock might avoid discrimination in the United States if he lived in the North rather than in Georgia. Northerners, according to this account, harbored the same prejudices against African Americans as southerners. The soldier insists that he prefers the more open racial prejudice of the South or of Hitler. "I like it better if they do it the way the South does. No double talk. Just like Hitler and the Jews. He said what he was going to do, and whether you liked it or not he did what he said. That's the way a *man* does."[106] Hitler is thus lauded for his manliness, inflected in that instance as forthrightness, in his genocidal policies. Masculinity offered little rhetorical purchase from which to mount a critique of Nazism's crimes.

Moreover, demands to be granted the rights of manhood left the implicit foundation of such rights on the subordination of women's rights unquestioned and even reinvigorated. If German anxieties about African Americans found their most convenient victims in the German women who associated with them, competing African American demands to be accorded the rights of manhood offered limited safeguards to those same women.

How much significance for the subsequent history of American race relations did developments in occupied Germany really contain? Demands for civil rights for African Americans in the postwar years obviously found expression in many forums beyond claims of manhood for black soldiers in Germany. The right to vote, access to education, freedom from lynching, and claims to other fundamental aspects of human dignity mobilized postwar African American action in ways that differed importantly from the dynamics sketched here. Framing the debate in the German context, however, remains important. The American historian David Brion Davis, who served as a GI in occupied Mannheim, writes that "the early years of American occupation were . . . a microcosm of the racial and civil rights struggles that would dominate America in the 1950s and 1960s and finally succeed in eradicating much of the evil of a Jim Crow South."[107] Davis may press the case a bit, but American-occupied Germany indeed provided a setting where the treatment of African Americans stood out in especially sharp relief against the background of discredited Nazi race hatred. The German context illuminates the sometime incompatibility between rhetorics of civil rights and women's rights as they were expressed in the 1940s, a tension that would long remain.

Beyond the implicit subordination of women in the rhetoric of interracial sexual relations, relationships between black men and white German women also paradoxically reinscribed race as a biological fact. In contemporaries' descriptions of the physical attributes of "blonde, buxom" German women in sexual relationships with virile, black men, the allure of the exotic racial Other is unmistakable. Race as a somatic category was especially underscored in the couples' progeny. The liberal sociologist Vernon Stone, for example, who clearly sought to critique

American racism in his study of how German women came to accept African American men as sexual partners, exhibited a fascination with the physical exoticism of biracial children. After reporting the children's age range, he endeavored to provide a racial taxonomy of the children according to their physical qualities: "Though there is a wide difference in their appearance, most of them have dark brown eyes, light tan skin, and soft dark curly hair. But the variation is indicated by the fact that 31 of the children have white complexions, while 56 are very dark; 21 have blue eyes, 95 have silky, straight hair, and 21 have hair of hard, knotty texture."[108] Stone's detailing of the children's appearance and his categorizing of them according to an elaborated racial classificatory system effectively reinscribed the importance of racial markers.

His description of the children further reflected the propensity to highlight the aesthetic qualities of biracial children in Germany. Descriptions of the children were remarkable for their repeated emphasis on their physical attractiveness. Besides the children's skin color, their hair often received special attention, described in one report as "sweet, black, poodle hair-dos."[109] To turn once again to *Last of the Conquerors,* in one scene Hayes meets the three-year-old biracial son of an African American soldier and an Afro-German dancer in Berlin. Hayes's first reaction is an aesthetic appreciation of the child's attractiveness. "He was an extremely handsome boy, with thick black curls piled uncombed upon his head." The attention of the reader is then directed to the boy's skin color: "His skin was the most beautiful I had ever seen, like cocoa with a lot of cream in it."[110] When Hayes and Ilse take the boy on the streetcar, the German passengers similarly comment approvingly on the boy's sweetness, as Hayes and Ilse consider the possibility of parenting their own biracial child in the utopia of racial equality that is postwar Germany. Race mixing brought not the disappearance of racial categories but their elaboration and fetishization.

In Germany, the biracial children came to stand for a special problem, as their African American fathers had, despite claims of many that Germans had no race prejudice. As the children reached school age early in the 1950s, their futures became the subject of public debate. That discussion linked the children's fate to the legacy of Nazi anti-Semitism. During a 1951 Bundestag committee session on the question, the CDU's Dr. Luise Rehling asserted that the children presented Germany with a chance "to atone at least in part for the guilt" of Nazi racism.[111] Thus, the children of African American fathers again suggested the existence of a link between Nazi racial anti-Semitism and attitudes toward blacks. In the 1950s, efforts by German liberals to successfully integrate this supposedly foreign group into German society testified to a desire to normalize Germany and in some measure overcome past racial crimes. The willingness to make the attempt at all and its phrasing in such terms indicated that Germans recognized the problem as an aspect of racism and sought to address it as such.[112]

Did it make sense to link the situation of biracial occupation children in the Federal Republic to the Final Solution? The children were not targeted by a murderous racial policy but rather became the subject of well-intentioned efforts to assimilate these ostensibly alien elements. That campaign, however, could not dispel the firm conviction that the children stood as a racially foreign group in a manner that bore similarities to the earlier framing of the "Jewish question." If liberal-minded social scientists hoped to resolve the question in a humane way, the very conception of the matter in such terms indicated that race retained meaning as a mental category. At least one child of an African American father sought in the 1960s to escape the difficulties of trying to live as a black German by emigrating. Adopted by a Jewish couple, she intended to move to Israel after attaining the college preparatory diploma, the *Abitur,* in Paris. Her destination suggested that into the 1960s the Third Reich provided a crucial point of comparison for German attitudes toward blacks and the response to such attitudes.[113]

The biracial children, as Heide Fehrenbach has shown, further cemented the recast typology of race in terms of the black/white divide. They came to be seen as "Negroes" living among West German "whites." A study of the children published in West Germany in 1960 placed its contribution in the context of American sociology of race. The study's authors reported that they could contribute to answering in the negative the question "Are Negroes on average less intelligent than whites?"[114] These days Germans are conventionally described as whites in opposition to African Americans or their biracial children.[115]

The postwar fate of Afro-German children thus was discussed in different terms than those that had characterized the Nazi era but did not leave behind racial categories. Over time, though, biological race would cede precedence as a meaningful way of understanding the biracial children and white Germans. In its place, Afro-Germans and white Germans increasingly came to speak of different cultures. The memoir of the Afro-German Ika Hügel-Marshall poignantly describes the difficulty she faced growing up where "[n]o black culture existed" and the only culture was "the white one."[116] The complex relation between race and culture became especially prominent in postwar discussions of black music, which is the subject of the next chapter.

CHAPTER FIVE

Black Music and German Culture

"Berlin Philharmonic conducted by a Negro" announced a headline in the September 8, 1945, edition of the *Frankfurter Rundschau*. Musician and war correspondent W. Rudolph Dunbar led the orchestra as it performed African American composer William Grant Still's *Afro-American Symphony*, as well as Tchaikovsky's Sixth Symphony. The performance represented the German premiere of Still's work and the first time that a "Negro" had directed the Berlin Philharmonic. The paper observed that the event "would have been impossible" only a short time before.[1] Indeed, coming four months after the Third Reich's capitulation, it symbolized black music's conquest of Germany's cultural institutions, refuting Joseph Goebbels's assertion that "America's contribution to the music of the world consists merely of jazzed-up Nigger music, not worthy of a single mention."[2]

In fact, Nazism's defeat signaled only the opening of a new phase in a struggle over German culture and African American music that continued through the postwar period and into the 1950s. "Black music" attracted considerable attention and careful comment during the American occupation, as Germans re-encountered African American jazz, spirituals, and, less frequently, symphonic works in a political setting transformed by the defeat of Nazism, with its legacy of strident denunciations of blacks and black music.

The field of cultural policy during the American military occupation and the years beyond, which had long been relatively ignored, has received increasing attention from historians in recent years. We now know a good deal about the efforts by occupying powers to effect a cultural re-education of the defeated Germans.[3] Scholarship on changes in the German music world after the war, building on an impressive and growing body of work on music during the Third Reich, has focused on the halfhearted denazification effort.[4] Pamela Potter has insightfully argued that denazification represented a difficult challenge because the Third Reich was less notable for its musical innovations than the manner in which it brought long-standing tendencies to malignant development.[5]

Important studies by Michael Kater and Uta Poiger have included consideration of the story of jazz in postwar Germany. In his work focused principally on the Third Reich, Kater celebrates the rebirth of "jazz triumphant" with the end of the Nazis' public campaign against it, although he acknowledges that jazz fans remained heavily outnumbered in Germany after 1945.[6] Poiger, who deals mainly with the 1950s, has brought the question of race more clearly into focus. She convincingly argues that in the eyes of German authorities fearful of youth rebellion during the 1950s, jazz and rock 'n' roll represented a threat to "bourgeois respectability."[7]

This chapter reconsiders the postwar German reception of jazz and black music within the context of changing ideas about race. The attack on Nazi race hatred had important implications for the fate of black music in Germany. Historians have failed to recognize that some American officials in fact attempted, albeit tentatively, to persuade Germans of the virtues of jazz during the years of the military occupation.[8] Those efforts reflected the broader campaign to re-educate Germans on the question of race. German discussions of black music changed in the immediate postwar years, as Germans for the most part refrained from asserting publicly that black music was inferior simply because it was created or performed by black musicians. Where Germans openly disparaged black music, they generally did so on other grounds, often asserting that the music was simply too foreign for Germans to appreciate. In postwar accounts of the greatness of German music, race likewise disappeared as an explanatory category. German musical gifts instead were depicted as reflecting the particular richness of German culture, not the musical gifts of a biologically distinct

German race. Although praise for black music sometimes attributed its beauty to the supposed special musical gifts of members of the "Negro race," Germans after 1945 slowly came to interpret music through a cultural, rather than a racial, lens.

Our understanding of postwar readings of jazz may be deepened by placing them within the same context as the notably enthusiastic postwar German reaction to spirituals. The widespread appreciation of spirituals among Germans is not unknown, but it has received comparatively little attention.[9] Neither Poiger nor Kater deals with the subject. If conservative middle-class opponents of jazz viewed it as a threat to bourgeois respectability, which Poiger has convincingly shown, how may we account for the fact that African American spirituals evidently posed no similar threat? Spirituals were as closely associated with blacks and as alien to Germans as jazz, suggesting that the racial origins of jazz alone were insufficient to account for the vigorous condemnations of jazz. Spirituals, of course, had religious themes, but that fact seems inadequate to explain the vastly different reactions to the two musical forms, which cut across class lines.

German audiences enthusiastically greeted African American spirituals in large measure because that music appeared as an authentic expression of a black folk art. "Negro spirituals," as they were conventionally termed, promised Germans unmediated access to an authentic folk musical form, an experience that the German music world had long searched for in its own folk music. Postwar readings of this black music still drew on older racial ideas, but biology receded into the background of that discussion.

Whereas the spirituals struck Germans as authentic folk culture, jazz appeared as inauthentic, modern, and corrupt. The racial foreignness of jazz was certainly central to German readings of the genre, but much of the antipathy toward jazz stemmed from its perceived chameleon-like character. Almost any tune could be "jazzed up," and the music thus uniquely threatened to cross cultural boundaries and corrupt Germanness, conceived in terms of a pure cultural essence. Jazz, to its detractors, appeared as the inauthentic twin of real black music, the spirituals, a musical form that seemed comfortably fixed and devoid of any possibility of seeping into German culture.

Although the majority of Germans disliked jazz, some young Germans celebrated the musical form. These German jazz fans prized in jazz many of the same qualities that its critics condemned, greeting it as a Dionysian force that might revitalize music in terms that drew on a durable racial dyad that opposed vigorous, natural blacks to sterile, overly civilized Europeans.[10] Jazz fans likewise wanted only the most authentic cultural forms, in this case, authentic jazz.

Discussions of black music in the postwar years proceeded under the burden of competing meanings of the term *culture*. Both Germans and

Americans in the postwar period often used the word *culture,* or especially the German term *Kultur,* to mean the endowments attained by cultivated people. It was according to that sense of the word that Germans (and some Americans) spoke of Germany as a cultured nation and the United States as a country "without culture."[11] On the other hand, the anthropological understanding of culture, as articulated by anthropologist Franz Boas and his students, was gaining currency through the 1940s. As American cultural anthropologist Ruth Benedict phrased it in her landmark polemic against racism, anthropology held that "culture is not a function of race."[12] Roughly stated, spirituals gained increasing acceptance as reflecting African Americans' culture, in the anthropological sense, as sophisticated audiences and critics reveled in the authentic "genius of the Negro folk" expressed in spirituals. This appreciation of the exotic correlated to a nascent cultural relativism in Germany: as spirituals were to African American culture, so yodeling was to Bavarian or German culture. Although arguments were made in the same vein for jazz, it seemed less obviously the music of another authentic culture than non-culture.

Black and German Music in Germany, 1918–1945

African American music burst on the German scene following World War I, as German musicians formed jazz bands to play the new style of music and German audiences turned out to see touring African American performers like Josephine Baker and the Chocolate Kiddies. The efflorescence of a jazz scene centered in Berlin sparked a conflict over the music that continued throughout the troubled life of the Weimar Republic.[13] The most vehement opponents of jazz were found mainly, but not exclusively, on the Right, including the National Socialists. They regarded jazz variously, and in somewhat contradictory terms, as modern, American, sexual, primitive, Jewish, and black. Jazz, closely linked in the public imagination to dancing and black sexuality, struck German conservatives as a threat to public decency and to the integrity of German culture. One noted music historian of the time contended that jazz, which he claimed had been invented by "a Nigger in Chicago," constituted an assault on "Occidental civilized music." The jazz mania, in the eyes of such critics, reflected the degeneracy of the Weimar Republic.[14]

German proponents of jazz, on the other hand, looked to blackness as a means of rescuing Western music from the sterility that seemed to follow the cataclysm of the Great War. That vision, which depended in large measure on the belief in African Americans' putative natural vitality, shaped Ernst Krenek's successful 1927 opera *Jonny spielt auf* (*Jonny strikes up*). Although the opera's title character, Jonny, is an African American jazz-violinist, the work's real protagonist is Max, a European composer in the throes of a creative crisis. Through a variety of opéra bouffe plot twists, Jonny proves instrumental in helping Max to make a break with European convention, symbolized when Max jumps onto a train that will carry him and his lover to Amsterdam, from where they will take a ship to America.[15]

African American music, which Krenek first encountered at a 1925 performance by the Chocolate Kiddies, provided the inspiration for the opera. Between its premiere in 1927 and 1930, Krenek's opera was staged more than seventy times, more than any other opera of the period, although it flopped in Paris and New York.[16] The character Jonny stood for modern, vigorous creativity, a function signaled through the vernacular of minstrelsy. The opera borrowed blackface conventions in numerous ways, most obviously through the use of blacked-up European white performers for the role of Jonny. At one point in the opera Jonny pulls out a white handkerchief and mops his brow as he sings "Swannee River." He grins and sings minstrel style. The libretto presented stereotypic black sensuality, as in one scene where his "animalistic, sensual, enraged sneer turns into a broad grin."[17] In the finale, Jonny plays the violin as the chorus celebrates the triumph of the New World over the Old.[18] The Nazis would cite *Jonny spielt auf* as an exemplar of the degradation of German art by African American influences.[19]

The arrival of black music in Germany was a shock to cultural conservatives. Richard Wagner had stated in 1878 that the German national character found its truest expression in music, and few voiced disagreement in the following years. German claims to cultural greatness had traditionally depended in significant part on the accomplishments of German composers and musicians like Bach and Beethoven.[20] The effort to discern Germanness in music extended beyond the realm of the great composers to folk music, which had long been a primary concern of German musicologists. Scholars studied folk music as a means of uncovering an authentic culture untainted by foreign influences under whose spell educated composers might have fallen.[21]

The biological world view that lay at the core of Nazism carried direct implications for readings of both German and African American music. Nazi musical theory held that music expressed the racial characteristics of its composer. German music purportedly reflected the superior racial character of the Aryan or Nordic race.[22] The Nazis thus put a biological twist on traditional Wagnerian German musical chauvinism. The Nazis further brought a new intensity to the long-standing veneration of German folk music and culture more generally in defining the German spirit.[23]

Richard Eichenauer, an SS member and music enthusiast, formulated a Nazi synthesis in his book *Musik und Rasse* (*Music and Race*). Eichenauer's work originated in an attempt to ground his own aesthetic objections to much of the new music of the 1920s on something more than judgments of taste. He claimed to have found that assurance in racial science, which he believed demonstrated that blood determined musical taste. Central to Eichenauer's racial musical aesthetic was the rejection of the existence of a "white race." As noted earlier, Eichenauer argued that the Nordic race alone in fact had monopolized musical greatness in Europe.[24]

With the Nazi seizure of power, Eichenauer's ideas acquired respectability, although his critique of the charade of common European whiteness was unusually pointed. German musicologists made new efforts to discern the racial bases for German music, devoting a 1938 conference to the theme of "Music and Race."[25] Jazz, according to Nazi ideologues, amounted to an inferior musical form (or noise masquerading as music) created by members of inferior racial stock, which threatened to poison German music. In the imaginings of race theorists, immersion in racially foreign music brought corruption of the Aryan racial soul. The Nazis' exhibitions of "degenerate" works in the fields of the visual arts and music were intended to persuade the German public that jazz and modernist works debased healthy expressions of German racial genius.[26]

The Nazi assault on jazz during the twenties and thirties distinguished itself by linking jazz to the perceived Jewish menace. Jewish performers and managers occupied prominent positions in the German jazz scene, a fact seized on by the Nazis as they asserted that jazz was Jewish music. The canard that the Jews deviously used blacks and jazz to seduce racially pure German girls was a staple of Nazi jazz rhetoric. The Nazis also linked the Jews to their other musical bête noir, modern music, some of whose leading exponents, like Arnold Schönberg, were Jewish.[27] The 1938 "Degenerate Music" exhibit printed on its program guide a simian caricature of a black playing the saxophone (the quintessential jazz instrument) with a Star of David pin in his lapel.[28] Jazz also served the regime as a propaganda weapon against the United States. The Nazis, continuing a European tradition, pilloried the United States for its lack of culture.[29]

The party's first steps in the cultural field targeted jazz. Following Nazi success in January 1930 state elections in Thuringia, Wilhelm Frick became the first Nazi to head a state ministry, taking the education and culture portfolio as part of a coalition government. During his short tenure in that post, he issued a notice that trade regulations would be applied to prohibit cultural offerings like jazz, "Negro dances, Negro songs, Negro plays," or other offerings that "glamorized the nature or feeling of the Negro and thereby injured the German national feeling." In April 1931, following a cabinet reshuffle that brought Frick's ouster, the ordinance was repealed, but Frick's policy initiative suggested that with the Nazi seizure of power at the national level in 1933, the days of jazz were numbered.[30] Once the Nazis came to power, however, the state's policy toward jazz proved to be more complicated than the official line might have led one to expect. The Third Reich avoided a complete ban on jazz but instead made a number of compromises with the music over the years, sacrificing an ideological crusade in order to avoid alienating that sector of the public that enjoyed listening to the music. The jazz scene nevertheless faded to virtual nonexistence after the defeat at Stalingrad and during the grim final months of the war following the unsuccessful attempt on Hitler's life of July 20, 1944.[31]

Throughout the Nazi period, comparatively small numbers of Germans continued to define themselves as jazz fans. They were commonly regarded as deviant and somehow un-German in their embrace of the foreign, black musical form. Their appreciation for the music was often interpreted (and sometimes intended) as a means of resisting the demands of the regime. The German jazz musician Carlo Bohländer, for example, recalls that during the Third Reich, his "love for jazz made [him] completely immune to the racism of the Nazis." The Nazi campaign against jazz fostered the growth of the myth of jazz as inherently antifascist or democratic. Enjoying jazz, however, by no means equated with a rejection of the importance of the category of race. Jazz fans, like the Nazis, often viewed jazz as foreign, sexual, primitive, modern, and black. They, however, admired those qualities.[32]

After 1945, Germans continued to insist on the unique greatness of German music, but it became unacceptable to maintain, as Nazi musical theorists had, that German music reflected the special musical gifts of the Aryan race. The distinctiveness of German music needed to be accounted for in cultural terms. Black music represented a more complicated case, as the existence of a "Negro race" remained largely unquestioned. Germans remained racially, as well as culturally, distinct from African Americans, while linked by ties of race and culture to the white West. The racially based vitriol heaped by the Nazis on black music nevertheless had discredited baldly racial critiques of jazz, and the general tenor of discussions of black music in the press changed dramatically. Race, however, remained acceptable as an explanatory musical category, so long as the commentator expressed appropriate approval for black music.

A New Day for Black Music

Nazism's defeat promised to turn the German music world upside down as previously proscribed music was now in favor. American officials responsible for cultural re-education of the defeated Germans faced a formidable knot of problems in mobilizing music for political purposes. Confronted with the difficult task of identifying suitably democratic musical works, American military government officers in 1945 adopted the rough expedient of encouraging, whenever possible, the performance of music banned by the Nazis.[33] If the Nazis had prohibited it, then the Americans would encourage it, whether it was jazz, modern music, or pieces by Jewish composers. Of course, such radical changes did not immediately persuade the

German listening public, the bulk of which had never had a taste for the works that the Nazis had blacklisted. Some, like the anonymous author of a letter to the Archbishop of Freiburg who railed against "Jewish-simian imitators" of great German musicians and their "atonal, nigger, monkey-noise," continued to espouse explicitly Nazi musico-racial doctrine.[34]

German invocations of the accomplishments of great German composers could be regarded as a form of resistance to American occupation, or at least mitigating evidence to be considered in punishing Germans for Nazism's crimes.[35] Germans widely regarded the United States as rich in material goods and poor in culture, and after the war many Germans continued to see American musical offerings as limited to jazz.[36] Germany, on the other hand, was the land of culture. As policy guidelines for Radio Munich phrased it, "Germans when brought up face to face with the enormity of the nazi crimes habitually point to German creations in cultural lines of endeavor as . . . ameliorative factors."[37] Even where Germans tried to sound an encouraging note in supporting the American re-education effort, the tone could be patronizing. A 1947 article in the Coburg *Neue Presse*, for example, damned American music with the faint praise that Americans, who had earlier seemed "unmusical," were gradually joining the international music world.[38]

American officials disagreed on how deeply the roots of Nazism extended. The extreme view, exemplified in the educational film *Your Job in Germany*, held that World War II was the product of a malignant German culture, which was thoroughly authoritarian, militaristic, nationalistic, undemocratic, and racist.[39] The musical field posed a difficult problem, since the Nazi culture apparatus had lashed itself to German musical greatness as tightly as possible. But the mere fact that the Nazis liked Bach and Beethoven obviously did not mean that their works would be blacklisted. The case of Wagner exemplified the dilemma: what to do about the works of a German musical genius in which protofascist elements could be identified and that Hitler had glorified as the expression par excellence of Nazi culture? An early programming policy statement for Radio Munich, for example, explained that "a disproportionate emphasis on Wagner's compositions—particularly music from his so-called 'heathen' operas—would have an effect on most listeners which . . . would be clearly detrimental to our objectives in respect to the eradication of nationalism and militerism [*sic*]." The difficulties with Wagner, according to the statement, included his operas' "romantic subject matter," the operas' characters, and Nazism's Wagner cult.[40]

Wagner represented a special case, but even his music soon returned to German radio. Official American policy after 1946 treated German high culture as free from intrinsic taint and identified the real danger as the exploitation of that culture by the Nazis. In 1946, for example, State-War-Navy Coordinating Committee Policy Statement No. 269 portrayed

German high culture as neither inherently militaristic nor undemocratic. Indeed, a draft of the statement regarded German "literary, artistic, scholarly, scientific and religious contributions to civilization" as a "potential basis for German self-respect," achievements in which Germans could take "justifiable pride."[41]

There was a tension in U.S. policy on musical re-education for Germans. On the one hand, American officials hoped to rebut the presumption that the United States was completely lacking in European-style high culture. Peter Kappell, an official within OWI, explained how American music might serve in the democratization of Germany after the war in a memorandum of April 16, 1945. In his view, the American music sent to Germany should demonstrate that American art did not "originate on a far-away planet, but rather embodies trends and qualities familiar to central European . . . developments." American art music works, including those by William Grant Still, fit the bill for this purpose.[42]

On the other hand, a current in favor of musical pluralism ran through American cultural affairs planning. American cultural officials agreed on the need to bring more foreign works into German concert halls, including especially works from the putatively democratic, peaceful, and open culture of the United States.[43] American re-education policy proclaimed that "toleration between diverse cultural and racial groups" formed the basis for peace, whereas "coerced unity of culture, after the manner of Nazism, is the source of tyranny and anarchy." In the postwar understanding of cultural and racial groups, the culture part of the pair was gaining favor over the racial as a means of defining such differences.[44]

Policy makers in military government's music branch believed that it was necessary to counteract the effects of the Nazi state's insistence on the "supremacy" of German art and music by showing that other nations also produced excellent music. The head of the music branch, Eric Clarke, claimed that American music and musicians numbered among "the best assets in the reorientation of Germans." He wrote that "top-rank American Negro vocalists," like Marian Anderson and Dorothy Maynor, "would be of great importance," and he also recommended presenting to German audiences Gershwin's operetta dealing with African American life, *Porgy and Bess*.[45] Marian Anderson likewise found favor from OWI's German Committee, which approved for distribution in Germany a recording of Anderson singing both spirituals and German lieder.[46] If Germans could hear talented African Americans performing artistic works capably, they could be convinced that blacks were not racially inferior. Although Marian Anderson did not perform in Germany until 1950 and *Porgy and Bess* arrived somewhat later, American military government brought black music to German audiences in a number of other ways.[47]

Black music represented a battleground between officials who believed the United States needed to show that it had real cultural achievements as

measured by the traditions of European art music and those who tried
to expand the musical and cultural canon. Although hardcore opponents
and some jazz enthusiasts may have viewed Nazi Germany's defeat as a
victory for jazz, the political meaning of jazz was ambiguous.[48] Opposition
to National Socialism did not necessarily equate with a taste for hot jazz.
Nor were all aesthetic objections to jazz specifically based on Nazi doctrine, although they could have roots in ideas about African Americans
that were consistent with Nazi thinking.[49] Indeed, the German reception of jazz shared much in common with readings of the music by other
Europeans, as well as by black and white Americans.[50]

Jazz nevertheless figured significantly in American plans to democratize German music, although officials recognized that, at a minimum, a
considerable "philistine stiffness" stood in the way of German acceptance
of jazz.[51] Some Americans and Germans hoped to persuade Germans that
jazz was real music. In June 1945 a German civilian, Will Fischer, who had
worked in the German film industry volunteered to produce a number
of documentaries to be used in the re-education of the German people,
including a short with the tentative title "Jazz or Beethoven?" The entre-
preneurial Dr. Fischer proposed that the movie could demonstrate that the
two musical forms could coexist peacefully, although he cautioned that
the subject should not receive a treatment that was "too 'hot.'" American
officials favorably commented on the proposal but declined to advance
any money to support filming in 1945.[52]

In spring 1945 the London bureau of OWI pushed successfully to
include a short 1943 RKO film of a performance by Duke Ellington's orchestra in a test program of documentary films to be shown to German audiences. Officials working on the emerging American cultural re-education
program put together sets of American films to gauge and to refine the
effectiveness of their film propaganda. During the last week of June 1945
they showed a set of four short documentary films, *Die Welt im Film II*,
Pipeline, *Duke Ellington's Orchestra* (*Duke Ellington und seine Kapelle*), and
Der Cowboy, to packed houses in Erlangen. Youth was overrepresented in
the audiences, making up 46 percent of the three crowds tested. At three of
the screenings, the Information Control Division (ICD) distributed questionnaires, the responses to which would guide officials as they planned
methods for democratizing Germans.[53]

The Ellington film proved, in the words of one American official, "a
smashing failure." It aroused the most negative reaction among the four,
with 166 out of 269 people marking it as their least favorite. (The *Welt im
Film* newsreel was a distant runner-up with sixteen people naming it as the
worst of the films.) The audiences regarded it as "'trashy,' un-German and
discordant." Indeed, ICD believed that the film had a "blighting effect" on
the other films' persuasive power.[54] American officials unanimously read
the experiment as demonstrating that Germans were not ready for African

American jazz. The Psychological Warfare Division urged that the picture "[d]efinitely should NOT be shown anywhere in Germany as it raises a racial and hence emotional reaction which is dynamite and would only throw our attempts at re-education of the German people back far beyond where we started."[55] Another American officer criticized the use of the film even more sharply.

> An unfortunate choice: Goebbels has been telling the Germans that the moment the US gains control over them, it will force negro jazz down their throats. Here it is, and badly done, with a camera that barely moves. With so many people in the US who refuse to accept negroes, it is perhaps asking a little too much from the Germans to consider this anything but another bitter pill they'll have to swallow.[56]

Military government was no hotbed of jazz fans. At least a few American officials in the re-education effort shared Goebbels's contempt for jazz, and the thrust of military government's music program aimed to show that American musical culture amounted to more than mere jazz. OMGUS concentrated on highlighting American musical achievement in the area of art music. ICD expended considerable effort promoting performances of serious American composers in order "to prove that life in the United States is conducive to musical authorship." The works of William Grant Still did not reappear frequently in records of such performances, although Daniel Gregory Mason's "String Quartet on Negro Themes" was performed in Erlangen in summer 1947 and radio broadcasts of George Gershwin's music aired in 1945 and 1948.[57]

American officials seeking to convince Germans of the quality of African American music favored spirituals. America House institutions played recordings of spirituals for small German audiences and organized programs that described how art music composers had esteemed black folk music. A September 1948 lecture at the Karlsruhe Information Center, for example, explained that Anton Dvorak had been so "greatly impressed" by spirituals that he borrowed from them in his own New World Symphony.[58] African American spirituals also received limited airtime on Radio Munich, including a midnight broadcast of Paul Robeson singing "Mississippi songs."[59]

The capstone of official efforts to bring spirituals to German audiences was an African American choir's 1949 tour of every major city in the American zone. The choir was composed of men from the Kitzingen Basic Training Center, which the European Command had established to provide supplemental training exclusively to black soldiers in Germany. Military government's Information Centers and Exhibits Branch organized the tour, with most performances held in America Houses. In seeking approval for the tour, planners assured the director that the choir was "excellent both as to repertoire and the quality of performance." German and American sources indicated that "the presentation of negro music of the Choir would be beyond criticism." The question of quality was crucial, because American cultural officials were convinced that Germans disposed to doubt American musical ability would regard performances of anything but the highest caliber as further support for a belief in German cultural superiority. Beyond the undisputed high quality of the music, the tour was touted as making "a real contribution to the Reorientation Program in presenting music which is indigenous to the United States of America and which is a colorful part of our music tradition."[60]

The response by German audiences validated American officials' predictions. The America House institutions where the choir's concerts were staged reported unanimously positive reactions by the German audiences.[61] In Munich, "[o]ver 800 people jammed the theater and the hall immediate outside of the theater and gave overwhelming applause to the Choir." The choir's performance in Nuremberg was also a "triumphant success," and its concert in Regensburg "was the musical event of Regensburg." In Augsburg, the choir drew an "enthusiastic" audience of 2,200. "People came from all walks of life and every age."[62] The reception was equally positive in Württemberg-Baden. The U.S. Information Center in Heidelberg reported that the choir's "success was so great that we asked them to come back. We received letters, personal visits, and telephone calls asking us if it wouldn't be possible for them to return." The audiences for the performances grew from at least 800 at the first concert to 2,000 at the second. The chief of the information center in Heidelberg wrote a letter of thanks to the choir's commander: "We feel that an activity of this nature is one of the best aspects of our reorientation program."[63]

The America House centers had every reason to hail the success of their program, but in fact German audiences indeed seem to have reacted remarkably positively to African American spirituals. (In this, Germans conformed to the tastes of other Europeans, who also demonstrated a fondness for spirituals.)[64] German commentary is notable for the absence of any opposition to spirituals. Moreover, the appeal of spirituals seems to have reached across generational lines to older Germans.

As the Duke Ellington documentary experiment suggested, German audiences did not demonstrate a similar receptivity where jazz was concerned.[65] A 1946 Radio Munich survey revealed the full extent of the antipathy for jazz in the American zone. The station's publication, *Radiowelt*, had asked listeners to characterize their attitude regarding each of twenty-five different programming formats, including jazz. Jazz stood out as arousing sharply negative listener reaction. Over 55 percent of respondents stated that they always turned off jazz, which thus repelled more listeners than any other format save calisthenics. (In the hunger years, 64 percent of listeners evidently saw little need for slimming.) Only 8 percent of respondents professed to particularly enjoying jazz. In contrast, dance music was quite popular, with 37 percent of the listeners saying that they particularly

The Jazz Pirates, a band composed of members of the 427th Army Band, in rehearsal in January 1948. The Jazz Pirates performed for German children as part of the U.S. Army's German youth program and in clubs, sometimes in jam sessions with German jazz musicians. Courtesy National Archives, U.S. Army Signal Corps, photo no. SC297357.

enjoyed listening to that format. An additional 23 percent of respondents, although not especially devoted to dance music, reported enjoying listening to it. Just over 12 percent of those surveyed indicated that they always turned off dance music.[66]

American officials inclined to favor highbrow culture tried to explain that American music included much more than jazz, but it could not be gainsaid that for most Germans in the postwar period jazz figured as the characteristic American musical form. Some advocates continued to believe that it could attract Germans if it were promoted deftly enough.[67] Jazz remained a presence in American-occupied Germany through performances in clubs, presentations in America Houses, and Armed Forces Network (AFN) broadcasts.[68]

The locus for the ongoing debate on how best to push jazz quickly shifted to the radio stations in the American zone, including Radio Munich, which later became Bayerischer Rundfunk. Radio Munich promoted jazz but never propagandized too overtly for it. American officials who formulated radio policy at the station, like their colleagues at Radio Frankfurt, generally used music to attract listeners who, it was hoped, would stay tuned for the more serious re-education programming, such as news and commentary.[69] Responsibility for music programming quickly devolved to the German employees at the station. By June 1946, Radio Munich employed almost 400 people, overseen by only 7 Americans.[70]

German disc jockey Jimmy Jungermann soon dominated the jazz field at Radio Munich. Brought in by American officials in fall 1945 as a jazz expert to create a jazz-appreciation program, he enjoyed remarkable autonomy in selecting the music he played.[71] His approach seems to have represented an effort to give the radio audience mostly what he thought it wanted, while taking available opportunities to gently educate his listeners.[72] The popular program "The Ten of the Week" played the ten most-requested American songs of the week, which some listeners believed helped reverse Goebbels's anti-jazz line.[73] Once station programmers recognized that their listeners were tuning jazz out, they moved to reduce the amount of airtime they devoted to jazz. It received airplay throughout the occupation period but in decreasing amounts, such that programming devoted exclusively to jazz quickly became ghettoized in the "Midnight in Munich" broadcast.[74] Jazz never disappeared, however, and the station evidently saw its low-key promotion of the musical form as part of its re-education effort.[75] Beyond spinning jazz records and discussing them on the air, station officials attempted to educate the public through *Radiowelt*.[76] The magazine generally applied a light touch in guiding the opinions of its listeners, and it affected a somewhat agnostic tone on the subject of jazz, although in the early postwar period the station certainly hoped to foster acceptance of jazz.[77] It published, for example, stories celebrating Glenn Miller and the saxophone.[78]

Radiowelt's first in-depth exploration of the subject appeared in February 1946 with three pieces considering "the problem of jazz music." The first article attempted to clarify the musical basics and the second and third pieces set out the cases of the "jazz opponents" and the "jazz friends." The series exemplified the American propaganda approach that adopted a moderate, objective tone, including making allowances for shortcomings, but that nevertheless suggested that opposition to jazz was illegitimate. The opening article asked, was jazz "really only typical 'Nigger music,' as the Nazis preached, is it a musical form to be taken seriously, is it a branch of entertainment music, is it really not music at all, is it a pleasure or a torment?" The article suggested that since jazz aroused views on both sides of the divide, jazz was something different to everyone. The article's foregrounding of National Socialist racial dogma as the basis for opposition to jazz served a double purpose. By associating opposition to jazz with Nazism, the article condemned that opinion. In addition, the editors' purported courage in airing both sides of the argument testified to their democratic credentials, because it was only in an open society that opposing views could be freely debated.[79]

The next article in the series advanced arguments expressly in favor of jazz, phrased in terms of praise for youth and modernity. The young people who, the article claimed, favored the displacing of old sentimental songs with jazz were ascendant against the decreasing numbers of jazz opponents. Jazz was the music of the time.[80] The last of the three articles on jazz described the position of the enemies of jazz in such a way as to make clear that the editors' sympathies lay with jazz. Unlike the arguments in favor of jazz, which had been articulated by Dr. Panofsky, the anti-jazz position was culled from statements by listeners. The magazine itself thus did not express objections to jazz but rather, "true to the democratic principle," published the views of jazz opponents. The article again employed the tactic of associating anti-jazz views with Nazis and cranks who lacked the decency to sign their names to their letters. The piece began by quoting epithets hurled anonymously against jazz. " 'I was never a Nazi, but I could never stand jazz.' 'Enough with jazz!' 'Jazz is musical non-culture.' " The editors explained that such remarks, usually in anonymous letters to Radio Munich, were on principle tossed into the trash. If, however, people were willing publicly to take a stand, their views could be aired. The editors printed five excerpts from listeners' objections to jazz, which purportedly represented the five major sources of anti-jazz sentiment: objectionable rhythms, violent instrumentation, the jazzing-up of art music works, the foreignness of the music, and opposition to jazz tunes sung in English instead of German dance music.[81]

The Blackness of Black Music

Jazz clearly represented black music.[82] Many Germans doubtless continued to regard it as an inferior musical form expressing the inferior racial quality of blacks. One Frau Stephan expressed her objections to jazz in a letter to the Bavarian minister of culture in October 1947. She opened her letter by explaining that she enjoyed listening to "lively tunes and dance music," so long as the music was "decent" (*vernünftig*). On the radio and in clubs, however, she heard only the "Negro howling" of American jazz. Stephan apparently realized that the Bavarian cultural ministry could not simply outlaw black jazz, so she proposed instead establishing a prize for the benefit of musicians who performed "beautiful, sensible dance music." She asked, though, that no "negrified prize judges" decide on the awards. The author asserted that even the Nazis, who had in other ways "trod culture under foot," had at least suppressed jazz.[83] One young housewife sharply rejected the Duke Ellington film in terms that mixed racial and national categories and emphasized the alien nature of jazz. She stated: "It fills me with disgust to look at these bestial faces and to listen to this horrible music. It is depressing for us white people to attend such a session. Give each race its own. Let the Negro listen to his own music; he might like it better. We Germans delight in the creations of the great German masters of German music."[84]

Public objections to jazz that included references to "bestial" African Americans were uncommon in American-occupied Germany, but the call to leave black music to black people recurred, usually in the politer tones of a racialized musical relativism. One listener, quoted in *Radiowelt*'s series on jazz, maintained that as black music, jazz could not appeal to members of other races. "The Negro origins in the American South of jazz" could not be denied, and the predominance of African Americans in the percussion sections of even American jazz bands testified to whites' inability to master the rhythms of jazz. If jazz were truly to be a "supranational musical affair," its "principal element — rhythm — would have to correspond to general conceptions and not the elemental drive [*Urtrieb*] of an individual race."[85] The musical form, according to that understanding, expressed the character of the Negro race, one foreign to both white Europeans and Americans, who were united by their race.

Jazz, as quintessentially African American music, struck most Germans as unfamiliar and un-German. *Radiowelt*'s series on jazz noted that many people complained to the station that jazz was too foreign. The editors quoted one letter asserting that just as "scarcely any American musician could perform a true waltz," so jazz was the exclusive property of Americans. One writer from Bamberg similarly opined that jazz was fundamentally American and was simply too foreign for people with a "European, German, Bavarian ear [*Klangempfinden*]." In this vision, Bavarian music fit seamlessly into broader categories of German and European culture, to which jazz remained foreign. Another writer, a stenographer, expressed support for jazz but, as a jazz nationalist, awaited a "German jazz-style that corresponds to our thought and feeling."[86] Radio Frankfurt officials cited the objection of one woman who herself enjoyed American dance music but objected to its inclusion in a youth broadcast "because the American spirit should not be injected into German youth before these children have been able to develop their German characteristics."[87] A forty-year-old wife of a neurologist, after seeing the Duke Ellington documentary, recommended that the occupiers "go easy with jazz music because the ears of the population of Germany are not yet used to this type of music."[88]

Spirituals too were black music.[89] The prevailing logic dictated that black artists best performed black music and that black performers were at their best performing black music, as illustrated by German commentary on Marian Anderson, the leading female singer of spirituals during the 1940s. Anderson had studied in Berlin and her voice was obviously classically trained. Her repertory included dozens of German lieder and her most-requested number was Schubert's "Ave Maria." Indeed, recordings of Anderson's renderings of the spirituals are jarring today for their remarkably precise enunciation of the lyrics' black dialect. Nevertheless, to German ears, what was "really most her own" were the spirituals, "the songs and melodies of her race."[90]

Although both spirituals and jazz were read as black music, commentators sharply distinguished between the two musical forms, which could have been viewed as closely related. Richard Hey played on the sharply divergent reactions, noting that jazz, the "profane descendant of the spirituals," was rejected by the same polite society that thronged to hear black religious music.[91] When performances of black music had first reached European audiences early in the twentieth century, they generally included a mélange of jazz, spirituals, ragtime, and minstrel tunes.[92] Jazz and spirituals continued to be performed together during the war. Roland Hayes's 1943 performance at the Royal Albert Hall, where he appeared with the London Symphony Orchestra and a "U.S. Army Negro Chorus," included, in addition to standard spirituals like "Go Down, Moses," a new composition titled *Freedom Morning*, which featured "fast material . . . of the 'jazz' type, skillfully and authentically employed."[93] The admonition by German musicologist Erich von Hornbostel in 1926 that it was "a mistake to divide Negro songs into two classes and to despise dance tunes while glorifying spirituals" generally went unheeded.[94]

The postwar assault on Nazi race hatred produced an asymmetry in the discussions of the blackness of black music. Although it was no longer acceptable to criticize jazz publicly simply on the ground that it was black music, proselytizers for jazz frequently resorted to the language of race in their arguments. A writer in the *Süddeutsche Zeitung* referred to jazz as a "dark-colored foundling."[95] The leading German jazz critic similarly hoped to enlighten that majority of "whites" in Germany who believed that "Negroid" music had nothing meaningful to offer them.[96] In the valorization of the blackness of jazz, postwar fans picked up a tradition that had characterized the Weimar era. Postwar jazz aficionados, however, demonstrated greater sensitivity in their use of race language than had Weimar jazz writing, as the admiring references to "niggers" that marked the earlier period disappeared among postwar publications celebrating jazz's blackness.[97] Jazz music's black character indeed was central to its attraction for fans like Oliver Hassencamp, who prized jazz's roots in the "slave songs originating from the cotton fields of the southern states."[98]

The blackness of black music, however, proved difficult to specify precisely. The riddle of black music's African roots had not been conclusively solved by 1945, despite the efforts of musicologists, historians, and racial theorists.[99] Music critics commonly believed that real blackness in music amounted to a black "style." A critic in the *Frankfurter Rundschau*, for example, wrote that it was not the song itself but its expression that constituted the heart of black music.[100] That argument had been made as early as 1926 by Hornbostel, who asserted that what made black music "totally different from [that] of any other race" was not its content but the *way* it was sung. He was obliged to confess, though, that the black style was "difficult, if not impossible, to describe or analyse."[101] Walter Dirks, writing in the *Frankfurter Hefte,* asserted that jazz ought to be understood as a product of the big city to which "Negroes" had contributed their musical gifts and "unselfconsciousness" (*Unbefangenheit*).[102]

Radiowelt explained that jazz really was "no more and no less than a particular joy in a rollicking, playful musical impulse." The language was implicitly racial, as it depicted jazz in the same terms that had been used to describe blacks. The description of the music as rollicking or wild, as well as "playful," drew explanatory force from the vision of blacks as unruly children. The unusual term *musical impulse* or *musical drive* hinted at other, sexual drives, which were commonly associated with African Americans and their music.[103]

Camill Schwarz argued that the sources of both spirituals and jazz lay in traditions of Psalm singing that originated in Europe. The "dialogue between soloist and ensemble," in Schwarz's view, originated not in African call and response but in Calvinism. Although that interpretation thus suggested that black musical excellence was ultimately derivative, Schwarz closed by lauding the blackness of jazz. The "touchstone of blackness" consisted in the "spirit of Negro music," which was "unknown in white music."[104] The obfuscatory resort to a "Negro spirit" to describe jazz works failed to recognize, as Scott DeVeaux has shown so convincingly, that much of the innovation in jazz in the 1930s and 1940s owed to African American jazz musicians' increasing technical mastery as they pursued the rewards of professionalism.[105]

Love of jazz could lead jazz fans to extend a broader embrace for all things African American. The dynamics of attraction were complex, but racial exoticism seems to have played a role. Immediately upon the war's conclusion, a few ardent jazz fans eagerly pursued contacts with African American musicians and music fans in the occupying army. Knowledgeable black musicians and fans exercised a real magnetism for some young jazz fans who had for years known blackness only through recordings of disfavored jazz. Fred Noll, a young German bassist active in the postwar Frankfurt jazz scene, testified to his enthusiasm for African Americans in the first edition of the Frankfurt Jazz Club's postwar newsletter in August 1945. He related to his fellow jazz fans the success of the Jazz Club Rhythm Band's latest performances before audiences of American soldiers. The most prized encomium for the combo of German musicians came from an African American musician who stopped by after one of the group's performances and demonstrated some of the latest techniques on the bass and drums. Noll rhapsodized over receiving validation from an African American: "What could be better than the praise of a Negro?"[106]

Herr Henken of the Frankfurt Symphony Orchestra (center) instructs William Gibbs (right) of the 427th Army Band as Larry Thomas (left) looks on in Frankfurt, Germany, in January 1948. Courtesy National Archives, U.S. Army Signal Corps, photo no. SC297359.

German jazz fans regarded black musicians as the real jazz men. The ability of the machinist Hans Massaquoi to reinvent himself as a jazz saxophone player after the war probably depended as much on the desire of

German audiences to see jazz performed by blacks as on his musician-ship.[107] The 1948 German tour by noted African American horn player Rex Stewart, on hiatus from Duke Ellington's orchestra, marked an important moment in the revival of jazz in Germany. His July 1948 Amiga session produced the first recording by a black musician in Germany since the Nazi seizure of power. His blackness featured prominently in attracting jazz fans, as he was billed on his German tour as "Rex Stewart and his Negro Band." Army Special Services had recruited "dark people" from Ceylon and Trinidad to perform with Stewart in order to meet audiences' desire for exotic color in their American jazz groups. On some nights the group was filled out by German jazz performers, whose playing dispelled Stewart's initial trepidation that they would be a bit "rusty" after winter-ing over the Nazi period.[108]

Jazz fans often equated blackness with raw vigor and whiteness with cold, desiccated, technical mastery.[109] One critic described jazz as an "eruptive and primitive form of elemental music-making, which strives not for intellectual clarity, but a trance." Jazz represented the victory of heart over intellect. Such descriptions of jazz might have been penned by the most virulent critics of jazz, but the author lauded these attributes as the antidote for intellectual sterility that had left music (and perhaps Western culture generally) an archaic, lifeless husk. In jazz, the "forest primeval" broke in against the "ossified, demystified (and desacralized) stone of civilization." It was precisely this dynamic force that was required to complete the "purification process" in music and to end the "intellectu-alized stagnation" that had overcome music.[110] *Radiowelt* described jazz as a "fresh wind," whose "easy-going freshness, problem-free nature" met "the general demand for light fare."[111] Richard Hey regarded bebop as the meeting of "African vitality and European finesse." Jazz was unlike European music, which needed to be "heard with the head." Jazz had to be "experienced bodily" (*körperlich erlebt*), although Hey believed that bebop represented an exception in this regard.[112]

The image of the vigorous black rescuing decaying Europe, depicted in biological terms as an impotent organism unable to reproduce, appeared in Koeppen's *Pigeons on the Grass,* whose message might be summarized as European culture required the sexual healing that virile black men could give. The black GI Odysseus Cotton strides manfully through the novel as the embodiment of American blackness, signaled by his cash crop sur-name and his sexual prowess. Strong and wealthy, he guzzles Coca-Cola, the American distillate bottled, and spits out the last mouthful onto the ground with what can only be described as gusto.[113] At his entry in the novel, Odysseus carries a radio playing African American music, which serves to encapsulate blackness, as well as all of black history from Africa through the Jim Crow era. The singer's voice on the radio evokes "night on the Mississippi, Judge Lynch rides over the land, oh day of Gettysburg,

Lincoln enters Richmond, forgotten the slave ship, the brand singed forever into the flesh, Africa, lost earth, the tangle of the forests, voice of a
Negress."[114]

Odysseus arrives as potential liberator of Europe, freeing it from its
worn-out, effeminate civilization, someone who can bring a return to the
lusty vigor of the forest primeval. Odysseus's mission as sexual liberator
appears in his relations with the prostitute Susanne toward the novel's
conclusion. At the black soldiers' club, Odysseus and Susanne dance "like
a single body across the dance floor, like a fourfooted, writhing snake."
The two dancers form a sexualized interracial alliance as they merge into
a single being with "four legs and two heads, one white and one black
face," becoming "a single being against the world." When an angry white
mob shows up at the club seeking vengeance for the rumored murder of a
child, Susanne hurries Odysseus out of the club by a back exit. The novel's
conclusion confirms that their dance performance was merely foreplay.
They end up in a small room where, continuing the snake metaphor, they
"writhed, black skin[,] white skin."[115]

Spirituals and Authenticity

Much of the spirituals' popularity stemmed directly from their perceived authenticity, which owed partly to their character as black music.
The authentic folk quality of spirituals had long been a staple of descriptions of the music by African Americans.[116] The linkages between African
American celebrations of spirituals and folk culture are signaled in the
person of W.E.B. Du Bois. Although no direct genealogy from Johann
Gottfried Herder to Du Bois can be traced, the African American schol-
ar's *The Souls of Black Folk* suggests that his study in Germany informed
his project of valorizing black culture.[117] William Grant Still believed
that African Americans possessed a "natural and deep-rooted feeling for
music."[118] The spirituals, in the view of James Weldon Johnson, were produced "naturally" and drew on a rhythmic ability that was an "innate
characteristic of the Negro in America." In his introduction to his influential collection, Johnson cited approvingly Henry Krehbiel's 1914 study of
African American folk songs, which had operated wholly within the racial
paradigm according to which folk songs expressed the racial or national
character of the group.[119] The program to a 1943 concert by Roland Hayes
and the U.S. Army Negro Chorus informed the British audience: "Musical
ability is an inherent part of the American Negro's physical make-up.
Group singing is as natural to him as eating or sleeping."[120] In 1949 Paul
Robeson discerned a "remarkable musicality" among African Americans,
which they "inherited from their African ancestors." African Americans,
Robeson asserted, had a gift for harmony, which he believed was a "natural phenomenon among the people."[121]

Authentic folk music had special appeal in Germany, which had traditionally glorified its own folk music and culture. The quest for authenticity had animated in large measure the search for and valorization of
folk music in societies that had grown increasingly urbanized, industrial-
ized, and atomized through the nineteenth and twentieth centuries. The
German folk music tradition, however, had witnessed as many disappointments as successes in isolating authentic Germanness over the years,
as cultural authenticity, even in something as seemingly "natural" as folk
music, proved a will-o-the-wisp. Although Nazism dealt serious damage
to the legitimacy of celebrating the German *Volk*, the tradition continued
after 1945.[122]

Folk culture in the American zone meant regional cultures as much
as it meant German culture, for Germans continued to cultivate their distinctive local characters after 1945, nowhere more so than in Bavaria.[123]
Bavarian cultural officials asserted that their land possessed a distinctive
culture that validated and delimited Bavarian identity. Dieter Sattler, state
secretary for the fine arts in Bavaria's Ministry of Culture, for example,
defined Bavaria's "cultural tasks," which he asserted were central to postwar renewal, as preserving Bavarian culture, working out (*Aufarbeiten*)
the past, rebuilding, and providing roots for youth. Bavaria's traditional
Christian and federal character, according to Sattler, could play an important role beyond its borders in addressing the "general cultural crisis of
Europe or even of the white race [*der weissen Rasse*]," the roots of which lay
in processes of secularization and industrialization.[124] Postwar Germans
made many such calls for Germany to awaken from its cultural "lethargy
and sterility" to rescue the "West," but Sattler's is striking for its mixing of
Germany's cultural project with a role in the "white" West.[125]

For German audiences disposed to see African Americans as natural and unaffected, spirituals promised unmediated access to an authentic
folk tradition unsullied by the sterile overrefinement of European music
of the twentieth century. A favorable review of the Kitzingen choir's performance in the *Rhein-Neckar-Zeitung* noted that many of the spirituals
had a "great essential kinship" with German folk songs. The piece found
in the spirituals all the essential attributes of authentic folk culture. Their
lyrics possessed "fresh directness . . . drawn without modification from
everyday life." The songs' "nativeness" continually breathed through the
performance, giving the religious message of the songs a "strong naturalness." The article further discerned an "unintentional purity" in the
alternation between the solo voice and the choral response. Spirituals
struck Germans as somehow more "natural" than white, European culture.[126] Although some commentators at times continued to use the old
distinction between "natural peoples" (*Naturvölkern*) and cultured peoples (*Kulturvölkern*), the express language of primitiveness was generally
eschewed in descriptions of black musical culture.[127]

Of course, even with the spirituals, any staging of the music, especially for white audiences, threatened the music's elusive authenticity. In the 1930s, Zora Neale Hurston had asserted flatly, "There never has been a presentation of genuine Negro spirituals to any audience anywhere."[128] Germany's leading postwar jazz expert, Joachim-Ernst Berendt, who was one of the few postwar German writers to emphasize a connection between spirituals and jazz, saw the authenticity of the spirituals as endangered by the loss of folk tradition. He bemoaned the fact that for decades "white teachers" had been teaching spirituals to African American children. As a result, he declared: "[M]any African Americans had come to regard and admire spirituals as 'art.' And that marks their end."[129] Although doubts about the spirituals' authenticity may have nagged at critical German listeners, most were inclined to set aside such concerns and hear the spirituals as living folk culture.

The predominantly religious content of the lyrics contributed to the music's appeal.[130] In addition, German commentators demonstrated sensitivity to the spirituals' origins in slavery, as they discerned connections between the context in which the songs originated and the situation of contemporary audiences. Critics typically described the songs as melancholy or as expressing the African Americans' "ancient fate."[131] A critic in the *Frankfurter Rundschau*, on the other hand, read the spirituals as testifying to African Americans' ability, even in the face of slavery, "[t]o enjoy life," which itself provided them with an "inner liberation" that comforted them in their misery. That writer suggested that perhaps that function of the music could explain the acceptance of the "music of the American Negro" by the "youth of the West."[132]

The Ambiguity of Jazz and Cultural Miscegenation

Jazz is notoriously difficult to define.[133] Like all cultural forms, jazz has a long tradition of experts who pronounce on what is "real" jazz—that is, aesthetically good—and what is "pseudojazz," and bad.[134] The ambiguity at the heart of jazz fostered such debates and placed disagreements about the aesthetic value of jazz on continually shifting ground. That was especially true in postwar Germany, where American jazz entered Germany in the baggage train of an alien occupying force. Soon jazz seemed everywhere, as even traditional German tunes were "jazzed up" in the new idiom. The perceived tendency of jazz to produce a sort of cultural miscegenation aroused considerable antipathy. That opposition could be phrased in expressly racial, nationalist, or cultural terms, as all of those modes of understanding difference were premised on understanding Germanness (whether racial, national, and/or cultural) as a pure homogenous essence.[135]

Jazz opponents expressed particular annoyance when German tunes were performed with jazz styles, rhythms, or instruments.[136] *Radiowelt* found that "[d]ance music, in so far that it is not jazzed-up, is popular on the whole. Jazz on the other hand is sharply rejected."[137] Thus Frau Stephan expressed outrage to Bavarian cultural officials because when she tuned her radio to hear promised dance music, she found instead what she regarded as American jazz. She complained that the situation was so bad that "typical American jungle music passes for dance music." She protested, "Beautiful pieces like 'Kaprifischer, Violetta' among many others are jazzed up to the point that they are unrecognizable, such that one can no longer even pick out the melody."[138]

Among the first victims of the propensity for "jazzing up" numbers had been the spirituals, which provoked objections to the assault on the purity of the spirituals from African Americans.[139] Paul Robeson, one of the leading African American performers of spirituals during the 1930s and 1940s, did not admire jazz at the time. In a 1949 piece in a Soviet music journal he condemned "[c]ommercial jazz" for having "prostituted and ruthlessly perverted many splendid models of Negro folk music."[140]

The ambiguity of jazz caused it to irritate particularly that segment of the German listening public who, like Frau Stephan, wanted to hear light dance music in the German style. The large number of music fans who tuned their radios to the light music programming could not know whether they would hear German dance music or American jazz, forms difficult to distinguish. Disc jockeys would inevitably stray over the line on occasion and offend listeners who wished for no jazz offerings among the dance music. The divide between jazz fans and dance music fans was deep but difficult to locate. By contrast, art music elitists, who viewed jazz as merely the most loathsome form of light music, could insulate themselves from jazz fairly easily, since they were unlikely to listen to the light music portions of the programming schedule. The jazzing-up of classics, however, struck highbrow listeners as a singular desecration.[141]

Folk music experts made arguments for preserving German culture from the pollution of jazz in a more sophisticated language that nevertheless resorted to biological metaphors. In December 1949 the Bavarian association for folk culture (*Heimatpflege*) submitted to the Bavarian culture ministry a twelve-page paper by Toni Grad, a Bavarian folk music specialist, concerning the "renewal of folk music culture in Bavaria." Grad called for the establishment of a professorship for folk music, whose occupant would work for "enlightenment about the borders of international jazz music, predominantly associated with large cities, as opposed to the European folk musics, predominantly associated with the countryside." The holder of the chair would educate the public concerning the "negligent blurring of these borders with a resultant miserable bastardization."[142]

Grad published a fuller statement of his views on the means of renewing authentic folk culture in July 1950. He again lamented that the corruption of authentic rural folk dance by jazz threatened to spawn a misborn musical half-breed. The article did not attack jazz per se as inferior, noting that it demanded technical expertise. The real trouble came when jazz infected Bavarian folk music, producing "horrifying monstrosities [*grausigen Mißgeburten*] and mixtures [*Zwitter*] between Bavarian rural and American seaport dance music, in which the previously faultless [*saubere*] musicians become sloppy hacks [*Schmierfinken*]." The dancing to such jazzed-up folk music similarly, according to Grad, degenerated from "well-ordered (and nevertheless natural) [*wohlgeordnete (und trotz-dem urwüchsig)*]" folk dances into chaos.[143] In Grad's description, what was native German or Swabian was clean, orderly, technically correct, and natural. The admixture of American jazz elements created only dirty disorder.

The mutability of jazz posed an opportunity and a problem for its advocates. On the one hand, jazz fans could always argue that objections to jazz in fact really amounted only to dislike for a particular form of jazz and a misapprehension of what real jazz was. *Radiowelt,* for example, explained that "Hot and Swing" constituted only two forms, not the sum, of jazz. (Of course, that view had its critics, who would charge that only such forms represented "real" jazz, as opposed to watered-down, com-promised versions.) On the other hand, nearly all jazz aficionados dis-liked some forms of jazz, which were treated as inferior. *Radiowelt* thus applauded the replacement after 1945 of the "lukewarm" jazz played by the Third Reich's German Dance and Entertainment Orchestra with "pure and undistorted jazz music" from the United States.[144] Defenders of jazz regularly maintained that the problem was that few Germans had heard authentic jazz.[145] The serious jazz enthusiasts of the Hot Club Dortmund picketed against the film *Hallo Fräulein* in summer 1949 for misrepresent-ing real jazz. One person held a sign insisting "Hallo Fräulein is no jazz film."[146] Both jazz fans and jazz opponents wanted the genuine article.

There were cases where musical innovators believed in the possibili-ties of productively combining European art music and African American music. In 1950 twenty-year-old Heinz Werner Zimmermann came to Heidelberg to study music and discovered jazz. His work expressly sought to combine jazz and European musical traditions, rejecting the notion that jazz could only bastardize European culture. He also empha-sized the affinities between jazz and spirituals in his work. Zimmermann writes that he believed that "jazz music had to be grafted as a vital new branch to the old tree of our sophisticated European music tradition."[147] His biological metaphor attributing to jazz the possibility of spawning new life is consistent with more expressly racial ways of thinking about music.

Jazz proponents endeavored without much success in the postwar years to mobilize a relativistic appreciation for the music as an expres-sion of African American culture in the Boasian sense. Olaf Hudtwalker informed his readers that George Gershwin had been the first to recognize that jazz was real American folk music.[148] *Radiowelt* argued that jazz was the authentic, natural expression of American culture. Jazz was not the invention of some composer. Rather, "jazz grew much more out of itself from joy in rhythm, from exuberance of a melody — it grew out of old Negro spirituals, farmer songs, cowboy calls, and singing rounds." The article explained that just as Bavarian folk music expressed the Bavarian rural character, so was the musical joy of the "farmer, cowboy, and black cotton-pickers tied-up with the basic elements of jazz: rhythm, instrumental wildness and virtuosity." Different countries simply had different customs. Germans had the same right to be amazed by a "Negro or Indian dance" as Americans could be with German folk customs. The question had nothing to do with "racial doctrine or prejudices." It was simply a matter of taste. Jazz struck many German listeners as noise because they were unaccustomed to the musical form. With time it would be possible for them to develop an appreciation for it.[149] Most Germans, to whom jazz signified not a different culture in the anthropological sense but pure non-culture, remained unmoved by that argument.[150]

The Politics of Music

The politics of jazz were ambiguous. German, as well as black and white American, devotees of jazz conventionally read jazz as somehow recounting and resisting the enslavement of African Americans and, to a lesser degree, their continuing disadvantaged position in American society.[151] That element of jazz thus represented a political difficulty for the American democratization effort, although not an insurmountable one, as Americans could point to their own achievements and continuing efforts toward achieving racial justice as a model for Germans. Within the German political context, the Nazis had politicized jazz by treating it as a threat to the regime and a "slap in the face" of German culture.[152] Joachim-Ernst Berendt, Germany's leading postwar jazz expert, noted in *Die Neue Zeitung* that the rancor involved in discussions of jazz stemmed from the German habit of equating music with an entire world view.[153]

Young German jazz fans indeed typically connected support for jazz with opposition to Nazism and German conservatism more broadly.[154] For such fans, listening to music, even after the war, was not merely a leisure activity. Letters in favor of jazz addressed to Radio Munich usually included declarations of allegiance as a "jazz supporter" (*jazz Anhänger*) or "jazz friend" (*jazz Freund*), terms that implied that jazz devotees did not simply enjoy listening to this music but had made a decision to follow a certain way of life.[155]

Part of the attraction of the music for some of its young fans rested in the fact that the decision to be a jazz fan conferred a particular identity.

The feeling of being a member of a hard core of devotees likely gained strength from the fact that one could hear jazz mostly at odd hours. "Jazz fanatics" could prove their devotion by tuning in to the "Dancing at Dawn" program on AFN.[156] Listeners to Radio Munich needed to stay up late to listen to the "Midnight in Munich" broadcast of jazz, which could be heard throughout Germany and much of western Europe. No doubt a frisson of rebellion added to the pleasure in staying up late to listen to jazz rather than engaging in useful work. The embrace of blackness by young Germans could serve as a convenient means of rejecting adulthood's norms.

Despite the hopes of some advocates, appreciation of jazz did not necessarily produce committed democrats or racial egalitarians. German jazz fans sometimes demonstrated a fascination with exotic African Americans that could reinforce the potency of race as a category. And yet, in occupied Germany enthusiasm for jazz could open the way to social relations across the color line and foster among Germans a genuine commitment to racial equality. The small group of young German jazz fans of the Frankfurt Jazz Club actively sought out African American jazz musicians and fans as soon as the fighting ended in 1945. German and African American musicians joined together in jam sessions in American and German clubs and bars. The Germans in the Frankfurt Jazz Club were remarkably well-informed about the cutting edge of jazz in the United States. By October 1945 the club's newsletter reported that Dizzy Gillespie and Charlie Parker were rising stars in the jazz firmament.[157]

Through their listening, reading, and socializing, members of the Frankfurt Jazz Club, such as Günter Boas and Horst Lippmann, became critical of racial discrimination against African Americans. Club members could read, for example, a critique of racism in the United States in a short biography of Bessie Smith, the great African American singer, which appeared in the club's April 1946 newsletter. Günter Boas, drawing from American jazz critic John Hammond's writings, repeated the legend that Bessie Smith had bled to death after a car accident because as an African American in the segregated South, she was refused care at a hospital reserved for whites only. Boas closed the article by opining that such a fate could never meet jazz greats Count Basie and Duke Ellington, and he credited jazz with having advanced "the principle of racial equality."[158] Boas's account of Bessie Smith's death was inaccurate, and his assessment of the role of jazz in American race relations is debatable, but he (and potentially his readers) clearly had become sensitive to racial injustice.[159] Jazz played a role in the emergence of that critical awareness.

Young jazz enthusiast Oliver Hassencamp hoped that jazz had the power to overcome "the borders between races and the fraternization prohibition." A Munich jam session led by Rex Stewart achieved in Hassencamp's recollection a moment of interracial harmony when

Jam session including Germans and African American GIs. From Horst Lippmann Nachlaß.

Hassencamp joined in to sing in Yiddish with the group as it played the old swing tune "Bei Mir Bist Du Scheen." Stewart then took over and brought the session to a breathtaking musical climax.[160] Spirituals had a similar potential to facilitate interracial understanding. One review of a Kitzingen choir performance noted that people who might have expected "wild bizarreness" had been disappointed, and the evening had instead been characterized by "fraternal fellowship."[161]

Music in Koeppen's novel likewise served to inform political commitments. As the music playing from Odysseus's case signified blackness, white appreciation of the music implied acceptance of blackness. Music figures prominently in the efforts by Odysseus's porter, Josef, to do penance for killing a French colonial soldier during World War I. As Josef expires, the voice of Marian Anderson rises from the radio, "as if the voice were trying to make amends to the slain man."[162] Marian Anderson's benediction indicates that Josef has atoned for his killing of the black colonial soldier. The music derives its racial meaning from the fact that Anderson sings, of course, a spiritual. Music's political meaning appears as well in the relationship between Carla and her father, Herr Behrend, who accepts her and her African American lover, Washington Price. Carla's father's racial liberalism is signaled by his affinity for jazz. He leads the jazz band performing at the black soldiers' club, and he claims to Carla that he can even play "real hot jazz." Although Herr Behrend's heart is in the right place, his race continues to limit his musical ability. Carla smiles at her father's naiveté: "Poor father. He imagined he could play real jazz. The blacks were the only ones who could play real jazz." He nevertheless provides a stark contrast to Carla's mother, who at that moment is reveling in traditional German music and race hatred. At the beer hall, white Germans and Americans unite in enjoyment of a Hitler favorite, the Badenweiler March. With the appropriate musical indoctrination, the crowd is primed for an attack on a black soldiers' club.[163]

The novel highlights the importance of music to postwar German understanding of blackness, whiteness, and the continuing relevance of race. Music was stamped with a racial character, as black music expressed the whole of African American history, and Germans, no matter how good-willed, could never completely master jazz. Koeppen, though, believed in the possibility of interracial reconciliation through white acceptance of black music, a theme that has had enduring force. Jazz often figured as the device for achieving a racial utopia, where differences of "skin color or nationality" become irrelevant.[164]

Jazz fans' political commitments were not always so clear, as the America House in Mannheim's "experiment" with twice-weekly jazz group meetings suggested. Officials discontinued the meetings when they decided that "the majority of those who attended were undisciplined, and disinterested, other than jazz, in what the [America House] has to offer."[165]

The Mannheim center intended to hold more jazz concerts and discussions every two or three weeks, but the episode underscored the ambiguity of jazz's political message. Other cultural forms, like performances of Gotthold Ephraim Lessing's classic plea for religious toleration, *Nathan the Wise*, seemed to promise a more direct payoff in "spreading racial tolerance among the Germans."[166] There could be no guarantee that jazz audiences were getting the message.

The fate of Rex Stewart's 1948 tour of American-occupied Germany likewise suggested that jazz proved a troublesome vehicle for democratizing Germany in the eyes of American officials. The tour came to an abrupt end when a brawl involving his group erupted at a bar. According to a report by Walter White, executive secretary of the NAACP, trouble arose when a black musician in Stewart's band "upbraided a waitress who was slow in serving him a drink." The comments were "resented by a white soldier," and a "general free-for-all resulted." General Huebner of EUCOM responded by canceling Stewart's contract and ordering him out of Germany. Stewart asked for White to intervene with General Clay on his behalf, and White reported to the NAACP that he planned to raise the issue with Clay. It is unknown whether he did so.[167] Huebner's action suggested that bringing black jazz to Germany was seen as fraught with risks that could outweigh its value in the re-education effort.

Jazz and American music more broadly met great skepticism from Germans who denied that Nazism reflected rot at the heart of German culture. Following World War II, German music and culture more broadly provided Germans with a usable past, purportedly defining and rescuing a core of Germanness untainted by Nazism's crimes.[168] In the eyes of many Germans and Americans, that culture manifested the greatest human achievements. Germany was the land of Beethoven, Goethe, and a national culture of which its bearers could be proud.[169] The common assertion that civilized Germany had been hijacked by a band of uncultured criminals suggested that after the elimination of the Nazis, the real Germany could again find expression through its cultural works.[170]

That vision had considerable currency among the German elites, and it found its most prominent expression in Friedrich Meinecke's *The German Catastrophe*, published in 1946. The work manifested the palpable anguish of a German nationalist who, appalled by the crimes of Nazism, strove to rehabilitate Germany. Meinecke placed his hope in German high culture, which effectively defined Germanness. He asked, for example, "What is more individual and German than the great German music from Bach to Brahms?" German music expressed the German spirit and had a "universal Occidental effect." The same was true for Italy's Raphael and for England's Shakespeare. Meinecke asserted, "In order to exert a universal influence, spiritual possessions of this kind must always blossom forth naturally, uniquely, and organically out of any given folk spirit."[171]

Walter White, executive secretary of the NAACP, pictured in the U.S. Information Center at Kitzingen, Germany, during his 1948 visit. By the time of White's visit, the Cold War framed American policy toward the Germans and influenced policy makers' thinking about the effect of American race relations on German views of the United States. Courtesy National Archives, U.S. Army Signal Corps, photo no. SC308768.

Meinecke articulated a fundamentally nationalist vision in which culture defined the nation.

Meinecke implicitly contrasted authentic culture that blossomed "naturally, uniquely, and organically" out of a national spirit with a culture that did not. Cultural products that did not originate naturally amounted, presumably, to what Meinecke called a "pale, empty, abstract cosmopolitanism." Meinecke thus expressed the common feeling that authenticity, regarded as the natural expression of national culture, provided the measure of cultural value. Although Meinecke did not take up the subject of American music, jazz, conceived of as a deracinated, transnational musical form, would have been repellent to him. In contrast, African American spirituals fitted well into Meinecke's vision of culture as the "organic" products of a black folk spirit and thus qualified as expressing the black essence in a manner that could appeal universally. Taking as his model the Sunday radio program of German music and poetry that Goebbels had instituted as an alternative to church services, Meinecke proposed establishing "Goethe Communities," which would cherish and spread the greatness of German culture by "offering the noblest music and poetry together." The meetings would open and close with "great German music—by Bach, Mozart, Beethoven, Schubert, Brahms, and so forth." Music and poetry would convey and regenerate the essence of Germanness.[172]

Music, Sexuality, Culture, and Race

The fields of music and sexual morality, although I have for the most part examined them separately, in fact were intimately connected in the postwar imagination. Jazz had long been associated with black sexual license.[173] To its critics, the wildness of jazz music was bad enough. What was worse, it could lead to dancing. Jitterbugging and African American–influenced dance styles, along with jazz recordings and musicians, made their way across the Atlantic. The dancing struck conservative observers as unbridled indecency. As black newspaperman Louis Martin wrote in 1948, were Hitler still alive, "nothing would probably klli [sic] him any quicker than the sight of American Negro soldiers teaching German girls the delicate art of jitterbugging."[174] Jazz provided the soundtrack to Germans' mental picture of postwar decadence: slatternly German women consorting with black GIs in a seedy club.[175]

The sexualized aspect of jazz appeared as well in descriptions of the importation of foreign black culture into defeated Germany using metaphors of contamination, defilement, and rape.[176] *Radiowelt* quoted an anonymous doctor of philosophy as saying, "Bach, Mozart, yes even Beethoven's Moonlight Sonata, but also Tschaikowsky and Dvorak are apparently not holy enough to be safe before a jazz-violation [*Jazz-Vergewaltigung*]."[177] Frau Stephan likewise equated the musical violation of German culture through jazz with the sexual violation of rape in her complaint to the Bavarian culture ministry. "Now we as the vanquished are apparently even to be violated [*soll . . . vergewaltigen lassen*]."[178] Music critic Olaf Hudtwalker asserted that by the same token, jazz fans objected to George Gershwin's "violation" (*Vergewaltigung*) of jazz by notating the music in his works based on jazz, instead of affording the musicians the freedom to improvise.[179]

Postwar discussions of music, sexuality, race, and culture revealed a complicated and untidy mixture of metaphors and categories. Amid the confusion, though, there was a general movement away from publicly attributing differences in sexual mores primarily to biological race and toward describing such differences as attributes of culture. Descriptions of German women's sexuality illustrated that change. As noted in Chapter 3, Saul Padover described German women as "perhaps the easiest white women in the world."[180] His colleague Cedric Belfrage, a British resident of the United States, subsequently authored a fictionalized critical account of American democratization efforts in which he included a character based on Padover. Belfrage's character updated Padover's formulation in a cultural idiom, stating, "The accessibility of young German women is without parallel in the modern western world. There is nothing like it this side of Tahiti."[181] With an apparent indirect reference to Margaret Mead, German women's sexuality in Belfrage's account represented deviance from the West instead of from whiteness. The difference in the descriptions owed less to nationality or historical period (since Belfrage's work was written soon after Padover's but delayed in publication) than to a politically oriented awareness of race. Elsewhere in his account, Belfrage highlighted American prejudices against blacks in order to expose what he saw as the hypocrisy at the core of the supposed American denazification and democratization effort.[182] The fictionalized liberal Padover thus was credited with a culturalist understanding that in fact differed from the real Padover's continued reliance on racial categories. Belfrage signaled that differences between groups would be described increasingly as cultural difference rather than racial difference.

Conclusion

After World War II, largely through the encounter with black Americans, the race of the Germans was recast from that of the blond, blue-eyed Aryan to the white-skinned Caucasian. The Nazi effort to persuade Germans that they were Aryans locked in a Darwinian struggle with alien Jewish and Slavic racial enemies gave way to a racial orthodoxy that lumped such groups together in racially undifferentiated whiteness. The defeat of Nazism marked a lasting victory of whiteness as a transnational racial category and the demise of the notion of the Aryan race.

The significance of the postwar ban on public racism in American-occupied Germany may be illuminated by considering the earlier implementation of Nazi racial ideology. Ulrich Herbert, in examining the origins of the Final Solution, highlights the importance of the shift that occurred with the Nazi seizure of power in 1933 when "anti-antisemitism" became unacceptable in public discourse.[1] Herbert argues persuasively that the suppression of public opposition to racism represented an important precondition to realizing the horrors of racial genocide. By the same token, the prohibition of public racism in 1945 could open the way toward racial equality and even the rejection of race as a biological category. The public discrediting of virulent racism represented a predicate for the changes in ideas and practices concerning blacks and Jews in Germany that followed. Subsequent generations grew up observing that anti-Semitism, although still voiced in private by many Germans, was continually condemned in public.[2] Publicly professed racism has remained disfavored in Germany since 1945. The sociologists studying the *Besatzungskinder* in the 1950s found that although many West Germans harbored prejudices against the children, they were reluctant to openly express those prejudices when asked about their attitudes toward the children.[3] I do not mean to suggest that racism has been permanently defeated, but Nazi-style practice and rhetoric have been relegated to the fringe of German political life.[4]

Racial categories exercised a markedly less pernicious influence in occupied Germany than they had before May 1945. Nazi genocide ended. Germans' victimization or open denigration of blacks declined dramatically. Likewise, white Americans in Germany mostly refrained from open avowals of white supremacy. Although some officials called for the removal of black troops from occupied Germany, such proposals eschewed arguments that black GIs were doomed by their biological makeup to permanent inferiority. They argued rather that misconduct by African Americans impeded the military's mission in Germany. Most importantly, African Americans continued to serve in the occupying forces. Although segregation persisted, it was on the wane.

Race still mattered. Banning racist statements did not convince Germans that African Americans were their equals. Most Germans felt disquiet over sexual relationships between German women and black soldiers and remained convinced that black music was profoundly alien. In German eyes, race mattered, especially because real white German women would refuse sexual relations with black men. Anxieties about race mixing found expression in a language that condemned immorality and in measures directed against the women involved in relations with African Americans. Although German women participating in relationships with black men bore the brunt of punitive measures, gender did not simply trump race. The women came to official attention because of their companions' race, and ideas about race led the women to be characterized as prostitutes and the soldiers as their dupes. Racial thought thus formed a principal ingredient in the mix of motives, which also included the political realities of military occupation and the sexual double standard that moved the authorities to mount roundups of putatively immoral and diseased women.

Race mattered in occupied Germany for Americans too. African American civil rights advocates found in occupied Germany an excellent rhetorical weapon to attack segregation and the racism of white American society. The absurdity of attacking Nazi race hatred with a Jim Crow army became evident to growing numbers of Americans. Occupied Germany represented the international arena in which Americans tried to explain their inability to live up to the ideals of the Declaration of Independence for a foreign audience. That effort would spread beyond occupied Germany to the world during the Cold War.

Germans' distinctiveness within the white race was typically expressed after 1945 in terms of culture, not race (although the two categories remained linked). Although culture increasingly won primacy over race as explaining differences in human groups, differences between groups were often depicted as virtually immutable. Indeed, it is sometimes difficult to determine what difference the new cultural understanding has made. Race usually served as a convenient shorthand for defining the boundaries of cultural groups. Terms such as *black culture* and *black music* purport to define a body of material unique to African Americans. Germans, as well as white and black Americans, experienced African American spirituals as an authentic expression of blackness in terms often indistinguishable from the older vision in which biological race determined a group's cultural products. The cultural model, which borrowed from preexisting racial ideas, could render difference nearly as immutably as if it were in the blood.

Abbreviations

AG	Adjutant General
AGCT	Army General Classification Test
BayHStA	Bayerisches Hauptstaatsarchiv
CAD	Civil Administration Division
CDU	Christian Democratic Union
CIC	Counter-Intelligence Corps
CMH	U.S. Army Center of Military History, Washington, D.C.
CSU	Christian Social Union
EAF	Erzbischöfliches Archiv Freiburg

ETO	European Theater of Operations
ETOUSA	European Theater of Operations, U.S. Army
EUCOM	European Command
FOD	Field Operations Division
GK	Generallandesarchiv Karlsruhe
ICD	Information Control Division
ICEB	Information Centers and Exhibits Branch
IfZ	Institut für Zeitgeschichte, Munich
ISD	Information Services Division
MK	Staatsministerium für Unterricht und Kultus
NACP	United States National Archives, College Park
OMGBY	Office of Military Government for Bavaria
OMGUS	Office of Military Government for Germany, United States
OMGW-B	Office of Military Government for Wuerttemberg-Baden
OWI	Office of War Information
PWD	Psychological Warfare Division
RLSO	Resident Liaison & Security Office
SB	Staatsarchiv Bamberg
SD	Security Service
SHAEF	Supreme Headquarters of the Allied Expeditionary Forces
SM	Stadtarchiv Mannheim
SN	Staatsarchiv Nürnberg
SPD	Social Democratic Party
StK	Bayerische Staatskanzlei
SW	Stadtarchiv Weißenburg
USFET	United States Forces, European Theater

Notes

Introduction

1. George Mosse, *Toward the Final Solution: A History of European Racism* (New York: Oxford University Press, 1978), 235–36; Robert Moeller, "Introduction: Writing the History of West Germany," in *West Germany under Construction: Politics, Society, and Culture in the Adenauer Era*, Social History, Popular Culture, and Politics in Germany, ed. Geoff Eley (Ann Arbor: University of Michigan Press, 1997), 20–21. See also Fatima El-Tayeb, *Schwarze Deutsche: Der Diskurs um "Rasse" und nationale Identität, 1890–1933* (Frankfurt a.M.: Campus Verlag, 2001), 209; Werner Bergmann, *Antisemitismus in öffentlichen Konflikten: Kollektives Lernen in der politischen Kultur der Bundesrepublik, 1949–1989*, Schriftenreihe des Zentrums für Antisemitismusforschung, Berlin, vol. 4 (Frankfurt a.M.: Campus Verlag, 1997), 510–11.

2. See Heide Fehrenbach, *Race after Hitler: Black Occupation Children in Postwar Germany and America* (Princeton, N.J.: Princeton University Press, 2005); Peter

Martin, ". . . Als wäre gar nichts geschehen," in *Zwischen Charleston und Stechschritt: Schwarze im Nationalsozialismus*, ed. Peter Martin and Christine Alonzo (Hamburg: Dölling und Galitz Verlag, 2004), 700–10; Brenda Gayle Plummer, "Brown Babies: Race, Gender, and Policy after World War II," in *Window on Freedom: Race, Civil Rights, and Foreign Affairs, 1945–1988*, ed. Brenda Gayle Plummer (Chapel Hill: University of North Carolina Press, 2003), 67–92; Maria Höhn, *GIs and Fräuleins: The German-American Encounter in 1950s West Germany* (Chapel Hill: University of North Carolina Press, 2002); Yara-Colette Lemke Muniz de Faria, *Zwischen Fürsorge und Ausgrenzung: Afrodeutsche "Besatzungskinder" im Nachkriegsdeutschland*, Reihe Dokumente, Texte, Materialien: Veröffentlicht vom Zentrum für Antisemitismusforschung, vol. 43 (Berlin: Metropol Verlag, 2002); Heide Fehrenbach, "Of German Mothers and 'Negermischlingskinder': Race, Sex, and the Postwar Nation," in *The Miracle Years: A Cultural History of West Germany, 1949–1968*, ed. Hanna Schissler (Princeton, N.J.: Princeton University Press, 2001), 164–86; Fehrenbach, "'Ami-Liebchen' und 'Mischlingskinder': Rasse, Geschlecht und Kultur in der deutsch-amerikanischen Begegnung," in *Nachkrieg in Deutschland*, ed. Klaus Naumann (Hamburg: Hamburger Edition, 2001), 178–205; Fehrenbach, "Rehabilitating Father*land*: Race and German Remasculinization," *Signs: Journal of Women in Culture and Society* 24 (1998): 107–27; Maria Höhn, "*Heimat* in Turmoil: African-American GIs in 1950s West Germany," in *The Miracle Years*, 145–63; Höhn, "GIs, Veronikas and Lucky Strikes: German Reactions to the American Military Presence in the Rhineland-Palatinate during the 1950s" (Ph.D. diss., University of Pennsylvania, 1995); Uta G. Poiger, *Jazz, Rock, and Rebels: Cold War Politics and American Culture in a Divided Germany* (Berkeley: University of California Press, 2000); Fatima El-Tayeb, "'Blood Is a Very Special Juice': Racialized Bodies and Citizenship in Twentieth-Century Germany," in *Complicating Categories: Gender, Class, Race and Ethnicity*, ed. Eileen Boris and Angélique Janssens, *International Review of Social History*, Supplement 7 (Cambridge: Press Syndicate of the University of Cambridge, 1999), 149–69; Tina Marie Campt, Pascal Grosse, and Yara-Colette Lemke Muniz de Faria, "Blacks, Germans, and the Politics of Imperial Imagination, 1920–1960," in *The Imperialist Imagination: German Colonialism and Its Legacy*, ed. Sara Friedrichsmeyer, Sara Lennox, and Susanne Zantop, Social History, Popular Culture, and Politics in Germany, ed. Geoff Eley (Ann Arbor: University of Michigan Press, 1998), 205–29; David Braden Posner, "Afro-America in West German Perspective, 1945–1966" (Ph.D. diss., Yale University, 1997).

3. Fehrenbach, *Race after Hitler*. The two quotations come from pages 19 and 18.

4. Höhn, *GIs and Fräuleins*.

5. Poiger, *Jazz, Rock, and Rebels*, 9.

6. See Johannes Kleinschmidt, *"Do Not Fraternize": Die schwierigen Anfänge deutsch-amerikanischer Freundschaft, 1944–49*, Mosaic: Studien und Texte zur amerikanischen Kultur und Geschichte, vol. 1 (Trier: WVT Wissenschaftler Verlag, 1997), 237–38; Höhn, *GIs and Fräuleins*, 90–94, 222; Rosemarie K. Lester, "Blacks in Germany and German Blacks: A Little-Known Aspect of Black History," in *Blacks and German Culture*, ed. Reinhold Grimm and Jost Hermand (Madison: University of Wisconsin Press, 1986), 120; Erin Leigh Crawley, "Challenging Concepts of Cultural and National Homogeneity: Afro-German Women and the Articulation of Germanness" (Ph.D. diss., University of Wisconsin–Madison, 1996), 96; Morris J. MacGregor Jr., *Integration of the Armed Forces, 1940–1965*, Defense Studies

Series (Washington, D.C.: Center of Military History, United States Army, 1981), 214–15.

7. Lester, "Blacks in Germany," 120.

8. Höhn, *GIs and Fräuleins,* 234.

9. See, e.g., Birgit Brander Rasmussen et al., eds., *The Making and Unmaking of Whiteness* (Durham, N.C.: Duke University Press, 2001); Matthew Frye Jacobson, *Whiteness of a Different Color: European Immigrants and the Alchemy of Race* (Cambridge, Mass.: Harvard University Press, 1998); Grace Elizabeth Hale, *Making Whiteness: The Culture of Segregation in the South, 1890–1940* (New York: Pantheon Books, 1998); Eric Lott, *Love and Theft: Blackface Minstrelsy and the American Working Class* (New York: Oxford University Press, 1993); Ruth Frankenberg, *White Women, Race Matters: The Social Construction of Whiteness* (Minneapolis: University of Minnesota Press, 1993); David Roediger, *The Wages of Whiteness: Race and the Making of the American Working Class* (New York: Verso, 1991). For criticisms of whiteness studies, see Eric Arnesen, "Whiteness and the Historians' Imagination," *International Labor and Working-Class History* 60 (Fall 2001): 3–32; Barbara J. Fields, "Whiteness, Racism, and Identity," *International Labor and Working-Class History* 60 (Fall 2001): 48–56.

10. The most sensitive application of whiteness studies to the German context has been made by Heike Paul in analyzing the work of German writers on the United States in the nineteenth century. See *Kulturkontakt und Racial Presences: Afro-Amerikaner und die deutsche Amerika-Literatur, 1815–1914,* American Studies — a Monograph Series, vol. 126 (Heidelberg: Universitätsverlag Winter, 2005). For the twentieth century, see Ursula Wachendorfer, "Weiß-Sein in Deutschland: Zur Unsichtbarkeit einer herrschenden Normalität," in *AfrikaBilder: Studien zu Rassismus in Deutschland,* ed. Susan Arndt (Münster: Unrast, 2001), 87–101; Tina Campt, *Other Germans: Black Germans and the Politics of Race, Gender, and Memory in the Third Reich* (Ann Arbor: University of Michigan Press, 2004); Campt, "'Afro-German': The Convergence of Race, Sexuality and Gender in the Formation of a German Ethnic Identity, 1919–1960" (Ph.D. diss., Cornell University, 1996), 20; Uta Poiger, "A New, 'Western' Hero? Reconstructing German Masculinity in the 1950s," in *The Miracle Years,* 420; Uli Linke, *German Bodies: Race and Representation after Hitler* (New York: Routledge, 1999); Crawley, "Challenging Concepts." On whiteness as a means of domination, see Linke, *German Bodies,* 32; Charles W. Mills, *The Racial Contract* (Ithaca, N.Y.: Cornell University Press, 1997).

11. See, e.g., Martha Hodes, ed., *Sex, Love, Race: Crossing Boundaries in North American History* (New York: New York University Press, 1999), 1.

12. See, e.g., Linke, *German Bodies,* 31–33.

13. W.E.B. Du Bois, *The Souls of Black Folk,* with an introduction by Dr. Nathan Hare and Alvin F. Poussaint, M.D. (1903; reprint, New York: A Signet Classic, New American Library, 1982), 54.

14. W.E.B. Du Bois, "The Superior Race," in *The Oxford W.E.B. Du Bois Reader,* ed. Eric J. Sundquist (New York: Oxford University Press, 1996), 68. See also Michael Omi and Howard Winant, *Racial Formation in the United States: From the 1960s to the 1980s,* Critical Social Thought, ed. Michael Apple (New York: Routledge & Kegan Paul, 1986), 62.

15. See, e.g., George Mosse, *Nationalism and Sexuality: Respectability and Abnormal Sexuality in Modern Europe* (New York: Fertig, 1985).

16. See Bergmann, *Antisemitismus in öffentlichen Konflikten,* 44. The McCloy quotation is found at ibid., 67.

17. See Jacobson, *Whiteness of a Different Color*, 91–135; Bergmann, *Antisemitismus in öffentlichen Konflikten*; Frank Stern, *The Whitewashing of the Yellow Badge: Antisemitism and Philosemitism in Postwar Germany*, trans. William Templer (New York: Pergamon Press, published for the Vidal Sassoon International Center for the Study of Antisemitism, the Hebrew University of Jerusalem, 1992); Karen Brodkin, *How Jews Became White Folks: And What That Says about Race in America* (New Brunswick, N.J.: Rutgers University Press, 1998); Ruth Benedict, *Race: Science and Politics*, rev. ed., with "The Races of Mankind," Ruth Benedict and Gene Weltfish (New York: Viking, 1945). This study also raises the question of how Germans and Americans came to think about Slavs after 1945. Slavs too increasingly seem to have been lumped into the white race after 1945, but the subject remains to be explored.

18. See Lora Wildenthal, *German Women for Empire, 1884–1945* (Durham, N.C.: Duke University Press, 2001), 10; Ira Berlin, *Many Thousands Gone: The First Two Centuries of Slavery in North America* (Cambridge, Mass.: Belknap Press of Harvard University Press, 1998), 1; Evelyn Brooks Higginbotham, "African-American Women's History and the Metalanguage of Race," *Signs: Journal of Women in Culture and Society* 17 (1992): 251–74; Barbara Fields, "Race and Ideology in American History," in *Region, Race and Reconstruction: Essays in Honor of C. Vann Woodward*, ed. J. Morgan Kousser and James M. McPherson (New York: Oxford University Press, 1983), 143–77; Jonathan Marks, *Human Biodiversity: Genes, Race, and History*, Foundations of Human Behavior (New York: Aldine de Gruyter, 1995).

19. See Neil MacMaster, *Racism in Europe, 1870–2000,* European Culture and Society, ed. Jeremy Black (New York: Palgrave, 2001), 27; Katrin Sieg, *Ethnic Drag: Performing Race, Nation, Sexuality in West Germany*, Social History, Popular Culture, and Politics in Germany, ed. Geoff Eley (Ann Arbor: University of Michigan Press, 2002), 252.

20. See Elazar Barkan, *The Retreat of Scientific Racism: Changing Concepts of Race in Britain and the United States between the World Wars* (Cambridge: Cambridge University Press, 1992). On the long-standing tension between race and culture in understanding difference, see Paul Gilroy, *Against Race: Imagining Political Culture beyond the Color Line* (Cambridge: Harvard University Press, 2000), 33–34, 282, 299; Richard Handler, "Raymond Williams, George Stocking, and Fin-de-Siècle U.S. Anthropology," *Cultural Anthropology* 13 (1998): 458–59; George Stocking Jr., *Victorian Anthropology* (New York: Free Press, 1987); Stocking, *Race, Culture, and Evolution: Essays in the History of Anthropology* (New York: Free Press, 1968).

21. I am mindful of the fear voiced by Hanna Schissler that the very term *race* carries with it "a racist mindset." Schissler, "Introduction: Writing about 1950s West Germany," in *The Miracle Years: A Cultural History of West Germany, 1949–1968*, ed. Hanna Schissler (Princeton, NJ: Princeton University Press, 2001), 13; see also Leslie A. Adelson, *Making Bodies, Making History: Feminism and German Identity* (Lincoln: University of Nebraska Press, 1993), 93–99. I believe, however, the term can and must be used but with attention to its pitfalls.

22. Imanuel Geiss, *Geschichte des Rassismus* (Frankfurt a.M.: Suhrkamp Verlag, 1988), 15. See also Martin N. Marger, *Race and Ethnic Relations: American and Global Perspectives,* 5th ed. (Stamford, Conn.: Wadsworth/Thomson Learning, 2000), 26–27; George M. Fredrickson, *Racism: A Short History* (Princeton, N.J.: Princeton University Press, 2002); Susan Arndt, "Impressionen: Rassismus und der deutsche Afrikadiskurs," in *AfrikaBilder*, 11–70.

Chapter 1: Germans, Blacks, and Race through 1945

1. See, e.g., Gilroy, *Against Race,* 57; Ivan Hannaford, *Race: The History of an Idea in the West* (Washington, D.C.: Woodrow Wilson Center Press, 1996); Mosse, *Toward the Final Solution;* Stocking, *Victorian Anthropology,* 18.

2. See Geiss, *Geschichte des Rassismus,* 14–15.

3. See Marger, *Race and Ethnic Relations,* 28; Robert Proctor, *Racial Hygiene: Medicine under the Nazis* (Cambridge, Mass.: Harvard University Press, 1988), 13; Wim F. Wertheim, "Netherlands-Indian Colonial Racism and Dutch Home Racism," in *Imperial Monkey Business: Racial Supremacy in Social Darwinist Theory and Colonial Practice,* ed. Jan Breman (Amsterdam: Vu University Press, 1990), 75; Benedict Anderson, *Imagined Communities* (London: Verso, 1983), 136; Fields, "Race and Ideology in American History."

4. Barkan, *The Retreat of Scientific Racism,* 17; Mosse, *Toward the Final Solution;* Mosse, *Nationalism and Sexuality.*

5. Hodes, *Sex, Love, Race,* 1; Ronald Hyam, *Empire and Sexuality: The British Experience* (Manchester: Manchester University Press, 1990), 203; Kathleen M. Brown, *Good Wives, Nasty Wenches, and Anxious Patriarchs: Gender, Race, and Power in Colonial Virginia* (Chapel Hill: University of North Carolina Press, published for the Institute of Early American History and Culture, Williamsburg, Virginia, 1996); Helmut Bley, *South-West Africa under German Rule, 1894–1914,* trans. Hugh Ridley (Evanston, Ill.: Northwestern University Press, 1971), 110, 212–16; George S. Schuyler, "Our White Folks," in *Black on White: Black Writers on What It Means to Be White,* ed. David Roediger (New York: Schocken Books, 1998), 78; Trudier Harris, "Exorcising Blackness: Historical and Literary Lynching and Burning Rituals," in *Black on White,* ed. Roediger, 300–301; Grace Halsell, *Black/White Sex* (New York: William Morrow and Company, 1972); Winthrop D. Jordan, *White over Black: American Attitudes towards the Negro, 1550–1812* (Chapel Hill: University of North Carolina Press, 1968); Ann Laura Stoler, *Race and the Education of Desire: Foucault's History of Sexuality and the Colonial Order of Things* (Durham, N.C.: Duke University Press, 1995); Frankenberg, *White Women, Race Matters.*

6. Piet de Rooy, "Of Monkeys, Blacks, and Proles: Ernst Haeckel's Theory of Recapitulation," in *Imperial Monkey Business,* 7–34.

7. See Campt, "'Afro-German,'" 2; Peter Martin, *Schwarze Teufel, edle Mohren* (Hamburg: Junius Verlag, 1993); Sander Gilman, *On Blackness without Blacks: Essays on the Image of the Black in Germany* (Boston: G. K. Hall and Co., 1982).

8. See Amadou Booker Sadji, *Das Bild des Negro-Afrikaners in der Deutschen Kolonialliteratur (1884–1945): Ein Beitrag zur literarischen Imagologie Schwarzafrikas* (Berlin: Dietrich Reimer Verlag, 1985).

9. See H. Glenn Penny and Matti Bunzl, "Introduction: Rethinking German Anthropology, Colonialism, and Race," in *Worldly Provincialism: German Anthropology in the Age of Empire,* ed. H. Glenn Penny and Matti Bunzl, Social History, Popular Culture, and Politics in Germany, ed. Geoff Eley (Ann Arbor: University of Michigan Press, 2003), 11–17.

10. "Negro" entry in *Allgemeine deutsche Real-Encyklopädie für die gebildeten Stände: Conversations-Lexikon,* 9th ed., vol. 10, *Moskau bis Patricier* (Leipzig: Brockhaus, 1846).

11. See Benoit Massin, "From Virchow to Fischer: Physical Anthropology and 'Modern Race Theories' in Wilhelmine Germany," in *Volksgeist as Method and*

Ethic: Essays on Boasian Ethnography and the German Anthropological Tradition, ed. George W. Stocking Jr., History of Anthropology, vol. 8 (Madison: University of Wisconsin Press, 1996), 80, 86–87, 95, 97.

12. Massin, "From Virchow to Fischer," 133–34. For a similar tradition in Victorian British anthropology, see Stocking, *Victorian Anthropology*, 224–25, 234–35.

13. Johann Gottfried Herder, *Sämtliche Werke*, vol. 13, ed. Bernhard Suphan (1887; reprint, Hildesheim: Georg Olms Verlag, 1978), 235. For an English translation, see Hans Adler and Ernst A. Menze, eds., *On World History: Johann Gottfried Herder: An Anthology*, trans. Ernest A. Menze with Michael Palma, Sources and Studies in World History (Armonk, N.Y.: M. E. Sharpe, 1997), 183.

14. Johann Gottfried Herder, *Reflections on the Philosophy of the History of Mankind*, abridged, with an introduction by Frank E. Manuel (reprint, Chicago: University of Chicago Press, 1968), 64, 186, 189.

15. Georg Wilhelm Friedrich Hegel, *Vorlesungen über die Philosophie der Weltgeschichte*, vol. 1, *Die Vernunft in der Geschichte*, ed. Johannes Hoffmeister (Hamburg: Verlag von Felix Meiner, 1955), 218–34; G.W.F. Hegel, *The Philosophy of History*, trans. J. Sibree (New York: Dover Publications, 1956), 93–98.

16. See Mosse, *Nationalism and Sexuality*, 79, 133–34; Susanne Zantop, *Colonial Fantasies: Conquest, Family, and Nation in Precolonial Germany, 1770–1870*, Post-Contemporary Interventions (Durham, N.C.: Duke University Press, 1997), 75–84; Michael H. Kater, *Different Drummers: Jazz in the Culture of Nazi Germany* (New York: Oxford University Press, 1992), 20; Sander L. Gilman, "Black Sexuality and Modern Consciousness," in *Blacks and German Culture*, ed. Grimm and Hermand, 35–53.

17. Erwin Baur, Eugen Fischer, and Fritz Lenz, *Menschliche Erblehre*, 4th ed. (Munich: J. F. Lehmanns Verlag, 1936), 716. An earlier edition of the work is discussed in Proctor, *Racial Hygiene*, 52–59.

18. Michael Schubert, *Der schwarze Fremde: Das Bild des Schwarzafrikaners in der parlamentarischen und publizistischen Kolonialdiskussion in Deutschland von den 1870er bis in die 1930er Jahre*, Beiträge zur Kolonial- und Überseegeschichte, no. 86 (Stuttgart: Franz Steiner Verlag, 2003), 46; MacMaster, *Racism in Europe*, 58; Margarete Dörr, *"Wer die Zeit nicht miterlebt hat . . .": Frauenerfahrungen im Zweiten Weltkrieg und in den Jahren danach*, vol. 2, *Kriegsalltag* (Frankfurt a.M.: Campus Verlag, 1998), 395.

19. See, e.g., Herder, *Reflections*, 6–7, 85, 103, 179. See also Isaiah Berlin, *Three Critics of the Enlightenment: Vico, Hamann, Herder*, ed. Henry Hardy (Princeton, N.J.: Princeton University Press, 2000), 233.

20. Alfred Kelly, *The Descent of Darwin: The Popularization of Darwinism in Germany, 1860–1914* (Chapel Hill: University of North Carolina Press, 1981), 117.

21. *Stenographische Berichte über die Verhandlungen des deutschen Reichstages, 1912*, vol. 284, 56th meeting, 8 May 1912, 1745, quoted in Helmut Walser Smith, "The Talk of Genocide, the Rhetoric of Miscegenation: Notes on Debates in the German Reichstag Concerning Southwest Africa, 1904–14," in *The Imperialist Imagination: German Colonialism and Its Legacy*, ed. Sara Friedrichsmeyer, Sara Lennox, and Susanne Zantop (Ann Arbor: University of Michigan Press, 1998), 121.

22. See Proctor, *Racial Hygiene*, 136; Gilroy, *Against Race*, 59, 64. On physical anthropologists, see Massin, "From Virchow to Fischer," 104–5. On Fischer, see Massin, "From Virchow to Fischer," 123, 143. Eugen Fischer's 1911 study found the "mixed race" Rehoboth to be "healthy, strong and fertile." Eugen Fischer, *Die Rehobother Bastards und das Bastardierungsproblem beim Menschen* (Jena, 1913), quoted

in Paul Weindling, *Health, Race and German Politics between National Unification and Nazism, 1870–1945,* Cambridge History of Medicine (Cambridge: Cambridge University Press, 1989), 237. On Darwin, see Kelly, *The Descent of Darwin,* 101; Proctor, *Racial Hygiene,* 13–14. For Hitler's views, see Adolf Hitler, *Mein Kampf,* trans. Ralph Manheim (Boston: Houghton Mifflin, 1971), 284–96.

23. Smith, "The Talk of Genocide," 109, 118.

24. *Fränkischer Kurier Nürnberg,* 24 November 1920, quoted in Campt, Grosse, and Lemke Muniz de Faria, "Blacks, Germans, and the Politics of Imperial Imagination," 213.

25. See Schubert, *Der schwarze Fremde;* Gilroy, *Against Race,* 33–34, 282, 299; Richard Handler, "Raymond Williams, George Stocking," 458–59; Stocking, *Victorian Anthropology;* Stocking, *Race, Culture, and Evolution.*

26. On Herder's synthesis, see Berlin, *Three Critics,* 170–75. For the quotation, see ibid., 186. See also Matti Bunzl, "Franz Boas and the Humboldtian Tradition: From *Volksgeist* and *Nationalcharakter* to an Anthropological Concept of Culture," in *Volksgeist as Method and Ethic: Essays on Boasian Ethnography and the German Anthropological Tradition,* ed. George W. Stocking Jr., History of Anthropology, vol. 8 (Madison: University of Wisconsin Press, 1996), 73.

27. Herder, *Reflections,* 7.

28. Berlin, *Three Critics,* 220–25.

29. Frank E. Manuel, "Editor's Introduction," xxi; Herder, *Reflections,* 23.

30. See Alfred Kelly, *The Descent of Darwin,* 117; MacMaster, *Racism in Europe,* 23–24. For Nazism's continued belief in a white race, see Alfred Rosenberg, *Race and Race History and Other Essays by Alfred Rosenberg,* ed. and Introduction by Robert Pois, Roots of the Right: Readings in Fascist, Racist and Elitist Ideology, ed. George Steiner (New York: Harper & Row, 1974), 80; Saul Friedländer, *Nazi Germany and the Jews,* vol. 1, *The Years of Persecution, 1933–1939* (New York: HarperCollins, 1997), 181. Hitler wrote, "It is the Jews who bring the Negroes into the Rhineland, always with the same secret thought and clear aim of ruining the hated *white race.*" Hitler, *Mein Kampf,* 325; emphasis added.

31. See Pascal Grosse, "Turning Native? Anthropology, German Colonialism, and the Paradoxes of the 'Acclimatization Question,' 1885–1914," in *Worldly Provincialism,* ed. Penny and Bunzl, 181; Grosse, *Kolonialismus, Eugenik und bürgerliche Gesellschaft in Deutschland, 1850–1918,* Campus Forschung vol. 815 (Frankfurt: Campus Verlag, 2000); Sadji, *Das Bild des Negro-Afrikaners.*

32. *Stenographische Berichte über die Verhandlungen des deutschen Reichstages, 1903–5,* vol. 5, 106th meeting, 3391, quoted in Smith, "The Talk of Genocide," 115.

33. See Wildenthal, *German Women for Empire,* 79–130; Annegret Ehmann, "From Colonial Racism to Nazi Population Policy: The Role of the So-Called Mischlinge," in *The Holocaust and History: The Known, the Unknown, the Disputed, and the Reexamined,* ed. Michael Berenbaum and Abraham J. Peck (Bloomington: Indiana University Press in association with the United States Holocaust Memorial Museum, 1998), 122–23.

34. Lora Wildenthal, "Race, Gender, and Citizenship in the German Colonial Empire," in *Tensions of Empire: Colonial Cultures in a Bourgeois World,* ed. Frederick Cooper and Ann Laura Stoler (Berkeley: University of California Press, 1997), 266–67.

35. Wildenthal, *German Women for Empire,* 79–121; Bley, *South-West Africa under German Rule,* 212.

36. Bley, *South-West Africa under German Rule,* 214–16.

37. On Togo, see Woodruff D. Smith, *The German Colonial Empire* (Chapel Hill: University of North Carolina Press, 1978), 66–73, 207–9, 217–19.

38. Smith, "The Talk of Genocide," 117, quoting *Stenographische Berichte über die Verhandlungen des deutschen Reichstages, 1912,* vol. 284, 53rd meeting, 2 May 1912, 1648. On Solf, see Smith, *The German Colonial Empire,* 217–19.

39. Quoted in Bley, *South-West Africa under German Rule,* 217.

40. Wildenthal, *German Women for Empire,* 126–27; Smith, "The Talk of Genocide," 117.

41. See Katharina Oguntoye, *Eine afro-deutsche Geschichte: Zur Lebenssituation von Afrikanern und Afro-Deutschen in Deutschland von 1884 bis 1950* (Berlin: Hoho Verlag, Christine Hoffmann, 1997).

42. *Stenographische Berichte über die Verhandlungen des deutschen Reichstages, 1905–6,* vol. 3, 73rd meeting, 23 March 1906, 2228; *Stenographische Berichte über die Verhandlungen des deutschen Reichstages, 1903–5,* vol. 6, 164th meeting, 15 March 1905, 5275, quoted in Smith, "The Talk of Genocide," 116; ellipsis in Smith.

43. Andrew D. Evans, "Anthropology at War: Racial Studies of POWs during World War I," in *Worldly Provincialism,* ed. Penny and Bunzl, 198–229; Massin, "From Virchow to Fischer," 126.

44. See Campt, *Other Germans,* 50–62; Campt, " 'Afro-German,' " 33–60; MacMaster, *Racism in Europe,* 129–32; Campt, Grosse, and Lemke Muniz de Faria, "Blacks, Germans, and the Politics of Imperial Imagination," 208–14; Sally Marks, "Black Watch on the Rhine: A Study in Propaganda, Prejudice and Prurience," *European Studies Review* 13 (1983): 297–334; Gisela Lebzelter, "Die 'Schwarze Schmach': Vorurteile, Propaganda Mythos," *Geschichte und Gesellschaft* 11 (1985): 37–58; Reiner Pommerin, "*Sterilisierung der Rheinlandbastarde": Das Schicksal einer farbigen deutschen Minderheit, 1918–1937* (Düsseldorf: Droste Verlag, 1979), 18–22; Keith Nelson, "The 'Black Horror on the Rhine': Race as a Factor in Post–World War I Diplomacy," *Journal of Modern History* 42 (December 1970): 606–27; Robert C. Reinders, "Racialism on the Left: E. D. Morel and the 'Black Horror on the Rhine,' " *International Review of Social History* 13 (1968): 1–28.

45. Marks, "Black Watch on the Rhine"; Nelson, "The 'Black Horror on the Rhine' "; Reinders, "Racialism on the Left."

46. Pommerin, "*Sterilisierung der Rheinlandbastarde,"* 18.

47. Ibid., 21–22, quoting Friedrich Ebert, *Schriften, Aufzeichnungen, Reden,* vol. 2 (Dresden, 1926), 290.

48. Marks, "Black Watch on the Rhine," 312.

49. Campt, " 'Afro-German,' " 56; Mosse, *Toward the Final Solution,* 176.

50. Marks, "Black Watch on the Rhine," 302.

51. "Die Schwarze Schmach," *Hamburger Nachrichten,* 30 July 1921, quoted in Campt, " 'Afro-German,' " 46–47.

52. The *Leipziger Tageszeitung* is quoted in Campt, Grosse, and Lemke Muniz de Faria, "Blacks, Germans, and the Politics of Imperial Imagination," 210. The *Grenzland Korrespondent* is quoted in ibid., 211. See also "Die Farbigenherrschaft in Rheinlande," *Die Deutsche Zeitung,* 28 May 1921, quoted in Campt, " 'Afro-German,' " 38.

53. For the quotation, see Campt, Grosse, and Lemke Muniz de Faria, "Blacks, Germans, and the Politics of Imperial Imagination," 213; see also Campt, " 'Afro-German,' " 48–51.

54. See Proctor, *Racial Hygiene*; Michael Burleigh and Wolfgang Wippermann, *The Racial State: Germany 1933–1945* (Cambridge: Cambridge University Press, 1991).

55. Jeremy Noakes, "The Development of Nazi Policy towards the German-Jewish '*Mischlinge*' 1933–1945," *Leo Baeck Yearbook* 34 (1989): 303, quoting Lösener minute for Frick, 24 July 1933.

56. Campt, *Other Germans,* 255n12, quoting "Erläuterungen zum § 2 des Reichsbürgergesetzes," in Stuckart and Globke, *Kommentare,* 55–57.

57. See Richard Eichenauer, *Musik und Rasse,* 2nd ed. (Munich: Lehmanns Verlag, 1937), 9–11, 22, 280. For quotations, see ibid., 9, 280.

58. Rosenberg, *Race and Race History,* 110–11.

59. Alfred Rosenberg, Aktennotiz für den Führer, 16 March 1942, Document 045-PS, *Trial of the Major War Criminals before the International Military Tribunal, Nuremberg, 14 November 1945–1 October 1946,* vol. 25 (Washington, D.C.: Government Printing Office, 1951), 97–98; Alexander Dallin, *German Rule in Russia, 1941–1945: A Study of Occupation Policies,* 2nd ed. (London: Macmillan Press, 1981), 148; Directive by Goebbels to the Reichsleiters, Gauleiters, and Gau Propaganda leaders of the NSDAP, 15 February 1943, in Jeremy Noakes and Geoffrey Pridham, ed., *Nazism 1919–1945,* vol. 3, *Foreign Policy, War and Racial Extermination: A Documentary Reader,* Exeter Studies in History No. 13 (Exeter: Exeter University Publications, 1988), 917.

60. See Reiner Pommerin, "The Fate of Mixed Blood Children in Germany," *German Studies Review* 5 (1982): 320; Walter Groß, *Rassenpolitische Erziehung* (Berlin: Junker und Dünnhaupt Verlag, 1935), 10.

61. Rosenberg, *Race and Race History,* 80.

62. Johnpeter Horst Grill and Robert L. Jenkins, "The Nazis and the American South in the 1930s: A Mirror Image?" *The Journal of Southern History* 58 (November 1992): 674.

63. Ibid., 671–73; on jazz, see Kater, *Different Drummers*; Michael Kater, "The Jazz Experience in Weimar Germany," *German History* 6 (1988): 154–58.

64. Pommerin, "The Fate of Mixed Blood Children in Germany," 357; see also Hitler, *Mein Kampf,* 430, 438, 624.

65. Kater, *Different Drummers,* 33.

66. See Burleigh and Wippermann, *The Racial State,* 304; Robert Proctor, *Racial Hygiene,* 112–14; Susann Samples, "African Germans in the Third Reich," in *The African-German Experience: Critical Essays,* ed. Carol Aisha Blackshire-Belay (Westport, Conn.: Praeger, 1996), 54; Grill and Jenkins, "The Nazis and the American South," 676; Pommerin, "*Sterilisierung der Rheinlandbastarde,*" 60, 86.

67. Campt, *Other Germans*; Clarence Lusane, *Hitler's Black Victims: The Historical Experiences of Afro-Germans, European Blacks, Africans, and African Americans in the Nazi Era,* Crosscurrents in African American History, ed. Graham Russell Hodges and Margaret Washington (New York: Routledge, 2003); Oguntoye, *Eine afro-deutsche Geschichte.*

68. See Campt, *Other Germans,* 91–135.

69. Hans J. Massaquoi, *Destined to Witness: Growing Up Black in Nazi Germany* (New York: William Morrow and Company, 1999).

70. See Samples, "African Germans in the Third Reich," in *African-German Experience,* ed. Carol Aisha Blackshire-Belay, 61–64.

71. Oguntoye, *Eine afro-deutsche Geschichte*, 118–19; Friedländer, *Nazi Germany and the Jews*, 208.

72. See Robert W. Kesting, "Forgotten Victims: Blacks in the Holocaust," *Journal of Negro History* 77 (1992): 30–36; David Killingray, "Africans and African Americans in Enemy Hands," in *Prisoners of War and Their Captors in World War II*, ed. Bob Moore and Kent Fedorowich (Oxford: Berg, 1996), 181–204; Raffael Scheck, " 'They Are Just Savages': German Massacres of Black Soldiers from the French Army in 1940," *The Journal of Modern History* 77 (2005): 325–44. On recollections of comparatively favorable treatment, see Monroe H. Little Jr., "The Black Military Experience in Germany: From the First World War to the Present," in *Crosscurrents: African Americans, Africa, and Germany in the Modern World*, ed. David McBride, Leroy Hopkins, and C. Aisha Blackshire-Belay (Columbia, S.C.: Camden House, 1998), 185.

73. See Robert G. Moeller, *Protecting Motherhood: Women and the Family in the Politics of Postwar West Germany* (Berkeley: University of California Press, 1993), after 108, figure 3, reprinted courtesy of the Hoover Institution Archives, Poster Collection.

74. See Annette F. Timm, "The Ambivalent Outsider: Prostitution, Promiscuity, and VD Control in Nazi Berlin," in *Social Outsiders in Nazi Germany*, ed. Robert Gellately and Nathan Stoltzfus (Princeton, N.J.: Princeton University Press, 2001), 200; "Introduction: Women in Weimar and Nazi Germany," in *When Biology Became Destiny: Women in Weimar and Nazi Germany*, ed. Renate Bridenthal, Atina Grossmann, and Marion Kaplan (New York: Monthly Review Press, 1984), 20–24; Gisela Bock, "Racism and Sexism in Nazi Germany: Motherhood, Compulsory Sterilization, and the State," in *When Biology Became Destiny*, ed. Bridenthal, Grossmann, and Kaplan, 271–96; Claudia Koonz, *Mothers in the Fatherland: Women, the Family, and Nazi Politics* (New York: St. Martin's Press, 1987), 3; Ute Frevert, *Women in German History: From Bourgeois Emancipation to Sexual Liberation*, trans. Stuart McKinnon-Evans (New York: Berg, 1988), 229–33; Jill Stephenson, *Women in Nazi Society* (London: Croom Helm, 1975), 37–51.

75. See Proctor, *Racial Hygiene*, 6, 61, 112, 197; Pommerin, "*Sterilisierung der Rheinlandbastarde*," 86.

76. See "Negro" entry in *Meyers Lexikon*, 8th ed., vol. 8, *Muskete-Rakete* (Leipzig: Bibliographisches Institut, 1940); Earl R. Beck, "German Views of Negro Life in the United States, 1919–1933," *Journal of Negro History* 48 (1963): 22–32; Matthias Reiß, "*Die Schwarzen waren unsere Freunde*": *Deutsche Kriegsgefangene in der amerikanischen Gesellschaft, 1942–1946*, Krieg in der Geschichte, vol. 11, ed. Stig Förster, Bernhard R. Kroener, and Bernd Wegner (Paderborn: Ferdinand Schöningh, 2002), 81. On German interest in the celebrated Scottsboro case in the interwar period, see James A. Miller, Susan D. Pennybacker, and Eve Rosenhaft, "Mother Ada Wright and the International Campaign to Free the Scottsboro Boys, 1931–1934," *AHR* 106 (2001): 387–430.

77. See, e.g., Saul K. Padover, "How the Nazis Picture America," *The Public Opinion Quarterly* (October 1939): 665; Grill and Jenkins, "The Nazis and the American South"; Lusane, *Hitler's Black Victims*, 183–84; Andreas Hüneke, "Die Propaganda gegen die 'Negerkunst,' " in *Zwischen Charleston und Stechschritt: Schwarze im Nationalsozialismus*, ed. Peter Martin and Christine Alonzo (Hamburg: Dölling und Galitz Verlag, 2004), 231.

78. G. M. Gilbert, *Nuremberg Diary* (1947; reprint, New York: Da Capo Press, 1995), 57.

79. "Reactions of Germans to Negro Troops," Information Control Intelligence Summary No. 16, 27 October 1945, 2, Records Re: Public Opinion, Opinion Surveys Branch, ICD, RG 260, NACP.

80. Friedrich Percyval Reck-Malleczewen, *Tagebuch eines Verzweifelten* (Stuttgart, 1966), 46, 110, quoted in Reinhold Grimm, "Germans, Blacks, and Jews; or Is There a German Blackness of Its Own?" in *Blacks and German Culture*, ed. Grimm and Hermand, 153.

81. Unsigned, undated [1945] Denkschrift, EAF, Nachlaß Conrad Gröber, Nb8/63.

82. Stefan Kühl, *The Nazi Connection: Eugenics, American Racism, and German National Socialism* (New York: Oxford University Press, 1994); Proctor, *Racial Hygiene*, 52, 97–101, 174, 286; Peter Weingart, Jürgen Kroll, and Kurt Bayertz, *Rasse, Blut und Gene: Geschichte der Eugenik und Rassenhygiene in Deutschland* (Frankfurt a.M.: Suhrkamp, 1992), 286–88; Gisela Bock, *Zwangssterilisation im Nationalsozialismus: Studien zur Rassenpolitik und Frauenpolitik* (Opladen: Westdeutscher Verlag, 1986), 112–16; Erwin Baur, Eugen Fischer, and Fritz Lenz, *Human Heredity*, trans. Eden Paul and Cedar Paul (New York: Macmillan, 1931), 629–33. For comparative studies of American and German approaches to racism, see Larry Eugene Jones, ed., *Crossing Boundaries: The Exclusion and Inclusion of Minorities in Germany and the United States* (New York: Berghahn Books, 2001); Norbert Finzsch and Dietmar Schirmer, eds., *Identity and Intolerance: Nationalism, Racism, and Xenophobia in Germany and the United States* (Cambridge: Cambridge University Press and the German Historical Institute, Washington, D.C., 1998).

83. J. A. Simpson and E.S.C. Weiner, *The Oxford English Dictionary*, vol. 6, *Follow–Haswed*, 2nd ed. (Oxford: Clarendon Press, 1989), 151.

84. Lucius D. Clay, *Decision in Germany* (Garden City, N.Y.: Doubleday and Co., 1950), 62.

85. For my understanding of the army's dealings with the race question during the war, I am heavily indebted to Ulysses Lee, *The Employment of Negro Troops*, The United States Army in World War II: Special Studies (Washington, D.C.: U.S. Government Printing Office, 1966). Daniel Kryder convincingly argues that pragmatism, not principle, motivated policy-making elites, but he fails to credit the long-term significance of the rhetorical justifications that accompanied public policy statements. See *Divided Arsenal: Race and the American State during World War II* (Cambridge: Cambridge University Press, 2000). I share the view that the fight against Nazism helped to delegitimize white supremacist thought. See Thomas Borstelmann, *The Cold War and the Color Line: American Race Relations in the Global Arena* (Cambridge, Mass.: Harvard University Press, 2001), 29, 31, 44; Sherie Mershon and Steven Schlossman, *Foxholes and Color Lines: Desegregating the U.S. Armed Forces*, A RAND Book (Baltimore: Johns Hopkins University Press, 1998), 94, 109.

86. Assistant Secretary of War to Judge Hastie, 2 July 1942, File X-Hastie, Judge Wm. H., Decimal File 291.2, General Correspondence of John J. McCloy, 1941–1945, Sec. of War, RG 107, NACP.

87. Lee, *The Employment of Negro Troops*, 331.

88. "South Carolina Speaks: 'Damned Agitators of North' Warned on Racial Interference," ProQuest Historical Newspapers, *The Washington Post*, 1 March 1944, 1. The resolution is discussed in Sterling A. Brown, "Count Us In," in *What the Negro Wants*, ed. Rayford W. Logan (Chapel Hill: University of North Carolina Press, 1944), 322.

89. Lee, *The Employment of Negro Troops,* 348–79; Harvard Sitkoff, "Racial Militancy and Interracial Violence in the Second World War," *Journal of American History* 58 (December 1971): 661–81; Neil A. Wynn, "The Impact of the Second World War on the American Negro," *Journal of Contemporary History* 6 (1971): 48–50; John Morton Blum, *V Was for Victory: Politics and American Culture during World War II* (San Diego: Harcourt Brace Jovanovich, 1976), 182–220.

90. Lee, *The Employment of Negro Troops,* 383–84.

91. War Department, Bureau of Public Relations, News Division, Future Release, January 1, 1945, 18–19, File 291.2, CMH.

92. Public Relations Section, HQ, Communications Zone, European Theater of Operations, Weekly Operations Bulletin No. 25, 13 August 1945, Bulletins, 1943–1946, Newspaper Clippings, Correspondence, Public Relations, USFET, RG 338, NACP.

93. Lee, *The Employment of Negro Troops,* 387–89; Mershon and Schlossman, *Foxholes and Color Lines,* 117–18.

94. *The Negro Soldier,* produced by the United States War Department, 42 min., 1944, distributed by National Audiovisual Center, 1979, videocassette. Memorandum to the War Department from Walter White, War Correspondent for the *New York Post,* and Secretary of the National Association for the Advancement of Colored People, 22 April 1944, 8, Decimal File 291.2, General Correspondence of John J. McCloy, 1941–1945, RG 107, NACP.

95. "Command of Negro Troops," War Department Pamphlet no. 20-6, 29 February 1944, 6–7, CMH; see also Lee, *The Employment of Negro Troops,* 389–91.

96. "Command of Negro Troops," 13, CMH.

97. "Leadership and the Negro Soldier," Army Service Forces Manual M5, October 1944, 26–34, CMH.

98. Benedict, *Race*; Margaret M. Caffrey, *Ruth Benedict: Stranger in This Land* (Austin: University of Texas Press, 1989), 282–300.

99. "Psychology for the Fighting Man: Prepared for the Fighting Man Himself by a Committee of the National Research Council with the Collaboration of Science Service as a Contribution to the War Effort," 2nd ed. (Washington, D.C.: Infantry Journal, Penguin Books, 1944), 335; Eva S. Moskowitz, *In Therapy We Trust: America's Obsession with Self-Fulfillment* (Baltimore: Johns Hopkins University Press, 2001), 116.

100. Lee, *The Employment of Negro Troops,* 393. In 1943, Congress cut funding for the Office of War Information after it was seen to push racial equality too vigorously. See Leila Rupp, *Mobilizing Women for War: German and American Propaganda, 1939–1945* (Princeton, N.J.: Princeton University Press, 1978), 92.

101. Sonya O. Rose, "Sex, Citizenship, and the Nation in World War II Britain," *AHR* 103 (1998): 1147–76; Graham Smith, *When Jim Crow Met John Bull: Black American Soldiers in World War II Britain* (London: I. B. Tauris & Co., 1987); Thomas E. Hachey, "Jim Crow with a British Accent: Attitudes of London Government Officials toward American Negro Soldiers in England during World War II," *Journal of Negro History* 59 (1974): 65–77; Lee, *The Employment of Negro Troops,* 627; Walter White, *A Man Called White* (New York: Arno Press and the New York Times, 1969), 257.

102. John J. McCloy to Assistant Chief of Staff, OPD, 19 September 1944, ASW 291.2 Negro Troops—F thru Z File, Decimal File 291.2, General Correspondence of John J. McCloy, 1941–1945, RG 107, NACP; Lieutenant General Thos. T. Handy,

Assistant Chief of Staff, War Department General Staff, Operations Division, to Assistant Secretary of War, John J. McCloy, 23 September 1944, ASW 291.2 Negro Troops—F thru Z File, Decimal File 291.2, General Correspondence of John J. McCloy, 1941–1945, RG 107, NACP.

103. Kleinschmidt, *"Do Not Fraternize,"* 172–73, quoting Memo for Record, 23 September 1944.

104. See "The Negro and Nazism," *Opportunity: Journal of Negro Life* (July 1940): 194–95; Jonathan Rosenberg, " 'Sounds Suspiciously Like Miami': Nazism and the U.S. Civil Rights Movement, 1933–1941," in *The Cultural Turn: Essays in the History of U.S. Foreign Relations,* ed. Frank Ninkovich and Liping Bu (Chicago: Imprint Publications, 2001), 105–30; Lee Finkle, "The Conservative Aims of Militant Rhetoric: Black Protest during World War II," *Journal of American History* 60 (December 1973): 701; Dan J. Puckett, "Hitler, Race, and Democracy in the Heart of Dixie: Alabamian Attitudes and Responses to the Issues of Nazi and Southern Racism, 1933–1946" (Ph.D. diss., Mississippi State University, 2005).

105. Finkle, "Conservative Aims," 692–713.

106. MacGregor, *Integration of the Armed Forces,* 56; Neil A. Wynn, *The Afro-American and the Second World War* (New York: Holmes & Meier Publishers, 1975), 21.

107. Gunnar Myrdal, *An American Dilemma: The Negro Problem and Modern Democracy* (New York: Harper & Brothers Publishers, 1944), 2:756; Bernard C. Nalty, *Strength for the Fight: A History of Black Americans in the Military* (New York: Free Press, 1986), 235–37; Renee C. Romano, *Race Mixing: Black-White Marriage in Postwar America* (Cambridge, Mass.: Harvard University Press, 2003), 13.

108. See Posner, "Afro-America in West German Perspective," 10, citing Günther Moltmann, "Amerikaklischees der deutschen Kriegspropaganda 1941–1945," *Amerikastudien* 31 (1986): 307; Beate Hoecker and Renate Meyer-Braun, *Bremerinnen bewältigen die Nachkriegszeit: Frauen, Alltag, Arbeit, Politik,* Frauen in Bremen, ed. Renate Meyer-Braun (Bremen: Steintor, 1988), 22–25; Lutz Niethammer, ed., *"Hinterher merkt man, daß es richtig war, daß es schiefgegangen ist": Nachkriegserfahrungen im Ruhrgebiet,* vol. 2, *Lebensgeschichte und Sozialkultur im Ruhrgebiet, 1930 bis 1960* (Berlin: Verlag J.H.W. Dietz Nachf., 1983), 23–34; Klaus Eyferth, Ursula Brandt, and Wolfgang Hawel, *Farbige Kinder in Deutschland: Die Situation der Mischlingskinder und die Aufgaben ihrer Eingliederung,* Schriftenreihe der Arbeitsgemeinschaft für Jugendpflege und Jugendfürsorge, no. 7 (Munich: Juventa Verlag, 1960), 73. See also the poster included in Moeller, *Protecting Motherhood,* after 108, figure 3.

109. See, e.g., Kleinschmidt, *"Do Not Fraternize,"* 98, 176–77; Lutz Niethammer, ed., *"Hinterher merkt man,"* 33–34; Eyferth, Brandt, and Hawel, *Farbige Kinder in Deutschland,* 73–74.

110. For the quotation, see Dörr, *"Wer die Zeit . . . ,"* 384–85. More generally, see ibid., 442; Bericht über Kriegsereignisse in Hockenheim, EAF, B2-35/150; unsigned, undated [1945] Denkschrift, EAF, Nachlaß Conrad Gröber, Nb8/63. On the wave of rapes committed by Soviet troops, see Norman M. Naimark, *The Russians in Germany: A History of the Soviet Zone of Occupation, 1945–1949* (Cambridge: Belknap Press of Harvard University Press, 1995), 69–140.

111. See generally Berichte über Kriegsereignisse, EAF, B2-35/147–150.

112. See, e.g., J. De Lattre de Tassigny to Archbishop of Freiburg Conrad Gröber, 6 May 1945, EAF, B2-35/142; see also F. Roy Willis, *The French in Germany, 1945–1949* (Stanford, Calif.: Stanford University Press, 1962), 70–74.

113. On rapes in the Bruchsal area, see Berichte über Kriegsereignisse in Stadtpfarramt St. Peter zu Bruchsal, 15 June 1945, Stadtpfarramt St. Paul, Bruchsal, and Stadtpfarramt der Hofkirche Bruchsal, 7 March 1945, EAF, B2-35/147. On "African law of war," see Berichte über Kriegsereignisse in Stadtpfarramt der Hofkirche Bruchsal, 7 March 1945, EAF, B2-35/147.

114. Joseph R. Starr, "Fraternization with the Germans in World War II," Occupation Forces in Europe Series 1945–1946, no. 67 (Frankfurt a.M.: Office of the Chief Historian, Headquarters European Command, 1947), 81–82.

115. Historischen Kommission bei der Bayerischen Akademie der Wissenschaften und der Generaldirektion der Staatlichen Archive Bayerns, ed., *Die Protokolle des Bayerischen Ministerrats, 1945–1954*, vol. 1, *Das Kabinett Schäffer: 28. Mai bis 28. September 1945*, ed. Karl-Ulrich Gelberg (Munich: R. Oldenbourg Verlag, 1995), 179; Fehrenbach, *Race after Hitler*, 56–61; Fehrenbach, "Rehabilitating Father*land*," 110–14; Atina Grossmann, "A Question of Silence: The Rape of German Women by Occupation Soldiers," in *West Germany under Construction: Politics, Society, and Culture in the Adenauer Era*, ed. Robert G. Moeller (Ann Arbor: University of Michigan Press, 1997), 46–47; Atina Grossmann, *Reforming Sex: The German Movement for Birth Control and Abortion Reform, 1920 to 1950* (New York: Oxford University Press, 1995), 192–93; Stephenson, *Women in Nazi Society*, 62.

116. Report of the Theater Judge Advocate European Theater of Operations, United States Army and United States Forces, European Theater, 4 April 1942 to 3 April 1946, 72, Records of the United States Army, Judge Advocate General, RG 153, NACP. A similar disproportion appeared in the number of whites and blacks convicted and executed for murder.

117. "A Double Standard of Morals," *Chicago Defender*, 28 April 1945, 12, and other clippings in April 1945 File; Press Items re: Negro Newspapers, 1944–1946 (Analysis Branch), Office of Public Information, Office of the Secretary of Defense, RG 330, NACP.

118. Two African Americans, e.g., were cleared of rape charges, notwithstanding serious contradictions in their stories, on the ground that the alleged victim had consented. Report of Confidential Investigation 508 CID, 10 November 1945, Special Courts Martial Case Files, JAG Section, Headquarters, Third Army, RG 338, NACP.

119. See Fehrenbach, *Race after Hitler*, 62; Fehrenbach, "Rehabilitating Father*land*," 113–14. I date the supplanting of the image of the German woman as victim by the woman as villain somewhat earlier than Fehrenbach.

120. Erzbischöfl. Pfarrkuratie Mannheim-Wallstadt, 11 June 1945, EAF, B2-35/149 (vol. 3, Dekenate: Konstanz-Neuenburg).

121. Bericht über Kriegsereignisse in Jöhlingen, 10 July 1945, 5, EAF, B2-35/147.

122. Rüdiger Overmans, *Deutsche militärische Verluste im Zweiten Weltkrieg*, Beiträge zur Militärgeschichte, Bd. 46 (Munich: R. Oldenbourg Verlag, 1999).

123. Hans-Ulrich Wehler, *Deutsche Gesellschaftsgeschichte*, vol. 4, *Vom Beginn des Ersten Weltkriegs bis zur Gründung der beiden deutschen Staaten, 1914–1949* (Munich: Verlag C. H. Beck, 2003), 941–46; Günter J. Trittel, "Ernährung," in *Deutschland unter alliierter Besatzung, 1945–1949/55*, ed. Wolfgang Benz (Berlin: Akademie Verlag, 1999), 117–23; Johannes-Dieter Steinert, "Flüchtlinge und Vertriebene," in *Deutschland unter alliierter Besatzung*, 123–29; Karl Christian Führer, "Wohnungen,"

in *Deutschland unter allierter Besatzung,* 206–9. For the calorie ration, see Clay, *Decision in Germany,* 264.

124. On the wave of rapes committed by Soviet troops, see Naimark, *The Russians in Germany,* 69–140. On the U.S. nonfraternization policy, see Starr, "Fraternization with the Germans"; Kleinschmidt, *"Do Not Fraternize."*

125. Werner Bührer, "Schwarzer Markt," in *Deutschland unter allierter Besatzung,* 365–66. For the calorie ration, see Clay, *Decision in Germany,* 268.

126. Carolyn Eisenberg, *Drawing the Line: The American Decision to Divide Germany, 1944–1949* (New York: Cambridge University Press, 1996); Naimark, *The Russians in Germany.*

127. Wolfgang Benz, "Währungsreform," in *Deutschland unter allierter Besatzung,* 190–94.

128. Benedict, *Race,* 176–77; see also Jacobson, *Whiteness of a Different Color,* 94–108.

129. Minutes of German Committee Meeting on 6 April 1945, 14, German Committee Minutes, October 1944, Agenda and Minutes of the German Committee, Central Control Division, 1944–1945, OWI, RG 208, NACP.

130. Information Control: Monthly Report of Military Governor No. 9, 20 April 1946, 3.

131. In 1946, Saul Padover referred to the Germans as "no longer members of the community of peoples but a race apart, cursed and feared as no race has ever been in recorded history." Saul K. Padover, *Experiment in Germany: The Story of an American Intelligence Officer* (New York: Duell, Sloan, and Pearce, 1946), 400; see also Michaela Hönicke, "'Know Your Enemy': American Interpretations of National Socialism, 1933–1945" (Ph.D. diss., University of North Carolina, 1998), 247, 249, 254, 260.

132. Dörr, *"Wer die Zeit . . . ,"* 393.

133. Hoecker and Meyer-Braun, *Bremerinnen bewältigen die Nachkriegszeit,* 22–23.

134. David Rodnick, *Postwar Germans: An Anthropologist's Account* (New Haven, Conn.: Yale University Press, 1948), 192.

135. Quoted in Reiß, *"Die Schwarzen waren unsere Freunde,"* 313–14; emphasis original. On race and the war against Japan, see John W. Dower, *War without Mercy: Race and Power in the Pacific War* (New York: Pantheon Books, 1986). Petra Goedde notes that "[r]acial and cultural similarities between Germans and white Americans" distinguished the American occupation of Germany from the occupation of Japan. Goedde, *GIs and Germans: Culture, Gender, and Foreign Relations, 1945–1949* (New Haven, Conn.: Yale University Press, 2003), xix.

136. Unsigned, undated [1945] Denkschrift, EAF, Nachlaß Conrad Gröber, Nb8/63.

137. Ika Hügel-Marshall, *Invisible Woman: Growing Up Black in Germany,* trans. Elizabeth Gaffney (New York: Continuum, 2001), 18.

138. Richard L. Gunn, *Art and Politics in Wolfgang Koeppen's Postwar Trilogy,* Germanic Languages and Literatures, vol. 26 (New York: Peter Lang, 1983), 18.

139. Wolfgang Koeppen, *Pigeons on the Grass,* trans. David Ward (New York: Holmes & Meier, 1988), 11; Koeppen, *Tauben im Gras* (Stuttgart: Scherz & Goverts Verlag, 1951), 21.

140. Koeppen, *Pigeons on the Grass,* 49; Koeppen, *Tauben im Gras,* 59.

141. Koeppen, *Pigeons on the Grass,* 143, 145.

142. Ibid., 184, 185, 191–93.

143. G-1 Division, Supreme Headquarters Allied Expeditionary Force, Memorandum regarding Conduct of Allied Troops and German Characteristics in Defeat, August 1944, 1, Division Records, G-1, SHAEF, RG 331, NACP.

144. Civil Affairs Division, "Pocket Guide to Germany" (1945), 3, 4, 9, 16, 21, CMH; Non-fraternization Spot Announcement Number 18, attached to Lieutenant Colonel John S. Hayes, Associate Director, Troop Broadcasting Services, Supreme Headquarters Allied Expeditionary Force (Rear), G-1, Directorate of Troop Broadcasting Services, to Lieutenant Colonel R. M. Furber, G-1 Division, SHAEF (Main), 16 March 1945, Division Records, G-1 Division, RG 331, NACP, emphasis original. See also Kleinschmidt, *"Do Not Fraternize,"* 38.

145. Civil Affairs Division, "Pocket Guide to Germany," 16; emphasis original.

146. G-1 Division, Supreme Headquarters Allied Expeditionary Force, August 1944, 2, Div. Records, G-1, RG 331, NACP.

147. *Your Job in Germany,* produced by International Historic Films, 32 min., originally produced by the Army Pictorial Service for Army Information Branch, Information and Education Division, A.S.F., and by the Army Pictorial Service, Signal Corps, 1985, videocassette.

148. "U.S. to Be 'Hard' with Germans; Eisenhower Orders Strict Rule," *New York Times,* 23 September 1944, 1.

149. Military Government—Germany, Law No. 1, Abrogation of Nazi Law, Art. II, in Ruth Hemken, ed., *Sammlung der vom Allierten Kontrollrat und der Amerikanischen Militärregierung erlassenen Proklamationen, Gesetze, Verordnungen, Befehle, Direktiven* (Stuttgart: Deutsche Verlags-Anstalt, 1947). See also James K. Pollock, James H. Meisel, and Henry L. Bretton, eds., *Germany under Occupation: Illustrative Materials and Documents* (Ann Arbor, Mich.: George Wahr Publishing Co., 1949), 115–16.

150. Headquarters, Civil Censorship Division, U.S. Forces, European Theater, Censorship Order No. 43, 23 May 1946, Reports, Civil Censorship Division, RG 338, NACP. See also Control Council Order No. 4, Confiscation of Literature and Material of a Nazi and Militarist Nature," 13 May 1946, in *Sammlung der vom Allierten Kontrollrat,* ed. Hemken.

151. Policy Instruction Number 3 to all Licensees in German Information Services, 30 September 1946, Policy File, Records of the Director and Deputy Director, 1945–1949, Records of the Division Headquarters, ICD, RG 260, NACP; see also Joseph Dunner, "Information Control in the American Zone of Germany, 1945–1946," in *American Experiences in Military Government in World War II,* ed. Carl J. Friedrich and Associates (New York: Rinehart & Company, 1948), 284; Report, U.S. Group Control Council, Information Control in Germany, 28 September 1945, quoted in Boyd L. Dastrup, *Crusade in Nuremberg: Military Occupation, 1945–1949* (Westport, Conn.: Greenwood Press, 1985), 78.

152. Lieutenant Colonel Richard J. Jackson, Chief, Governmental Affairs Branch, OMGBY, to Minster of Justice for Bavaria, 14 November 1945, with attachment, BayHStA, StK 13630.

153. Headquarters, Civil Censorship Division, U.S. Forces, European Theater, Censorship Order No. 30, 28 March 1946, Reports, Civil Censorship Division, RG 338, NACP. On censorship policies generally, see Office of the Chief Historian, European Command, "Censorship," Occupation Forces in Europe Series 1945–1946 (Frankfurt a.M.: Office of the Chief Historian, European Command, 1947).

154. African Americans Baxter Scruggs, Marcus Ray, and Barrington Dunbar spoke before America House audiences. See Report from Exhibitions and Information Centers Branch, ISD, OMGBY, to Director, Office of Military Government for Bavaria, 12 May 1949, Records re: activities of the ICEB 1945–1949, ICEB, ICD, RG 260, NACP; America House Regensburg, Narrative Statement to Weekly Report 2 April to 3 May 1949, 2, Records re: activities of the ICEB 1945–1949, ICEB, ICD, RG 260, NACP; Marcus Ray, "Der Amerikanische Neger," Records relating to U.S. Information Centers, 1949, ICEB, ICD, RG 260, NACP; Patrick H. Byrne to Chief, IC & E Branch, 19 January 1949, Records relating to U.S. Information Centers, 1949, ICEB, ICD, RG 260, NACP; Report of Activities at U.S. Information Center Karlsruhe, 21 April to 20 May 1949, Records re: activities of the ICEB 1945–1949, ICEB, ICD, RG 260, NACP; Information Services (Cumulative Review): Report of the Military Governor No. 48, 1 July 1948–30 June 1949, 59; Maritta Hein-Kremer, *Die amerikanische Kulturoffensive: Gründung und Entwicklung der amerikanischen Information Centers in Westdeutschland und West-Berlin, 1945–1955*, Beiträge zur Geschichte der Kulturpolitik, ed. Kurt Düwell, vol. 6 (Köln: Böhlau Verlag, 1996), 312–13. On African American music, see Chapter 5.

155. C. S. Wright, Text of Radio Address, December 1948, Script for Military Government Broadcast over Radio Munich File, General Records, 1945–1949, Weißenburg RLSO, FOD, OMGBY, RG 260, NACP.

156. Brigadier General Robert A. McClure memorandum on Documentary Films, 11 May 1946, appendix A-2, U.S. Official Documentaries File, Records Relating to Motion Picture Production and Distribution, 1945–1949, Records of the Motion Picture Branch, ICD, RG 260, NACP. See Comments forwarded by Major Edward T. Peeples, Executive Officer to Reorientation Branch, Civil Affairs Division, War Department, Attn: Colonel McRae, 16 September 1946, Documentaries: General File, Records Relating to Motion Picture Production and Distribution, 1945–1949, Records of the Motion Picture Branch, ICD, RG 260, NACP; Information Services (Cumulative Review): Report of the Military Governor No. 48, 1 July 1948–30 June 1949, 39, 64.

157. For this issue in the context of the American effort to re-educate German prisoners of war in the United States, see Reiß, *"Die Schwarzen waren unsere Freunde,"* 282–305.

158. Joseph Dunner, Memorandum on German Ideas about the United Nations, especially the U.S.A., 1 May 1945, 2, German Committee–London File, Records of the Historian, Psychological Warfare Branch, 1942–1945, RG 208, NACP.

159. Cardinal Graf von Galen's speech in Rome, March 1946, 8, IfZ, Nachlaß Hoegner, Bd. 127.

160. On Soviet criticisms of American mistreatment of African Americans and the American reaction, see Information Control Division, "Soviet Propaganda Practices in Germany," November 1947, Records re: Information Control, Control Office Headquarters, RG 260, NACP; Clay, *Decision in Germany*, 157; Posner, "Afro-America in West German Perspective," 33; "Die falsche Stimme," *Tägliche Rundschau*, 13 April 1947, 2. The article asserted that the Voice of America "claims that the American constitution grants all citizens of the USA the same rights, regardless of race, but forgets that the situation of Negroes in the USA is known in the Soviet Union."

161. Thomas Borstelmann and Mary Dudziak convincingly argue that domestic American battles over civil rights became inseparable from their foreign policy

implications, but they do not examine the German setting where that connection emerged. See Borstelmann, *The Cold War and the Color Line*; Mary Dudziak, *Cold War Civil Rights: Race and the Image of American Democracy* (Princeton, N.J.: Princeton University Press, 2000); Dudziak, "Desegregation as a Cold War Imperative," *Stanford Law Review* 41 (November 1988): 61–120. Although the German context does not receive consideration in Brenda Gayle Plummer's *Rising Wind: Black Americans and U.S. Foreign Affairs, 1935–1960* (Chapel Hill: University of North Carolina Press, 1996), she considers the children born to German mothers and African American fathers in Plummer, "Brown Babies." The issue of race figured prominently in ICD's October 1947 study of means to effectively answer Soviet propaganda. See ICD Opinion Survey No. 73, "A Guide to Some Propaganda Problems," 28 October 1947, Political Information Program File, Records of the Director and Deputy Director, 1945–1949, Division Headquarters, ICD, RG 260, NACP.

162. Roi Ottley, "Tan GIs Attacked Unfairly," *Pittsburgh Courier*, 28 December 1946, clipping in Press Items re: Negro Newspapers, 1944–1946 (Analysis Branch), Office of Public Information, RG 330, NACP.

163. Marcus Ray, "Der Amerikanische Neger"; Patrick H. Byrne to Chief, IC & E Branch, 19 January 1949.

164. Marcus Ray, "Der Amerikanische Neger," 7.

165. Bergmann, *Antisemitismus in öffentlichen Konflikten*, 65–66. See also, e.g., Dr. Johannes Grünig, Staatsanwalt beim Amtsgericht in Wunsiedel, Vorschlag zur Neuorganisation der deutschen Jugend, November 1945, 3–4, IfZ, Nachlaß Hoegner, Bd. 117. For a wartime critique of the Nazi idolatry of the Nordic race, see Gröber to Pius XII, 2 February 1944, in Ludwig Volk, ed., *Akten deutscher Bischöfe über die Lage der Kirche 1933–1945*, vol. 6, *1943–1945*, Veröffentlichungen der Kommission für Zeitgeschichte, Bd. 38 (Mainz: Matthias-Grünewald-Verlag, 1985), 310.

166. See Stern, *The Whitewashing of the Yellow Badge*, xii, xv; MacMaster, *Racism in Europe*, 167–77. See also Dewey A. Browder, *Americans in Post–World War II Germany: Teachers, Tinkers, Neighbors and Nuisances* (Lewiston, N.Y.: Edwin Mellen Press, 1998), 103; René Klein to Archbishop Gröber, 15 April 1946, EAF, Nachlaß Conrad Gröber, Nb8/67, charging that war crimes committed by Germans included the "lynching" of Negro aviators who parachuted onto German territory.

167. Wilhelm Karl Gerst, "Rassismus: Die Lehre von der Vernichtung der 'niederen' Rassen," *Frankfurter Rundschau*, 15 September 1945, 4.

168. On the Cologne statement, see Rolf Steininger, *Deutsche Geschichte seit 1945: Darstellung und Dokumente in vier Bänden*, vol. 1, *1945–1947* (Frankfurt a.M.: Fischer Taschenbuch Verlag, 1996), 122–24. For the Bavarian CSU's statement, see "Die dreißig Punkte der Union: Richtlinien der Christlich-Sozialen Union in Bayern zur Überwindung der inneren und äußeren Not unseres Volkes," in *Nachkriegsdeutschland, 1945–1949*, ed. Peter Bucher, Quellen zum politischen Denken der Deutschen im 19. und 20. Jahrhundert, vol. 10 (Darmstadt: Wissenschaftliche Buchgesellschaft, 1990), 246.

169. "Dr. Hoegners Münchner Rede: Der Weg in Bayern," *Frankfurter Rundschau*, 4 December 1945, 1. See also Ansprache des bayerischen Ministerpräsidenten am 27.1.1946 vor dem Ausschuss der befreiten Juden in Bayern, IfZ, Nachlaß Hoegner, Bd. 281.

170. On conservative assessments, see Axel Schildt, *Zwischen Abendland und Amerika: Studien zur westdeutschen Ideenlandschaft der 50er Jahre*, Ordnungssyteme:

Studien zur Ideengeschichte der Neuzeit, ed. Dietrich Beyrau, Anselm Doering-Manteuffel, and Lutz Raphael, vol. 4 (Munich: R. Oldenbourg Verlag, 1999); Maria Mitchell, "Materialism and Secularism: CDU Politicians and National Socialism, 1945–1949," *The Journal of Modern History* 67 (1995): 278–308.

171. See Grimm, "Germans, Blacks, and Jews"; Mosse, *Toward the Final Solution,* xi; Gilman, *On Blackness without Blacks.* The Nazi Party certification form is quoted in Proctor, *Racial Hygiene,* 114. On European-wide pairings of blacks and Jews, see MacMaster, *Racism in Europe,* 209–17; Robert Philipson, *The Identity Question: Blacks and Jews in Europe and America* (Jackson: University Press of Mississippi, 2000).

172. Maggie M. Morehouse, *Fighting in the Jim Crow Army: Black Men and Women Remember World War II* (Lanham, Md.: Rowman & Littlefield, 2000), 194; Dr. Halter to Dr. Pierre M. Purves, 28 April 1949, BayHStA, StK 14950.

173. See Bergmann, *Antisemitismus in öffentlichen Konflikten,* 67, 184; Stern, *Whitewashing the Yellow Badge*; Stern, "The Historic Triangle: Occupiers, Germans and Jews in Postwar Germany," in *West Germany under Construction,* ed. Moeller, 199–229. Jacobson notes that the mid-twentieth-century American critique of the national/racial typology in favor of the tripartite division lent further weight to the black/white racial distinction. Jacobson, *Whiteness of a Different Color,* 102–8. Jews remained in occupied Germany, as Atina Grossmann explores in "Trauma, Memory, and Motherhood: Germans and Jewish Displaced Persons in Post-Nazi Germany, 1945–1949," in *Life after Death: Approaches to a Cultural and Social History of Europe during the 1940s and 1950s,* ed. Richard Bessel and Dirk Schumann (Cambridge: German Historical Institute, Washington, D.C., and Cambridge University Press, 2003), 93–127. On anti-Semitism among the American occupiers, see Suzanne Brown-Fleming, "'The Worst Enemies of a Better Germany': Postwar Antisemitism among Catholic Clergy and U.S. Occupation Forces," *Holocaust and Genocide Studies* 18 (2004): 379–401.

174. Headquarters, USFET, Office of the Assistant Chief of Staff, G-2, Weekly Intelligence Summary No. 29, 31 January 1946, 58, Weekly Intelligence Summary–U.S. Forces, European Theater, Publications ("P") Files, 1946–1951, Document Library Branch, Administrative Division, Asst. Chief of Staff (G-2) Intelligence, Records of the Army Staff, RG 319, NACP.

175. See, e.g., Leo Bogart, *How I Earned the Ruptured Duck: From Brooklyn to Berchtesgaden in World War II* (College Station: Texas A&M University Press, 2004), 103. On the postwar taboo on the subject of race, see Sieg, *Ethnic Drag,* 2; Otger Autrata et al., "Ausgangspunkte und Fragestellungen," in *Theorien über Rassismus: Eine Tübinger Veranstaltungsreihe,* ed. Otger Autrata et al. (Hamburg: Argument-Verlag, 1989), 26; Poiger, *Jazz, Rock, and Rebels,* 8. On the dramatic change in scientific and medical work, see Proctor, *Racial Hygiene,* 303–5. Although it is true that many scientists who had collaborated eagerly with the Nazi regime managed to continue their work after 1945, nevertheless such continuities depended on skillful adaptation to a significantly altered political landscape. See Mitchell G. Ash, "Verordnete Umbrüche—Konstruierte Kontinuitäten: Zur Entnazifizierung von Wissenschaftlern und Wissenschaften nach 1945," *Zeitschrift für Geschichtswissenschaft* 43 (1995): 903–23. Werner Bergmann's analysis is instructive, as he points out that with the defeat of the Third Reich, Nazi anti-Semitism was discredited on the public level practically "over night," leaving a tension between the public repudiation of anti-Semitism and many individuals' private anti-Semitism. Bergmann, *Antisemitismus in öffentlichen Konflikten,* 12.

176. Hans Fischer, *Völkerkunde im Nationalsozialismus: Aspekte der Anpassung, Affinität und Behauptung einer Wissenschaftlichen Disziplin,* Hamburger Beiträge zur Wissenschaftsgeschichte, Bd. 7 (Berlin: Dietrich Reimer Verlag, 1990), 47–50, quoting on page 49 Robert Pfaff-Giesberg, *Die Sklaverei: Ein wirtschaftliches, soziales und kulturelles Problem* (Stuttgart, 1935), 36; Pfaff-Giesberg, *Geschichte der Sklaverei* (Meisenheim/Glan, 1955), 49.

177. Rodnick, *Postwar Germans,* 191–92.

Chapter 2: Blackness and German Whiteness through American Eyes

1. Brigadier General R. B. Lovett to the AG, War Department, 1 October 1945, 13, File 291.2, AG Correspondence, 1945, RG 338, NACP; Headquarters, Seventh Army, to Commanding General, USFET, 7 August 1945, 16, File 291.2, AG Correspondence, 1945, RG 338, NACP.

2. Lieutenant Colonel Walter E. Forry to Commanding General, Third U.S. Army, 8 July 1945, 9, File 291.2, AG Correspondence, 1945, RG 338, NACP.

3. Major George J. Balog to Commanding General, Third U.S. Army, 15 July 1945, 2, File 291.2, AG Correspondence, 1945, RG 338, NACP.

4. G-2 Weekly Intelligence Report No. 52, 15, File 319.1, G-2 General Correspondence 1944–1947, Third Army, RG 338, NACP.

5. "Reactions of Germans to Negro Troops," Information Control Intelligence Summary No. 16, 27 October 1945, 1, 2, Records Relating to Public Opinion, 1945–1949, Opinion Surveys Branch, ICD, RG 260, NACP.

6. Robert Schmid, Daily Intelligence Digest No. 246, 11 September 1946, File 291.2, Classified General Correspondence, 1946, Secretary, General Staff, RG 338, NACP; Office of the Inspector General, Headquarters, Continental Base Section, USFET, to Commanding General, Continental Base Section, USFET, 17 August 1946, File 333.5, Classified General Correspondence 1946, AG, RG 338, NACP.

7. ICD Opinion Survey No 24, "Mannheim Attitudes toward Negro Troops," 22 October 1946, 4–5, Records Relating to Public Opinion, 1945–1949, Opinion Surveys Branch, ICD, RG 260, NACP. The survey is discussed in Anna J. Merritt and Richard L. Merritt, eds., *Public Opinion in Occupied Germany: The OMGUS Surveys, 1945–1949,* with a Foreword by Frederick W. Williams (Urbana: University of Illinois Press, 1970), 10, 107–8.

8. ICD Opinion Survey No. 24, "Mannheim Attitudes toward Negro Troops," 22 October 1946, 3, 5; Merritt and Merritt, *Public Opinion,* 10, 107–8.

9. Ibid., 31, 99, 39, 210, 146.

10. Major General W. S. Paul to Chief of Staff, 21 January 1947, 4, File 291.2, G-1 Decimal File, 1946–1948, War Department General and Special Staffs, RG 165, NACP.

11. MacGregor, *Integration of the Armed Forces,* 130–43; War Department Theater AG to Commander-in-Chief, Southwest Pacific Area et al., 23 May 1945, in *Planning for the Postwar Employment of Black Personnel,* vol. 7, *Blacks in the United States Armed Forces: Basic Documents,* ed. Morris J. MacGregor Jr. and Bernard C. Nalty (Wilmington, Del.: Scholarly Resources, 1977), 11–15.

12. Lovett to the AG, War Department, 1 October 1945, 9–10. For a similar assessment crediting successes to white officers, see Major Bell I. Wiley, "The Training of Negro Troops," Army Ground Forces Study No. 36, 1946, in *Planning for the Postwar Employment of Black Personnel,* ed. MacGregor and Nalty, 266.

13. MacGregor, *Integration of the Armed Forces,* 136–38, 151.

14. Brigadier General T. M. Obsorne [*sic*], Memorandum for the Assistant Secretary of War, 1 November 1946, 4, File 333.5, Classified General Correspondence, 1945–1946, Secretary, General Staff, RG 338, NACP.

15. Lee, *The Employment of Negro Troops,* 241–44. Anthropologist Alfred Kroeber had shown that northern blacks scored better than southern whites on predecessor army mental tests. Barkan, *The Retreat of Scientific Racism,* 94.

16. See Margaret L. Geis, "Negro Personnel in the European Command, 1 January 1946–30 June 1950," Occupation Forces in Europe Series (Karlsruhe: Historical Division, European Command, 1952), 60, CMH. The view continued to hold currency long after the war. See Brian Arthur Libby, "Policing Germany: The United States Constabulary, 1946–1952" (Ph.D. diss., Purdue University, 1977), 44; Lee, *The Employment of Negro Troops,* 244–45, 273–74. A few commanders believed that AGCT scores had little or no bearing on their soldiers' aptitude. Ibid., 255.

17. Transcript of Press Conference given by Mr. Marcus Ray, Frankfurt, Germany, 23 November 1946, 2, File 291.2, Classified General Correspondence, 1946, Secretary, General Staff, RG 338, NACP.

18. MacGregor, *Integration of the Armed Forces,* 184–85.

19. Forry to Commanding General, Third U.S. Army, 8 July 1945, 2.

20. Lovett to the AG, War Department, 1 October 1945, 10.

21. Geis, "Negro Personnel in the European Command," in *Segregation under Siege,* vol. 8, *Blacks in the United States Armed Forces: Basic Documents,* ed. Morris J. MacGregor Jr. and Bernard C. Nalty (Wilmington, Del.: Scholarly Resources, 1977), 148. On the method of calculating the rate and a defense of the conduct of troops in Germany, see Clay, *Decision in Germany,* 230–31. On the postwar "explosion of GI crime," see John Willoughby, *Remaking the Conquering Heroes: The Social and Geopolitical Impact of the Post-War American Occupation of Germany* (New York: Palgrave, 2001), 16–18. For an attempt to explain the higher venereal disease rate among black troops, see John Willoughby, "The Sexual Behavior of American GIs during the Early Years of the Occupation of Germany," *The Journal of Military History* 62 (1998): 166n31.

22. MacGregor, *Integration of the Armed Forces,* 206–7.

23. War Department Circular No. 188, 26 June 1946, File 291.2, G-1 Decimal File, 1946–1948, RG 165, NACP; Marcus H. Ray to Howard C. Petersen, 23 May 1946, File 291.2, G-1 Decimal File, 1946–1948, RG 165, NACP; Summary by Major General W. S. Paul, Director of Personnel and Administration, 11 June 1946, File 291.2, G-1 Decimal File, 1946–1948, RG 165, NACP.

24. See, e.g., "GI's in Europe Hounded by Bias," Baltimore *Afro-American,* 22 June 1946; Bill Smith, "Innocent Soldier Goes on Rampage; Kills 1, Wounds 3," *Pittsburgh Courier,* 25 January 1947, clippings in Press Items re: Negro Newspapers, 1944–1946 (Analysis Branch), Office of Public Information, RG 330, NACP; see also Alice Kaplan, *The Interpreter* (New York: Free Press, 2005).

25. Forry to Commanding General, Third U.S. Army, 8 July 1945, 3.

26. Brigadier General Edward T. Williams to G-3, 9 July 1945, 4, File 291.2, AG Correspondence, 1945, RG 338, NACP.

27. The eight recommendations were taken almost verbatim from the artillery officer's report. Compare Williams to G-3, 9 July 1945, 2–3, and Lovett to AG, War Department, 1 October 1945, 8.

28. See Appendix D, "Summary of Venereal Disease Statistics during World War II," in Medical Department, United States Army, *Preventive Medicine in World War II,* vol. 5, *Communicable Diseases Transmitted through Contact or by Unknown Means,* prepared and published under the direction of Lieutenant General Leonard D. Heaton, the Surgeon General, United States Army (Washington, D.C.: Office of the Surgeon General, Department of the Army, 1960), 469.

29. MacGregor, *Integration of the Armed Forces,* 207; see also Willoughby, *Remaking the Conquering Heroes,* 67–69.

30. Lieutenant Colonel John F. George to Commanding General, XII Corps, Attention: Assistant Chief of Staff, G-3, 12 July 1945, 4, File 291.2, AG Correspondence, 1945, RG 338, NACP. Major Bell Wiley likewise believed that white officers would prefer not to command black units. See Wiley, "The Training of Negro Troops," in *Planning for the Postwar Employment of Black Personnel,* ed. MacGregor and Nalty, 269. For attitudes of white officers early in the war, see MacGregor, *Integration of the Armed Forces,* 37.

31. Forry to Commanding General, Third U.S. Army, 8 July 1945, 11.

32. Captain Paul V. Lenz to Commanding General, XII Corps, 12 July 1945, 1, File 291.2, AG Correspondence, 1945, RG 338, NACP.

33. Williams to G-3, 9 July 1945, 9.

34. Testimony of Lieutenant Colonel John D. Salmon, Exhibit B-1, to Lieutenant Colonel D. M. Witt, Inspector General, Headquarters VI Corps, Office of the Inspector General, Report of Investigation of Alleged Misconduct of U.S. Troops in Kreis Kunzelsau, Germany, to Commanding General, VI Corps, 30 November 1945, 10, File 333.5, AG Classified General Correspondence, 1945, RG 338, NACP.

35. "Command of Negro Troops," 11, quoted in Lee, *The Employment of Negro Troops,* 391.

36. MacGregor, *Integration of the Armed Forces,* 212. The fact that African Americans were court-martialed at a disproportionately high rate does not mean that white officers pressed all cases or felt pressure not to bring cases against African Americans.

37. Nelson Peery, *Black Fire: The Making of an American Revolutionary* (New York: New Press, 1994), 89; Major Robert F. Shearer to Commanding General, Continental Base Section, 6 August 1946, Tab B, File 291.2, AG Classified Correspondence, 1946, RG 338, USFET, NACP.

38. Lovett to the AG, War Department, 1 October 1945, 12.

39. The quotation comes from Colonel A. J. deLorimer to Commanding General, Third U.S. Army, 14 July 1945, 4, File 291.2, AG Correspondence, 1945, RG 338, NACP. See also Lenz to Commanding General, XII Corps, 12 July 1945, 2; Captain Lewis H. Keyes to Commanding General, Headquarters XII Corps, 12 July 1945, 2, File 291.2, AG Correspondence, 1945, RG 338, NACP.

40. Brigadier General L. S. Ostrander to Commanding Generals, 19 April 1946, File 291.2, AG Classified Correspondence, 1946, RG 338, USFET, NACP.

41. Note from G-3 to C/S, 2 December 1946, File 291.2, Classified General Correspondence, 1946, Secretary, General Staff, RG 338, NACP; SGS USFET to AC/S G-3, 25 November 1946, attaching memo for record by General Huebner, Chief of Staff, File 291.2, Classified General Correspondence, 1946, Secretary, General Staff, RG 338, NACP.

42. Report AG-(OT)-70 regarding utilization of Negro personnel, to the AG, War Department, 15 April 1947, File 291.2, General Correspondence, 1947, AG Division, EUCOM, RG 338, NACP.

43. Lenz to Commanding General, XII Corps, 12 July 1945, 2.

44. Brigadier General Roderick R. Allen to General Huebner, 11 September 1946, File 291.2, Classified General Correspondence, 1946, Secretary, General Staff, RG 338, NACP.

45. See Harald Thomas Oskar Leder, "Americans and German Youth in Nuremberg, 1945–1956: A Study in Politics and Culture" (Ph.D. diss., Louisiana State University, 1997), 92–93. On relations between African Americans and the police, see Myrdal, *An American Dilemma,* 1:527–59.

46. Colonel Lester J. Abele to Commanding General, XII Corps, 13 July 1945, File 291.2, AG Correspondence, 1945, RG 338, NACP; John Willoughby likewise believes "superior mobility" of black GIs played a role in higher misconduct. See *Remaking the Conquering Heroes,* 67.

47. See Colonel C. M. Spainhour to Commanding General, United States Air Forces in Europe, 2 February 1946, File 333.5, Classified General Correspondence, 1945, USFET AG, RG 338, NACP; Geis, "Negro Personnel in the European Command," 18; Morehouse, *Fighting in the Jim Crow Army,* 185–90.

48. Special Inspector General Board, Headquarters European Theater, to Chief of Staff, Headquarters USFET, 23 July 1946, Tab E, 18, File 320.2, AG Classified Correspondence, 1946, RG 338, NACP.

49. Report of the Negro Newspaper Publishers Association to the Honorable Secretary of War, Judge Robert P. Patterson, on Troops and Conditions in Europe, 18 July 1946, in *Segregation under Siege,* ed. MacGregor and Nalty, 23.

50. Office of Military Government for Greater Hesse, Office of Chief of Intelligence, "Misconduct of Troops," 5 March 1947, quoted in Kleinschmidt, *"Do Not Fraternize,"* 181.

51. Truman K. Gibson Jr. to Assistant Secretary McCloy, 8 August 1945, in *Planning for the Postwar Employment of Black Personnel,* ed. MacGregor and Nalty, 19.

52. Lieutenant Colonel J. W. Dougherty to Commanding General, XII Corps, 11 July 1945, 2–3, File 291.2, AG Correspondence, 1945, RG 338, NACP.

53. DeLorimer to Commanding General, Third U.S. Army, 14 July 1945, 5.

54. Lieutenant Colonel Edmund G. Murphy, Asst. XII Corps Chaplain, Headquarters, XII Corps, Office of the Chaplain, 9 July 1945, File 291.2, AG Correspondence, 1945, RG 338, NACP.

55. Memorandum, Ground AG for Chief of Staff, U.S. Army, 28 November 1945, in *Planning for the Postwar Employment of Black Personnel,* ed. MacGregor and Nalty, 103, 118; MacGregor, *Integration of the Armed Forces,* 139.

56. Memorandum, Ground AG for Chief of Staff, U.S. Army, 28 November 1945, in *Planning for the Postwar Employment of Black Personnel,* ed. MacGregor and Nalty, 119.

57. Ibid.

58. Wiley, "The Training of Negro Troops," in *Planning for the Postwar Employment of Black Personnel,* ed. MacGregor and Nalty, 283.

59. War Department Circular No. 124, "Utilization of Negro Manpower in the Postwar Army Policy," 27 April 1946, in *Planning for the Postwar Employment of Black Personnel,* ed. MacGregor and Nalty, 395.

60. One sees here a continuing vulgar neo-Lamarckism or social Darwinism after its delegitimation in the social sciences. On the hold of Lamarckism in the U.S. academy into the twentieth century, see George W. Stocking Jr., "Lamarckianism

in American Social Science, 1890–1915," in *Race, Culture, and Evolution: Essays in the History of Anthropology* (New York: Free Press, 1968), 234–69. On similar views during the nineteenth century, see George M. Fredrickson, *The Black Image in the White Mind: The Debate on Afro-American Character and Destiny, 1817–1914* (Middletown, Conn.: Wesleyan University Press, 1987).

61. George to Commanding General, XII Corps, Attention: Assistant Chief of Staff, G-3, 12 July 1945, 2.

62. Lieutenant Colonel James L. Baker to Commanding General, XII Corps, 7 July 1945, 2, File 291.2, AG Correspondence, 1945, RG 338, NACP.

63. Dwight David Eisenhower to General Bruce Clarke, 29 May 1967, quoted in MacGregor, *Integration of the Armed Forces,* 227.

64. Quoted in MacGregor, *Integration of the Armed Forces,* 410. In fact, sexual rivalry had occasioned violence in Britain between white and black troops. See Smith, *When Jim Crow Met John Bull*; Lovett to the AG, War Department, 1 October 1945, 14.

65. Myrdal, *An American Dilemma,* 1:587. See also Eileen Boris, " 'You Wouldn't Want One of 'em Dancing with Your Wife': Racialized Bodies on the Job in World War II," *American Quarterly* 50 (1998): 77–108.

66. Lovett to the AG, War Department, 1 October 1945, 11. See also Douglas Allanbrook, *See Naples: A Memoir* (Boston: Houghton Mifflin, 1995), 213; Mershon and Schlossman, *Foxholes and Color Lines,* 71.

67. Colonel Theodore J. Krokus to Brigadier General Walter J. Muller, 7 July 1945, 4, File 291.2, AG Correspondence, 1945, RG 338, NACP.

68. Baker to Commanding General, XII Corps, 7 July 1945, 4.

69. DeLorimer to Commanding General, Third U.S. Army, 14 July 1945, 4, 6.

70. Lovett to the AG, War Department, 1 October 1945, 15.

71. Report of the Negro Newspaper Publishers Association, in *Segregation under Siege,* ed. MacGregor and Nalty, 22.

72. Captain D. G. MacWilliams to Unit Commanders and Section Chiefs, 5 December 1946, File 291.2, Classified General Correspondence, 1946, Secretary, General Staff, RG 338, NACP.

73. Report AG-(OT)-70 regarding utilization of Negro personnel, to the AG, War Department, 15 April 1947.

74. "Negro Manpower in the Army," Department of the Army Basic Training Talk, in *Segregation under Siege,* ed. MacGregor and Nalty, 227–28. The organization of separate unit clubs is described in the inspector general's investigation of events in Mannheim. See Office of the Inspector General to Commanding General, Continental Base Section, USFET, 17 August 1946, with exhibits.

75. Lovett to the AG, War Department, 1 October 1945, 14.

76. Colonel T. J. Hartford to AC of S, G-3, Third U.S. Army, 12 July 1945, 5, 7, File 291.2, AG Correspondence, 1945, RG 338, NACP; Lieutenant Colonel R. V. Metzger to Commanding General, XII Corps, 10 July 1945, 4–5, File 291.2, AG Correspondence, 1945, RG 338, NACP; Krokus to Brigadier General Walter J. Muller, 7 July 1945, 6. See also Brigadier General John F. Conklin to AC of S, G-3, 13 July 1945, 2, File 291.2, AG Correspondence, 1945, RG 338, NACP.

77. Williams to G-3, 9 July 1945, 8.

78. Chief of Staff Brigadier General Bryan L. Milburn to Commanding General, United States Forces, European Theater, 24 May 1946, File 250.1, General Correspondence, Office of the AG, RG 260, NACP. See also note of C/S to A/DMG,

stating "I agree that colored troops should not be over here but I doubt if we can get rid of them—at least not immediately." File 250.1, General Correspondence, Office of the AG, RG 260, NACP; Marvin Boyle, Colonel, Field Artillery, Chief of Branch, CA Div, PE Br, 29 July 1946, File 386.7, Central Files, Office of Director, CAD, RG 260, NACP. This document is discussed in Posner, "Afro-America in West German Perspective," 24.

79. Morris MacGregor Jr. rightly emphasizes the importance of a desire to improve efficiency in ending segregation in the military in the years after World War II. MacGregor, *Integration of the Armed Forces,* 123, 291–92.

80. War Department Circular No. 124.

81. MacGregor, *Integration of the Armed Forces,* 164–65, 232–33.

82. See Geis, "Negro Personnel in the European Command," 16–17. File labeled "Misconduct of US Troops. (Incidents Involving US Troops and German Civilians and Officials.) Report No. 205," Investigation Reports and Related Records, 1945–1947, USFET Inspector General, RG 338, NACP.

83. Unsigned, undated draft report, Utilization of Negro Troops, 1–2; File labeled "Misconduct of US Troops. (Incidents Involving US Troops and German Civilians and Officials.) Report No. 205," Investigation Reports and Related Records, 1945–1947, USFET Inspector General, RG 338, NACP.

84. Ibid., 3–4.

85. Ibid., 5–6.

86. "Supervision Survey of Colored Troops: Discussion of Salient Features," enclosure "L" to Major Robert F. Shearer, Assistant AG, Headquarters, USFET, to Commanding General, Continental Base Section, 6 August 1946.

87. Metzger to Commanding General, XII Corps, 10 July 1945, 4.

88. See G-1 to SGS, 15 July 1946, File 291.2, Classified General Correspondence, 1946, Secretary, General Staff, RG 338, NACP. See also Major Richard F. Wagner, Weekly Intelligence Report, 6 July 1946, File 250.1, Classified General Correspondence, AG, Admin. Branch, RG 338, NACP.

89. Geis, "Negro Personnel in the European Command," 54; see also attachments F and G to Brigadier General Roderick R. Allen to the Chief of Staff, 16 November 1946, File 291.2, Classified General Correspondence, 1946, Secretary, General Staff, RG 338, NACP. Civilian Aide Marcus Ray reported that there were still no African Americans in Austria as of December 1946 but that a railroad car company of "selected Negro personnel" had been ordered to move to Vienna. Marcus H. Ray, Civilian Aide, to Secretary of War, Robert P. Patterson, "Report of Tour of European Installations," 16 November to 17 December 1946, in *Segregation under Siege,* ed. MacGregor and Nalty, 70.

90. Cable VX-33193 from CG US HQ Berlin District, Gavin, to CG USFET Main, 22 September 1945, File 291.2, Classified General Correspondence, 1944–1945, Secretary, General Staff, RG 338, NACP.

91. Major R. P. Rosser Jr. to SGS, 25 October 1946, File 291.2, Classified General Correspondence, 1946, Secretary, General Staff, RG 338, NACP.

92. Geis, "Negro Personnel in the European Command," 54.

93. MacGregor, *Integration of the Armed Forces,* 179.

94. Allen to the Chief of Staff, 16 November 1946. The 24 August 1946 CIC study, "Security Threat Provoked by Use of Negro Troops in the European Theater," was not included with Allen's letter.

95. Major General Paul to Chief of Staff, 21 January 1947, 4–5.

96. MacGregor, *Integration of the Armed Forces,* 330–31.

97. See George Meader, Chief Counsel, Special Senate Committee Investigating the National Defense Program, "Confidential Report to the Senate Special Committee Investigating the National Defense Program on the Preliminary Investigation of Military Government in the Occupied Areas of Europe," 22 November 1946, in U.S. Senate Special Committee Investigating the National Defense Program, *Investigation of the National Defense Program,* Hearings before a Special Committee Investigating the National Defense Program, 80th Cong., 1st sess., 5 April, 14 August, 26 September, and 18 November 1946 and 21–24 October 1947, Part 42, 26163.

98. Clay, *Decision in Germany,* 47.

99. Meader, "Confidential Report," 26163. The quotation comes from Division Staff Meeting Minutes, 3 May 1947, 37, Minutes of Division Staff Meetings, Office of Director, CAD, RG 260, NACP. See also Geis, "Negro Personnel in the European Command," 81, 98.

100. Geis, "Negro Personnel in the European Command," 56.

101. "Supervision Survey of Colored Troops: Discussion of Salient Features," enclosure "L" to Major Robert F. Shearer, Assistant AG, Headquarters, USFET, to Commanding General, Continental Base Section, 6 August 1946; Memorandum re: "Supervision Survey of Colored Companies," to Chief of Staff, U.S. Forces, European Theater, 18 June 1946, File 291.2, Classified General Correspondence, 1946, Secretary, General Staff, RG 338, NACP. USFET had similarly recommended to the War Department in 1945 that the "isolation of small detachments under supervision of Negro non-commissioned officers where they are left responsible for maintenance of expensive equipment and in control of large quantities of pilferable material should be avoided." Lovett to AG, War Department, 1 October 1945, 6.

102. Allen to the Chief of Staff, 16 November 1946; see also Boyle, 29 July 1946; Lieutenant Colonel Louis Kelly to Colonel Boyle, 26 July 1946, File 386.7, Central Files, Office of Director, CAD, RG 260, NACP. See also the recommendation "[t]hat every effort be made to concentrate Negro troops in isolated Kasernes." (The word *isolated* had been struck out, with the edit initialed by Major General Bevans.) Major General J. M. Bevans to SGS, 26 August 1946, File 333.5, Classified General Correspondence 1946, AG, RG 338, NACP. In November 1946 General McNarney ordered the housing of all African American units in Mannheim in the Kaiser Wilhelm Kaserne and nearby facilities. Message SX-6506 from McNarney to CG, Third United States Army and CG, Continental Base Section, 18 November 1946, File 291.2, Classified General Correspondence, 1946, Secretary, General Staff, RG 338, NACP.

103. Report AG-(OT)-70 regarding utilization of Negro personnel, to the AG, War Department, 15 April 1947.

104. Geis, "Negro Personnel in the European Command"; Major General Edward F. Witsell to Commanding Generals, 4 February 1946, File 291.2, Classified Decimal File 1946–1947, Communications Branch, RG 407, NACP; MacGregor, *Integration of the Armed Forces,* 152–53. African Americans had volunteered in disproportionate numbers for the military before the war. Lee, *The Employment of Negro Troops,* 90.

105. MacGregor, *Integration of the Armed Forces,* 178–79.

106. Witsell to Commanding Generals, 4 February 1946.

107. MacGregor, *Integration of the Armed Forces,* 179.

108. Major General W. S. Paul, Assistant Chief of Staff, G-1, for the Secretary of War, 9 March 1946, File 291.2, Classified Decimal File 1946–1947, RG 407, NACP.

109. Major General Paul to Chief of Staff, 21 January 1947, 2.

110. MacGregor, *Integration of the Armed Forces,* 183.

111. Major General Edward F. Witsell to Commanding Generals, 16 April 1946, File 291.2, Classified Decimal File 1946–1947, RG 407, NACP.

112. Geis, "Negro Personnel in the European Command," 16–17; Colonel William A. Walker, Memorandum for General Arnold, 7 August 1946, Reference Book, European and Mediterranean Theaters, File 322, General Correspondence 1944–1947, Secretary, General Staff, RG 338, NACP; Brigadier General L. S. Ostrander to Commanding Generals, 22 June 1946, File 291.2, Classified General Correspondence, 1946, Secretary, General Staff, RG 338, NACP. USFET remained skittish on the issue. Days after the War Department agreed to stop sending black troops to Europe, General McNarney cabled the War Department that USFET had been informed that 1,572 African Americans were scheduled to be shipped the next day from Brooklyn to Europe aboard the *George Washington.* He asked that they not be sent. The War Department responded that no black soldiers were aboard the *George Washington.* Cable S-5688 from McNarney to War Department, 14 June 1946, File 291.2, G-1 Decimal File, 1946–1948, RG 165, NACP; WARCOS to Commanding General U.S. Forces European Theater, 18 June 1946, File 291.2, G-1 Decimal File, 1946–1948, RG 165, NACP.

113. Cable from War Department to USFET, 4 July 1946, Correspondence, Directives and Messages, 1944–1947, G-3, RG 338, NACP; see also Geis, "Negro Personnel in the European Command," 19; MacGregor, *Integration of the Armed Forces,* 184.

114. MacGregor, *Integration of the Armed Forces,* 186. After the oversupply diminished, the War Department took gradual steps to reopen enlistment. After October 31, 1946, African Americans who had a score of 100 or higher on the AGCT were eligible to serve in the regular army. Whites needed only to score a 70. MacGregor, *Integration of the Armed Forces,* 185.

115. Geis, "Negro Personnel in the European Command," 64–65; Minutes of Nineteenth Meeting of the Theater Commander with Major Commanders and Deputy Military Governor, 23 January 1947, 2–3, File 337, General Correspondence 1943–1946, ETO G-1 Section, Admin. Branch, RG 338, NACP; Report AG-(OT)-70 regarding utilization of Negro personnel, to the AG, War Department, 15 April 1947; Major General Paul to Chief of Staff, 21 January 1947, 5–7; Office of Advisor on Negro Affairs, Headquarters, European Command, "Resume of Activities" [1948], Operations Reports, 1948, Office of Advisor on Negro Affairs, EUCOM, RG 338, NACP.

116. See, e.g., Cable SX 3418, CINCEUR, Frankfurt, Germany, sgd Huebner, to War Department, 24 March 1947, File 291.2, G-1 Decimal File, 1946–1948, RG 165, NACP; Colonel John H. Riepe, memorandum regarding Quotas for Enlistment of Negroes, 12 October 1948, File 291.2, G-1 Decimal File, 1946–1948, RG 165, NACP; Geis, "Negro Personnel in the European Command," 29–31.

117. Testimony of Colonel Francis P. Miller, U.S. Senate Special Committee Investigating the National Defense Program, *Investigation of the National Defense Program,* 25831–32. See Kevin Conley Ruffner, "The Black Market in Postwar Berlin: Colonel Miller and an Army Scandal," *Prologue* 34 (Fall 2002): 170–83.

118. Testimony of Colonel Francis P. Miller, 25832–33.

119. Ibid., 25832; Exhibit No. 2690, 26144–47.

120. Testimony of Howard C. Petersen, Assistant Secretary of War, U.S. Senate Special Committee Investigating the National Defense Program, *Investigation of the National Defense Program,* 25846.

121. Obsorne [*sic*], Memorandum for the Assistant Secretary of War, 1 November 1946, 4.

122. Meader, "Confidential Report," in U.S. Senate Special Committee Investigating the National Defense Program, *Investigation of the National Defense Program,* 26163–64.

123. Ibid., 26163.

124. Ibid., 26164, 26166–68.

125. Ibid., 26151.

126. Felix Belair Jr., "Senators Reject Occupation Study," *New York Times,* 27 November 1946, 10.

127. U.S. Senate Special Committee Investigating the National Defense Program, *Investigation of the National Defense Program,* Executive Session, Investigation of Military Government, 13 November 1946, 29–32, 38. On Byrnes's opinions of African Americans, see Borstelmann, *The Cold War and the Color Line,* 24, 36, 49.

128. U.S. Senate Special Committee Investigating the National Defense Program, Executive Session, 30–32.

129. Belair, "Senators Reject Occupation Study," *New York Times,* 27 November 1946, 10; Anthony Leviero, "Political Conflict Rages around AMG in Germany," *New York Times,* 8 December 1946, section E.

130. Colonel Robert S. Allen, "Suppressed Report on Germany Lays Immorality to U.S. Forces," *New York Times,* 2 December 1946, 3. The article, e.g., quoted the report as stating that "frauleins" who associated with black soldiers "have been propagandized by Hitler into a psychology of moral laxness, and, in view of the food shortage, are unusually receptive to the generosity of the Negro troops." The analogous section of the version released by the Senate dealt only with economic matters, removing the reference to Hitlerite propaganda and moral laxness. It stated simply, "In view of food shortages, some German women have been unusually receptive to the generosity of the Negro troops." Meader, "Confidential Report," in U.S. Senate Special Committee Investigating the National Defense Program, *Investigation of the National Defense Program,* 26163–64.

131. Robert S. Allen, "Meader Report Says U.S. Is Victim of Displaced Persons in Europe," *New York Times,* 3 December 1946, 13.

132. Anthony Leviero, "Truman Opposes Occupation Study," *New York Times,* 4 December 1946, 1; "Supplemental Data" to U.S. Senate Special Committee Investigating the National Defense Program, *Investigation of the National Defense Program,* 26149; Felix Belair Jr., "Senators Reject Occupation Study," *New York Times,* 27 November 1946, 10; Colonel Robert S. Allen, "Suppressed Report on Germany Lays Immorality to U.S. Forces," *New York Times,* 2 December 1946, 3.

133. Statement by NAACP on Charges of Misconduct by Negro Troops by George Meader, Counsel to the Senate War Investigating Committee in *Papers of the NAACP,* part 9, *Discrimination in the U.S. Armed Forces, 1918–1955,* Series A: General Office Files on Armed Forces' Affairs, 1918–1955 (Frederick, Md.: University Publications of America, 1989), reel 12, frame 615.

134. Walter White to Honorable Harry S. Truman, December 3, 1946, and Walter White to Senators Brewster, Ball, Ferguson, and Knowland, 3 December 1946, in *Papers of the NAACP,* part 9, *Discrimination in the U.S. Armed Forces, 1918–1955,* series A, reel 12, frames 616–20.

135. For objections in the black press to the Meader report, see, e.g., Truman K. Gibson Jr., "Meader's Report Seeks to Remove GIs: Drive on to Smear Overseas Soldiers," *Pittsburgh Courier,* 14 December 1946, 1; "Still Smearing Our Soldiers," *Pittsburgh Courier,* 14 December 1946, 6; Louis Lautier, "Ray Discredits Meader Report on GI Misconduct in Germany," *Pittsburgh Courier,* 28 December 1946, 3.

136. For the poll, see Hazel Gaudet Erskine, "The Polls: Race Relations," *Public Opinion Quarterly* 26 (1962): 138. More generally, see Robert J. Norrell, *The House I Live In: Race in the American Century* (Oxford: Oxford University Press, 2005), 112–47.

137. Truman Gibson emphasized during the war that the growing political clout of African Americans required recognition in planning for the utilization of Negro manpower. Truman K. Gibson Jr. to Assistant Secretary of War John J. McCloy, 20 July 1944, in *Planning for the Postwar Employment of Black Personnel,* ed. MacGregor and Nalty, 3–5; Truman K. Gibson Jr. to Assistant Secretary McCloy, 5 September 1944, in *Planning for the Postwar Employment of Black Personnel,* ed. MacGregor and Nalty, 8–10. See also MacGregor, *Integration of the Armed Forces,* 123; National Urban League to James Forrestal, 26 August 1948, in *Segregation under Siege,* ed. MacGregor and Nalty, 695; Berman, *The Politics of Civil Rights,* 237–40; Mershon and Schlossman, *Foxholes and Color Lines,* 26; Lee, *The Employment of Negro Troops,* 84.

138. See Mershon and Schlossman, *Foxholes and Color Lines,* 168–86.

139. Major General Paul to Chief of Staff, 21 January 1947, 2. On broader white attitudes, see MacGregor, *Integration of the Armed Forces,* 165, 229.

140. Truman K. Gibson Jr., "Nazis in Army: American Officers Abroad Propagating Race Hatred," *Pittsburgh Courier,* 8 June 1946, 3; Cable WCL 43733 from AGWAR SGD Parks WDSPR to USFET for Eyster, 13 September 1946, File 291.2, Classified General Correspondence, 1946, Secretary, General Staff, RG 338, NACP.

141. Cable S-3850 from HQ U.S. Forces European Theater, Public Relations Division, McNarney, to AGWAR, 21 September 1946, File 291.2, Classified General Correspondence, 1946, Secretary, General Staff, RG 338, NACP; quotation from "McNarney Denies Slur on Negroes," *New York Times,* 22 September 1946, 22.

142. Statement Issued by General Joseph T. McNarney, Commanding General, USFET, in Reply to a Query on the Subject of U.S. Negro Troops, USFET Release No. 2116, 21 September 1946, 3, attached to Public Relations Division Report of Operations, 1 July 1946 to 30 September 1946, Records of the Public Relations Section, RG 338, NACP.

143. See Rosenberg, " 'Sounds Suspiciously Like Miami.' "

144. Report of the Negro Newspaper Publishers Association, in *Segregation under Siege,* ed. MacGregor and Nalty, 21–22.

145. Ibid., 23–24, 28.

146. Ibid., 27–28.

147. Major General Lauris Norstad to Commanding General, USFET, 5 September 1946, File 291.2, Classified General Correspondence, 1946, Secretary, General Staff, RG 338, NACP; Comments on the Report of the Negro Publishers

Association by Lieutenant Colonel Louis A. Kunzig Jr., 30 September 1946, File 291.2, Classified General Correspondence, 1946, Secretary, General Staff, RG 338, NACP.

148. Allen to Huebner, 11 September 1946.

149. First Lieutenant Kimball S. Green to Commanding General, USFET, 14 March 1946, File 291.2, AG Classified Correspondence, 1946, RG 338, USFET, NACP.

150. Captain R. A. Knecht to Commanding General, USFET, 3 April 1946, File 291.2, AG Classified Correspondence, 1946, RG 338, NACP.

151. Colonel Charles V. Bromley to G-4, 30 April 1946, File 291.2, AG Classified Correspondence, 1946, RG 338, NACP.

152. Ray later recalled that Patterson had sent him to Europe to investigate in response to the Meader report after having rejected the recommendation to remove African Americans from Germany. See Geis, "Negro Personnel in the European Command," in *Segregation under Siege,* ed. MacGregor and Nalty, 153. The fact, however, that Ray left for Europe on November 17, before Meader's report was publicized, suggests that the trip did not originate in response to Meader's recommendation. In addition, a note from the Personnel and Administration Division of November 1, 1946, indicated that the purpose of the visit was to study the current employment of black troops with a "view to possible reduction or redeployment." Note, Personnel and Administration Division, WDGS, 1 November 1946, File 291.2, G-1 Decimal File, 1946–1948, RG 165, NACP.

153. Transcript of Press Conference given by Mr. Marcus Ray, Frankfurt, Germany, 23 November 1946, File 291.2, Classified General Correspondence, 1946, Secretary, General Staff, RG 338, NACP; "Patterson Aide Finds Negro GI's Maligned," *New York Times,* 21 December 1946, 8; "Ray Defends GIs Serving Overseas," *Chicago Defender,* 28 December 1946; "Marcus Ray Gives the Lie to Slanders of GIs in Germany," *California Eagle,* 26 December 1946, clippings in Press Items re: Negro Newspapers, 1944–1946 (Analysis Branch), Office of Public Information, RG 330, NACP.

154. Marcus H. Ray, "Report of Tour," 66–67.

155. Ibid., 67, 70–71.

156. The quotation is from Lieutenant General C. R. Huebner to Major General Willard S. Paul, 1 November 1947, File 291.2, G-1 Decimal File, 1946–1948, RG 165, NACP. See also Headquarters, European Command, Office of the Director of Personnel and Administration, Report of Operations 1 July 1947–30 September 1947, 6, Quarterly Operations Reports, Personnel and Administration Division, EUCOM, RG 338, NACP. Major General W. S. Paul to Lieutenant General C. R. Huebner, 2 December 1947, File 291.2, G-1 Decimal File, 1946–1948, RG 165, NACP; MacGregor, *Integration of the Armed Forces,* 216–19; Geis, "Negro Personnel," in *Segregation under Siege,* ed. MacGregor and Nalty, 123–44.

157. Jean Edward Smith, ed., *The Papers of General Lucius D. Clay: Germany, 1945–1949,* vol. 1 (Bloomington: Indiana University Press, 1974), 310; Shirley Griffith, "Co. C Guards the Palace of Justice," *Nürnberg Post-Spade,* 5 March 1948, Stadtarchiv Nürnberg; "Palace of Justice Guard Changes Hands: Co. A, 18th Relieved by Co. C, 371st," *Nürnberg Post-Spade,* 20 February 1948, 1, Stadtarchiv Nürnberg.

158. "Army Talk 170," 12 April 1947, in *Segregation under Siege,* ed. MacGregor and Nalty, 81.

159. Thomas W. Young, "ETO Tour of Newsmen Called 'Greatest Show on Earth,'" *Norfolk Journal and Guide,* 24 April 1948, and other clippings in Press Items re: Negro Newspapers, 1944–1946 (Analysis Branch), Office of Public Information, RG 330, NACP.

160. Report to Secretary of the Army Kenneth C. Royall on the Tour of the U.S. Occupied Zones of Germany and Austria by Negro Newspaper Publishers Group, 18 March–5 April 1948, 21 April 1948, 2–4, File 291.2, G-1 Decimal File, 1946–1948, RG 165, NACP.

161. Ibid., 6–7.

162. Conference Report, National Defense Conference on Negro Affairs, The Pentagon, 9:00 A.M. Monday, 26 April 1948, 19, in *Segregation under Siege,* ed. MacGregor and Nalty, 473.

163. Secretary of the Army Kenneth C. Royall to Chief of Staff, no date, File 291.2, G-1 Decimal File, 1946–1948, RG 165, NACP; Lieutenant General W. S. Paul to Deputy Chief of Staff, 21 June 1948, File 291.2, G-1 Decimal File, 1946–1948, RG 165, NACP.

164. Statement of Grant Reynolds, National Chairman of the Committee Against Jim Crow in Military Service and Training and New York State Commissioner of Correction, New York, and Statement of A. Philip Randolph, National Treasurer of the Committee Against Jim Crow in Military Service and Training and President of the Brotherhood of Sleeping-Car Porters, A. F. of L., New York City, U.S. Senate, Hearings before the Senate Committee on Armed Services, *Universal Military Training,* 80th Cong., 2nd sess., 1948, in *Segregation under Siege,* ed. MacGregor and Nalty, 645–70.

165. Berman, *The Politics of Civil Rights,* 239.

166. Executive Order 9981, in *Segregation under Siege,* ed. MacGregor and Nalty, 687–88; Clark Clifford, Advisor to the President, Memorandum for the President, 17 August 1948, in *Segregation under Siege,* ed. MacGregor and Nalty, 685–86; Extract from the President's News Conference of 29 July 1948, *Public Papers of the Presidents,* 1948, in *Segregation under Siege,* ed. MacGregor and Nalty, 689.

167. MacGregor, *Integration of the Armed Forces,* 331, 375–78, 428–30.

168. Ibid., 448–52; Ronald Sher, "Integration of Negro and White Troops in the U.S. Army, Europe, 1952–1954" (n.p.: Historical Division Headquarters, United States Army, Europe, 1956), Historical Manuscripts Collection, CMH; Richard M. Dalfiume, *Desegregation in the Armed Forces: Fighting on Two Fronts, 1939–1953* (Columbia: University of Missouri Press, 1969), 216–17.

Chapter 3: "Bad Girls" and "Boys Who Never Had It So Good": Sex and Race in American-Occupied Germany

1. On the negative German reactions to relations between African American soldiers and German women, see, e.g., Fehrenbach, *Race after Hitler*; Fehrenbach, "Of German Mothers and 'Negermischlingskinder'"; Höhn, "*Heimat* in Turmoil"; Poiger, *Jazz, Rock, and Rebels,* 35–36; Fehrenbach, "Rehabilitating Father*land*"; Browder, *Americans in Post–World War II Germany,* 162–63; Posner, "Afro-America in West German Perspective," 9–18.

2. Mire Koikari has discerned a similar dynamic operating during the American occupation of Japan, whereby Japanese women who associated with

American soldiers (white or black; Koikari does not assess the race of American soldiers as an issue) were deemed "'immoral' [and] constructed as racially different from the rest of the normal and virtuous Japanese." Koikari, "Rethinking Gender and Power in the U.S. Occupation of Japan, 1945–1952," *Gender & History* 11 (1999): 328. Perry Biddiscombe, who focuses on the issue of fraternization in general and accordingly devotes most of his attention to women who fraternized with white Americans, suggests no such rhetorical exclusion of German women from whiteness or Germanness occurred. Biddiscombe, "Dangerous Liaisons: The Anti-Fraternization Movement in the U.S. Occupation Zones of Germany and Austria, 1945–1948," *Journal of Social History* 34 (2001): 630.

3. Perry Biddiscombe discerns "a classic case of transferrance [*sic*]" in attacks by German men on women who associated with American soldiers. Biddiscombe, "Dangerous Liaisons," 615. The move to blame the women, however, was socially determined rather than an expression of irrational, psychological "transference," a phenomenon whose validity seems open to question. For an effective critique of over-reliance on the displacement dynamic, see Gordon W. Allport, *The Nature of Prejudice*, 25th anniversary ed., with an introduction by Kenneth Clark and foreword by Thomas Pettigrew (Reading, Mass.: Addison-Wesley, 1979), 343–53.

4. On Nazism and women see, e.g., Timm, "The Ambivalent Outsider," 192–211; Koonz, *Mothers in the Fatherland*; Bridenthal, Grossmann, and Kaplan, eds., *When Biology Became Destiny*; Stephenson, *Women in Nazi Society*. On the similarities in images of the ideal woman as mother of the race and nation during the 1930s in the United States and the Third Reich, see Rupp, *Mobilizing Women for War*, 11–71. On women's special responsibility to the postwar nation, see Poiger, *Jazz, Rock, and Rebels*; Elizabeth D. Heineman, *What Difference Does a Husband Make? Women and Marital Status in Nazi and Postwar Germany* (Berkeley: University of California Press, 1999); Heide Fehrenbach, *Cinema in Democratizing Germany: Reconstructing National Identity after Hitler* (Chapel Hill: University of North Carolina Press, 1995); Moeller, *Protecting Motherhood*; Annette Kuhn, "Power and Powerlessness: Women after 1945, or the Continuity of the Ideology of Femininity," *German History* 7 (1989): 35–46; Barbara Willenbacher, "Zerrüttung und Bewährung der Nachkriegs-Familie," in *Von Stalingrad zur Währungsreform: Zur Sozialgeschichte des Umbruchs in Deutschland*, ed. Martin Broszat, Klaus-Dietmar Henke, and Hans Woller (Munich: R. Oldenbourg Verlag, 1989), 595–618. On the history of this idea generally, see Uli Linke, *Blood and Nation: The European Aesthetics of Race*, Contemporary Ethnography, ed. Dan Rose and Paul Stoler (Philadelphia: University of Pennsylvania Press, 1999), 235; Mosse, *Nationalism and Sexuality*; for the Weimar period, Frevert, *Women in German History*, 198–99. For British concerns over sexual morality during the war, see Rose, "Sex, Citizenship, and the Nation in World War II Britain."

5. For the quotation, see Fehrenbach, *Cinema in Democratizing Germany*, 95. For the statistic, see Monthly Report of the Military Governor No. 21, 1–31 March 1947, Statistical Annex, fig. 1.

6. See Fehrenbach, *Race after Hitler*, 46–73; Hanna Schissler, "'Normalization' as Project: Some Thoughts on Gender Relations in West Germany during the 1950s," in *The Miracle Years*, 361; Fehrenbach, "Rehabilitating Fatherland," 110–15; Gerda Lerner, *The Creation of Patriarchy* (New York: Oxford University Press, 1986), 450; Naimark, *The Russians in Germany*; Ingrid Schmidt-Harzbach, "Eine Woche im April: Berlin 1945—Vergewaltigung als Massenschicksal," *Feministische Studien* 2 (1984): 56.

7. See Jennifer Victoria Evans, "Reconstruction Sites: Sexuality, Citizenship, and the Limits of National Belonging in Divided Berlin, 1944–58" (Ph.D. diss., Binghamton University, State University of New York, 2001); Poiger, *Jazz, Rock, and Rebels*; Heineman, *What Difference Does a Husband Make?*; Fehrenbach, *Cinema in Democratizing Germany*, 94–97; Moeller, *Protecting Motherhood*, 23–37; Kuhn, "Power and Powerlessness"; Willenbacher, "Zerrüttung und Bewährung der Nachkriegs-Familie"; Christoph Boyer and Hans Woller, " 'Hat die deutsche Frau versagt?' Die 'neue Freiheit' der Frauen in der Trümmerzeit, 1945–1949," *Journal für Geschichte* 2 (1983): 32–36.

8. Information Control Intelligence Summary No. 12, Week ending 29 September 1945, 9–10, Opinion Surveys, Opinion Surveys Branch, Information Control Service, United States Group Control Council, RG 260, NACP; "Reactions of Germans to Negro Troops," Information Control Intelligence Summary No. 16, 27 October 1945, 2; Records Relating to Public Opinion, 1945–1949, Opinion Surveys Branch, ICD, RG 260, NACP; Public Safety: Monthly Report of Military Governor No. 3, 20 October 1945, 1; Monthly Report of Military Governor No. 5, 20 December 1945, 5. See also Biddiscombe, "Dangerous Liaisons"; Kleinschmidt, *"Do Not Fraternize,"* 154–63; Elizabeth Heineman, "The Hour of the Woman: Memories of Germany's 'Crisis Years' and West German National Identity," *AHR* 101 (1996): 380–84; Heineman, *What Difference Does a Husband Make?* 95–106; Petra Goedde, "From Villains to Victims: Fraternization and the Feminization of Germany, 1945–1947," in The American Occupation of Germany in Cultural Perspective: A Roundtable, *Diplomatic History* 23 (1999): 1–20; Harald Thomas Oskar Leder, "Americans and German Youth in Nuremberg, 1945–1956: A Study in Politics and Culture" (Ph.D. diss., Louisiana State University, 1997), 174–75; Michael John, "Das 'Haarabschneiderkommando' von Linz: Männlicher Chauvinismus oder national-sozialistische Wiederbetätigung? Ein Fallbeispiel aus den Jahren 1945–1948," in *Historisches Jahrbuch der Stadt Linz, 1995: Entnazifizierung und Wiederaufbau in Linz,* ed. Fritz Mayrhofer and Walter Schuster (Linz: Archiv der Stadt Linz, 1996), 335–59; Elfrieda Berthiaume Shukert and Barbara Smith Scibetta, *War Brides of World War II* (Novato: Presidio Press, 1988), 126–27; Boyer and Woller, " 'Hat die deutsche Frau versagt?' " 36.

9. Klaus-Jörg Ruhl, ed., *Frauen in der Nachkriegszeit, 1945–1963* (Munich: Deutscher Taschenbuch, 1988), 37. For the text of an often-cited example of objections to fraternization with American troops, see Hans Woller, *Gesellschaft und Politik in der amerikanischen Besatzungszone: Die Region Ansbach und Fürth* (Munich: R. Oldenbourg Verlag, 1986), 71.

10. Headquarters, United States Forces European Theater, Office of the Assistant Chief of Staff, G-2, Weekly Intelligence Summary No. 52, July 1946, 7, Weekly Intelligence Summaries, 1945–1946, G-2 Section, ETO, RG 338, NACP.

11. Major Nicolaus Harithas, "VI Corps, U.S. Constabulary, Reports of Operations," April 1946, Constabulary Section, U.S. Army Units, RG 338, NACP. See also Headquarters, Third United States Army, Office of the Assistant Chief of Staff, G-2, G-2 Weekly Intelligence Report No. 54, June 1946, 13, File 319.1, G-2 General Correspondence 1944–1947, Third Army, RG 338, NACP. For an example of an anonymous flier condemning shameless German women who carried on relations with "Negroes," see Oberbürgermeister der Stadt Nürnberg to Herrn Ministerpräsident Dr. Högner, 3 December 1945, attaching copy of flier, BayHStA, StK 13630. More generally, see Goedde, *GIs and Germans*, 65; Kleinschmidt,

"Do Not Fraternize," 181; Hoecker and Meyer-Braun, *Bremerinnen bewältigen die Nachkriegszeit,* 35.

12. Special Agent N. De Vyner, Memorandum for the Officer in Charge, 14 December 1945, 3, File 333.5, Classified General Correspondence, 1945, USFET AG, RG 338, NACP.

13. Sonya Rose discerns a similar dynamic in wartime Britain. Rose, "Sex, Citizenship, and the Nation in World War II Britain," 1149.

14. G-2 Weekly Intelligence Report No. 54, June 1946, 13.

15. For events in Meitingen, see Headquarters, 74th Constabulary Squadron, report to Commanding General, U.S. Constabulary, Attn: A C of S, G-2, 29 August 1946, General Correspondence 1944–1947, G-2, Third Army, RG 338, NACP. On Weißenburg, see Lieutenant Colonel Allen D. Raymond Jr. to Commanding General, Third U.S. Army, 23 July 1946, File 333.5, General Correspondence of AG, 1945–1947, Third Army, RG 338, NACP. On Waghäusel, see Pf. Jos. Weiskopf to Bürgermeisteramt Bruchsal, 9 May 1946, Records of the Public Safety Officer, 1945–1949, Bruchsal RLSO, FOD, OMGW-B, RG 260, NACP. On Mannheim, see Office of the Inspector General, Headquarters, Continental Base Section, USFET, to Commanding General, Continental Base Section, USFET, 17 August 1946, with exhibits, File 333.5, Classified General Correspondence 1946, AG, RG 338, NACP.

16. Hugo Freiherr von Imhoff to Military Government, 17 July 1946, File 250.1, General Correspondence, Office of the AG, RG 260, NACP; Chef der Landpolizei im Reg.-Bez. Ober- u. Mittelfranken to Regierungspräsident im Reg.Bez. Ober- u. Mittelfranken, in Abschrift an: Präsidium der Landpolizei von Bayern, C.O. der Constabulary; Militär-Regierung Ober- u. Mittelfranken, 17 July 1946, SN, Regierung von Mittelfranken, Rep. 270, Nr. 1464 [the German original]. The English version of Imhoff's memorandum is mentioned in Posner, "Afro-America in West German Perspective," 17–18. The events in Wirsberg are also discussed in Fehrenbach, *Race after Hitler,* 64; Fehrenbach, "Of German Mothers and 'Neger-mischlingskinder,'" 167.

17. Imhoff to Military Government, 17 July 1946. The memorandum refers to this officer as an "American officer" and describes another officer at the hotel as a "colored officer," following the settled contemporary practice of describing whites without indicating their race but always noting the race of blacks.

18. Ibid.

19. Ibid.; emphasis added.

20. Ibid.

21. Military Government Liaison and Security Office, Det B-211, Stadtkreis-Landkreis Nürnberg to Commanding Officer, Headquarters Company B, 3rd Military Government Regiment, Public Safety Weekly Report, 21 June 1946, RLSO, Nürnberg, FOD, OMGBY, RG 260, NACP; "Der Mord in der Peter-Henlein-Straße," *Nürnberger Nachrichten,* 23 March 1946, 7. The race of the perpetrator was not given in the report or the article but had he been black, that certainly would have been stated.

22. Incident Report, 22 May 1946, RLSO, Nürnberg, FOD, OMGBY, RG 260, NACP.

23. Office of Military Government for Kreis Nürnberg, Regierungsbezirk Oberfranken und Mittelfranken to Director, Office of Military Government for Regierungsbezirk Oberfranken und Mittelfranken, Bavaria, 4 May 1946, RLSO,

Nürnberg, FOD, OMGBY, RG 260, NACP; Office of Military Government for Kreis Nürnberg, Regierungsbezirk Oberfranken und Mittelfranken to Director, Office of Military Government for Regierungsbezirk Oberfranken und Mittelfranken, Bavaria, 19 April 1946, RLSO, Nürnberg, FOD, OMGBY, RG 260, NACP. Other weekly public safety reports clearly indicated that the activities of both the *Stadtpolizei* and the *Landpolizei* were covered. The German policemen attacked thus could have been members of the Rural Police. See Military Government Liaison and Security Office Det B-211, Stadtkreis-Landkreis Nürnberg to Commanding Officer, Company B, 3rd Mil. Gov. Regt., 4 April 1947, RLSO, Nürnberg, FOD, OMGBY, RG 260, NACP.

24. "Fight over German Girls," *New York Times*, 1 July 1946, 12.

25. Imhoff to Military Government, 17 July 1946.

26. Geißler to Militärregierung in Altdorf b/Nbg., 6 May 1946, SN, Rep. 270, Nr. 1704.

27. Compare, e.g., Geißler's statement, "Folgende Einzelfälle beweisen, wie diese Protistuierten [*sic*] mit Hilfe ihrer Liebhaber gegen Gesetz und Ordnung vorstoßen und sich mit Gewalt durchzusetzen versuchen," with that of Imhoff, "Nachstehende Einzelfälle beweisen, wie diese Dirnen mit Hilfe ihrer Liebhaber gegen Gesetz und Ordnung verstossen und sich mit Gewalt durchzusetzen versuchen." Ibid.; Imhoff to Military Government, 17 July 1946.

28. Geißler to Militärregierung in Altdorf b/Nbg., 6 May 1946.

29. Ibid.

30. Georg Lowig to Regierungspräsidenten Ober- und Mittelfranken, 31 May 1946, SN, Rep. 270, Nr. 1704.

31. Dr. Hans Schregle, Regierungspräsident, to Military Government Headquarters, Regierungsbezirk Ober- and Mittelfranken, 14 June 1946, SN, Rep. 270, Nr. 1704 [English translation]; Der Regierungspräsident, to Militärregierung für Ober- und Mittelfranken in Ansbach, 14 June 1946, SN, Rep. 270, Nr. 1704 [German original]. The enclosed draft letter was from Dr. Hans Schregle, Regierungspräsident, to Oberbürgermeister and Landräte, all Stadt and Landkreise of Regierungsbezirk Ober- and Mittelfranken, 13 June 1946.

32. Major James T. Tillinghast to Regierungspräsident, Regierungsbezirk Ober und Mittelfranken, Bavaria, 25 June 1946, SN, Rep. 270, Nr. 1704.

33. The *Fränkische Landeszeitung, Die Neue Zeitung,* the *Nürnberger Nachrichten,* and *Die Neue Presse* were all silent on the Wirsberg and Feucht incidents and trouble involving African American soldiers generally through 1946. *Der Ruf* demonstrated the boldness that would lead it into difficulties with American officials by including one piece that mentioned the subject of relations between German women and black soldiers. See Hans Werner Richter, "Unterhaltungen am Schienenstrang," *Der Ruf,* 1 October 1946, 6.

34. Imhoff to Military Government, 17 July 1946; Chef der Landpolizei im Reg.-Bez. Ober- u. Mittelfranken to Regierungspräsident, 17 July 1946 [German original].

35. See, e.g., Second Lieutenant Chester F. O'Brien to Company A, 3rd Military Government, Regierungsbezirk Unterfranken, 6 August 1946, File 291.2, Classified Correspondence, 1946, Office of the AG, RG 338, NACP. The term *Neger* could be offensive to Afro-Germans as well. It was especially objectionable to the young Afro-German Hans Massaquoi growing up in Hamburg in the 1920s and 1930s. Massaquoi, *Destined to Witness,* 17–18. Nelson Peery reports having mistaken the

German word *Neger* for *nigger*. Nelson Peery, *Black Fire: The Making of an American Revolutionary* (New York: New Press, 1994), 334.

36. Marginal note on Röder, "Report for the month of July 1946," Correspondence and Related Records, 1945–1949, Kulmbach RLSO, FOD, OMGBY, RG 260, NACP.

37. Compare Geißler to Militärregierung in Altdorf b/Nbg., 6 May 1946, and Imhoff to Military Government, 17 July 1946.

38. See Imhoff to Captain Smith, 23 October 1946, Denazification Files 1946–1948, Public Safety Branch, OMGBY, RG 260, NACP; Dr. Schade to Imhoff, 13 August 1942, SN, Rep. 270, Nr. 1873; Dr. Otto Schwaab to Imhoff, 16 September 1942, SN, Rep. 270, Nr. 1873. It is unknown whether Imhoff and his wife suffered further persecution under the Nazis. Many Jewish spouses of "Aryan" men survived the Third Reich. See Nathan Stoltzfus, "The Limits of Policy: Social Protection of Intermarried German Jews in Nazi Germany," in *Social Outsiders in Nazi Germany*, ed. Robert Gellately and Nathan Stoltzfus (Princeton, N.J.: Princeton University Press, 2001), 117–44.

39. Dr. Mathern to Director, Office of Military Government for Bavaria, 2 October 1946, Denazification Files 1946–1948, Public Safety Branch, OMGBY, RG 260, NACP.

40. On the strength of Nazi support in Upper and Middle Franconia, see Rainer Hambrecht, *Der Aufstieg der NSDAP in Mittel- und Oberfranken, 1925–1933* (Nürnberg: Stadtarchiv Nürnberg, 1976).

41. On the blurring of prostitution's borders, see Goedde, "From Villains to Victims," 8. For more on the difficult question of defining prostitution, see Chapter 4.

42. Imhoff to Military Government, 17 July 1946; Chef der Landpolizei im Reg.-Bez. Ober- u. Mittelfranken to Regierungspräsident, 17 July 1946 [the German original]; Geißler to Militärregierung in Altdorf b/Nbg., 6 May 1946.

43. The idea of gullible blacks used by (often Jewish) manipulators was a staple of Nazi rhetoric. Blacks, e.g., were often portrayed as the unthinking partners used by Jews to corrupt German music. See Kater, *Different Drummers*, 20. White Americans also stereotyped African Americans as easily duped. Myrdal bemoaned "the ease with which the Negro masses can be duped—because they are distressed, poorly educated, politically inexperienced, tractable, and have old traditions of dependence and carelessness." Myrdal, *An American Dilemma*, 1:508; see also ibid., 1: 454.

44. Joachim Irek, *Mannheim in den Jahren 1945–1949: Geschichte einer Stadt zwischen Diktatur und Republik*, Veröffentlichungen des Stadtarchivs Mannheim, Bd. 9 (Stuttgart: Verlag W. Kohlhammer, 1983), 167–69.

45. Hoecker and Meyer-Braun, *Bremerinnen bewältigen die Nachkriegszeit*, 24.

46. William J. Moran to Police President Pitzer, 16 December 1946, Miscellaneous Reports and Correspondence File, General Records of Munich RLSOs, 1945–1949, Munich RLSO, FOD, OMGBY, RG 260, NACP.

47. Based on the body of Moran's correspondence with German officials, it does not appear that Moran's comment reflected disagreement with prevailing notions about African Americans. See General Records of Munich RLSOs, 1945–1949, Munich RLSO, FOD, OMGBY, RG 260, NACP.

48. For other instances of blaming German women for inciting black soldiers to criminal acts, see, e.g., Goedde, *GIs and Germans*, 65–66; Letter from "several

people living at the Speckweg" to Polizei-Prasidium, 17 June 1946, and Testimony of Hans Moeller, exhibits to Office of the Inspector General, Headquarters, Continental Base Section, USFET, to Commanding General, Continental Base Section, USFET, 17 August 1946, File 333.5, Classified General Correspondence 1946, AG, RG 338, NACP.

49. The Archbishop of Freiburg, 7 May 1946, Enclosure No. 2 to Morris O. Edwards, Memorandum regarding Troop-Civilian Relations to Deputy Military Governor, 16 May 1946, File 250.1, General Correspondence, Office of the AG, RG 260, NACP. The archbishop borrowed heavily from the earlier letter by Father Sales of the monastery in Waghäusel. P. Franz Sales to Military Government Bruchsal, 30 April 1946, GK, Der Präsident des Landesbezirks Baden (1945–1952) Präsidialstelle, Rep. 481, Nr. 723.

50. Bürgermeister Bläsi to Military Government, Det. H-87, Bruchsal, 10 May 1946, Records of the Public Safety Officer, 1945–1949, Bruchsal RLSO, FOD, OMGW-B, RG 260, NACP. The file includes the German original and the English translation.

51. Ibid.; Jos. Weiskopf to Bürgermeister, Bruchsal, 9 May 1946, Enclosure No. 5 to Morris O. Edwards to Deputy Military Governor, 16 May 1946. The German original of the report is in the papers of the Bruchsal Liaison and Security Office. Pf. Jos. Weiskopf to Bürgermeisteramt Bruchsal, 9 May 1946; Records of the Public Safety Officer, 1945–1949, Bruchsal RLSO, FOD, OMGW-B, RG 260, NACP.

52. The Archbishop of Freiburg, 7 May 1946.

53. Else Feldbinder, "Mütter ohne Liebe: Einen Tag unterwegs mit der Jugendfürsorgerin," *Sie* (15 December 1946): 2; Feldbinder, "Zwischen Tanzbar und Gesundheitsamt: Ein Kapitel vom Kampf gegen die Seuchengefahr," *Sie* (20 October 1946): 9; see also Biddiscombe, "Dangerous Liaisons," 622–23.

54. A. Beier to the Chief of the Military Police, 25 June 1946, OMGUS (3) File, Office of the Chief, 1946–1949, OMGBY Public Safety, RG 260, NACP; emphasis original.

55. Proclamation by the mayor of Kunzelsau, 18 October 1945, Exhibit E to Lieutenant Colonel D. M. Witt, Inspector General, Headquarters VI Corps, Office of the Inspector General, Report of Investigation of Alleged Misconduct of U.S. Troops in Kreis Kunzelsau, Germany, to Commanding General, VI Corps, 30 November 1945, File 333.5, AG Classified General Correspondence, 1945, RG 338, NACP.

56. Testimony of Doctor Lorenz Burkert, Exhibit B-4, to Witt to Commanding General, VI Corps, 30 November 1945, 24–25.

57. Rücksprache mit der Militärverwaltung am 24 January 1946, SW, Files of Weißenburg Government, Bestand 412, Bd. 4.

58. Ibid.

59. Gesetz zur Bekämpfung der Geschlechtskrankheiten, 18 February 1927, *Reichsgesetzblatt* 9, 61; Major General J. M. Bevans, GSC, to Chief of Staff, 12 September 1946, File 726.1 Venereal Disease, General Correspondence, Office of the AG, RG 260, NACP; Memorandum regarding program for incarceration of German women afflicted with venereal disease, 5 November 1946, File 700, Decimal File, 1942–1946, Records of the Judge Advocate General Section, Records of the Special Staff, RG 338, NACP. See also Lutz Sauerteig, *Krankheit, Sexualität, Gesellschaft: Geschlechtskrankheiten und Gesundheitspolitik in Deutschland im 19. und frühen 20. Jahrhundert*, Medizin, Gesellschaft und Geschichte, Jahrbuch des Instituts für Geschichte der Medizin der Robert Bosch Stiftung, ed. Robert Jütte,

no. 12 (Stuttgart: Franz Steiner Verlag, 1999); Elisabeth Meyer-Renschhausen, "The Bremen Morality Scandal," in *When Biology Became Destiny,* ed. Bridenthal, Grossmann, and Kaplan, 98.

60. Colonel Ernest L. McLendon, Chief, Administration of Justice Branch, Memorandum regarding V.D. control program, 3 October 1946, File 726.1 Venereal Disease, General Correspondence, Office of the AG, RG 260, NACP.

61. Translated in Lieutenant Colonel G. H. Garde, AG, for the Military Governor, OMGUS, to Headquarters, European Command, April 1948, Central Files, 1945–1949, Office of Director, CAD, RG 260, NACP.

62. Röder, Landrat des Kreises Kulmbach to Regierungspräsident, Ober und Mittelfranken, 15 May 1946, SN, Rep. 270, Nr. 1704. On the efforts of American military government in Bavaria to negotiate the thicket of German law regarding prostitution, see Lieutenant Colonel Robert A. Reese, Memorandum re: Prohibition of Houses of Prostitution in the U.S. Zone, 28 March 1946, with attachments, Office of the Chief, OMGBY Public Safety, RG 260, NACP. On the historical local variation within Germany in the interpretation and application of prostitution laws, see Timm, "The Ambivalent Outsider," 198–99.

63. *Bayerisches Gesetz- und Verordnungsblatt* Nr. 15, 15 April 1946, 219.

64. Ibid. See also "Anstalten für verwahrloste Frauen," *Fränkische Landeszeitung,* 17 August 1946, 6.

65. On the ambiguity of *Verwahrlost* in German law, see Helmut Vent, *Verwahrlosung Minderjähriger: Die Verdeutlichung eines unbestimmten Rechtsbegriffes unter Berücksichtigung pädagogischer und soziologischer Kriterien* (Frankfurt a.M.: Haag Herchen Verlag, 1979). Mannheim officials urged that Württemberg-Baden should adopt a similar measure. Minutes of Stadtratssitzung, 7 November 1946, Stadtarchiv Mannheim.

66. Ordinance No. 1, section 43, in *Sammlung der vom Allierten Kontrollrat und der Amerikanischen Militärregierung erlassenen Proklamationen.*

67. Office of Military Government for Bavaria, Legal Division, Manual for Military Government Courts, 20 May 1947, 33–34, IfZ, Nachlaß Walter Muller, MA-1427/2, Box 16, item 101.

68. USFET, Directive regarding control of Venereal Disease, 23 April 1946, File 726.1 Venereal Disease, General Correspondence, Office of the AG, RG 260, NACP; Brigadier General Walter J. Muller, Memorandum regarding venereal disease control, 24 September 1946, VD Control File, Office of the Chief, Public Safety Branch, OMGBY, RG 260, NACP. Muller stated that the venereal disease rate in the European Theater had increased from 70 per thousand per annum on V-E day to 254 per thousand per annum during June 1946.

69. See, e.g., "Das Uebel, von dem niemand spricht," *Fränkische Landeszeitung,* 27 July 1946, 3; Walter Gong, "Veronika Dankeschön," *Frankfurter Rundschau,* 26 July 1946, 4; *Die Neue Zeitung,* 8 November 1945, 3; "Verwahrloste Jugend — zerrüttete Ehen: Gibt es noch eine öffentliche Moral?" newspaper clipping, GK, Rep. 481, Nr. 1727.

70. See, e.g., Venereal Disease Rates of Major Commands, 8 November 1946 through 29 November 1946, File 726.1 Venereal Disease, General Correspondence, Office of the AG, RG 260, NACP; Willoughby, *Remaking the Conquering Heroes,* 64–65. The rate of infection among African Americans in the military was disproportionately high throughout World War II. See Lee, *The Employment of Negro Troops,* 276–90.

71. See Elizabeth Fee, "Venereal Disease: The Wages of Sin?" in *Passion and Power: Sexuality in History,* ed. Kathy Peiss and Christina Simmons, with Robert A. Padgug (Philadelphia: Temple University Press, 1989), 178–98; James H. Jones, *Bad Blood: The Tuskegee Syphilis Experiment,* new and expanded ed. (New York: Free Press, 1993); Myrdal, *An American Dilemma,* 1:143; Fredrickson, *The Black Image in the White Mind,* 251. On the contemporaneous development of a sickle cell anemia discourse figuring the African American body as diseased, see Melbourne Tapper, *In the Blood: Sickle Cell Anemia and the Politics of Race,* Critical Histories, ed. David Ludden (Philadelphia: University of Pennsylvania Press, 1999).

72. Lieutenant Colonel Hyman Y. Chase, Venereal Disease Control among Negro Troops in EUCOM, 3, included in EUCOM Venereal Disease Indoctrination Course, 20 November 1947, attachment 30 to Report of Operations for the Personnel and Administration Division, EUCOM, for the reporting period 1 October through 31 December 1947, Quarterly Operations Reports, Personnel and Administration Division, EUCOM, RG 338, NACP; emphasis original.

73. See Zantop, *Colonial Fantasies,* 50, 62; Campt, Grosse, and Lemke Muniz de Faria, "Blacks, Germans, and the Politics of Imperial Imagination," 211; Smith, "The Talk of Genocide," 121; Lester, "Blacks in Germany," 120. One Weimar-era writer for the German Society for Combating Venereal Disease blamed "the mixing of very different races" for the outbreak of venereal disease in Europe. Dr. Seger, "Wie schützen wir unsere Jugend vor sexuellen Gefahren? Ein Mahnwort für Eltern," *Flugschriften der deutschen Gesellschaft zur Bekämpfung der Geschlechtskrankheiten,* number 22 (Leipzig: Verlag von Johann Ambrosius Barth, [n.d.]), 4. Klaus Theweleit, *Male Fantasies,* trans. Stephen Conway, vol. 2 (Minneapolis: University of Minnesota Press, 1987), 15–17; Marks, "Black Watch on the Rhine," 301; Weindling, *Health, Race and German Politics,* 532. Sander Gilman detects a long-standing association of blacks, especially black females, with sexually transmitted disease. Gilman, "Black Sexuality and Modern Consciousness," 39. On the racing of venereal disease as black, see Hoecker and Meyer-Braun, *Bremerinnen bewältigen die Nachkriegszeit,* 34–35; Annette F. Timm, "The Legacy of *Bevölkerungspolitik*: Venereal Disease Control and Marriage Counselling in Post–WW II Berlin," *Canadian Journal of History* 33 (1998): 188–89; Andreas Dinter, "Die Seuchen im Berlin der Nachkriegszeit 1945–1949" (Ph.D. diss., Frei Universität Berlin, 1994), 560–61; Baur, Fischer, and Lenz, *Menschliche Erblehre,* 717. For British readings of venereal disease in the imperial context, see Philippa Levine, *Prostitution, Race, and Politics: Policing Venereal Disease in the British Empire* (New York: Routledge, 2003), 64–66.

74. On Weimar-era concerns about venereal disease, see Richard Bessel, *Germany after the First World War* (Oxford: Clarendon Press, 1993), 233–39; Cornelie Usborne, *The Politics of the Body in Weimar Germany: Women's Reproductive Rights and Duties,* Social History, Popular Culture, and Politics in Germany, ed. Geoff Eley (Ann Arbor: University of Michigan Press, 1992), 74–75, 83–84, 109–12. British discussion of venereal disease during World War I similarly described venereal disease as a threat to the race and nation. David Michael Simpson, "The Moral Battlefield: Venereal Disease and the British Army during the First World War" (Ph.D. diss., University of Iowa, 1999), 6, 13, 74, 256–58.

75. See Abt. Innere Verwaltung, Der Präsident des Landesbezirks Baden, to Military Government in Stuttgart, 25 June 1946, GK, Rep. 481, Nr. 537.

76. Minutes of Division Staff Meeting, Saturday, 9 March 1946, 4, Minutes of Division Staff Meetings, Office of Director, CAD, RG 260, NACP; H. M. Leet

to Colonel P. V. Kieffer Jr., 6 November 1946, File 700, Decimal File, 1942–1946, Records of the Judge Advocate General Section, Records of the Special Staff, RG 338, NACP.

77. Office of the Chief Historian, European Command, "Medical Policies and Operations," Occupation Forces in Europe Series 1945–1946 (Frankfurt a.M.: Office of the Chief Historian, European Command, 1947), 139. Black soldiers in Italy were punished for contracting venereal diseases more often than white soldiers, and it seems likely this differing treatment was the case in Germany also. See the U.S. Army Research Branch, *The American Soldier in World War II*, Attitudes of white and black troops toward venereal disease: S-233, August 1945, data tapes, response to question 53, The American Soldier Survey, RG 330, NACP. McNarney initiated "an intensive Venereal Disease control" program in September 1946 as he continued to be dismayed by the command's high infection rate through summer 1946. See Headquarters, U.S. Forces, European Theater, to Commanding Generals, 22 August 1946, Office of the Chief, OMGBY Public Safety, RG 260, NACP. Jennifer Evans discusses some cases where the army took disciplinary action against enlisted men for contracting venereal disease. See Evans, "Reconstruction Sites," 78–81.

78. On the punitive policies against German women, see Heineman, *What Difference Does a Husband Make?* 99–104; Hoecker and Meyer-Braun, *Bremerinnen bewältigen die Nachkriegszeit,* 30–36. The concentration of punitive measures on infected women has been fairly common in efforts to control venereal disease. See, e.g., Simpson, "The Moral Battlefield," 60, 186, 322, 377–88. The campaign in postwar Germany was notable, however, for its severity and for the striking difference between its targeting of the women and the campaign against the "Black Horror" after World War I, which had blamed French colonial troops for rising rates of infection. See Campt, Grosse, and Lemke Muniz de Faria, "Blacks, Germans, and the Politics of Imperial Imagination," 211; Lester, "Blacks in Germany," 120; Marks, "Black Watch on the Rhine," 301.

79. Abt. Innere Verwaltung, Der Präsident des Landesbezirks Baden, to Military Government in Stuttgart, 25 June 1946, GK, Rep. 481, Nr. 537.

80. Monthly Report of the Military Governor No. 15, 1–30 September 1946, 18.

81. Chief of Staff Brigadier General J. D. Barker to Commanding General, USFET, 21 August 1946, File 726.1 Venereal Disease, General Correspondence, Office of the AG, RG 260, NACP. Office of the Inspector General, Headquarters, Continental Base Section, USFET, to Commanding General, Continental Base Section, USFET, 17 August 1946, with exhibits, File 333.5, Classified General Correspondence 1946, AG, RG 338, NACP.

82. The measures OMGUS took to combat the spread of venereal disease in Germany echoed the vigorous quarantine measures enacted around military bases inside the United States during the war. See Allan M. Brandt, *No Magic Bullet: A Social History of Venereal Disease in the United States since 1880* (New York: Oxford University Press, 1985), 167.

83. Adjutant General G. Garde, by direction of the Military Governor, to Director, Office of Military Government for Land Wuerttemberg-Baden, 30 September 1946, File 333.5, Classified General Correspondence 1946, AG, RG 338, NACP.

84. "Arbeit verkürzt Strafe: Frauen im Arbeitserziehungslager — ein Versuch unserer Stadt," *Mannheimer Morgen,* 10 January 1948, in SM, Ortsgeschichte, S2, 449-1.

85. Adjutant General G. Garde to Director, Office of Military Government for Land Wuerttemberg-Baden, 30 September 1946; Testimony of Oberbürgermeister Joseph [sic] Braun, exhibit to Office of the Inspector General, Headquarters, Continental Base Section, USFET, to Commanding General, Continental Base Section, USFET, 17 August 1946, question 340, File 333.5, Classified General Correspondence 1946, AG, RG 338, NACP.

86. Woller, *Gesellschaft und Politik in der amerikanischen Besatzungszone*, 319. See also Testimony of Friedrick Roos, Exhibit B-3 to Office of the Inspector General, Headquarters, Continental Base Section, USFET, to Commanding General, Continental Base Section, USFET, 17 August 1946, question 158, File 333.5, Classified General Correspondence 1946, AG, RG 338, NACP.

87. Pastor Boschert to Landrat, Bamberg, 16 May 1947, SB, Bezirksamt/LRA Bamberg K5, Nr. 10214.

88. See "German Police in the U.S. Zone," 30 November 1948, Central Files, 1945-1949, Office of Director, CAD, RG 260, NACP; Office of the Chief Historian, European Command, "Public Safety," Occupation Forces in Europe Series, 1945-1946 (Frankfurt a.M.: Office of the Chief Historian, European Command, 1947), 42, CMH.

89. Division Staff Meeting Minutes, Meeting of Saturday, 11 May 1946, 6, Minutes of Division Staff Meetings, Office of Director, CAD, RG 260, NACP.

90. There were numerous instances in which African American soldiers prevented members of the German police from taking action against German women who associated with them. See, e.g., Offenbach incidents described in Special Agent N. De Vyner, Memorandum for the Officer in Charge, 14 December 1945, File 333.5, Classified General Correspondence, 1945, USFET AG, RG 338, NACP; Affidavit of Philipp Walch, Policeman, 6 January 1946, File 333.5, Classified General Correspondence, 1945, USFET AG, RG 338, NACP. Events in Wertinger, where black troops assaulted the Bürgermeister on suspicion of having reported their girlfriends to military government, came to national attention in the Meader report. See Chapter 2; Meader, "Confidential Report," Part 42, 26150-75. On Meitingen, see Captain Dana L. Todd, Interrogation of Bürgermeister Karl Liepert of Meitingen, 28 September 1946, Insp. & Inv. PSFT "E" File, Office of the Chief, 1946-1949, OMGBY Public Safety, RG 260, NACP. On Kunzelsau, see Lieutenant Colonel D. M. Witt, Report of Investigation of Alleged Misconduct of U.S. Troops in Kreis Kunzelsau, Germany, to Commanding General, VI Corps, 30 November 1945, 8, File 333.5, Classified General Correspondence, 1945, AG, RG 338, NACP. For Karlstadt, see O'Brien to Company A, 3rd Military Government, Regierungsbezirk Unterfranken, 6 August 1946. For Mannheim, see Moeller, Krim. Secretary, Notice from the Moral Police, exhibit to Office of the Inspector General, Headquarters, Continental Base Section, USFET, to Commanding General, Continental Base Section, USFET, 17 August 1946, File 333.5, Classified General Correspondence 1946, AG, RG 338, NACP; see also Karl Jering, *Überleben und Neubeginn: Aufzeichnungen eines Deutschen aus den Jahren 1945/46*, Dokumente Unserer Zeit, ed. Rudolf Birkl and Günter Olzog, Band 1 (Munich: Günter Olzog Verlag, 1979), 229; Willoughby, *Remaking the Conquering Heroes*, 63-64.

91. Lieutenant Colonel G. H. Garde to Office of Military Government for Land Bavaria, 20 December 1946, Central Files, 1945-1949, Office of Director, CAD, RG 260, NACP.

92. See Edward N. Peterson, *The American Occupation of Germany: Retreat to Victory* (Detroit: Wayne State University Press, 1977), 86.

93. See Division Staff Meeting Minutes, Meetings of Saturday, 9 March 1946, 6; 16 March 1946, 10; 27 April 1946, 10; 4 May 1946, 9; 18 May 1946, 11–12; 1 June 1946, 12; 15 June 1946, 9–10; 5 October 1946, 12–13, Minutes of Division Staff Meetings, Office of Director, CAD, RG 260, NACP; Headquarters, United States Forces European Theater, Office of the Assistant Chief of Staff, G-2, Weekly Intelligence Summary No. 36, March 1946, 2, Weekly Intelligence Summaries, 1945-1946, G-2 Section, ETO, RG 338, NACP; Draft Intelligence Summary for two-week period ending 26 July 1946, Minutes of Division Staff Meetings, Office of Director, CAD, RG 260, NACP.

94. Lieutenant Colonel Roy Cochrane, Asst. AG, by command of Lieutenant General Truscott, memorandum on cooperation with German police, 22 April 1946, File 014.12 Civil Authorities, 1946, Nuremberg RLSO, FOD, OMGBY, RG 260, NACP.

95. See Division Staff Meeting Minutes, Meeting of Saturday, 20 April 1946, Minutes of Division Staff Meetings, Office of Director, CAD, RG 260, NACP; Brigadier General T. M. Obsorne [sic], Memorandum for the Assistant Secretary of War, 1 November 1946, 3, File 333.5, Classified General Correspondence, 1945–1946, Secretary, General Staff, RG 338, NACP.

96. Lieutenant Colonel D. M. Witt, Report of Investigation of Alleged Misconduct of U.S. Troops in Kreis Kunzelsau, Germany, to Commanding General, VI Corps, 30 November 1945, 7, File 333.5, Classified General Correspondence, 1945, AG, RG 338, NACP. See also O'Brien to Company A, 3rd Military Government, Regierungsbezirk Unterfranken, 6 August 1946, reporting an incident in which the local public safety officer told a group of African American soldiers that one of their fellow soldiers had been injured in a motorcycle accident. The soldiers urged the injured soldier to tell them if he had actually been beaten by members of military government or the constabulary, so that they could exact revenge.

97. See, e.g., Major Charles M. O'Donnell to Director, Office of Military Government for Bavaria, 26 October 1946, File 250.1, General Correspondence, Office of the AG, RG 260, NACP; Leder, "Americans and German Youth in Nuremberg," 103–4; O'Brien to Company A, 3rd Military Government, Regierungs-bezirk Unterfranken, 6 August 1946.

98. Annual historical report — 23 April 1945 to 30 June 1946, 33, Correspondence and Related Records, 1945–1949, Weißenburg RLSO, FOD, OMGBY, RG 260, NACP.

99. "Rücksprache mit der Militärregierung am 10.4.1946," SW, Rep. 412, Bd. 4.

100. Peter Zeitler, *Neubeginn in Oberfranken, 1945–1949: Die Landkreise Kronach und Kulmbach* (Kronach: 1000 Jahre Kronach e.V., 1997), 125.

101. File in Case No. 191, Summary Military Court, Summary Court Case Files, August 1947–September 1948, Weißenburg RLSO, FOD, OMGBY, RG 260, NACP.

102. Testimony of Ilse Matthisson, taken by Lieutenant Colonel Allen D. Raymond Jr. on 8 July 1946, 14, Exhibit B to Lieutenant Colonel Allen D. Raymond Jr., Assistant Inspector General, Headquarters, Third U.S. Army, to Commanding General, Third U.S. Army, 23 July 1946.

103. Ibid., 14. See also First Lieutenant Woodburn C. Williams to Colonel F. J. Pearson, 8 June 1946, 5, Exhibit A-1 to Lieutenant Colonel Allen D. Raymond Jr. to

Commanding General, Third U.S. Army, 23 July 1946. (It is unclear whether clemency was granted.)

104. In late March the Weißenburg police compiled for military government a list of all incidents involving African American soldiers, dating back to September 1945, before the 351st moved into the area. Chief of Town Police Strassner, "List of especial affairs with American colored soldiers," 28 March 1946, SW, Bestand 412, Bd. 1. Lieutenant Williams evidently used the material as the basis for a letter alerting the USFET inspector general's office to the situation in Weißenburg. See Williams to Pearson, 8 June 1946.

105. Testimony of Major Linton S. Boatwright, Exhibit B, to Lieutenant Colonel Allen D. Raymond Jr. to Commanding General, Third U.S. Army, 23 July 1946, 97, 100, 109, File 333.5, General Correspondence of AG, 1945–1947, Third Army, USFET, RG 338, NACP.

106. Raymond to Commanding General, Third U.S. Army, 23 July 1946, 5 and Exhibit B, testimony of Second Lieutenant Thomas J. Carney, 41–42, and testimony of Boatwright, 119.

107. Second Lieutenant Glen Bowser to Director, Office of Military Government for Bavaria, 30 June 1946, File 250.1, General Correspondence, Office of the AG, RG 260, NACP; Testimony of Ilse Matthisson, 8 July 1946, 18. For similar plans elsewhere, see, e.g., Willoughby, "The Sexual Behavior of American GIs," 164–65.

108. First Lieutenant Woodburn C. Williams to Director, Office of Military Government for Bavaria, 5 June 1946, 1, File 250.1, General Correspondence, Office of the AG, RG 260, NACP.

109. Williams's prejudice did not prevent him from signing off on the paperwork necessary for a Frenchwoman in town to marry a soldier from the unit, who must have been black. See application in SW, Bestand 412, Bd. 1.

110. Woodburn C. Williams to Director, Office of Military Government for Bavaria, 5 June 1946, 3.

111. Ibid., 1.

112. Ibid., 2. Lieutenant Williams stated that offenses by the African American troops were difficult to prosecute because "identification is impossible because they [look] so much alike to outsiders." Ibid.

113. "Rücksprache mit der Militärregierung am 10.4.1946," SW, Rep. 412, Bd. 4.

114. Annual historical report—23 April 1945 to 30 June 1946, 33, Correspondence and Related Records, 1945–1949, Weißenburg RLSO, FOD, OMGBY, RG 260, NACP.

115. Williams to Director, Office of Military Government for Bavaria, 5 June 1946, 2.

116. On the responsibilities of the constabulary and procedures for cooperation with military government and German police officials, see H. M. Page, Asst. AG, Directive and Policies Governing the Formation and Operation of the U.S. Constabulary, U.S. Zone, Germany, 12 March 1946, incl. 2, Operational Procedure, U.S. Constabulary, Military Government, and German Police Agencies, Cases Closed File, Reports, 1945–1949, Kulmbach RLSO, FOD, OMGBY, RG 260, NACP; Untitled Report, Public Safety Branch, Office of Military Government for Bavaria, 29 July 1946, File 333.5, AG Decimal File, 1945–1946, RG 260, NACP. Relations between the constabulary and military government seem to have been smooth.

See, e.g., Inspection Trip report by Office of the Inspector General, USFET, to Deputy Director, Military Government, U.S. Army, 7 September 1946, 2, File 336.7-1, Central Files, Office of Director, CAD, RG 260, NACP.

117. In Meitingen, sixty-one women were arrested and subjected to a VD check. Thirty-one of the women had improper registration. Headquarters, 74th Constabulary Squadron, to Commanding General, U.S. Constabulary, Attn: A. C. of S., G-2, 29 August 1946, General Correspondence 1944–1947, G-2, Third Army, RG 338, NACP.

118. Deputy Military Governor Lucius Clay testified before a Senate committee investigating military government that "[e]xcept in emergency [the members of the constabulary] do not arrest Germans, only at the request of the military government." Testimony of Lieutenant General Lucius D. Clay, deputy governor, American military government, Germany, U.S. Senate Special Committee Investigating the National Defense Program, *Investigation of the National Defense Program,* Hearings before a Special Committee Investigating the National Defense Program, 80th Cong., 1st sess., 18 November 1946, Part 42, 25877.

119. See David Brion Davis, "World War II and Memory," *The Journal of American History* 77 (1990): 585–86.

120. Libby, "Policing Germany," 16, 115, quoting Harmon, Personal Memoirs of Harmon, 181, box 3, Harmon Papers, Army War College, Carlisle Barracks, Pennsylvania.

121. Headquarters, U.S. Constabulary, Staff Conference Notes, 5 July 1946, 1, Daily Staff Conference Notes, 1946–December 1947, Constabulary, EUCOM, RG 338, NACP.

122. Libby, "Policing Germany," 22, 38–50.

123. Libby lists the constabulary's VD rate in July 1946 as 190.72 per 1,000 per year. Libby, "Policing Germany," 51. The rate for white troops at that time was 203 per 1,000, whereas the average for Negro units was 806 per 1,000 per annum, yielding a weighted average VD rate of 276. "The Relations of Occupation Personnel with the Civil Population, 1946–1948," Occupation Forces in Europe Series, 1946–1948 (Karlsruhe: Historical Division, European Command, 1951), 37, CMH. During the war, Harmon had instituted a divisional brothel while his unit was stationed in Oran, Algeria, as a means of combating venereal disease, but he did not attempt such measures in postwar Germany. Major General E. N. Harmon, with Milton Mackaye and William Ross Mackaye, *Combat Commander: Autobiography of a Soldier* (Englewood Cliffs, N.J.: Prentice-Hall, 1970), 146–47.

124. Headquarters, 53rd Constabulary Squadron, Report of Operations (1 August 1946–31 August 1946), 4 September 1946, Constabulary Section, U.S. Army Units, RG 338, NACP; Cliford Robinson, Individual Report of Case of Venereal Disease, 1 October 1946, Records of the Public Safety Officer, 1945–1949, Bruchsal RLSO, FOD, OMGW-B, RG 260, NACP. A pastor in Ermershausen-Birkenfeld reported to his superiors that members of the constabulary were encouraging prostitution in the neighboring community. Report from Evang.-Luth. Pfarramt, Ermershausen-Birkenfeld in Mainfranken, to Evang.-Luth. Landeskirchenrat Muenchen, 2 September 1946, Landeskirchliches Archiv, Nuremberg, LkR V, Nr. 904a.

125. Bürgermeister of Philippsburg to Militärregierung Bruchsal, 3 January 1947, Records of the Public Safety Officer, 1945–1949, Bruchsal RLSO, FOD, OMGW-B, RG 260, NACP.

126. See Special Agent Robert M. Weldon, Memorandum to Officer in Charge, 16 May 1946, File 250.1, General Correspondence, 1946, Admin. Branch, Office of the AG, RG 338, NACP.

127. Analysis and Reports Section, Office of the Director of Intelligence, OMGUS, Intelligence summary for the two-week period ending 12 July 1946, 12 July 1946, Minutes of Division Staff Meetings, Office of Director, CAD, RG 260, NACP. See also O'Brien to Company A, 3rd Military Government, Regierungsbezirk Unterfranken, 6 August 1946, attributing trouble in Karstadt over one weekend to the dispensing of liquor in bottles during the time that the local club was closed.

128. Lieutenant Colonel Walter E. Forry to Commanding General, Third U.S. Army, 8 July 1945, 9, File 291.2, AG Correspondence, 1945, RG 338, NACP. This comment was repeated in the report of the XX Corps's Ordnance Officer. See Lieutenant Colonel M. L. De Guire to Commanding General XX Corps (Attn: Chemical Officer), 8 July 1945, 5, File 291.2, AG Correspondence, 1945, RG 338, NACP.

129. Dr. Köhler to the American Military Government for Wuerttemberg-Baden, c/o Colonel Dawson, 8 July 1946, GK, Rep. 481, Nr. 723; see also Zimmerman, Präsident Landesbezirks Baden—Abt. Innere Verwaltung, to Herrn Präsidenten des Landsbezirks Baden, 28 June 1946, GK, Rep. 481, Nr. 723. The Department of the Interior in Landesbezirk Baden forwarded Father Sales's sensational account of the situation in Waghäusel to the president of Landesbezirk Baden with the note that the "troubles depicted therein apply not only to Waghäusel, but to all locations in the district where colored soldiers are stationed."

130. Major Frank Meszar to Office of Military Government for Bavaria, Public Safety Office for Regierungsbezirk Oberfranken and Mittelfranken, Ansbach, 30 August 1946, File 250.1, General Correspondence, Office of the AG, RG 260, NACP. In addition, one man who worked for the soldiers was arrested. The report erroneously stated that twenty-three women had been arrested. The records from Amtsgerichtsgefängnis Kulmbach indicate that twenty-two women and one man were brought to the jail at 1:00 A.M. on the morning of 30 August 1946. Gefängnisverwalter, Amtsgerichtsgefängnis Kulmbach, undated report, Correspondence and Related Records, 1945–1949, Kulmbach RLSO, FOD, OMGBY, RG 260, NACP.

131. Major H. C. Kauffman to Lieutenant Colonel R. A. Reese, 5 September 1946, File 250.1, General Correspondence, Office of the AG, RG 260, NACP.

132. Gefängnisverwalter, Amtsgerichtsgefängnis Kulmbach, undated report. There is some disagreement on the number of women suffering from venereal disease. The prison report indicates that six women were infected, but according to Major Kauffman, six of the women were suffering from gonorrhea and four from syphilis. Major H. C. Kauffman to Lieutenant Colonel R. A. Reese, 5 September 1946.

133. Captain Norman E. Petty to Commanding Officer, Company B, 3rd Mil. Govt. Regt., Regierungsbezirk Ober- und Mittelfranken, 18 September 1946, and attached report, Correspondence and Related Records, 1945–1949, Kulmbach RLSO, FOD, OMGBY, RG 260, NACP.

134. Glen Bowser to Director, Office of Military Government for Bavaria, 26 July 1946, General Records, 1945–1949, Weißenburg RLSO, FOD, OMGBY, RG 260, NACP; Testimony of Second Lieutenant Glen Bowser, Exhibit B, 20, to Lieutenant Colonel Allen D. Raymond Jr., Assistant Inspector General, Headquarters, Third United States Army, to Commanding General, Third U.S. Army, 23 July 1946.

135. Bowser to Director, Office of Military Government for Bavaria, 26 July 1946.

136. Case No. 210, Summary Court Case Files, August 1947–September 1948, Weißenburg RLSO, FOD, OMGBY, RG 260, NACP.

137. Bowser to Director, Office of Military Government for Bavaria, 26 July 1946.

138. Weißenburg Summary Military Court Case No. 225, Summary Court Case Files, August 1947–September 1948, Weißenburg RLSO, FOD, OMGBY, RG 260, NACP.

139. Ibid.

140. Bowser to Director, Office of Military Government for Bavaria, 26 July 1946.

141. Testimony of Dr. Ruppercht Schaumberg, Exhibit B, 88, attached to Raymond to Commanding General, Third U.S. Army, 23 July 1946, Weekly Reports of the Summary Court Weißenburg, 2 August 1946 and 24 August 1946, General Records, 1945–1949, Weißenburg RLSO, FOD, OMGBY, RG 260, NACP.

142. In Waghäusel the unit had been transferred to another town before the complaints against it were investigated. The commander of the unit explained that he would make "[e]very effort . . . to indoctrinate . . . the troops . . . [with] high moral and disciplinary standards." Lieutenant Colonel Norman H. Gold to Commanding General, Third United States Army, 14 June 1946, File 250.1, General Correspondence, 1946, Admin. Branch, Office of the AG, RG 338, NACP. African American soldiers in Mannheim likewise seem to have largely escaped punishment for attacks on German police in 1946, a fact attributed by a member of the local security police to the "hesitancy" of tactical unit commanders to take disciplinary action against soldiers arrested by the security police. Testimony of First Lieutenant Wellington C. Livingston, exhibit to Office of the Inspector General, Headquarters, Continental Base Section, USFET, to Commanding General, Continental Base Section, USFET, 17 August 1946, question 220, File 333.5, Classified General Correspondence 1946, AG, RG 338, NACP.

143. Testimony of Boatwright, 109. The inspector general investigation into the situation in Weißenburg also disclosed that the white commander of the battalion, Lieutenant Colonel Palmer, had been cohabiting with a married German woman, had allegedly threatened her husband, and had attempted to assist her in obtaining an abortion, which actions the investigator determined had lowered the prestige of the army. The investigator initiated charges against Palmer for those actions. See Raymond to Commanding General, Third U.S. Army, 23 July 1946, and attached exhibits.

144. Second Lieutenant Glen Bowser to Commanding Officer, 351st Field Artillery Battalion, Schwabach (Attention: Lieutenant Colonel Palmer), 3 July 1946, copies to 53rd Constabulary, General Records, 1945–1949, Weißenburg RLSO, FOD, OMGBY, RG 260, NACP.

145. Rücksprache mit der Militärregierung, 2 July 1946, SW, Files of Weißenburg Government, Rep. 412, Bd. 4.

146. Artillery Section Report for the Month of May 1946, Appendix IX, Section B, 7, Third Army Records, Reports, 1945–1947, RG 338, USFET, NACP.

147. Unit History of 351st Field Artillery Battalion, Unit Histories File, CMH; Rücksprache mit der Militärregierung, 3 August 1946, SW, Files of Weißenburg Government, Rep. 412, Bd. 4.

148. Major Frank Meszar to Office of Military Government for Bavaria, Public Safety Office for Regierungsbezirk Oberfranken and Mittelfranken, Ansbach, 30 August 1946, File 250.1, General Correspondence, Office of the AG, RG 260, NACP; Major H. C. Kauffman to Lieutenant Colonel R. A. Reese, 5 September 1946.

149. The OMGBY security report for the period described events in Wirsberg as the "attempts of undisciplined colored troops to intimidate the population." Periodic Report for Week ending 4 September 1946, Investigative Correspondence and Reports, Land Director, OMGBY, RG 260, NACP. See also Major Charles M. O'Donnell to Director, Office of Military Government for Bavaria, 26 October 1946, File 250.1, General Correspondence, Office of the AG, RG 260, NACP.

150. Meszar to Office of Military Government for Bavaria, Public Safety Office for Regierungsbezirk Oberfranken and Mittelfranken, Ansbach, 30 August 1946.

151. Major H. C. Kauffman to Lieutenant Colonel R. A. Reese, 5 September 1946.

152. Georg Lowig, Landrat des Landkreises Nürnberg to Regierungspräsidenten Ober- und Mittelfranken, 31 May 1946, SN, Rep. 270, Nr. 1704.

153. Incident Report Reference No. TUSA/TPM 01266, Colonel Frederick R. Lafferty, Deputy Theater Provost Marshal, Headquarters, USFET, Office of the Theater Provost Marshal, 3 July 1946, File 250.1, General Correspondence, 1946, Admin. Branch, Office of the AG, RG 338, NACP. The incident report contains the English translation of a report by German authorities. The German original was not included.

154. Captain T. W. Suchara, by command of General McNarney, to Commanding General, Third U.S. Army Area, 22 July 1946, File 250.1, General Correspondence, 1946, Admin. Branch, Office of the AG, RG 338, NACP.

155. Colonel P. W. Brown to Adjutant General, 7 October 1946, File 250.1, General Correspondence, 1946, Admin. Branch, Office of the AG, RG 338, NACP.

156. Division Staff Meeting Minutes, 24 August 1946, 9, Minutes of Division Staff Meetings, Office of Director, CAD, RG 260, NACP.

157. See Testimony of Boatwright, 95–97; Major H. C. Kauffman to Lieutenant Colonel R. A. Reese, 5 September 1946; Note to Major Kauffman, 4 September 1946, File 250.1, General Correspondence, Office of the AG, RG 260, NACP.

158. Röder to Regierungspräsident, 15 May 1946, SN, Rep. 270, Nr. 1704.

159. Lucius Clay to Colonel Robinson, 31 October 1946, File 250.1, General Correspondence, Office of the AG, RG 260, NACP, commenting on letter from Brigadier General Walter J. Muller to Deputy Military Governor, OMGUS, 26 October 1946, File 250.1, General Correspondence, Office of the AG, RG 260, NACP.

160. Weißenburg historical report — 23 April 1945 to 30 June 1946, 33.

161. Hoecker and Meyer-Braun, *Bremerinnen bewältigen die Nachkriegszeit*, 24.

162. See, e.g., "Die Trauer um Dr. Gröber: Weihbischof Dr. Burger zum Kapitularvikar gewählt," *Badische-Zeitung*, 20 February 1948, quoting a statement by the Baden government eulogizing Archbishop Gröber of Freiburg upon his death as a "German patriot, in the noblest sense of the word." GK, Rep. 481, Nr. 339.

163. Quoted by Peter Seewald, "'Grüß Gott, ihr seid frei': Passau 1945," in *1945: Deutschland in der Stunde Null*, ed. Wolfgang Malanowski (Reinbek bei Hamburg: SPIEGEL Verlag, 1985), 114–15.

164. Letter to the editor, *Stern*, 8 August 1948, quoted in Kleinschmidt, *"Do Not Fraternize,"* 184.

165. This relationship has been noted by historians in the German and other contexts. See, e.g., Martha Hodes, "The Mercurial Nature and Abiding Power of Race: A Transnational Family Story," *AHR* 108 (2003): 84–118.

166. Padover, *Experiment in Germany,* 263. Edward Peterson describes Padover as "an avid liberal army propagandist." Peterson, *The American Occupation of Germany,* 140.

167. Testimony of Captain Tyrone J. McCullough, Exhibit B-16, to Witt to Commanding General, VI Corps, 30 November 1945, 64.

168. Gemeinde Wiesental Polizei Report to American Military Government in Bruchsal, 17 May 1946 (English translation and German original), Records of the Public Safety Officer, 1945–1949, Bruchsal RLSO, FOD, OMGW-B, RG 260, NACP.

169. Ibid.

170. Herder, *Sämtliche Werke,* vol. 13, 235. I have used Ernst Menze's translation. Adler and Menze, ed., *On World History,* 183. The "Negro" entry in *Allgemeine deutsche Real-Encyklopädie für die gebildeten Stände: Conversations-Lexikon,* vol. 10, *Moskau bis Patricier* (Leipzig: Brockhaus, 1846), listed among the "Negro" race's physical characteristics "thick, thrust out lips" (*dicken, aufgeworfenen Lippen*).

171. Karl Friedrich Schaller, "Polizei und Geschlechtskrankheitenbekämpfung," *Zeitschrift für Haut- und Geschlechtskrankheiten* 4 (1948): 297. This rhetorical exclusion is similar to that discerned by Mire Koikari with respect to Japanese prostitutes and Ruth Frankenberg with U.S. women. See Koikari, "Rethinking Gender and Power," 328; Frankenberg, *White Women,* 104. For similar views of poor white South African amateur prostitutes, see Karen Jochelson, *The Colour of Disease: Syphilis and Racism in South Africa, 1880–1950* (Houndsmills: Palgrave, 2001), 72.

172. The Archbishop of Freiburg, 7 May 1946, Enclosure No. 1, to Morris O. Edwards, Memorandum regarding Troop-Civilian Relations to Deputy Military Governor, 16 May 1946, File 250.1, General Correspondence, Office of the AG, RG 260, NACP. Imhoff likewise warned that the attacks on the police threatened to undermine all respect for law and order. Imhoff to Military Government, 17 July 1946.

173. On the postwar idealization of the Third Reich as a period of sexual rectitude, see Heineman, *What Difference Does a Husband Make?* 72. I detect more disquiet about sexuality in postwar German attitudes than appears in the work of Dagmar Herzog. See Herzog, *Sex after Fascism: Memory and Morality in Twentieth-Century Germany* (Princeton, N.J.: Princeton University Press, 2005); Herzog, "Desperately Seeking Normality: Sex and Marriage in the Wake of the War," in *Life after Death: Approaches to a Cultural and Social History of Europe during the 1940s and 1950s,* ed. Richard Bessel and Dirk Schumann (Cambridge: German Historical Institute, Washington, D.C., and Cambridge University Press, 2003), 161–92.

174. Report from Evang.-Luth. Pfarramt, Ermershausen-Birkenfeld in Mainfranken, to Evang.-Luth. Landeskirchenrat Muenchen, 2 September 1946, Landeskirchliches Archiv, Nuremberg, LkR V, Nr. 904a.

175. Weekly Intelligence Report No. 57, week ending 26 June 1946, General Correspondence 1944–1947, Office of the Assistant Chief of Staff, G-2, Headquarters, Third Army, RG 338, NACP.

176. Testimony of Dr. Lorenz Burkert, Bürgermeister, Exhibit B-4, to Witt to Commanding General, VI Corps, 30 November 1945, 26.

177. *Amtsblatt für die Erzdiözese Freiburg,* 12 May 1945, 14.

Chapter 4: Fräuleins and Black GIs: Race, Sex, and Power

1. Du Bois, *The Souls of Black Folk*, 45; Roi Ottley, *No Green Pastures* (New York: Charles Scribner's Sons, 1951); Morehouse, *Fighting in the Jim Crow Army*, 201; Myrdal, *An American Dilemma*, 2:928. Myrdal wrote that Negro culture was "*a distorted development, or a pathological condition, of the general American culture*" (emphasis original). C. G. Jung detected a "negroid" influence on all Americans. Quoted in Dan Diner, *America in the Eyes of the Germans: An Essay on Anti-Americanism*, trans. Allison Brown (Princeton, N.J.: Marcus Wiener Publishers, 1996), 72.

2. See Ute Frevert, *Frauen-Geschichte: Zwischen bürgerlicher Verbesserung und neuer Weiblichkeit* (Frankfurt a.M.: Suhrkamp Verlag, 1986), 244–52.

3. On the loss of place in white American society in this period for white women who married black men, see Romano, *Race Mixing*, 74, 89, 106–7, 134. In her study of interracial rape in twentieth-century Virginia, Lisa Lindquist Dorr has described how white Virginian women who deviated from "middle-class morality" risked losing their "status as innocent victims," even where the alleged perpetrator was black. Lisa Johanna Lindquist Dorr, "'Messin' White Women': White Women, Black Men, and Rape in Virginia, 1900–1960" (Ph.D. diss., University of Virginia, 2000), 19.

4. Koeppen, *Pigeons on the Grass*, 110–11; Koeppen, *Tauben im Gras*, 123.

5. Landpolizei Ober/Mittelfranken Posten Neuenmarkt to Bez.-Insp. der Landpolizei in Kulmbach, 22 November 1947, SB, K13, Nr. 7827.

6. The quotation comes from Dörr, "*Wer die Zeit nicht miterlebt hat . . . ,*" 444. See Goedde, *GIs and Germans*, 64–65. For recollections of African Americans' friendly dealings with children, see Leder, "Americans and German Youth," 88; Niethammer, "*Hinterher merkt man,*" 22–23; Hügel-Marshall, *Invisible Woman*, 18. On the tradition of viewing blacks as childlike, see Gilman, "Black Sexuality and Modern Consciousness," 39; Massin, "From Virchow to Fischer," 95, 98–99; Sadji, *Das Bild des Negro-Afrikaners*, 133; Fredrickson, *The Black Image in the White Mind*; Richard Wright, "The American Problem—Its Negro Phase," in *Richard Wright: Impressions and Perspectives*, ed. David Ray and Robert M. Farnsworth (Ann Arbor: University of Michigan Press, 1971), 11.

7. Note to Major Kauffman, 4 September 1946, File 250.1, General Correspondence, Office of the AG, RG 260, NACP.

8. Trial Record, Summary Military Court, Case No. 217, Summary Court Case Files, August 1947–September 1948, Weißenburg RLSO, FOD, OMGBY, RG 260, NACP.

9. Statement of Karoline R., in report of Dr. Güntner, Public Prosecutor, to Military Government, Special Branch, Mannheim, 8 July 1948, 3, General Records, 1946–1949, Mannheim RLSO, FOD, OMGW-B, RG 260, NACP.

10. Historians of the question have taken pains to refute the commonly held belief of the time. See Fehrenbach, *Race after Hitler*, 66–67; Fehrenbach, "Of German Mothers and 'Negermischlingskinder,'" 168, 182; Fehrenbach, "Rehabilitating Father*land*," 115; Lester, "Blacks in Germany," 122.

11. Special Agent N. De Vyner, Memorandum for the Officer in Charge, 14 December 1945, 3, File 333.5, Classified General Correspondence, 1945, USFET AG, RG 338, NACP.

12. Lieutenant Colonel Hyman Y. Chase, Venereal Disease Control among Negro Troops in EUCOM, 3, Quarterly Operations Reports, Personnel and Administration Division, EUCOM, RG 338, NACP.

13. See Round Table, "Are Negroes Good Soldiers?" *Negro Digest,* December 1945, 30, quoting Senator James O. Eastland of Mississippi as stating that Negro soldiers had crossed the color line in Europe and had relations with "white girls of the very lowest caliber." More generally, see Martha Hodes, *White Women, Black Men: Illicit Sex in the Nineteenth-Century South* (New Haven, Conn.: Yale University Press, 1997).

14. See Eyferth, Brandt, and Hawel, *Farbige Kinder in Deutschland,* 16, 27; Fehrenbach, "Of German Mothers and 'Negermischlingskinder,'" 168, 182; Fehrenbach, "Rehabilitating Father*land*," 115; Lester, "Blacks in Germany," 122.

15. Vernon W. Stone, "German Baby Crop Left by Negro GI's," *The Survey,* November 1949, 581.

16. See "The Position of Women in German Society," extracted from a report by Intelligence Section, Office of Military Government for Bavaria, 6870th District Information Services Control Command, 7 January 1946, included as Annex No. 7 to G-2 Weekly Intelligence Report No. 34, Third Army, G-2, General Correspondence 1944–1947, RG 338, NACP. "In a nation at war the social mobility of women was greatly enhanced. Social disorganization was considerable. Women moved to new jobs, homes were bombed out, husbands and lovers were killed at the front. Interpenetration of social classes was accelerated." Neither Stone nor Eyferth provided information on the situation of the women at the time that they conceived their children.

17. Eyferth's study testified to the continuing importance of the act of having crossed the color line for women's status in West Germany, observing that the situation of mothers of biracial children was largely determined by the fact that they had borne biracial children. Eyferth, Brandt, and Hawel, *Farbige Kinder in Deutschland,* 30. For a discussion of the perceived taint of blackness for white women in relationships with black men in a different historical context, see Hodes, "Mercurial Nature," 107.

18. Arrest Report of Gertrud W., 7 June 1946, Records of the Public Safety Officer, 1945–1949, Bruchsal RLSO, FOD, OMGW-B, RG 260, NACP.

19. Ibid.

20. See, e.g., Sitzung des Bezirksverbandstages Ober- und Mittelfranken, 28 January 1946, SN, Rep. 270, Nr. 23.

21. Rücksprache mit der Militärverwaltung 24 January 1946, SW, Files of Weißenburg Government, Rep. 412, Nr. 4; Bowser to Director, Office of Military Government for Bavaria, 26 July 1946.

22. Röder to Regierungspräsident, Ober und Mittelfranken, 15 May 1946, SN, Rep. 270, Nr. 1704. On the stereotypical characteristics of *Amiliebchen* in general as foreign, work-shy, and immoral, see Dörr, *"Wer die Zeit nicht miterlebt hat . . . ,"* 430. The army survey of Giessen residents' attitudes toward African American troops asserted that most of the women who associated with the soldiers were transients, without explaining the basis for that conclusion. "Reactions of Germans to Negro Troops," Information Control Intelligence Summary No. 16, 27 October 1945, Records Relating to Public Opinion, 1945–1949, Opinion Surveys Branch, ICD, RG 260, NACP.

23. Frevert, *Women in German History,* 191; Mosse, *Nationalism and Sexuality,* 90–100. On American attitudes, see Kathy Peiss and Christina Simmons, "Passion and Power: An Introduction," in *Passion and Power,* 5.

24. On African Americans' awareness of Nazi racism, see Grill and Jenkins, "The Nazis and the American South," 668, 677; Rex Stewart, *Boy Meets Horn,*

ed. Claire P. Gordon, Michigan American Music Series, ed. Richard Crawford (Ann Arbor: University of Michigan Press, 1991), 180; Rosenberg, " 'Sounds Suspiciously Like Miami' "; Finkle, "The Conservative Aims of Militant Rhetoric," 701. On resistance of African American GIs' family members to relations with German women, see Romano, *Race Mixing*, 82–88; Höhn, "*Heimat* in Turmoil," 161n42.

25. The "psychosocial study" of African Americans published by Abram Kardiner and Lionel Ovesey in 1951 included an admittedly "impressionistically" based study of the "sexual mores of the urban Negro," which concluded that for middle- and upper-class African American men, "sex relations with white women have a high demonstrative value in terms of pride and prestige." Abram Kardiner and Lionel Ovesey, *The Mark of Oppression: A Psychosocial Study of the American Negro* (New York: W. W. Norton & Co., 1951), 69.

26. Frevert, *Frauen-Geschichte*, 252.

27. Sierra A. Bruckner, "Spectacles of (Human) Nature: Commercial Ethnography between Leisure, Learning, and *Schaulust*," in *Worldly Provincialism*, ed. Penny and Bunzl, 144–51.

28. Marks, "Black Watch on the Rhine," 302.

29. Campt, Grosse, and Lemke Muniz de Faria, "Blacks, Germans, and the Politics of Imperial Imagination," 221.

30. Heinz Boberach, ed., *Meldungen aus dem Reich, 1938–1945: Die geheimen Lageberichte des Sicherheitsdienstes der SS*, vol. 5 (Herrsching: Pawlak Verlag, 1984), 1358.

31. Heineman, *What Difference Does a Husband Make?* 56–59; Rupp, *Mobilizing Women for War*, 124; Robert Gellately, *The Gestapo and German Society: Enforcing Racial Policy, 1935–1945* (Oxford: Clarendon Press, 1990), 251; Ulrich Herbert, *Hitler's Foreign Workers: Enforced Foreign Labor in Germany under the Third Reich*, trans. William Templer (Cambridge: Cambridge University Press, 1997), 75–77, 128–33, 268–69; Boberach, *Meldungen aus dem Reich*, 5:3201.

32. Margot Dominika Kreuzer, "Die Entwicklung der heterosexuellen Prostitution in Frankfurt am Main von 1945 bis zur Gegenwart unter besonderer Betrachtung des Einflusses von Syphilis und AIDS" (Doktorgrades der Medizin diss., Johann Wolfgang Goethe–Universität, 1987), 218–33.

33. On the habit of regarding all women who associated with African American soldiers as prostitutes, see Fehrenbach, *Race after Hitler*, 66; Fehrenbach, "Of German Mothers and 'Negermischlingskinder,' " 168–69; Höhn, "*Heimat* in Turmoil," 154. On the difficulty of defining prostitution, see Goedde, *GIs and Germans*, 91; Goedde, "From Villains to Victims," 8.

34. Translation of arrest report for suspicion of prostitution and VD of Magdalene E., 30 April 1946, Records of the Public Safety Officer, 1945–1949, Bruchsal RLSO, FOD, OMGW-B, RG 260, NACP.

35. Quoted in John Costello, *Virtue under Fire: How World War II Changed Our Social and Sexual Attitudes* (New York: Fromm International Publishing, 1987), 13–15. See also Goedde, *GIs and Germans*, 90–91.

36. "The Position of Women in German Society," Third Army, G-2, General Correspondence 1944–1947, RG 338, NACP. The literature appears unanimous on this point. See Heineman, *What Difference Does a Husband Make?* 96; Tamara Domentat, *"Hallo Fräulein": Deutsche Frauen und amerikanische Soldaten* (Berlin: Aufbau-Verlag, 1998), 163.

37. See Biddiscombe, "Dangerous Liaisons," 613. On bourgeois expectations for women's work and marriage strategies, see Frevert, *Women in German History*, 37–49. On such expectations and the realities in the 1930s, see Stephenson, *Women in Nazi Society*, 80–83, who concludes that during the Depression "most married women worked out of dire necessity." Ibid., 83.

38. Allied Control Council Order No. 3, 17 January 1946, in *Sammlung der vom Allierten Kontrollrat und der Amerikanischen Militärregierung erlassenen Proklamationen*, Hemken; Testimony of Doctor Hugo Swart, Oberbürgermeister, Heidelberg, taken by Captain Paul Peltcs, IGD, 30 September 1946, at question 52, attachment to report of investigation to Office of the Inspector General, Headquarters, Third United States Army, 8 October 1946, File 333.5, General Correspondence of AG, 1945–1947, Third United States Army, RG 338, NACP; Heineman, *What Difference Does a Husband Make?* 87–89; Heineman, "The Hour of the Woman"; Nori Möding, "Die Stunde der Frauen? Frauen und Frauenorganisationen des bürgerlichen Lagers," in *Von Stalingrad zur Währungsreform: Zur Sozialgeschichte des Umbruchs in Deutschland*, ed. Martin Broszat, Klaus-Dietmar Henke, and Hans Woller (Munich: R. Oldenbourg Verlag, 1990), 620–22.

39. See Heineman, *What Difference Does a Husband Make?* 87–89.

40. Weekly Intelligence Report No. 61, week ending 24 July 1946, General Correspondence 1944–1947, Office of the Assistant Chief of Staff, G-2, Headquarters, Third Army, RG 338, NACP.

41. Sitzung des Bezirksverbandstages Ober- und Mittelfranken, 28 January 1946, SN, Rep. 270, Nr. 23. See also the Archbishop of Freiburg, 7 May 1946, Enclosure No. 1, to Morris O. Edwards, Memorandum regarding Troop-Civilian Relations to Deputy Military Governor, 16 May 1946, File 250.1, General Correspondence, Office of the AG, RG 260, NACP.

42. Being confined for venereal disease treatment carried the stigma of prostitution with it, although the connection was not a necessary one. Indeed, the chief doctor of the Nussbaum venereal disease hospital, to which the women from Weißenburg were confined, referred to the women as black soldiers' "fiances" and "girl friends." Testimony of Hans Muggenthaler, Exhibit B, 79–80, to Lieutenant Colonel Allen D. Raymond Jr., Assistant Inspector General, Headquarters, Third United States Army, to Commanding General, Third U.S. Army, 23 July 1946, File 333.5, General Correspondence of AG, 1945–1947, Third Army, RG 338, NACP.

43. Georg Lowig to Regierungspräsidenten Ober- und Mittelfranken, 31 May 1946, SN, Rep. 270, Nr. 1704. See also Testimony of Friedrick Roos, Exhibit B-3, to Office of the Inspector General, Headquarters, Continental Base Section, USFET, to Commanding General, Continental Base Section, USFET, 17 August 1946, question 158, File 333.5, Classified General Correspondence 1946, AG, RG 338, NACP.

44. Trial Record, Summary Military Court, Case No. 226, Summary Court Case Files, August 1947–September 1948, Weißenburg RLSO, FOD, OMGBY, RG 260, NACP.

45. Trial Record, Summary Military Court, Case No. 235, Summary Court Case Files, August 1947–September 1948, Weißenburg RLSO, FOD, OMGBY, RG 260, NACP.

46. Domentat, *"Hallo Fräulein,"* 164; Shukert and Scibetta, *War Brides of World War II*, 130.

47. Hoecker and Meyer-Braun, *Bremerinnen bewältigen die Nachkriegszeit*, 35; Boyer and Woller, " 'Hat die deutsche Frau versagt?' " 34–36.

48. Trial Records, Summary Military Court, Case Nos. 211, 212, 213, 223, 214, and 222, Summary Court Case Files, August 1947–September 1948, Weißenburg RLSO, FOD, OMGBY, RG 260, NACP.

49. Annex No. 5 to G-2 Weekly Intelligence Report No. 71, HQ Third U.S. Army, October 1946, File 319.1, General Correspondence, 1944–1947, G-2, Third Army, RG 338, USFET, NACP.

50. Testimony of Doctor Hugo Swart, Oberbürgermeister, Heidelberg, taken by Captain Paul Peltcs, IGD, 30 September 1946, at question 54, attachment to report of investigation to Commanding General, Third U.S. Army, 8 October 1946, File 333.5, General Correspondence of AG, 1945–1947, Third United States Army, RG 338, NACP. See also Shukert and Scibetta, *War Brides of World War II,* 130.

51. Massaquoi, *Destined to Witness,* 306–7, 319.

52. Olen Conaway, Individual Report of Case of Venereal Disease, 13 June 1946, Records of the Public Safety Officer, 1945–1949, Bruchsal RLSO, FOD, OMGW-B, RG 260, NACP. On soldiers' celebration of "shabby and perfunctory" relations with women, see Henry Elkin, "Aggressive and Erotic Tendencies in Army Life," *American Journal of Sociology* 51 (1946): 412.

53. Osmar White, *Conquerors' Road* (Cambridge: Cambridge University Press, 1996), 146; Bogart, *How I Earned the Ruptured Duck,* 135; Stone, "German Baby Crop," 581.

54. Massaquoi, *Destined to Witness,* 288; Grace Halsell, *Black/White Sex* (New York: William Morrow and Company, 1972), 149–50.

55. Quoted in Boyer and Woller, "'Hat die deutsche Frau versagt?'" 34.

56. Statement of Helene H., 14 June 1946, Records of the Public Safety Officer, 1945–1949, Bruchsal RLSO, FOD, OMGW-B, RG 260, NACP; First Lieutenant K. A. Brown to Amtsgericht Bruchsal and Kreisjugendamt Bruchsal, 28 June 1946, Records of the Public Safety Officer, 1945–1949, Bruchsal RLSO, FOD, OMGW-B, RG 260, NACP.

57. Stone, "German Baby Crop," 582.

58. On courteousness, see ibid., 580; on the "more unaffected and childlike openhearted nature" of blacks, see Eyferth, Brandt, and Hawel, *Farbige Kinder in Deutschland,* 24.

59. "Reactions of Germans to Negro Troops," Information Control Intelligence Summary No. 16, 27 October 1945, 2, Records Relating to Public Opinion, 1945–1949, Opinion Surveys Branch, ICD, RG 260, NACP.

60. Roi Ottley, "Tan Yanks Shared Their Food and Won Hearts of German Girls: Now the Young Ladies Are Fat and Happy," *Pittsburgh Courier,* 8 December 1945, 13; Starr, "Fraternization with the Germans," 89; Hügel-Marshall, *Invisible Woman,* 18; Ernst von Salomon, *Der Fragebogen* (Hamburg: Rowohlt Verlag, 1951), 785. See also Boyer and Woller, "'Hat die deutsche Frau versagt?'" 34.

61. Captain Lewis H. Keyes to Commanding General, Headquarters XII Corps, 12 July 1945, 1, File 291.2, AG Correspondence, 1945, RG 338, NACP; Wiley, "The Training of Negro Troops," in *Planning for the Postwar Employment of Black Personnel,* ed. MacGregor and Nalty, 242. On the practices of African American style, see Shane White and Graham White, *Stylin': African American Expressive Culture from Its Beginnings to the Zoot Suit* (Ithaca: Cornell University Press, 1998).

62. Stone, "German Baby Crop," 580; see also Halsell, *Black/White Sex,* 149–59.

63. Dörr, "*Wer die Zeit nicht miterlebt hat . . . ,*" 395.

64. William Henry Mauldin, "The War Isn't Won," in *Responsibility of Victory: Report of the New York Herald Tribune Annual Forum on Current Problems* (New York: New York Tribune, 1945), 204–7. For other articles linking American racism and Nazism, see, e.g., Allan Morrison, "The Negro GI in Germany," *The Stars and Stripes Magazine* (Paris edition), 12 August 1945, vi; William Smith, "Half of Tan GIs Leaving Germany," *Pittsburgh Courier*, 21 December 1946, 1; Roi Ottley, "Italian Hospitality Hailed by Tan GIs; Resent U.S. Policies: Engaged Corporal Feted by Girl's Parents," *Pittsburgh Courier*, 23 November 1946, 2; Truman K. Gibson Jr., "Nazis in Army: American Officers Abroad Propagating Race Hatred," *Pittsburgh Courier*, 8 June 1946, 3; Albert E. Kahn, "America's Badge of Shame," *Negro Digest*, January 1946, 65–67; Oliver Harrington, "Frontiers Still Left in America: The Negro's Part," in *The Struggle for Justice as a World Force: Report of the New York Herald Tribune Annual Forum* (New York: New York Tribune, 1946), 50–55; Roi Ottley, "Tan Yanks," *Pittsburgh Courier*, 8 December 1945, 13; "Three Die in France Because War's End Left Untouched Nazi Race Ideas in Midst of Army," *Pittsburgh Courier*, 3 November 1945, 11; Roi Ottley, "Nazi Attitudes of White Soldiers Shock Robeson: Completes USO Tour," *Pittsburgh Courier*, 29 September 1945, 1. The *Pittsburgh Courier* continually condemned Bilbo as an American Nazi for his racist beliefs. See, e.g., Horace R. Cayton, "Hurrah for Bilbo: His 'Red Necked' Ignorance Is Making New Friends for the Negro Every Day," *Pittsburgh Courier*, 4 August 1945, 7.

65. Historian of slavery David Brion Davis describes the powerful impact of this incongruity on him as a young soldier in Mannheim in "The Americanized Mannheim of 1945–1946," in *American Places: Encounters with History: A Celebration of Sheldon Meyer*, ed. William E. Leuchtenburg (Oxford: Oxford University Press, 2000), 78–91. Davis reports that his experience in Germany likely contributed to his "later decision to devote over forty years to the study of slavery and race." Ibid., 91.

66. "Reactions of Germans to Negro Troops," Information Control Intelligence Summary No. 16, 27 October 1945, 1, Records Relating to Public Opinion, 1945–1949, Opinion Surveys Branch, ICD, RG 260, NACP. For recollections of better relations with Germans than with the white American civilian population during the war, see Charles Matthews Brown, Army Service Experiences Questionnaire, 6, U.S. Army Military History Institute, Carlisle Barracks, Pennsylvania. See also Morehouse, *Fighting in the Jim Crow Army*, 201. Petra Goedde and Heide Fehrenbach have noted that accounts of Germans' lack of racial prejudice implicitly critiqued U.S. race relations. Fehrenbach, *Race after Hitler*, 38; Goedde, *GIs and Germans*, 109.

67. William Gardner Smith, *Last of the Conquerors* (New York: Farrar, Straus and Co., 1948), 44, 238. On Smith's biography, see LeRoy S. Hodges, *Portrait of an Expatriate: William Gardner Smith, Writer*, Contributions in Afro-American and African Studies, no. 91 (Westport, Conn.: Greenwood, 1985).

68. During the war and soon after its conclusion, the black press emphasized the Nazi roots of Germans' racial prejudices. See, e.g., Lieutenant Robert Lewis, "Black Soldiers under Fire," *Negro Digest*, November 1945, 5.

69. "Germany Meets the Negro Soldier," *Ebony* (October 1946): 5.

70. Ibid., 5, 10.

71. Ollie Stewart, "Definite Advantage Seen in Limiting of Occupation Troops to Service Units," Baltimore *Afro-American*, 20 April 1946, in Press Items re: Negro

Newspapers, 1944–1946 (Analysis Branch), Office of Public Information, RG 330, NACP.

72. Roi Ottley, "Tan Yanks," *Pittsburgh Courier,* 8 December 1945, 13. Ottley described relations between African American soldiers and the Italian populace similarly. Ottley, "Italian Hospitality," *Pittsburgh Courier,* 23 November 1946, 2.

73. "Germany Meets the Negro Soldier," *Ebony* (October 1946): 5–11; Ollie Stewart, "Ammunition Outfit Likes German Occupation Duties," Baltimore *Afro-American,* 20 April 1946, in Press Items re: Negro Newspapers, 1944–1946 (Analysis Branch), Office of Public Information, RG 330, NACP.

74. "Germany Meets the Negro Soldier," *Ebony* (October 1946): 7.

75. Alfred A. Duckett, "U.S. White Supremacy Invades Germany; Tan GIs Brutalized," undated, unidentified clipping in Press Items re: Negro Newspapers, 1944–1946 (Analysis Branch), Office of Public Information, RG 330, NACP. For other examples, see Allan Morrison, "The Negro GI in Germany," *The Stars and Stripes Magazine* (Paris edition), 12 August 1945, vi; "Three Die in France Because War's End Left Untouched Nazi Race Ideas in Midst of Army," *Pittsburgh Courier,* 3 November 1945, 11; Ottley, "Nazi Attitudes of White Soldiers Shock Robeson: Completes USO Tour," *Pittsburgh Courier,* 29 September 1945, 1; "Bishop Walls Reports Shocking Conditions," *Norfolk Journal and Guide,* undated clipping in Press Items re: Negro Newspapers, 1944–1946 (Analysis Branch), Office of Public Information, RG 330, NACP.

76. Stone, "German Baby Crop," 579–80.

77. Smith, *Last of the Conquerors,* 149–54. For other examples of faithfulness, see 72, 93, 196.

78. Ibid., 147, 257.

79. See Bill Smith, "Few GIs Eager to Return to States," *Pittsburgh Courier,* 22 February 1947; Bill Smith, "Innocent Soldier Goes on Rampage; Kills 1, Wounds 3," *Pittsburgh Courier,* 25 January 1947; Bill Smith, "Crack QM Outfit 'Best in Berlin,'" *Pittsburgh Courier,* 27 July 1946, clippings in Press Items re: Negro Newspapers, 1944–1946 (Analysis Branch), Office of Public Information, RG 330, NACP.

80. Smith, *Last of the Conquerors,* 82–83.

81. The accuracy of the novel's characterization of relations between blacks and Germans has been the subject of rather pointed debate between Kleinschmidt and Meyer. See Kleinschmidt, "Antwort auf Martin Meyer," *Amerikastudien* 41 (1996): 499–500; Martin Meyer, "Replik: 'Schwarze GIs im Nachkriegsdeutschland,'" *Amerikastudien* 41 (1996): 497–99; Hodges, *Portrait of an Expatriate,* 105n53. Literary critics have observed that the novel's politics colored its depiction. See Georg Schmundt-Thomas, "America's Germany: National Self and Cultural Other after World War II" (Ph.D. diss., Northwestern University, 1992), 62; Martin Meyer, *Nachkriegsdeutschland im Spiegel amerikanischer Romane der Besatzungszeit, 1945–1955,* AAA, Buchreihe zu den Arbeiten aus Anglistik und Amerikanistik, no. 9 (Tübingen: Gunter Narr Verlag, 1994), 177–79, 189.

82. George S. Schuyler, column in *Pittsburgh Courier,* 1 February 1947, clipping in Press Items re: Negro Newspapers, 1944–1946 (Analysis Branch), Office of Public Information, RG 330, NACP.

83. On African American opposition to black soldiers' relations with white women, see Romano, *Race Mixing,* 82–88; Höhn, "*Heimat* in Turmoil," 161n42; Halsell, *Black/White Sex,* 139; Charley Cherokee, "National Grapevine," *Chicago Defender,* 12 January 1946, 13; Major J. L. Fenton to Theatre Censor, ETOUSA, 1

Sept 1943, 2, File 291.2, General Correspondence of John J. McCloy, 1941–1945, RG 107, NACP.

84. "Bishop Walls Reports Shocking Conditions," *Norfolk Journal and Guide,* undated clipping in Press Items re: Negro Newspapers, 1944–1946 (Analysis Branch), Office of Public Information, RG 330, NACP.

85. Such hurdles remained in place into the 1950s. See Romano, *Race Mixing;* Höhn, *GIs and Fräuleins,* 105–7.

86. On the rarity and danger of contact with white women for African American men, see, e.g., Peery, *Black Fire,* 17–18; Myrdal, *An American Dilemma,* 1:607–8. On the psychological meaning of relations with European women for African American soldiers, see Halsell, *Black/White Sex,* 138; Leder, "Americans and German Youth," 89. See also Frantz Fanon, *Black Skin, White Masks,* trans. Charles Lam Markmann (New York: Grove Press, 1967), 63.

87. Trezzzvant [*sic*] W. Anderson, "Germans Gradually Accepting Colored Occupational Troops," *Pittsburgh Courier,* 2 February 1946, 3, in Press Items re: Negro Newspapers, 1944–1946 (Analysis Branch), Office of Public Information, RG 330, NACP.

88. Massaquoi, *Destined to Witness,* 291.

89. Cable S-81213 from SHAEF Main, from Allen and Warden, signed Eisenhower, to AGWAR for Surles, 7 March 1945, File 291.2, Classified General Correspondence, 1944–1945, Secretary, General Staff, RG 338, NACP; Cable WX-51156 from AGWAR from Surles to SHAEF Main for Eisenhower for Allen and Warden, 11 March 1945, File 291.2, Classified General Correspondence, 1944–1945, Secretary, General Staff, RG 338, NACP.

90. The study by Kardiner and Ovesey included evidence of the importance of the "flash" that an attractive women could provide to the African American man in her company. Kardiner and Ovesey, *The Mark of Oppression,* 109. On the social value of sexual experiences in the army generally, see Elkin, "Aggressive and Erotic Tendencies in Army Life," 412–13.

91. Captain Norman E. Petty to Commanding Officer, Company B, 3rd Mil. Govt. Regt., Regierungsbezirk Ober- und Mittelfranken, 18 September 1946, and attached report, Correspondence and Related Records, 1945–1949, Kulmbach RLSO, FOD, OMGBY, RG 260, NACP.

92. Major H. C. Kauffman to Lieutenant Colonel R. A. Reese, 5 September 1946. The contrast between the situation in Germany and the situation of African Americans and white police officials in the rural southern United States is stark. See, e.g., Myrdal, *An American Dilemma,* 1:535–44.

93. Smith, *Last of the Conquerors,* 71.

94. Ibid., 72–73.

95. Ibid., 193–94.

96. Malcolm Cowley, "In Love with Germany," *New Republic* (27 September 1948): 33.

97. See McNarney's opposition to permitting unrestricted marriages between American soldiers and German women, discussed in Shukert and Scibetta, *War Brides of World War II,* 143; Willoughby, *Remaking the Conquering Heroes,* 43; Willoughby, "The Sexual Behavior of American GIs," 169; Goedde, *GIs and Germans,* 115. The issue is a central theme of Billy Wilder's film *A Foreign Affair,* Paramount, 1948.

98. My analysis of the power dynamics between African American men and German women suggests the importance of the societal barriers in the United

States to African American men's ability to realize the prerogatives of masculinity as conventionally defined at the time. In that respect it is consistent with the conclusions of Kardiner and Ovesey, who asserted that because African American men had fewer economic opportunities than African American women, relations between the sexes proved especially tense. In their view, the black man was "not infrequently at the mercy of the woman. Masculinity is closely tied to power in every form in our society. The male is much the more vulnerable to socioeconomic failure. He unconsciously interprets it as a loss in masculinity, i.e. as femininity." Kardiner and Ovesey, *The Mark of Oppression*, 70.

99. Urteil der Strafkammer bei dem Landgericht Nürnberg-Fürth gegen Martin W. (pseudonym) wegen Verbrechens der schweren Kuppelei, 27 March 1946, SN, Staatsanwaltschaft Nürnberg-Fürth, Strafsache, Landgericht Nürnberg-Fürth, Nr. 1693.

100. Ibid.

101. The trope of the white woman who duped her black lover retained life long after 1949. It surfaces, e.g., in Grace Halsell's generally insightful study of interracial sex, in which she describes the history of one black GI, who was cuckolded by his successive German wives, observing, "Any black woman might easily have predicted that Wiley would be used by white women for their devious purposes." Although Halsell notes that such behavior by women and soldiers was not limited to interracial liaisons, she goes on to describe the soldier as "entrapped in a world of white women, a dark Adam somehow innocently caught up in a garden of blond Eves." Halsell, *Black/White Sex*, 161–62.

102. Fehrenbach has recently noted the gendered construction of racial equality in occupied Germany. Fehrenbach, *Race after Hitler*, 40–41. For context on the denial of the manliness of African American men, see Gail Bederman, *Manliness and Civilization: A Cultural History of Gender and Race in the United States, 1880–1917* (Chicago: University of Chicago Press, 1995).

103. On the history of this dynamic in African American claims to equality, see, e.g., Michele Mitchell, "'The Black Man's Burden': African Americans, Imperialism, and Notions of Racial Manhood, 1890–1910," in *Complicating Categories*, ed. Eileen Boris and Angélique Janssens, *International Review of Social History*, Supplement 7 (Cambridge: Press Syndicate of the University of Cambridge, 1999), 77–99; Hazel V. Carby, *Race Men* (Cambridge, Mass.: Harvard University Press, 1998).

104. William Hastie, Survey and Recommendations Concerning the Integration of the Negro Soldier into the Army, Submitted to the Secretary of War by the Civilian Aide to the Secretary of War, 22 September 1941, 2, File 291.2, General Correspondence of John J. McCloy, 1941–1945, RG 107, NACP.

105. Smith, *Last of the Conquerors*, 67–68.

106. Ibid., 69; emphasis original.

107. Davis, "The Americanized Mannheim," 79.

108. Stone, "German Baby Crop," 580.

109. Fehrenbach, "Of German Mothers and 'Negermischlingskinder,'" 171. See also "Ute und Edgar fahren nach Amerika: Zwei farbige kleine Mannheimer wurden als erste von amerikanischen Eltern adoptiert," *Rhein-Neckar-Zeitung*, 4 October 1951, 3, SM, Zugang 3, Nr. 425; Hans Willauer, "Wenn uns die dunkle Haut ärgert," *Christ und Welt*, 6 October 1961, 10, Bayerischer Rundfunk Archiv (BRA), Signatur F-13 Besatzungskinder, Newspaper Clipping Files; Ilse Tubbesing, "Das dunkle Gesicht in der Menge: Porträt eines milchkaffeebraunen

'Besatzungskindes': Die Farbe ist ein Ehehindernis," *Mannheimer Morgen*, 22 July 1964, BRA, Signatur F-13 Besatzungskinder, Newspaper Clipping Files.

110. Smith, *Last of the Conquerors*, 90–91.

111. Lester, "Blacks in Germany," 121, citing *Das Parlament* (1951), no. 12.

112. For an outstanding analysis of that process, see Fehrenbach, *Race after Hitler*.

113. "Heidi mit der dunklen Haut," *Stern*, 24 June 1962, 35, BRA, Signatur F-13 Besatzungskinder, Newspaper Clipping Files. A considerable body of literature exists regarding the life histories of Afro-Germans. See, e.g., Hügel-Marshall, *Invisible Woman*; Carol Aisha Blackshire-Belay, ed., *The African-German Experience: Critical Essays* (Westport, Conn.: Praeger, 1996); Katharina Oguntoye, May Opitz, and Dagmar Schultz, eds., *Farbe Bekennen: Afro-Deutsche Frauen auf den Spuren ihrer Geschichte* (Berlin: Orlanda Frauenverlag, 1986); collections of newspaper clippings in BRA, S-201 Schwarze Deutsche, and F-13 Besatzungskinder, Newspaper Clipping Files.

114. Eyferth, Brandt, and Hawel, *Farbige Kinder in Deutschland*, 8.

115. See, e.g., Hügel-Marshall, *Invisible Woman*; Campt, "'Afro-German'"; Crawley, "Challenging Concepts."

116. Hügel-Marshall, *Invisible Woman*, 19.

Chapter 5: Black Music and German Culture

1. "Berliner Philharmoniker von einem Neger dirigiert," *Frankfurter Rundschau*, 8 September 1945, 4. The article wrongly reported that the performance was the European premiere of the *Afro-American Symphony*. Dunbar had conducted the work in London during the war and in Paris in July 1945. See "In Retrospect: W. Rudolph Dunbar: Pioneering Orchestra Conductor," *The Black Perspective in Music* 9 (1981): 193–225; Paul Gilroy, *Against Race*, 324–25.

2. Joseph Goebbels, "Der neue Stil," unidentified newspaper fragment [June 1939], Private Archive of Dr. Hans Otto Jung, Rüdesheim/Rhein (Germany), quoted in Kater, *Different Drummers*, 30.

3. See David Monod, *Settling Scores: German Music, Denazification, and the Americans, 1945–1953* (Chapel Hill: University of North Carolina Press, 2005); Poiger, *Jazz, Rock, and Rebels*, 37–43; Michael Kater, *Composers of the Nazi Era: Eight Portraits* (New York: Oxford University Press, 2000), 271–84; Jessica C.E. Gienow-Hecht, *Transmission Impossible: American Journalism as Cultural Diplomacy in Postwar Germany*, Eisenhower Center Studies on War and Peace (Baton Rouge: Louisiana State University Press, 1999); Gienow-Hecht, "Art Is Democracy and Democracy Is Art: Culture, Propaganda, and the *Neue Zeitung* in Germany, 1944–1947," in The American Occupation of Germany in Cultural Perspective: A Roundtable, *Diplomatic History* 23 (1999): 21–43; Rebecca Boehling, "Commentary: The Role of Culture in American Relations with Europe: The Case of the United States's Occupation of Germany," in The American Occupation of Germany in Cultural Perspective: A Roundtable, *Diplomatic History* 23 (1999): 57–69; Wolfgang Schivelbusch, *In a Cold Crater: Cultural and Intellectual Life in Berlin, 1945–1948*, trans. Kelly Barry (Berkeley: University of California Press, 1998); Reiner Pommerin, ed., *Culture in the Federal Republic of Germany, 1945–1995*, German Historical Perspectives, ed. Gerhard A. Ritter and Anthony J. Nicholls, no. 11 (Oxford: Berg,

1996); Hein-Kremer, *Die amerikanische Kulturoffensive*; Axel Schildt, "Die USA als 'Kulturnation': Zur Bedeutung der Amerikahäuser in den 1950er Jahren," in *Amerikanisierung: Traum und Alptraum im Deutschland des 20. Jahrhunderts,* ed. Alf Lüdtke, Inge Marßolek, and Adelheid von Saldern, Transatlantische historische Studien, ed. Detlef Junker, vol. 6 (Stuttgart: Franz Steiner Verlag, 1996), 256–69; Fehrenbach, *Cinema in Democratizing Germany*; Gabriele Clemens, ed., *Kulturpolitik im besetzten Deutschland, 1945–1949* (Stuttgart: Franz Steiner Verlag, 1994); Thomas Steiert, "Zur Musik- und Theaterpolitik in Stuttgart während der amerikanischen Besatzungszeit," in *Kulturpolitik im besetzten Deutschland,* 55–68; Reinhold Wagnleitner, *Coca-Colonization and the Cold War: The Cultural Mission of the United States in Austria after the Second World War,* trans. Diana Wolf (Chapel Hill: University of North Carolina Press, 1994); Hermann-Josef Rupieper, *Die Wurzeln der westdeutschen Nachkriegsdemokratie: Der amerikanische Beitrag, 1945– 1952* (Opladen: Westdeutscher Verlag, 1993); Reinhard Bassenge, "Radio München 1945–1949 – Eine Programmanalyse" (Wissenschaftliche Arbeit zur Erlangung des Magister Artium, Ludwig-Maximilians-Universität zu München, 1990).

   4. See Pamela M. Potter, *Most German of the Arts: Musicology and Society from the Weimar Republic to the End of Hitler's Reich* (New Haven, Conn.: Yale University Press, 1998); Kater, *Composers of the Nazi Era*; Kater, *The Twisted Muse: Musicians and Their Music in the Third Reich* (New York: Oxford University Press, 1997); Kater, *Different Drummers.*

   5. Potter, *Most German of the Arts,* 261–63.

   6. Kater, *Different Drummers,* 202–11; Kater, *Composers of the Nazi Era,* 275–76.

   7. Poiger, *Jazz, Rock, and Rebels,* 9.

   8. See, e.g., Penny M. Von Eschen, *Satchmo Blows up the World: Jazz Ambassadors Play the Cold War* (Cambridge, Mass.: Harvard University Press, 2004), 3; Poiger, *Jazz, Rock, and Rebels,* 38–39. Jennifer Fay's thoughtful article on the jazz film *Hallo Fräulein* notes that a short film on Duke Ellington was not widely released in German theaters, but it fails to examine fully American re-education officials' testing of the film with German audiences. Jennifer Fay, " 'That's Jazz Made in Germany!' *Hallo Fräulein!* and the Limits of Democratic Pedagogy," *Cinema Journal* 44:1 (2004): 20.

   9. Germans' favorable reception of African American spirituals, mainly in the 1950s, has been noted by Posner and Höhn. Posner, "Afro-America in West German Perspective," 175–77; Höhn, "GIs, Veronikas and Lucky Strikes," 78.

   10. On this theme in American thinking about black music, see Ronald Radano, "Hot Fantasies: American Modernism and the Idea of Black Rhythm," in *Music and the Racial Imagination,* ed. Ronald Radano and Philip V. Bohlman, with a foreword by Houston A. Baker Jr., Chicago Studies in Ethnomusicology, ed. Philip V. Bohlman and Bruno Nettl (Chicago: University of Chicago Press, 2000), 459–80.

   11. For a brief statement on *Kultur,* see Fritz K. Ringer, *The Decline of the German Mandarins: The German Academic Community, 1890–1933* (Cambridge, Mass.: Harvard University Press, 1969; Hanover, N.H.: Wesleyan University Press, published by University Press of New England, 1990), 86–90. On the perception of American cultural inferiority, see Monod, *Settling Scores,* 5, 58.

   12. Ruth Benedict, *Race: Science and Politics,* 14. See also Barkan, *The Retreat of Scientific Racism,* 18–20, 81.

   13. See Rainer E. Lotz, "Schwarze Entertainer in der Weimarer Republik," in *Zwischen Charleston und Stechschritt: Schwarze im Nationalsozialismus,* ed. Peter

Martin and Christine Alonzo (Hamburg: Dölling und Galitz Verlag, 2004), 255–61; Peter Jelavich, *Berlin Cabaret* (Cambridge, Mass.: Harvard University Press, 1993), 169–75; Jürgen Heinrichs, "'Blackness in Weimar': 1920s German Art Practice and American Jazz and Dance" (Ph.D. diss., Yale University, 1998); Kater, *Different Drummers,* 3–28; Kater, "The Jazz Experience in Weimar Germany," 145–58.

14. Kater, *Different Drummers,* 21, quoting Alfred Einstein, *Geschichte der Musik,* 3rd ed. (Leipzig, 1927), 130. More generally, see *Different Drummers,* 19–21, 25. White American jazz opponents made many of the same arguments in the 1920s. See Neil Leonard, *Jazz and the White Americans: The Acceptance of a New Art Form* (Chicago: University of Chicago Press, 1962), 29–46.

15. See Alan Lareau, "Jonny's Jazz: From *Kabarett* to Krenek," in *Jazz and the Germans: Essays on the Influence of "Hot" American Idioms on 20th-Century German Music,* ed. Michael J. Budds, Monographs and Bibliographies in American Music no. 17, series ed. Michael J. Budds (Hillsdale, N.Y.: Pendragon Press, 2002), 19–60.

16. See Liner Notes to "*Jonny spielt auf:* Between Jazz and New Music," Entartete Musik: Music Suppressed by the Third Reich (London: Decca, 1993); Charlotte Purkis, *Jonny spielt auf* entry in *New Grove Dictionary of Music and Musicians,* 2nd ed., ed. Stanley Sadie (New York: Grove Dictionaries, 2001, www.e-grove.com); John L. Stewart, *Ernst Krenek: The Man and His Music* (Berkeley: University of California Press, 1991), 81–89. Stewart's admiring biography insists that Krenek "was not and never would be a racist." Ibid., 83. On the opera's reception in New York, see Martin Bauml Duberman, *Paul Robeson* (New York: Alfred A. Knopf, 1988), 111.

17. Krenek, *Jonny spielt auf,* act I, scene 3, p. 56; act I, scene 3, p. 54.

18. See Liner Notes to *Jonny spielt auf.*

19. Hans Severus Ziegler, "Entartete Musik: Eine Abrechnung," in *Entartete Musik: Dokumentation und Kommentar zur Düsseldorfer Ausstellung von 1938,* revised and expanded edition, ed. Albrecht Dümling and Peter Girth (Düsseldorf: dkv, der kleine Verlag, 1993), 177, 182; Carl Hannemann, "Der Jazz als Kampfmittel des Judentums und des Amerikanismus," reprinted in *Entartete Musik,* 121.

20. Potter, *Most German of the Arts,* ix–xi; Kater, *Composers of the Nazi Era,* 268. On the effort to define Germanness in music, see Potter, *Most German of the Arts,* 200–34. Richard Wagner confessed in 1878 that he could not define the German essence in music. Ibid., 203. See also Celia Applegate, "What Is German Music? Reflections on the Role of Art in the Creation of a Nation," *German Studies Review: Special Issue, German Identity* (Winter 1992): 21–32.

21. Potter, *Most German of the Arts,* 213–20. On the importance to the folklorist project of obtaining information on folk music from the unadulterated source, see Béla Bartók, "Why and How Do We Collect Folk Music?" in *Béla Bartók Essays,* selected and edited by Benjamin Suchoff, New York Bartók Archive Studies in Musicology no. 8 (New York: St. Martin's Press, 1976), 13.

22. Ehrhard Bahr, "Nazi Cultural Politics: Intentionalism v. Functionalism," in *National Socialist Cultural Policy,* ed. Glenn R. Cuomo (New York: St. Martin's Press, 1995), 17–18.

23. Kater, *The Twisted Muse,* 76.

24. Eichenauer, *Musik und Rasse,* 9–11, 22, 280.

25. See Potter, *Most German of the Arts,* 78–79, 176–91; Guido Waldmann, ed., *Rasse und Musik,* Musikalische Volksforschung: Eine Schriftenreihe, vol. 3 (Berlin-Lichterfelde: C. F. Vieweg, 1939).

26. Ziegler, "Entartete Musik"; Hans Petsch, "Der Jazzbazillus," *Zeitschrift für Musik* 107 (1940): 455, reprinted in *Zwischen Charleston und Stechschritt*, ed. Peter Martin and Christine Alonzo, 266; Potter, *Most German of the Arts*, 17–19, 78–80, 176–91; David Snowball, "Controlling Degenerate Music: Jazz in the Third Reich," in *Jazz and the Germans*, 161. On the Degenerate Art exhibit, see Stephanie Barron, ed., *"Degenerate Art": The Fate of the Avant-Garde in Nazi Germany* (New York: Harry N. Abrams, 1991).

27. On the prominence of Jews in German jazz and the Nazi assault on jazz, see Kater, *Different Drummers*, 20–21, 32–33; Hannemann, "Der Jazz als Kampfmittel," in *Entartete Musik*, ed. Dümling and Girth, 121; Kater, *Composers of the Nazi Era*, 268–69. On sexual defilement, see Kater, *Different Drummers*, 22, 33.

28. On the degenerate music exhibit, see Dümling and Girth, eds., *Entartete Musik*; Potter, *Most German of the Arts*, 17–19.

29. See Alf Lüdtke, "Introduction," in *Amerikanisierung: Traum und Alptraum*, 13; Adelheid von Saldern, "Überfremdungsängste: Gegen die Amerikanisierung der deutschen Kultur in den zwanziger Jahren," in *Amerikanisierung: Traum und Alptraum*, 213–44.

30. "Wider die Negerkultur—für deutsches Volkstum: Bekanntmachung des Ministers Frick in Thüringen," *Völkischer Beobachter* [Munich edition], 15 April 1930, 1.

31. Kater, *Different Drummers*, 33, 52, 57, 111–12, 117, 163–65.

32. Carlo Bohländer, "The Evolution of Jazz Culture in Frankfurt: A Memoir," in *Jazz and the Germans*, ed. Budds, 169; Jelavich, *Berlin Cabaret*, 170–71; Kater, *Different Drummers*, 17–18; Detlev J. K. Peukert, *Inside Nazi Germany: Conformity, Opposition, and Racism in Everyday Life*, trans. Richard Deveson (New Haven, Conn.: Yale University Press, 1987), 66–68.

33. Harry Bogner to Dr. Arthur Bauckner, 16 August 1945, BayHStA, MK 50052.

34. Anonymous undated letter, EAF, Nachlaß Conrad Gröber, Nb8/62.

35. Boehling, "Commentary: The Role of Culture in American Relations with Europe," 57; Verena Botzenhart-Viehe, "The German Reaction to the American Occupation, 1944–1947" (Ph.D. diss., University of California, Santa Barbara, 1980), 141; Gienow-Hecht, *Transmission Impossible*, 79–94.

36. See, e.g., John Evarts to Chief, Film, Theater and Music, 22 December 1946, Records re: Music and Theater, 1945–1948, Cultural Affairs Branch, Records of the Education and Cultural Relations Division, RG 260, NACP; Steiert, "Zur Musik- und Theaterpolitik in Stuttgart," 63; Schildt, *Zwischen Abendland und Amerika*.

37. "Radio Munich Policy," undated, BRA, General Correspondence File, 24.4, RV 24, Mr. Horine Correspondence.

38. "Musikschaffendes Amerika," *Neue Presse*, 26 April 1947, 6.

39. *Your Job in Germany*; "Germany after the War, Round Table—1945," *American Journal of Orthopsychiatry* 15 (1945): 381–441; Monod, *Settling Scores*, 32–43.

40. "Radio Munich Policy," undated, BRA, General Correspondence File, 24.4, RV 24, Mr. Horine Correspondence.

41. Long-Range Policy Statement for German Re-education, SWNCC 269/5, 5 June 1946, in U.S. Department of State, *Germany, 1947–1949: The Story in Documents* (Washington, D.C.: U.S. Government Printing Office, 1950), 541–42. The draft is Cable W-85547 from AGWAR to OMGUS for Clay, 27 April 1946, Records of the

Director and Deputy Director, 1945–1949, Records of the Division Headquarters, ICD, RG 260, NACP.

42. Peter Kappell to Hans Meyer, 16 April 1945, German Committee Minutes, October 1944, Agenda and Minutes of the German Committee, Central Control Division, 1944–1945, RG 208, NACP.

43. See, e.g., "Radio Munich Policy," undated, BRA, General Correspondence File, 24.4, RV 24, Mr. Horine Correspondence; JCS 1779, in U.S. Department of State, *Germany, 1947–1949,* 40.

44. SWNCC 269/5, in U.S. Department of State, *Germany, 1947–1949,* 542.

45. Eric T. Clarke, Theater and Music Quarterly Progress Report, 15 April 1947, 22, 25–26, Records of the Director and Deputy Director, 1945–1949, Records of the Division Headquarters, ICD, RG 260, NACP.

46. Minutes of the Meeting of the German Committee on 18 May 1945, 4 and attachment 4, German Committee Minutes, October 1944, Agenda and Minutes of the German Committee, Central Control Division, 1944–1945, RG 208, NACP.

47. Anderson performed in Munich and Berlin to an enthusiastic response in 1950. Allan Keiler, *Marian Anderson: A Singer's Journey* (New York: Scribner, 2000), 253–55.

48. See WD [Walter Dirks], "Jazz," *Frankfurter Hefte* 3 (1948): 790–91; for political readings of jazz, see Kater, *Different Drummers,* 202–11. On fascist music, see Kater, *Composers of the Nazi Era,* 111, 114, 128. For an examination of connections between the political and the musical in the civil rights movement in the United States, see Brian Ward, *Just My Soul Responding: Rhythm and Blues, Black Consciousness and Race Relations* (London: UCL Press, 1998).

49. Adorno was the most notable anti-jazz antifascist. See, e.g., Theodor W. Adorno, "Perennial Fashion—Jazz," in *Prisms,* trans. Samuel Weber and Shierry Weber, Studies in Contemporary German Social Thought, ed. Thomas McCarthy (Cambridge, Mass.: MIT Press, 1981 [1967]), 119–32. The problem was analogous to that faced in the visual arts. See Walter Grasskamp, "'Degenerate Art' and Documenta I: Modernism Ostracized and Disarmed," in *Museum Culture: Histories, Discourses, Spectacles,* ed. Daniel J. Sherman and Irit Rogoff (Minneapolis: University of Minnesota Press, 1994), 163–95.

50. The French in the interwar period, e.g., certainly regarded jazz as "black music," whether they admired or condemned the music, and many jazz fans, identifying a black musical style at the core of jazz, insisted that African Americans had a special gift for playing jazz. See Jeffrey H. Jackson, "Making Jazz French: Music and Cosmopolitanism in Interwar Paris" (Ph.D. diss., University of Rochester, 1999), 2, 26, 128–35, 216–18; Ernst-Alexandre Ansermet, "Sur un orchestre nègre," translated by Walter Schaap for *Jazz Hot,* reprinted in *Reading Jazz: A Gathering of Autobiography, Reportage, and Criticism from 1919 to Now,* ed. Robert Gottlieb (New York: Pantheon Books, 1996), 744. For white Americans, see Leonard, *Jazz and the White Americans;* Lawrence W. Levine, "Jazz and American Culture," *Journal of American Folklore* 102 (1989): 6–22.

51. Captain Herbert C. Cross to Office of the Director of Information Control, OMGUS, Attn: Radio Control Branch, 14 May 1946, 4, BRA, General Correspondence File, 24.4, RV 24, Mr. Horine Correspondence.

52. Marginal note on PWB, P & PW Detachment, 12th Army Group to Chief, Psychological Warfare Division, SHAEF, Attn: Film, Theater and Music Control Officer, 23 June 1945, attaching Letter from Dr. Will Fischer to the Military

Government of Germany, Film Production File, Records Relating to Motion Picture Production and Distribution, 1945–1949, Records of the Motion Picture Branch, ICD, RG 260, NACP; Colonel V. W. Roche to Commanding General, Military Government, Bernburg, 7 July 1945, Film Production File, Records Relating to Motion Picture Production and Distribution, 1945–1949, Records of the Motion Picture Branch, ICD, RG 260, NACP.

53. Brigadier General Robert A. McClure, Chief, Psychological Warfare Division, 4 July 1945, Film, Test Screenings (Audience Reactions, Etc.) File, Records Relating to Motion Picture Production and Distribution, 1945–1949, Records of the Motion Picture Branch, ICD, RG 260, NACP; ICD, Headquarters, United States Forces, European Theater, Reactions of German Civilians to a Program of Short Films (Program No. 2), 6 August 1945, Film, Test Screenings (Audience Reactions, Etc.) File, Records Relating to Motion Picture Production and Distribution, 1945–1949, Records of the Motion Picture Branch, ICD, RG 260, NACP.

54. ICD, Headquarters, United States Forces, European Theater, Reactions of German Civilians to a Program of Short Films (Program No. 2), 6 August 1945, 3–4.

55. Comments by Gerard W. Van Loon on program summary by Davidson Taylor, Chief, Film, Theatre and Music Control Section, Psychological Warfare Division, SHAEF, to Brigadier General Robert A. McClure et al., 29 May 1945, Film, Test Screenings (Audience Reactions, Etc.) File, Records Relating to Motion Picture Production and Distribution, 1945–1949, Records of the Motion Picture Branch, ICD, RG 260, NACP.

56. Untitled memorandum by Second Lieutenant Henry C. Alter, undated, Film, Test Screenings (Audience Reactions, Etc.) File, Records Relating to Motion Picture Production and Distribution, 1945–1949, Records of the Motion Picture Branch, ICD, RG 260, NACP.

57. Still is not listed among the composers whose works were performed from June 1947 to June 1948. See Information Control (Cumulative Review): Report of the Military Governor No. 36, June 1947–June 1948, 35. For the quotation and on Mason, see Information Control (Bimonthly Review): Report of the Military Governor No. 26, 1 July–31 August 1947, 12, Annex E 14. On the Gershwin radio broadcast, see "Musik der Neuen Welt," *Frankfurter Rundschau,* 8 September 1945, 4; O. W. Studtmann, "Am Lautsprecher: Unser Radiobericht vom 15. bis 21. August," *Frankfurter Rundschau,* 24 August 1948, 3. More generally, see Steiert, "Zur Musik- und Theaterpolitik in Stuttgart," 63.

58. U.S. Information Center Karlsruhe, Program of Wednesday Evening Concert, 15 September 1948, ICD, RG 260, NACP; Information Services (Quarterly Review): Report of the Military Governor No. 39, July–September 1948, 49.

59. *Radiowelt,* 8 December 1947, 10.

60. Patricia Van Delden to Director, Information Services Division, 1 February 1949, Records re: activities of the ICEB 1945–1949, ICEB, ICD, RG 260, NACP.

61. Information Services (Cumulative Review): Report of the Military Governor No. 48, 1 July 1948–30 June 1949, 35; Van Delden to Director, Information Services Division, 1 February 1949; Patricia Van Delden to ISD Reports Officer, 18 February 1949, attaching reports, Records relating to U.S. Information Centers, 1949, ICEB, ICD, RG 260, NACP; Patrick H. Byrne to Chaplain Wittington, 2 February 1949, Records re: activities of the ICEB 1945–1949, ICEB, ICD, RG 260, NACP. On the choir's successes in Hesse, see Raymond J. Stover, Monthly Summary for Period

1–31 March 1949, 1 April 1949, Land Level Reports 1949, ICEB, ICD, RG 260, NACP. On performances in Württemberg-Baden, see Michael Barjansky, Monthly Summary April 1949, 29 April 1949, Land Level Reports 1949, ICEB, ICD, RG 260, NACP; U.S. Information Center Heilbronn, Monthly Report for the period 21 March – 20 April 1949, Land Level Reports 1949, ICEB, ICD, RG 260, NACP.

62. Report from Exhibitions and Information Centers Branch, ISD, OMGBY, to Director, Office of Military Government for Bavaria, 12 May 1949, Records re: activities of the ICEB 1945–1949, ICEB, ICD, RG 260, NACP.

63. U.S. Information Center Heidelberg, OMGW-B, 7780th OMGUS Group Wuerttemberg-Baden Section, ISD, to Chief, Information Centers and Exhibitions Branch, ISD, OMGW-B, 30 April 1949, Records re: activities of the ICEB 1945–1949, ICEB, ICD, RG 260, NACP; Kenneth Norquist to Colonel Henry C. Newton, 14 April 1949, Records re: activities of the ICEB 1945–1949, ICEB, ICD, RG 260, NACP.

64. See Keiler, *Marian Anderson,* 133–58, 248–55; Gilroy, *The Black Atlantic.*

65. On German dislike of jazz through 1946, see History of ICD, OMGUS, 8 May 1945 to 30 June 1946, 84–85, Records re: Information Control, Headquarters, Control Office, RG 260, NACP.

66. "Statistik des Geschmacks," *Radiowelt: Wochenschrift mit Funkprogramm,* 20 October 1946, 2.

67. Captain Herbert C. Cross to Office of the Director of Information Control, OMGUS, Attn: Radio Control Branch, 14 May 1946, 4, BRA, General Correspondence File, 24.4, RV 24, Mr. Horine Correspondence.

68. "Das Urteil unserer Leser," *Radiowelt,* 25 May 1947, 4–5, Information Services (Cumulative Review): Report of the Military Governor No. 48, 1 July 1948–30 June 1949, 59; Information Control (Cumulative Review): Report of the Military Governor No. 36, June 1947–June 1948, 24.

69. Bassenge, "Radio München 1945–1949," 126; "Radio Munich Policy," undated, BRA, General Correspondence File, 45.4, RV 24, Mr. Horine Correspondence; Captain Herbert C. Cross to Office of the Director of Information Control, OMGUS, Attn: Radio Control Branch, 14 May 1946, 2–3, BRA, General Correspondence File, 24.4, RV 24, Mr. Horine Correspondence.

70. Field Horine to Office of the Director of Information Control, OMGUS, Attention: Radio Control Branch, 19 June 1946, 1, BRA, General Correspondence File, 24.4, RV 24, Mr. Horine Correspondence.

71. Music Department weekly report 1 September to 7 September, BRA, RV 23, Mr. Brill Reports, Radio Control Branch.

72. See Bassenge, "Radio München 1945–1949," 147.

73. History of ICD, OMGUS, 8 May 1945 to 30 June 1946, 82, Records re: Information Control, Headquarters, Control Office, RG 260, NACP.

74. See Lieutenant Klaus Brill to Chief of Section, 4 March 1946, BRA, RV 23, Mr. Brill Reports, Radio Control Branch.

75. Bassenge, "Radio München 1945–1949," 119. Bassenge regards the promotion of jazz music as the one element of re-education work served by the light music programming of Radio Munich.

76. See Lieutenant Klaus Brill to Chief of Section, 17 November 1945, BRA, RV 23, Mr. Brill Reports, Radio Control Branch.

77. In an article summarizing listeners' generally negative views on jazz, e.g., the magazine asked whether the views could be altered by a disc jockey. "Statistik

des Geschmacks," *Radiowelt: Wochenschrift mit Funkprogramm,* 3 November 1946, 4.

78. "Glenn Miller: Das Portrait eines Amerikanischen Musikers," *Radiowelt,* 11 May 1947, 4; "Herr Sax hat Schwierigkeiten," *Radiowelt,* 11 May 1947, 4.

79. "Yes zum Jazz?" *Radiowelt: Bayerische illustrierte Wochenschrift mit Funkprogramm und Kulturspiegel,* 24 February 1946, 3.

80. "Yes zum Jazz!" *Radiowelt: Bayerische illustrierte Wochenschrift mit Funkprogramm und Kulturspiegel,* 3 March 1946, 2.

81. "No zum Jazz," *Radiowelt: Bayerische illustrierte Wochenschrift mit Funkprogramm und Kulturspiegel,* 10 March 1946, 4–5.

82. For a concise, perceptive exploration of the problematic blackness of jazz, see Scott DeVeaux, *The Birth of Bebop: A Social and Musical History* (Berkeley: University of California Press, 1997), 17–20.

83. Th. Stephan to Kultusminister, 29 October 1947, BayHStA, MK 51228.

84. ICD, Headquarters, USFET, Reactions of German Civilians to a Program of Short Films (Program No. 2), 6 August 1945, Film, Test Screenings (Audience Reactions, Etc.) File, Records Relating to Motion Picture Production and Distribution, 1945–1949, Records of the Motion Picture Branch, ICD, RG 260, NACP.

85. "No zum Jazz," *Radiowelt,* 4.

86. Ibid., 5.

87. Captain Herbert C. Cross to Office of the Director of Information Control, OMGUS, Attn: Radio Control Branch, 14 May 1946, 4, BRA, General Correspondence File, 24.4, RV 24, Mr. Horine Correspondence.

88. The 6870th District Information Services Control Command, Headquarters, Supreme Headquarters Allied Expeditionary Force, to Captain Ross, Chief of Intelligence, 6870 DISCC, SHAEF, 28 June 1945, Film, Test Screenings (Audience Reactions, Etc.) File, Records Relating to Motion Picture Production and Distribution, 1945–1949, Records of the Motion Picture Branch, ICD, RG 260, NACP.

89. See, e.g., "Negro Spirituals: Der Kitzinger Negerchor in Heidelberg," *Rhein-Neckar-Zeitung,* 2 April 1949, 7; "Religiöse Musik der Neger: Etwas über 'Spirituals,'" *Frankfurter Rundschau,* 21 April 1949, 5; Carl Heidt, "Vom Mississippi zum Nordseestrand," *Weser-Kurier,* 29 January 1949, 4. Race also figured centrally in the description of the Kitzingen Negro choir. See, e.g., "Gastspiel des Kitzinger Negerchors wird wiederholt," *Rhein-Neckar-Zeitung,* 1 April 1949, 4.

90. For Anderson's repertory, see Keiler, *Marian Anderson,* App. 1. The quotation is from "Schwarze Kunst: Mit Kochbuch und Kamera," *Der Spiegel,* 28 July 1949, 30–31.

91. Richard Hey, "Jazz ist Musik," *Frankfurter Allgemeine Zeitung,* 18 April 1950.

92. See, e.g., Ansermet, "Sur un orchestre nègre," in *Reading Jazz,* ed. Gottlieb, 741–46.

93. Programme of 29 September 1943 concert, Bulletins, 1943–1946, Newspaper Clippings, Correspondence, Public Relations, RG 338, NACP. The London Symphony Orchestra led off the program with an adaptation of American folk tunes, including the minstrel favorite "Turkey in the Straw." See also Eric A. Gordon, *Mark the Music: The Life and Work of Marc Blitzstein* (New York: St. Martin's Press, 1989), 237–43.

94. Erich M. von Hornbostel, "American Negro Songs," *The International Review of Missions* 15 (1926): 753. But see Joachim-Ernst Berendt, "Vom Choral zum Swing: Zur Genesis des Jazz," *Melos: Zeitschrift für neue Musik* 14:5 (March 1947): 134–38.

95. "Nachdenkliches zum Jazz," *Süddeutsche Zeitung*, 31 August 1948, 5.

96. Joachim-Ernst Berendt, "Jazz—einmal ernst betrachtet: Musik und Welt-anschauung—ein psychoanalytisches Problem," *Die Neue Zeitung*, 13 October 1949, 4.

97. For the unthinking Weimar-era use of such terms, see Jelavich, *Berlin Cabaret*, 170–71.

98. Oliver Hassencamp, *Der Sieg nach dem Krieg: Die gute schlechte Zeit* (Munich: Herbig, n.d.), 109.

99. See Hornbostel, "American Negro Songs," 748–53; Walter Jackson, "Melville Herskovits and the Search for Afro-American Culture," in *Malinowski, Rivers, Benedict and Others: Essays on Culture and Personality*, ed. George W. Stocking Jr., History of Anthropology, vol. 4 (Madison: University of Wisconsin Press, 1986), 95–126; Melville Herskovits, *The Myth of the Negro Past* (1941; reprint, Boston: Beacon Press, 1958).

100. "Religiöse Musik der Neger," *Frankfurter Rundschau*.

101. Hornbostel, "American Negro Songs," 752.

102. WD [Walter Dirks], "Jazz," *Frankfurter Hefte* 3 (1948): 790–91.

103. "Yes zum Jazz?" *Radiowelt: Bayerische illustrierte Wochenschrift mit Funk-programm und Kulturspiegel*, 24 February 1946, 3.

104. Camill Schwarz, "An den Quellen des Jazz," *Frankfurter Rundschau*, 22 February 1946, 4.

105. DeVeaux, *The Birth of Bebop*, 35–71.

106. Fred Noll, "Auf 'Show' mit dem 'Jazz—Club Rhythm,'" *Die Jazz-Club News!* 30 August 1945, 6, Jazz Institut Darmstadt, Horst Lippmann Nachlaß. The Frankfurt postwar jazz scene is described in Jürgen Schwab, *Der Frankfurt Sound: Eine Stadt und ihre Jazzgeschichte(n)* (Frankfurt a.M.: Societäts-Verlag, 2004).

107. See Massaquoi, *Destined to Witness*, 160–61, 286–88. This desire to see black musicians play black music was not new in 1945. See Ansermet, "Sur un orchestre nègre," in *Reading Jazz*, ed. Gottlieb, 742.

108. See Horst H. Lange, *Jazz in Deutschland: Die Deutsche Jazz-Chronik bis 1960* (Hildesheim: Olms Presse, 1996), 186, 201; Stewart, *Boy Meets Horn*, 216–17. Early in 1949, African American tenor saxophonist Don Byas's arrival in Germany was greeted with similar enthusiasm. "Internationale Jazz-Prominenz in Deutschland," *Frankfurter Rundschau*, 29 January 1949, 3.

109. The same theme recurred in readings of jazz in France, in Weimar Germany, and during the Harlem Renaissance. See Jackson, "Making Jazz French," 133–35, 217–25; Carl Hannemann, "Der Jazz als Kampfmittel des Judentums und des Amerikanismus," reprinted in *Entartete Musik*, ed. Dümling and Girth, 123; J. A. Rogers, "Jazz at Home," in *The New Negro*, ed. Alain Locke, with an introduction by Arnold Rampersad (1925; reprint, New York: Atheneum, 1992), 224.

110. "Nachdenkliches zum Jazz," *Süddeutsche Zeitung*, 31 August 1948, 5.

111. "Yes zum Jazz!" *Radiowelt: Bayerische illustrierte Wochenschrift mit Funk-programm und Kulturspiegel*, 3 March 1946, 2.

112. Hey, "Jazz ist Musik."

113. Koeppen, *Pigeons on the Grass*, 111; Koeppen, *Tauben im Gras*, 124.

114. Koeppen, *Pigeons on the Grass,* 17.

115. Ibid., 179–80, 197–98.

116. See James Weldon Johnson, ed., *The Book of American Negro Spirituals* (1925; reprint, New York: Viking Press, 1947); Albert C. Barnes, "Negro Art and America," in *The New Negro,* 19–25; Alain Locke, "The Negro Spirituals," in *The New Negro,* 199–213; Gilroy, *The Black Atlantic,* 90. Brian Ward describes unremitting subsequent efforts to locate pure black music. Ward, *Just My Soul Responding,* 11.

117. Du Bois, *The Souls of Black Folk*; Gilroy, *The Black Atlantic.* On Du Bois's studies in Germany, see David Levering Lewis, *W.E.B. Du Bois: Biography of a Race* (New York: Henry Holt, 1993), 117–49.

118. William Grant Still, "An Afro-American Composer's Point of View," in *American Composers on American Music: A Symposium,* ed. Henry Cowell, with a new introduction by the editor (1933; reprint, New York: Frederick Ungar Publishing, 1962), 182.

119. Johnson, ed., *The Book of American Negro Spirituals,* 17, 21–23, 31; Henry Edward Krehbiel, *Afro-American Folksongs: A Study in Racial and National Music* (1914; reprint, New York: Frederick Ungar Publishing, 1962), 4, 56–58. On Krehbiel, see Mark N. Grant, *Maestros of the Pen: A History of Classical Music Criticism in America* (Boston: Northeastern University Press, 1998), 80–86; Joseph Horowitz, Krehbiel entry in *New Grove Dictionary of Music and Musicians.*

120. "The Story of the Chorus," in Programme of 29 September 1943 concert; Bulletins, 1943–1946, Newspaper Clippings, Correspondence, Public Relations, RG 338, NACP.

121. Paul Robeson, "Songs of My People," *Sovietskaia muzyka* 7 (July 1949): 100–104, translated by Paul A. Russo, in *Paul Robeson Speaks: Writings, Speeches, Interviews, 1918–1974,* ed. with an Introduction and notes by Philip S. Foner (New York: Brunner/Mazel, 1978), 213–14.

122. On German musicologists' efforts to find the true expression of the German soul in folk music before and during the Nazi era, see, e.g., Potter, *Most German of the Arts,* 191–96, 213–20. For post-1945 statements, see Dr. Ernst H. Meyer, "Der Leidensweg der deutschen Musik," *Frankfurter Rundschau,* 22 February 1946, 4; Grad, "Die Lage der Musikkultur." On the inherent instability of the search for authentic national culture, see Richard Handler, *Nationalism and the Politics of Culture in Quebec,* New Directions in Anthropological Writing: History, Poetics, Cultural Criticism (Madison: University of Wisconsin Press, 1988).

123. On the relation among the national, provincial, and local in imperial Germany, see Alon Confino, *The Nation as a Local Metaphor: Württemberg, Imperial Germany, and National Memory, 1871–1918* (Chapel Hill: University of North Carolina Press, 1997); Celia Applegate, *A Nation of Provincials: The German Idea of Heimat* (Berkeley: University of California Press, 1990).

124. "Bayerns kulturelle Aufgabe," 17, IfZ, Nachlaß Sattler, Bd. 149.

125. For the quotation, see Toni Grad, "Die Lage der Musikkultur in Stadt und Land: Wege zu ihrer Erneuerung," *Schwäbische Blätter für Volksbildung und Heimatpflege* 1 (1950), IfZ, Nachlaß Sattler, Bd. 35. See also Dr. Ernst H. Meyer, "Der Leidensweg der deutschen Musik," *Frankfurter Rundschau,* 22 February 1946, 4. For more on Sattler, see also "Der Bayerische Rundfunk: Gestern, heute und morgen," IfZ, Nachlaß Sattler, Bd. 112; "Aufbau des Bayerischen Staatstheater," IfZ, Nachlaß Sattler, Bd. 2; Minutes 20 February 1947 meeting, IfZ, Nachlaß Sattler,

Bd. 16; Ulrike Stoll, *Kulturpolitik als Beruf: Dieter Sattler (1906–1968) in München, Bonn und Rom,* Veröffentlichungen der Kommission für Zeitgeschichte, Reihe B: Forschungen, Bd. 98 (Paderborn: Ferdinand Schöningh, 2005).

126. "Negro Spirituals: Der Kitzinger Negerchor," *Rhein-Neckar-Zeitung,* 2 April 1949, 7.

127. Fritz Jöde, "Der Rhythmus als Grundkraft," *Junge Musik: Zeitschrift für die Musikpflege in der Jugend* 7 (1950), 111, BayHStA, MK 51282.

128. Zora Neale Hurston, "Spirituals and Neo-Spirituals," in *Negro Anthology Made by Nancy Cunard, 1931–1933* (London: Nancy Cunard at Wishart & Co., 1934), 360.

129. Joachim-Ernst Berendt, "Vom Choral zum Swing: Zur Genesis des Jazz," *Melos: Zeitschrift für neue Musik* 14:5 (March 1947): 138.

130. See "Negro Spirituals: Der Kitzinger Negerchor," *Rhein-Neckar-Zeitung;* "Religiöse Musik der Neger," *Frankfurter Rundschau;* Hey, "Jazz ist Musik."

131. "Negro Spirituals: Der Kitzinger Negerchor," *Rhein-Neckar-Zeitung.*

132. "Religiöse Musik der Neger," *Frankfurter Rundschau.*

133. See Scott DeVeaux, *The Birth of Bebop,* 39–45; Kater, *Different Drummers,* 13–14.

134. Horst Lange asserts that even AFN, the supposed bastion of real American jazz in occupied Germany, actually played mostly "pseudojazz." See Lange, *Jazz in Deutschland,* 145, 185, 190.

135. See Handler, *Nationalism and the Politics of Culture.*

136. Jazz arrangements of popular tunes, long central to jazz, were common in postwar Germany. See Lange, *Jazz in Deutschland,* 148; Toni Grad, "Die Lage der Musikkultur."

137. "Statistik des Geschmacks," *Radiowelt: Wochenschrift mit Funkprogramm,* 3 November 1946, 4.

138. Th. Stephan to Kultusminister, 29 October 1947.

139. Levine, "Jazz and American Culture," 12–13.

140. Robeson, "Songs of My People," 217. For similar statements by Robeson in the 1930s, see Duberman, *Paul Robeson,* 176–77. Anthropologist Edward Sapir likewise regarded jazz as vulgarizing spirituals. See "Review of James Weldon Johnson, *The Book of American Negro Spirituals,*" in *The Collected Works of Edward Sapir,* vol. 3, *Culture,* ed. Regna Darnell and Judith T. Irvine (sections 1 and 3), and Richard Handler (sections 4 and 5) (New York: Mouton de Gruyter, 1999), 1029.

141. "No zum Jazz," *Radiowelt: Bayerische illustrierte Wochenschrift mit Funkprogramm und Kulturspiegel,* 10 March 1946, 4.

142. Toni Grad, Denkschrift über die Erneuerung der Volksmusikkultur in Bayern, enclosure to Prof. Dr. Hanika, Bayerischer Landesverein für Heimatpflege, to Bayer. Staatsministerium für Unterricht und Kultus, z.Hd. Herrn Dr. Martin Luible, 9, BayHStA, MK 51275.

143. Grad, "Die Lage der Musikkultur."

144. "Yes zum Jazz?" *Radiowelt: Bayerische illustrierte Wochenschrift mit Funkprogramm und Kulturspiegel,* 24 February 1946, 3; "Yes zum Jazz!" *Radiowelt: Bayerische illustrierte Wochenschrift mit Funkprogramm und Kulturspiegel,* 3 March 1946, 2.

145. Joachim-Ernst Berendt, "Jazz—einmal ernst betrachtet: Musik und Weltanschauung—ein psychoanalytisches Problem," *Die Neue Zeitung,* 13 October 1949, 4; Hey, "Jazz ist Musik."

146. Uta C. Schmidt, Andreas Müller, and Richard Ortmann, *Jazz in Dortmund: Hot – Modern – Free – New* (Essen: Klartext Verlag, 2004), 88. Jennifer Fay reads the film as domesticating jazz. See Fay, " 'That's Jazz Made in Germany!' " 3–24.

147. Heinz Werner Zimmermann, "The Influence of American Music on a German Composer," in *Jazz and the Germans*, ed. Budds, 181.

148. Olaf Hudtwalker, "Ein Mann der Volksmusik: Zu George Gershwins 50. Geburtstag am 26. September 1948," *Frankfurter Rundschau*, 25 September 1948, 5. Hudtwalker accurately described Gershwin's thought. See George Gershwin, "The Relation of Jazz to American Music," in *American Composers on American Music*, ed. Cowell, 186–87.

149. "Yes zum Jazz?" *Radiowelt: Bayerische illustrierte Wochenschrift mit Funkprogramm und Kulturspiegel,* 24 February 1946, 3.

150. For the history of similar American attitudes, see Levine, "Jazz and American Culture."

151. See, e.g., James E. Alsbrook, "Negro Syncopation," *Opportunity: Journal of Negro Life* (October 1940): 302.

152. Kater, *Different Drummers;* "Wider die Negerkultur – für deutsches Volkstum: Bekanntmachung des Ministers Frick in Thüringen," *Völkischer Beobachter* [Munich edition], 15 April 1930, 1.

153. Joachim-Ernst Berendt, "Jazz – einmal ernst betrachtet: Musik und Weltanschauung – ein psychoanalytisches Problem," *Die Neue Zeitung,* 13 October 1949, 4.

154. See "Statistik des Geschmacks," *Radiowelt: Wochenschrift mit Funkprogramm,* 3 November 1946, 4. American officials at Radio Frankfurt believed that "younger people appreciate jazz music." Captain Herbert C. Cross to Office of the Director of Information Control, OMGUS, Attn: Radio Control Branch, 14 May 1946, 4, BRA, General Correspondence File, 24.4, RV 24, Mr. Horine Correspondence; Kater, *Different Drummers.* Jennifer Fay finds a democratic spirit in authentic jazz. Fay, " 'That's Jazz Made in Germany!' " 3–24.

155. See also O. W. Studtmann, "Am Lautsprecher: Unser Radiobericht vom 15. bis 21. August," *Frankfurter Rundschau,* 24 August 1948, 3. On similar trends today, see Cathy Covell Waegner, "Rap, Rebounds, and Rocawear: The 'Darkening' of German Youth Culture," in *Blackening Europe: The African American Presence,* ed. Heike Raphael-Hernandez, with a Foreword by Paul Gilroy (New York: Routledge, 2004), 171–86.

156. "Quer durch den Tag mit AFN," *Radiowelt,* 31 August 1947, 5.

157. Horst Lippmann, "Letzte Neuheiten," *Die Jazz-Club News!* 3/4 (October/ November 1945): 22, Jazz Institut. For an excellent account of the Frankfurt jazz scene, see Schwab, *Der Frankfurt Sound.*

158. Günter Boas, "Die Jazzbiographie: IV. Bessie Smith," *Die Jazz-Club News!* 7/8 (March/April 1946): 10, Jazz Institut.

159. Chris Albertson, *Bessie,* revised and expanded edition (New Haven, Conn.: Yale University Press, 2003), 256–57.

160. Hassencamp, *Der Sieg nach dem Krieg,* 109–15.

161. "Gastspiel des Kitzinger Negerchors wird wiederholt," *Rhein-Neckar-Zeitung,* 1 April 1949, 4.

162. Koeppen, *Pigeons on the Grass,* 147; Koeppen, *Tauben im Gras,* 161.

163. Koeppen, *Pigeons on the Grass,* 179, 176.

164. The quotation comes from Hassencamp's description of jam sessions by

German and American jazz musicians in the postwar period. Hassencamp, *Der Sieg nach dem Krieg*, 110. See also Ward, *Just My Soul Responding*.

165. Monthly Summary of U.S. Information Center Mannheim, ISD, OMGW-B to Chief, Information Centers and Exhibition Branch W-B, ISD, regarding period from 21 January 1949–20 February 1949, 23 February 49, Records regarding activities of the ICEB 1945–1949, ICEB, ICD, OMGUS, RG 260, NACP.

166. Notes dated 7 October 1947, Records re: Music and Theater, 1945–1948, Cultural Affairs Branch, Records of the Education and Cultural Relations Division, RG 260, NACP. On the postwar popularity of *Nathan the Wise*, see Sieg, *Ethnic Drag*, 64–71.

167. Report of Walter White to the Office and Board on his trip to Germany, in *Papers of the NAACP, Part 9: Discrimination in the U.S. Armed Forces, 1918–1955, Series C: The Veterans' Affairs Committee, 1940–1950* (Frederick, Md.: University Publications of America, 1989), reel 8, F145–46.

168. Reiner Pommerin, "Some Remarks on the Cultural History of the Federal Republic of Germany," in *Culture in the Federal Republic of Germany*, 3.

169. See Massaquoi, *Destined to Witness*, 436.

170. See, e.g., Hassencamp, *Der Sieg nach dem Krieg*, 29–31.

171. Friedrich Meinecke, *The German Catastrophe: Reflections and Recollections*, trans. Sidney B. Fay (Cambridge, Mass.: Harvard University Press, 1950), 117–18.

172. Ibid., 118–19, 120.

173. DeVeaux, *The Birth of Bebop*, 124; Kater, *Different Drummers*, 20; Lewis A. Erenberg, *Swingin' the Dream: Big Band Jazz and the Rebirth of American Culture* (Chicago: University of Chicago Press, 1998), 37.

174. Louis Martin, "Tan Yanks in Germany Destroy Last of Nazi 'Culture': Swing Music Big Favorite," *Chicago Defender*, 8 May 1948, clipping in Press Items re: Negro Newspapers, 1944–1946 (Analysis Branch), Office of Public Information, RG 330, NACP.

175. For such a scene without black GIs, see Hans Habe, *Aftermath: A Novel* (New York: Viking Press, 1947), 140. Wolfram Knauer observes that in popular memory, the linking of GIs, Fräuleins, and jazz has become cliché. Knauer, " 'Jazz, GI's und German Fräuleins': Einige Anmerkungen zur deutsch-amerikanischen Beziehung im musikalischen Nachkriegsdeutschland," in *Ekkehard Jost: Festschrift zum 65. Geburtstag*, ed. Bernd Hoffmann et al., *Jazzforschung Jazz Research* 34 (2002): 77–88.

176. See, e.g., "Keine Jazzmusik mehr im Programm der Berliner Funk-Stunde," 8 March 1933, reprinted in *Entartete Musik*, ed. Dümling and Girth, 120.

177. "No zum Jazz," *Radiowelt: Bayerische illustrierte Wochenschrift mit Funkprogramm und Kulturspiegel*, 10 March 1946, 4. There was an established jazz tradition of borrowing from artworks. See DeVeaux, *The Birth of Bebop*, 57.

178. Stephan to Kultusminister, 29 October 1947.

179. Hudtwalker, "Ein Mann der Volksmusik," *Frankfurter Rundschau*, 25 September 1948, 5.

180. Padover, *Experiment in Germany*, 263.

181. Cedric Belfrage, *Seeds of Destruction: The Truth about the U.S. Occupation of Germany* (New York: Cameron & Kahn, 1954), 67. Kleinschmidt describes the connection between the two authors and juxtaposes the quotations. Kleinschmidt, *"Do Not Fraternize,"* 153n80.

182. Belfrage, *Seeds of Destruction*, viii–xvii, 68.

Conclusion

1. Ulrich Herbert, ed., *National Socialist Extermination Policies: Contemporary German Perspectives and Controversies,* War and Genocide, ed. Omer Bartov, no. 2 (New York: Berghahn Books, 2000), 22.

2. See Bergmann, *Antisemitismus in öffentlichen Konflikten,* 48.

3. Eyferth, Brandt, and Hawel, *Farbige Kinder in Deutschland,* 77.

4. Others are less convinced of the durable nature of changes in attitudes toward race. See, e.g., Gilroy, *Against Race,* 25.

Bibliography

Archival Sources

United States National Archives, College Park, Maryland

Record Group 107, Records of the Secretary of War
Record Group 153, Records of the United States Army, Judge Advocate General
Record Group 165, Records of the War Department General and Special Staffs
Record Group 200, Gift Collections
       Papers of General Lucius Clay
Record Group 208, Records of the Office of War Information
Record Group 260, Records of the Office of the Military Government for Germany, United States
Record Group 319, Records of the Army Staff
Record Group 330, The American Soldier Survey, data tapes

Record Group 331, Records of SHAEF
Record Group 338, Records of Commands in the European, Mediterranean, and
    Africa–Middle East Theaters of Operations, World War II, 1941–48
        Records of European Theater of Operations U.S. Army/U.S. Forces Euro-
            pean Theater
        Records of the European Command
Record Group 389, Records of the Provost Marshal General
Record Group 407, Records of the Communications Branch

Bayerischer Rundfunk Archiv
Newspaper Clipping Files
Signatur F-13, S-201
RV 23, Mr. Brill Reports
RV 24, Mr. Horine Correspondence

Bayerisches Hauptstaatsarchiv
StK
Nrs. 13630, 14950
MK
Nrs. 50052, 51228, 51275, 51282

Erzbischöfliches Archiv Freiburg
Rep. B2-35
Nachlaß Conrad Gröber (Nb8)
62, 63, 67

Generallandesarchiv Karlsruhe
Bestand 481, Der Präsident des Landesbezirks Baden (1945–1952) Präsidialstelle
Nrs. 339, 537, 723, 1727

Institut für Zeitgeschichte
Nachlaß Wilhelm Hoegner
        Bd. 117, 127, 281
Nachlaß Walter Muller
        MA-1427/2
Nachlaß Dieter Sattler
        Bd. 2, 16, 35, 112, 149

Jazz Institut, Darmstadt
Nachlaß Horst Lippmann

Landeskirchliches Archiv, Nürnberg
LkR V Nr. 904a

Staatsarchiv Bamberg
Bezirksamt/LRA Bamberg, K5
Nr. 10214
LRA Kulmbach, K13
Nr. 7827

Staatsarchiv Nürnberg
Regierung von Mittelfranken
Nrs. 23, 1464, 1704, 1873
Staatsanwaltschaft Nürnberg-Fürth, Strafsache; Landgericht Nürnberg-Fürth
Nr. 1693

Stadtarchiv Mannheim
Ortsgeschichte, S2
Nrs. 425, 449-1

Stadtarchiv Nürnberg
Zeitungsarchiv

Stadtarchiv Weißenburg
Files of Weißenburg Government

U.S. Army Center of Military History, Washington, D.C., Historical Manuscripts Collection

Geis, Margaret L. "Negro Personnel in the European Command, 1 January 1946–30 June 1950." Occupation Forces in Europe Series. Karlsruhe: Historical Division, European Command, 1952.

Geis, Margaret L., and George J. Gray. "The Relations of Occupation Personnel with the Civil Population 1946–1948." Occupation Forces in Europe Series, 1946–48, no. 69. Karlsruhe: Historical Division, European Command, 1951.

Geis, Margaret L., et al. "Morale and Discipline in the European Command, 1945–1949." Occupation Forces in Europe Series, 1945–49. Karlsruhe: Historical Division, European Command, 1951.

Historical Division, European Command. "Medical Policies and Operations, 1 July 1946–30 June 1947." Occupation Forces in Europe Series 1945–46. Frankfurt a.M.: Historical Division, European Command, 1948.

Office of the Chief Historian, European Command. "Censorship." Occupation Forces in Europe Series 1945–46. Frankfurt a.M.: Office of the Chief Historian, European Command, 1947.

Office of the Chief Historian, European Command. "Law, Order, and Security." Occupation Forces in Europe Series, 1945–46. Frankfurt a.M.: Office of the Chief Historian, European Command, 1947.

Office of the Chief Historian, European Command. "Medical Policies and Operations." Occupation Forces in Europe Series 1945–46. Frankfurt a.M.: Office of the Chief Historian, European Command, 1947.

Office of the Chief Historian, European Command. "Public Safety." Occupation Forces in Europe Series, 1945–46. Frankfurt a.M.: Office of the Chief Historian, European Command, 1947.

Sher, Ronald. "Integration of Negro and White Troops in the U.S. Army, Europe, 1952-1954." N.p.: Historical Division Headquarters, United States Army, Europe, 1956.

Starr, Joseph R. "Fraternization with the Germans in World War II." Occupation Forces in Europe Series 1945–46, no. 67. Frankfurt a.M.: Office of the Chief Historian, Headquarters European Command, 1947.

U.S. Army Military History Institute, Carlisle Barracks, Pennsylvania
Army Service Experiences Questionnaires

Films

A Foreign Affair. Directed by Billy Wilder. 1 hr., 56 min. Paramount, 1948, videocassette.
The Negro Soldier. Produced by the United States War Department, 42 min., 1944, distributed by National Audiovisual Center, 1979, videocassette.
Your Job in Germany. Produced by International Historic Films, 32 min., originally produced by the Army Pictorial Service for Army Information Branch, Information and Education Division, A.S.F., and by the Army Pictorial Service, Signal Corps, 1985, videocassette.

Periodicals

Badische-Zeitung
Bayerische Rundschau: Kulmbacher Nachrichten für Stadt und Land
Bayerisches Gesetz- und Verordnungsblatt
Ebony
Frankfurter Allgemeine Zeitung
Frankfurter Rundschau
Fränkische Landeszeitung
Melos: Zeitschrift für neue Musik
Negro Digest: A Magazine of Negro Comment
Die Neue Presse
Die Neue Zeitung
New Republic
New York Times
Newsweek
Nürnberg Post-Spade
Nürnberger Nachrichten
Opportunity: Journal of Negro Life
Pittsburgh Courier
Radiowelt
Rhein-Neckar-Zeitung
Der Ruf
Sie
Der Spiegel
Stars and Stripes (Paris edition)
Süddeutsche Zeitung
Völkischer Beobachter (Munich edition)
Washington Post
Weser-Kurier
Zeitschrift für Haut- und Geschlechtskrankheiten

Books and Articles

Adelson, Leslie A. *Making Bodies, Making History: Feminism and German Identity.* Lincoln: University of Nebraska Press, 1993.

Adler, Hans, and Ernst A. Menze, eds. *On World History: Johann Gottfried Herder: An Anthology,* trans. Ernest A. Menze with Michael Palma. Sources and Studies in World History. Armonk, N.Y.: M. E. Sharpe, 1997.

Adorno, Theodor W. "Perennial Fashion — Jazz." In *Prisms,* trans. Samuel Weber and Shierry Weber. Studies in Contemporary German Social Thought, ed. Thomas McCarthy, 119–32. 1967. Reprint, Cambridge, Mass.: MIT Press, 1981.

Albertson, Chris. *Bessie,* revised and expanded edition. New Haven, Conn.: Yale University Press, 2003.

Allanbrook, Douglas. *See Naples: A Memoir.* Boston: Houghton Mifflin, 1995.

Allgemeine deutsche Real-Encyklopädie für die gebildeten Stände: Conversations-Lexikon. 9th ed. Vol. 10, *Moskau bis Patricier.* Leipzig: Brockhaus, 1846.

Allport, Gordon W. *The Nature of Prejudice,* 25th anniversary ed., with an introduction by Kenneth Clark and foreword by Thomas Pettigrew. Reading, Mass.: Addison-Wesley, 1979.

Anderson, Benedict. *Imagined Communities.* London: Verso, 1983.

Applegate, Celia. *A Nation of Provincials: The German Idea of Heimat.* Berkeley: University of California Press, 1990.

———. "What Is German Music? Reflections on the Role of Art in the Creation of a Nation." *German Studies Review: Special Issue, German Identity* (Winter 1992): 21–32.

Arndt, Susan. "Impressionen: Rassismus und der deutsche Afrikadiskurs." In *AfrikaBilder: Studien zu Rassismus in Deutschland,* ed. Susan Arndt, 11–70. Münster: Unrast, 2001.

Arnesen, Eric. "Whiteness and the Historians' Imagination." *International Labor and Working-Class History* 60 (Fall 2001): 3–32.

Ash, Mitchell G. "Verordnete Umbrüche — Konstruierte Kontinuitäten: Zur Entnazifizierung von Wissenschaftlern und Wissenschaften nach 1945." *Zeitschrift für Geschichtswissenschaft* 43 (1995): 903–23.

Autrata, Otger, Gerrit Kaschuba, Rudolf Leiprecht, and Cornelia Wolf. "Ausgangspunkte und Fragestellungen." In *Theorien über Rassismus: Eine Tübinger Veranstaltungsreihe,* ed. Otger Autrata, Gerrit Kaschuba, Rudolf Leiprecht, and Cornelia Wolf. Hamburg: Argument-Verlag, 1989.

Bahr, Ehrhard. "Nazi Cultural Politics: Intentionalism v. Functionalism." In *National Socialist Cultural Policy,* ed. Glenn R. Cuomo, 5–22. New York: St. Martin's Press, 1995.

Baker, Lee D. *From Savage to Negro: Anthropology and the Construction of Race, 1896–1954.* Berkeley: University of California Press, 1998.

Barkan, Elazar. *The Retreat of Scientific Racism: Changing Concepts of Race in Britain and the United States between the World Wars.* Cambridge: Cambridge University Press, 1992.

Barron, Stephanie, ed. *"Degenerate Art": The Fate of the Avant-Garde in Nazi Germany.* New York: Harry N. Abrams, 1991.

Bartók, Béla. "Why and How Do We Collect Folk Music?" In *Béla Bartók Essays,* selected and edited by Benjamin Suchoff, 9–28. New York Bartók Archive Studies in Musicology no. 8. New York: St. Martin's Press, 1976.

Bassenge, Reinhard. "Radio München 1945–1949 – Eine Programmanalyse." Wissenschaftliche Arbeit zur Erlangung des Magister Artium, Ludwig-Maximilians-Universität zu München, 1990.

Baur, Erwin, Eugen Fischer, and Fritz Lenz. *Human Heredity*. Trans. Eden Paul and Cedar Paul. New York: Macmillan, 1931.

———. *Menschliche Erblehre*. 4th ed. Munich: J. F. Lehmanns Verlag, 1936.

Bausch, Ulrich M. *Die Kulturpolitik der US-amerikanischen Information Control Division in Württemberg-Baden von 1945 bis 1949: Zwischen militärischem Funktionalismus und schwäbischem Obrigkeitsdenken*. Stuttgart: Klett-Cotta, 1992.

Beck, Earl R. "German Views of Negro Life in the United States, 1919–1933." *Journal of Negro History* 48 (1963): 22–32.

Bederman, Gail. *Manliness and Civilization: A Cultural History of Gender and Race in the United States, 1880–1917*. Chicago: University of Chicago Press, 1995.

Belfrage, Cedric. *Seeds of Destruction: The Truth about the U.S. Occupation of Germany*. New York, 1954.

Benedict, Ruth. *Race: Science and Politics*. Rev. ed., with "The Races of Mankind," Ruth Benedict and Gene Weltfish. New York: Viking, 1945.

Benz, Wolfgang, ed. *Deutschland unter allierter Besatzung, 1945–1949/55*. Berlin: Akademie Verlag, 1999.

———. "Währungsreform." In *Deutschland unter allierter Besatzung, 1945–1949/55*, ed. Wolfgang Benz, 190–94. Berlin: Akademie Verlag, 1999.

Berenbaum, Michael, and Abraham J. Peck, eds. *The Holocaust and History: The Known, the Unknown, the Disputed, and the Reexamined*. Bloomington: Indiana University Press in association with the United States Holocaust Memorial Museum, 1998.

Berendt, Joachim-Ernst. "Vom Choral zum Swing: Zur Genesis des Jazz." *Melos: Zeitschrift für neue Musik* 14:5 (March 1947): 134–38.

Bergmann, Werner. *Antisemitismus in öffentlichen Konflikten: Kollektives Lernen in der politischen Kultur der Bundesrepublik, 1949–1989*. Frankfurt a.M.: Campus Verlag, 1997.

Berlin, Ira. *Many Thousands Gone: The First Two Centuries of Slavery in North America*. Cambridge: Belknap Press of Harvard University Press, 1998.

Berlin, Isaiah. *Three Critics of the Enlightenment: Vico, Hamann, Herder*, ed. Henry Hardy. Princeton, N.J.: Princeton University Press, 2000.

Berman, William C. *The Politics of Civil Rights in the Truman Administration*. N.p.: Ohio State University Press, 1970.

Bessel, Richard. *Germany after the First World War*. Oxford: Clarendon Press, 1993.

Biddiscombe, Perry. "Dangerous Liaisons: The Anti-Fraternization Movement in the U.S. Occupation Zones of Germany and Austria, 1945–1948." *Journal of Social History* 34 (2001): 611–47.

Blackshire-Belay, Carol Aisha, ed. *The African-German Experience: Critical Essays*. Westport, Conn.: Praeger, 1996.

———. Special Issue: The Image of Africa in German Society. *Journal of Black Studies* 23:2 (1992).

Bley, Helmut. *South-West Africa under German Rule, 1894–1914*. Trans. Hugh Ridley. Evanston, Ill.: Northwestern University Press, 1971.

Blum, John Morton. *V Was for Victory: Politics and American Culture during World War II*. San Diego: Harcourt Brace Jovanovich, 1976.

Boberach, Heinz, ed. *Meldungen aus dem Reich, 1938–1945: Die geheimen Lageberichte des Sicherheitsdienstes der SS*. Vol. 5. Herrsching: Pawlak Verlag, 1984.

Bock, Gisela. *Zwangssterilisation im Nationalsozialismus: Studien zur Rassenpolitik und Frauenpolitik*. Opladen: WDV, 1986.

Boehling, Rebecca. "Commentary: The Role of Culture in American Relations with Europe: The Case of the United States' Occupation of Germany." In The American Occupation of Germany in Cultural Perspective: A Roundtable. *Diplomatic History* 23 (1999): 57–69.

———. *A Question of Priorities: Democratic Reforms and Economic Recovery in Postwar Germany: Frankfurt, Munich, and Stuttgart under U.S. Occupation 1945–1949*. Monographs in German History, vol. 2. Providence: Berghahn Books, 1996.

Bogart, Leo. *How I Earned the Ruptured Duck: From Brooklyn to Berchtesgaden in World War II*. College Station: Texas A&M University Press, 2004.

Bohländer, Carlo. "The Evolution of Jazz Culture in Frankfurt: A Memoir." In *Jazz and the Germans: Essays on the Influence of "Hot" American Idioms on 20th-Century German Music*, ed. Michael J. Budds, Monographs and Bibliographies in American Music no. 17, series ed. Michael J. Budds, 167–78. Hillsdale, NY: Pendragon Press, 2002.

Boris, Eileen. "'You Wouldn't Want One of 'Em Dancing with Your Wife': Racialized Bodies on the Job in World War II." *American Quarterly* 50 (1998): 77–108.

Borstelmann, Thomas. *The Cold War and the Color Line: American Race Relations in the Global Arena*. Cambridge, Mass.: Harvard University Press, 2001.

Botzenhart-Viehe, Verena. "The German Reaction to the American Occupation, 1944–1947." Ph.D. diss., University of California, Santa Barbara, 1980.

Boyer, Christoph, and Hans Woller. "'Hat die deutsche Frau versagt?' Die 'neue Freiheit' der Frauen in der Trümmerzeit, 1945–1949." *Journal für Geschichte* 2 (1983): 32–36.

Brandt, Allan M. *No Magic Bullet: A Social History of Venereal Disease in the United States since 1880*. New York: Oxford University Press, 1985.

Breman, Jan, ed. *Imperial Monkey Business: Racial Supremacy in Social Darwinist Theory and Colonial Practice*. Amsterdam: Vu University Press, 1990.

Bridenthal, Renate, Atina Grossmann, and Marion Kaplan, eds. *When Biology Became Destiny: Women in Weimar and Nazi Germany*. New York: Monthly Review Press, 1984.

Bridgman, Jon M. *The Revolt of the Hereros*. Berkeley: University of California Press, 1981.

Brodkin, Karen. *How Jews Became White Folks: And What That Says about Race in America*. New Brunswick, N.J.: Rutgers University Press, 1998.

Broszat, Martin, Klaus-Dietmar Henke, and Hans Woller, eds. *Von Stalingrad zur Währungsreform: Zur Sozialgeschichte des Umbruchs in Deutschland*. Munich: R. Oldenbourg Verlag, 1990.

Browder, Dewey A. *Americans in Post–World War II Germany: Teachers, Tinkers, Neighbors and Nuisances*. Lewiston, N.Y.: Edwin Mellen Press, 1998.

Brown, Kathleen M. *Good Wives, Nasty Wenches, and Anxious Patriarchs: Gender, Race, and Power in Colonial Virginia*. Chapel Hill: University of North Carolina Press, published for the Institute of Early American History and Culture, Williamsburg, Virginia, 1996.

Brown, Sterling A. "Count Us In." In *What the Negro Wants*, ed. Rayford W. Logan. Chapel Hill: University of North Carolina Press, 1944.

Brown-Fleming, Suzanne. "'The Worst Enemies of a Better Germany': Postwar Antisemitism among Catholic Clergy and U.S. Occupation Forces." *Holocaust and Genocide Studies* 18 (2004): 379–401.

Bruckner, Sierra A. "Spectacles of (Human) Nature: Commercial Ethnography between Leisure, Learning, and *Schaulust*." In *Worldly Provincialism: German Anthropology in the Age of Empire*, ed. H. Glenn Penny and Matti Bunzl, Social History, Popular Culture, and Politics in Germany, ed. Geoff Eley, 127–55. Ann Arbor: University of Michigan Press, 2003.

Bucher, Peter, ed. *Nachkriegsdeutschland, 1945–1949*. Quellen zum politischen Denken der Deutschen im 19. und 20. Jahrhundert, vol. 10. Darmstadt: Wissenschaftliche Buchgesellschaft, 1990.

Budds, Michael J., ed. *Jazz and the Germans: Essays on the Influence of "Hot" American Idioms on 20th-Century German Music*. Monographs and Bibliographies in American Music no. 17, series ed. Michael J. Budds. Hillsdale, N.Y.: Pendragon Press, 2002.

Bührer, Werner. "Schwarzer Markt." In *Deutschland unter alliierter Besatzung, 1945–1949/55*, ed. Wolfgang Benz, 365–66. Berlin: Akademie Verlag, 1999.

Bunzl, Matti. "Franz Boas and the Humboldtian Tradition: From *Volksgeist* and *Nationalcharakter* to an Anthropological Concept of Culture." In *Volksgeist as Method and Ethic: Essays on Boasian Ethnography and the German Anthropological Tradition*, ed. George W. Stocking Jr. History of Anthropology, vol. 8, 17–78. Madison: University of Wisconsin Press, 1996.

Burleigh, Michael, and Wolfgang Wippermann. *The Racial State: Germany, 1933–1945*. Cambridge: Cambridge University Press, 1991.

Caffrey, Margaret M. *Ruth Benedict: Stranger in This Land*. Austin: University of Texas Press, 1989.

Campt, Tina. "'Afro-German': The Convergence of Race, Sexuality and Gender in the Formation of a German Ethnic Identity, 1919–1960." Ph.D. diss., Cornell University, 1996.

———. *Other Germans: Black Germans and the Politics of Race, Gender, and Memory in the Third Reich*. Ann Arbor: University of Michigan Press, 2004.

Campt, Tina Marie, Pascal Grosse, and Yara-Colette Lemke Muniz de Faria. "Blacks, Germans, and the Politics of Imperial Imagination, 1920–1960." In *The Imperialist Imagination: German Colonialism and Its Legacy*, ed. Sara Friedrichsmeyer, Sara Lennox, and Susanne Zantop, 205–29. Ann Arbor: University of Michigan Press, 1998.

Capeci, Dominic J., Jr. *Race Relations in Wartime Detroit: The Sojourner Truth Housing Controversy of 1942*. Philadelphia: Temple University Press, 1984.

Carby, Hazel V. *Race Men*. Cambridge, Mass.: Harvard University Press, 1998.

Clay, Lucius D. *Decision in Germany*. Garden City, N.Y.: Doubleday and Co., 1950.

Clemens, Gabriele, ed. *Kulturpolitik im besetzten Deutschland, 1945–1949*. Stuttgart: Franz Steiner Verlag, 1994.

Confino, Alon. *The Nation as a Local Metaphor: Württemberg, Imperial Germany, and National Memory, 1871–1918*. Chapel Hill: University of North Carolina Press, 1997.

Costello, John. *Virtue under Fire: How World War II Changed Our Social and Sexual Attitudes*. New York: Fromm International Publishing Corporation, 1987.

Cowell, Henry, ed. *American Composers on American Music: A Symposium*, with a new introduction by the editor. 1933. Reprint, New York: Frederick Ungar Publishing, 1962.

Crawley, Erin Leigh. "Challenging Concepts of Cultural and National Homogeneity: Afro-German Women and the Articulation of Germanness." Ph.D. diss., University of Wisconsin–Madison, 1996.

Dalfiume, Richard M. *Desegregation in the Armed Forces: Fighting on Two Fronts, 1939–1953*. Columbia: University of Missouri Press, 1969.

Dallin, Alexander. *German Rule in Russia, 1941–1945: A Study of Occupation Policies*. 2nd ed. London: Macmillan Press, 1981.

Dastrup, Boyd L. *Crusade in Nuremberg: Military Occupation, 1945–1949*. Westport, Conn.: Greenwood Press, 1985.

Davis, David Brion. "The Americanized Mannheim of 1945–1946." In *American Places: Encounters with History: A Celebration of Sheldon Meyer*, ed. William E. Leuchtenburg, 78–91. Oxford: Oxford University Press, 2000.

———. "World War II and Memory." *The Journal of American History* 77 (1990): 580–87.

DeVeaux, Scott. *The Birth of Bebop: A Social and Musical History*. Berkeley: University of California Press, 1997.

Diner, Dan. *America in the Eyes of the Germans: An Essay on Anti-Americanism*. Trans. Allison Brown. Princeton, N.J.: Marcus Wiener Publishers, 1996.

Dinter, Andreas. "Die Seuchen im Berlin der Nachkriegszeit, 1945–1949." Ph.D. diss., Frei Universität Berlin, 1994.

Domentat, Tamara. *"Hallo Fräulein": Deutsche Frauen und amerikanische Soldaten*. Berlin: Aufbau-Verlag, 1998.

Donaldson, Gary A. *Double V: The History of African-Americans in the Military*. Malabar, Fla.: Krieger Publishing Company, 1991.

Dorr, Lisa Johanna Lindquist. "'Messin' White Women': White Women, Black Men, and Rape in Virginia, 1900–1960." Ph.D. diss., University of Virginia, 2000.

Dörr, Margarete. *"Wer die Zeit nicht miterlebt hat . . .": Frauenerfahrungen im Zweiten Weltkrieg und in den Jahren danach*. Vol. 2, *Kriegsalltag*. Frankfurt a.M.: Campus Verlag, 1998.

Dower, John W. *War without Mercy: Race and Power in the Pacific War*. New York: Pantheon Books, 1986.

Duberman, Martin Bauml. *Paul Robeson*. New York: Alfred A. Knopf, 1988.

Du Bois, W.E.B. *The Souls of Black Folk*, with an introduction by Dr. Nathan Hare and Alvin F. Poussaint, M.D. 1903. Reprint, New York: A Signet Classic, New American Library, 1982.

Dudziak, Mary. *Cold War Civil Rights: Race and the Image of American Democracy*. Princeton, N.J.: Princeton University Press, 2000.

———. "Desegregation as a Cold War Imperative." *Stanford Law Review* 41 (November 1988): 61–120.

Dümling, Albrecht, and Peter Girth, eds., *Entartete Musik: Dokumentation und Kommentar zur Düsseldorfer Ausstellung von 1938*, revised and expanded edition. Düsseldorf: dkv, der kleine Verlag, 1993.

Dunner, Joseph. "Information Control in the American Zone of Germany, 1945–1946." In *American Experiences in Military Government in World War II*, ed. Carl J. Friedrich, 276–91. New York: Rinehart & Company, 1948.

Ebeling, Hermann. "Zum Problem der deutschen Besatzungskinder." *Bildung und Erziehung* 7 (1954): 612–30.

Ehmann, Annegret. "From Colonial Racism to Nazi Population Policy: The Role of the So-Called Mischlinge." In *The Holocaust and History: The Known, the Unknown, the Disputed, and the Reexamined*, ed. Michael Berenbaum and Abraham J. Peck, 115–33. Bloomington: Indiana University Press in association with the United States Holocaust Memorial Museum, 1998.

Eichenauer, Richard. *Musik und Rasse*, 2nd ed. Munich: Lehmanns Verlag, 1937.

Eisenberg, Carolyn. *Drawing the Line: The American Decision to Divide Germany, 1944–1949*. New York: Cambridge University Press, 1996.

Elkin, Henry. "Aggressive and Erotic Tendencies in Army Life." *American Journal of Sociology* 51 (1946): 408–13.

El-Tayeb, Fatima. "'Blood Is a Very Special Juice': Racialized Bodies and Citizenship in Twentieth-Century Germany." In *Complicating Categories: Gender, Class, Race and Ethnicity*, ed. Eileen Boris and Angélique Janssens, *International Review of Social History*, Supplement 7, 149–69. Cambridge: Press Syndicate of the University of Cambridge, 1999.

———. *Schwarze Deutsche: Der Diskurs um "Rasse" und nationale Identität, 1890–1933*. Frankfurt a.M.: Campus Verlag, 2001.

Emde, Helga. "Als Besatzungskind im Nachkriegsdeutschland." In *Farbe Bekennen: Afro-Deutsche Frauen auf den Spuren ihrer Geschichte*, ed. Katharina Oguntoye, May Opitz, and Dagmar Schultz, 103–113. Berlin: Orlanda Verlag, 1986.

Erenberg, Lewis A. *Swingin' the Dream: Big Band Jazz and the Rebirth of American Culture*. Chicago: University of Chicago Press, 1998.

Ermath, Michael, ed. *America and the Shaping of German Society, 1945–1955*. Providence: Berg, 1993.

Erskine, Hazel Gaudet. "The Polls: Race Relations." *Public Opinion Quarterly* 26 (1962): 137–48.

Evans, Jennifer Victoria. "Reconstruction Sites: Sexuality, Citizenship, and the Limits of National Belonging in Divided Berlin, 1944–58." Ph.D. diss., Binghamton University, State University of New York, 2001.

Eyferth, Klaus, Ursula Brandt, and Wolfgang Hawel. *Farbige Kinder in Deutschland: Die Situation der Mischlingskinder und die Aufgaben ihrer Eingliederung*. Schriftenreihe der Arbeitsgemeinschaft für Jugendpflege und Jugendfürsorge, no. 7. Munich: Juventa Verlag, 1960.

Fanon, Frantz. *Black Skin, White Masks*, trans. Charles Lam Markmann. New York: Grove Press, 1967.

Fay, Jennifer. "'That's Jazz Made in Germany!' *Hallo Fräulein!* and the Limits of Democratic Pedagogy." *Cinema Journal* 44:1 (2004): 3–24.

Fee, Elizabeth. "Venereal Disease: The Wages of Sin?" In *Passion and Power: Sexuality in History*, ed. Kathy Peiss and Christina Simmons, with Robert A. Padgug, 178–98. Philadelphia: Temple University Press, 1989.

Fehrenbach, Heide. "'Ami-Liebchen' und 'Mischlingskinder': Rasse, Geschlecht und Kultur in der deutsch-amerikanischen Begegnung." In *Nachkrieg in Deutschland*, ed. Klaus Naumann, 178–205. Hamburg: Hamburger Edition, 2001.

———. *Cinema in Democratizing Germany: Reconstructing National Identity after Hitler*. Chapel Hill: University of North Carolina Press, 1995.

———. "Of German Mothers and 'Negermischlingskinder': Race, Sex, and the Postwar Nation." In *The Miracle Years: A Cultural History of West Germany,*

1949–1968, ed. Hanna Schissler, 164–86. Princeton, N.J.: Princeton University Press, 2001.

———. *Race after Hitler: Black Occupation Children in Postwar Germany and America.* Princeton, N.J.: Princeton University Press, 2005.

———. "Rehabilitating Father*land*: Race and German Remasculinization." *Signs: Journal of Women in Culture and Society* 24 (1998): 107–27.

Fields, Barbara J. "Race and Ideology in American History." In *Region, Race and Reconstruction: Essays in Honor of C. Vann Woodward*, ed. J. Morgan Kousser and James M. McPherson. New York: Oxford University Press, 1983.

———. "Whiteness, Racism, and Identity." *International Labor and Working-Class History* 60 (Fall 2001): 48–56.

Finkle, Lee. "The Conservative Aims of Militant Rhetoric: Black Protest during World War II." *Journal of American History* 60 (December 1973): 692–713.

———. *Forum for Protest: The Black Press during World War II.* Rutherford, N.J.: Fairleigh Dickinson University Press, 1975.

Finzsch, Norbert, and Dietmar Schirmer, eds. *Identity and Intolerance: Nationalism, Racism, and Xenophobia in Germany and the United States.* Cambridge: Cambridge University Press and the German Historical Institute, Washington, D.C., 1998.

Fischer, Hans. *Völkerkunde im Nationalsozialismus: Aspekte der Anpassung, Affinität und Behauptung einer Wissenschaftlichen Disziplin.* Hamburger Beiträge zur Wissenschaftsgeschichte, Bd. 7. Berlin: Dietrich Reimer Verlag, 1990.

Flugschriften der deutschen Gesellschaft zur Bekämpfung der Geschlechtskrankheiten, number 22. Leipzig: Verlag von Johann Ambrosius Barth, n.d.

Frankenberg, Ruth. *White Women, Race Matters: The Social Construction of Whiteness.* Minneapolis: University of Minnesota Press, 1993.

Fredrickson, George M. *The Black Image in the White Mind: The Debate on Afro-American Character and Destiny, 1817–1914.* Middletown, Conn.: Wesleyan University Press, 1987.

———. *Racism: A Short History.* Princeton, N.J.: Princeton University Press, 2002.

Freier, Anna-Elisabeth, and Annette Kuhn, eds. *"Das Schicksal Deutschlands liegt in der Hand seiner Frauen": Frauen in der deutschen Nachkriegsgeschichte.* Düsseldorf: Schwann, 1984.

Frevert, Ute. *Frauen-Geschichte: Zwischen Bürgerlicher Verbesserung und Neuer Weiblichkeit.* Frankfurt a.M.: Suhrkamp Verlag, 1986.

———. *Women in German History: From Bourgeois Emancipation to Sexual Liberation.* Trans. Stuart McKinnon-Evans. New York: Berg, 1988.

Friedlander, Judith, Blanche Wiesen Cook, Alice Kessler-Harris, and Carroll Smith-Rosenberg, eds. *Women in Culture and Politics: A Century of Change.* Bloomington: Indiana University Press, 1986.

Friedländer, Saul. *Nazi Germany and the Jews.* Vol. 1, *The Years of Persecution, 1933–1939.* New York: HarperCollins, 1997.

Friedmann, Wolfgang. *The Allied Military Government of Germany.* The Library of World Affairs, no. 8. London: Stevens & Sons, 1947.

Friedrich, Carl J., ed. *American Experiences in Military Government in World War II.* New York: Rinehart & Company, 1948.

Friedrichsmeyer, Sara, Sara Lennox, and Susanne Zantop, eds. *The Imperialist Imagination: German Colonialism and Its Legacy.* Social History, Popular Culture, and Politics in Germany, ed. Geoff Eley. Ann Arbor: University of Michigan Press, 1998.

Führer, Karl Christian. "Wohnungen." In *Deutschland unter allierter Besatzung, 1945–1949/55,* ed. Wolfgang Benz, 206–9. Berlin: Akademie Verlag, 1999.

Gassert, Philipp. *Amerika im Dritten Reich: Ideologie, Propaganda und Volksmeinung, 1933–1945.* Stuttgart: Franz Steiner Verlag, 1997.

Geiss, Imanuel. *Geschichte des Rassismus.* Frankfurt a.M.: Suhrkamp Verlag, 1988.

Gellately, Robert. *The Gestapo and German Society: Enforcing Racial Policy, 1935–1945.* Oxford: Clarendon Press, 1990.

Gellately, Robert, and Nathan Stoltzfus, eds. *Social Outsiders in Nazi Germany.* Princeton, N.J.: Princeton University Press, 2001.

"Germany after the War, Round Table — 1945." *American Journal of Orthopsychiatry* 15 (1945): 381–441.

Gienow-Hecht, Jessica C.E. "Art Is Democracy and Democracy Is Art: Culture, Propaganda, and the *Neue Zeitung* in Germany, 1944–1947." In The American Occupation of Germany in Cultural Perspective: A Roundtable. *Diplomatic History* 23 (1999): 21–43.

———. *Transmission Impossible: American Journalism as Cultural Diplomacy in Post-war Germany.* Eisenhower Center Studies on War and Peace. Baton Rouge: Louisiana State University Press, 1999.

Gilbert, G. M. *Nuremberg Diary.* 1947. Reprint, New York: Da Capo Press, 1995.

Gilman, Sander L. "Black Sexuality and Modern Consciousness." In *Blacks and German Culture,* ed. Reinhold Grimm and Jost Hermand, 35–53. Madison: University of Wisconsin Press, 1986.

———. *Difference and Pathology: Stereotypes of Sexuality, Race, and Madness.* Ithaca, N.Y.: Cornell University Press, 1985.

———. *On Blackness without Blacks: Essays on the Image of the Black in Germany.* Boston: G. K. Hall and Co., 1982.

Gilroy, Paul. *Against Race: Imagining Political Culture beyond the Color Line.* Cambridge, Mass.: Harvard University Press, 2000.

———. *The Black Atlantic: Modernity and Double Consciousness.* Cambridge, Mass.: Harvard University Press, 1993.

Goedde, Petra. "From Villains to Victims: Fraternization and the Feminization of Germany, 1945–1947." In The American Occupation of Germany in Cultural Perspective: A Roundtable. *Diplomatic History* 23 (1999): 1–20.

———. *GIs and Germans: Culture, Gender, and Foreign Relations, 1945–1949.* New Haven, Conn.: Yale University Press, 2003.

Gottlieb, Robert, ed. *Reading Jazz: A Gathering of Autobiography, Reportage, and Criticism from 1919 to Now.* New York: Pantheon Books, 1996.

Grant, Mark N. *Maestros of the Pen: A History of Classical Music Criticism in America.* Boston: Northeastern University Press, 1998.

Grasskamp, Walter. "'Degenerate Art' and Documenta I: Modernism Ostracized and Disarmed." In *Museum Culture: Histories, Discourses, Spectacles,* ed. Daniel J. Sherman and Irit Rogoff, 163–94. Minneapolis: University of Minnesota Press, 1994.

Grill, Johnpeter Horst, and Robert L. Jenkins. "The Nazis and the American South in the 1930s: A Mirror Image?" *The Journal of Southern History* 58 (November 1992): 667–94.

Grimm, Reinhold. "Germans, Blacks, and Jews; or Is There a German Blackness of Its Own?" In *Blacks and German Culture,* ed. Reinhold Grimm and Jost Hermand, 150–84. Madison: University of Wisconsin Press, 1986.

Grimm, Reinhold, and Jost Hermand, eds. *Blacks and German Culture*. Madison: University of Wisconsin Press, 1986.

Groß, Walter. *Rassenpolitische Erziehung*. Berlin: Junker und Dünnhaupt Verlag, 1935.

Grosse, Pascal. *Kolonialismus, Eugenik und bürgerliche Gesellschaft in Deutschland, 1850–1918*, Campus Forschung vol. 815. Frankfurt: Campus Verlag, 2000.

———. "Turning Native? Anthropology, German Colonialism, and the Paradoxes of the 'Acclimatization Question,' 1885–1914." In *Worldly Provincialism: German Anthropology in the Age of Empire*, ed. H. Glenn Penny and Matti Bunzl, Social History, Popular Culture, and Politics in Germany, ed. Geoff Eley, 179–97. Ann Arbor: University of Michigan Press, 2003.

Grossmann, Atina. "A Question of Silence: The Rape of German Women by Occupation Soldiers." In *West Germany under Construction: Politics, Society, and Culture in the Adenauer Era*, ed. Robert G. Moeller, 33–52. Ann Arbor: University of Michigan Press, 1997.

———. *Reforming Sex: The German Movement for Birth Control and Abortion Reform, 1920 to 1950*. New York: Oxford University Press, 1995.

———. "Trauma, Memory, and Motherhood: Germans and Jewish Displaced Persons in Post-Nazi Germany, 1945–1949." In *Life after Death: Approaches to a Cultural and Social History of Europe during the 1940s and 1950s*, ed. Richard Bessel and Dirk Schumann, 93–127. Cambridge: German Historical Institute, Washington, D.C., and Cambridge University Press, 2003.

Gunn, Richard L. *Art and Politics in Wolfgang Koeppen's Postwar Trilogy*. Germanic Languages and Literatures, vol. 26. New York: Peter Lang, 1983.

Habe, Hans. *Aftermath: A Novel*. New York: Viking Press, 1947.

Hachey, Thomas E. "Jim Crow with a British Accent: Attitudes of London Government Officials toward American Negro Soldiers in England during World War II." *Journal of Negro History* 59 (1974): 65–77.

Hahn, Karl. *Chronik des Marktes Wirsberg*. Markt Wirsberg: n.p., 1984.

Hale, Grace Elizabeth. *Making Whiteness: The Culture of Segregation in the South, 1890–1940*. New York: Pantheon Books, 1998.

Halsell, Grace. *Black/White Sex*. New York: William Morrow and Company, 1972.

Hambrecht, Rainer. *Der Aufstieg der NSDAP in Mittel- und Oberfranken, 1925–1933*. Nürnberg: Stadtarchiv Nürnberg, 1976.

Handler, Richard. "Interpreting the Predicament of Culture Theory Today." *Social Analysis* 41:3 (1997): 72–83.

———. *Nationalism and the Politics of Culture in Quebec*. New Directions in Anthropological Writing: History, Poetics, Cultural Criticism. Madison: University of Wisconsin Press, 1988.

———. "Raymond Williams, George Stocking, and Fin-de-Siècle U.S. Anthropology." *Cultural Anthropology* 13 (1998): 447–63.

Hannaford, Ivan. *Race: The History of an Idea in the West*. Washington, D.C.: Woodrow Wilson Center Press, 1996.

Harmon, Major General E. N., with Milton Mackaye and William Ross Mackaye. *Combat Commander: Autobiography of a Soldier*. Englewood Cliffs, N.J.: Prentice-Hall, 1970.

Harrington, Oliver. "Frontiers Still Left in America: The Negro's Part." In *The Struggle for Justice as a World Force: Report of the New York Herald Tribune Annual Forum*, 50–55. New York: New York Tribune, 1946.

Harsch, Donna. "Public Continuity and Private Change? Women's Consciousness and Activity in Frankfurt, 1945–1955." *Journal of Social History* 27 (1993): 29–59.

Hassencamp, Oliver. *Der Sieg nach dem Krieg: Die gute schlechte Zeit.* Munich: Herbig, n.d.

Hegel, Georg Wilhelm Friedrich. *The Philosophy of History,* trans. J. Sibree. New York: Dover Publications, 1956.

———. *Vorlesungen über die Philosophie der Weltgeschichte.* Vol. 1, *Die Vernunft in der Geschichte,* ed. Johannes Hoffmeister. Hamburg: Verlag von Felix Meiner, 1955.

Heineman, Elizabeth D. "The Hour of the Woman: Memories of Germany's 'Crisis Years' and West German National Identity." *AHR* 101 (1996): 354–95.

———. *What Difference Does a Husband Make? Women and Marital Status in Nazi and Postwar Germany.* Berkeley: University of California Press, 1999.

Hein-Kremer, Maritta. *Die amerikanische Kulturoffensive: Gründung und Entwicklung der amerikanischen Information Centers in Westdeutschland und West-Berlin, 1945–1955.* Beiträge zur Geschichte der Kulturpolitik, ed. Kurt Düwell, vol. 6. Köln: Böhlau Verlag, 1996.

Heinrichs, Jürgen. "'Blackness in Weimar': 1920s German Art Practice and American Jazz and Dance." Ph.D. diss., Yale University, 1998.

Hemken, Ruth, ed. *Sammlung der vom Alliierten Kontrollrat und der Amerikanischen Militärregierung erlassenen Proklamationen, Gesetze, Verordnungen, Befehle, Direktiven: Im englischen Originalwortlaut mit deutscher Übersetzung.* 3 vols. Stuttgart: Deutsche Verlags-Anstalt, 1947.

Henke, Klaus-Dietmar. *Die amerikanische Besetzung Deutschlands.* Munich: R. Oldenbourg Verlag, 1995.

Herbert, Ulrich. *Hitler's Foreign Workers: Enforced Foreign Labor in Germany under the Third Reich.* Trans. William Templer. Cambridge: Cambridge University Press, 1997.

———, ed. *National Socialist Extermination Policies: Contemporary German Perspectives and Controversies.* War and Genocide, ed. Omer Bartov. New York: Berghahn Books, 2000.

Herder, Johann Gottfried. *Reflections on the Philosophy of the History of Mankind,* abridged, with an introduction by Frank E. Manuel. Reprint, Chicago: University of Chicago Press, 1968.

———. *Sämtliche Werke.* Vol. 23, 1887. Reprint, ed. Bernhard Suphan. Hildesheim: Georg Olms Verlag, 1978.

Hermand, Jost. "Artificial Atavism: German Expressionism and Blacks." In *Blacks and German Culture,* ed. Reinhold Grimm and Jost Hermand, 65–86. Madison: University of Wisconsin Press, 1986.

———. *Kultur im Wiederaufbau: Die Bundesrepublik Deutschland, 1945–1965.* Munich: Nymphenburger, 1986.

Herskovits, Melville. *The Myth of the Negro Past.* 1941. Reprint, Boston: Beacon Press, 1958.

Herzog, Dagmar. "Desperately Seeking Normality: Sex and Marriage in the Wake of the War." In *Life after Death: Approaches to a Cultural and Social History of Europe during the 1940s and 1950s,* ed. Richard Bessel and Dirk Schumann, 161–92. Cambridge: German Historical Institute, Washington, D.C., and Cambridge University Press, 2003.

————. *Sex after Fascism: Memory and Morality in Twentieth-Century Germany*. Princeton, N.J.: Princeton University Press, 2005.

Higginbotham, Evelyn Brooks. "African-American Women's History and the Metalanguage of Race." *Signs: Journal of Women in Culture and Society* 17 (1992): 251–74.

Historischen Kommission bei der Bayerischen Akademie der Wissenschaften und der Generaldirektion der Staatlichen Archive Bayerns, ed. *Die Protokolle des Bayerischen Ministerrats, 1945–1954*. Vol. 1, *Das Kabinett Schäffer: 28. Mai bis 28. September 1945*, ed. Karl-Ulrich Gelberg. Munich: R. Oldenbourg Verlag, 1995.

Hitler, Adolf. *Mein Kampf*. Trans. Ralph Manheim. Boston: Houghton Mifflin, 1971.

Hodes, Martha. "The Mercurial Nature and Abiding Power of Race: A Transnational Family Story." *AHR* 108 (2003): 84–118.

————, ed. *Sex, Love, Race: Crossing Boundaries in North American History*. New York: New York University Press, 1999.

————. *White Women, Black Men: Illicit Sex in the Nineteenth-Century South*. New Haven, Conn.: Yale University Press, 1997.

Hodges, LeRoy S. *Portrait of an Expatriate: William Gardner Smith, Writer*. Contributions in Afro-American and African Studies, no. 91. Westport, Conn.: Greenwood, 1985.

Hoecker, Beate, and Renate Meyer-Braun. *Bremerinnen bewältigen die Nachkriegszeit: Frauen, Alltag, Arbeit, Politik*. Frauen in Bremen, ed. Renate Meyer-Braun. Bremen: Steintor, 1988.

Höhn, Maria. *GIs and Fräuleins: The German-American Encounter in 1950s West Germany*. Chapel Hill: University of North Carolina Press, 2002.

————. "GIs, Veronikas and Lucky Strikes: German Reactions to the American Military Presence in the Rhineland-Palatinate during the 1950s." Ph.D. diss., University of Pennsylvania, 1995.

————. "*Heimat* in Turmoil: African-American GIs in 1950s West Germany." In *The Miracle Years: A Cultural History of West Germany, 1949–1968*, ed. Hanna Schissler, 145–63. Princeton, N.J.: Princeton University Press, 2001.

Hönicke, Michaela. "'Know Your Enemy': American Interpretations of National Socialism, 1933–1945." Ph.D. diss., University of North Carolina, 1998.

Horowitz, Joseph. Krehbiel entry in *New Grove Dictionary of Music and Musicians*, 2nd ed., ed. Stanley Sadie. New York: Grove Dictionaries, 2001, www.e-grove.com.

Hough, Patricia. "The Socio-Cultural Integration of German Women Married to American Personnel." Ph.D. diss., Frei Universität Berlin, 1979.

Hügel-Marshall, Ika. *Invisible Woman: Growing Up Black in Germany*. Trans. Elizabeth Gaffney. New York: Continuum, 2001.

Hüneke, Andreas. "Die Propaganda gegen die 'Negerkunst.'" In *Zwischen Charleston und Stechschritt: Schwarze im Nationalsozialismus*, ed. Peter Martin and Christine Alonzo, 227–39. Hamburg: Dölling und Galitz Verlag, 2004.

Hurston, Zora Neale. "Spirituals and Neo-Spirituals." In *Negro Anthology Made by Nancy Cunard, 1931–1933*. London: Nancy Cunard at Wishart & Co., 1934.

Hyam, Ronald. *Empire and Sexuality: The British Experience*. Manchester: Manchester University Press, 1990.

"In Retrospect: W. Rudolph Dunbar: Pioneering Orchestra Conductor." *The Black Perspective in Music* 9 (1981): 193–225.

Irek, Joachim. *Mannheim in den Jahren 1945–1949: Geschichte einer Stadt zwischen Diktatur und Republik*. Veröffentlichungen des Stadtarchivs Mannheim, Bd. 9. Stuttgart: Verlag W. Kohlhammer, 1983.

Jackson, Jeffrey H. "Making Jazz French: Music and Cosmopolitanism in Interwar Paris." Ph.D. diss., University of Rochester, 1999.

Jackson, Walter. "Melville Herskovits and the Search for Afro-American Culture." In *Malinowski, Rivers, Benedict and Others: Essays on Culture and Personality*, ed. George W. Stocking Jr., History of Anthropology, vol. 4, 95–126. Madison: University of Wisconsin Press, 1986.

Jacobson, Matthew Frye. *Whiteness of a Different Color: European Immigrants and the Alchemy of Race*. Cambridge, Mass.: Harvard University Press, 1998.

Jelavich, Peter. *Berlin Cabaret*. Cambridge, Mass.: Harvard University Press, 1993.

Jering, Karl. *Überleben und Neubeginn: Aufzeichnungen eines Deutschen aus den Jahren 1945/46*. Dokumente Unserer Zeit, ed. Rudolf Birkl and Günter Olzog, Band 1. Munich: Günter Olzog Verlag, 1979.

Jochelson, Karen. *The Colour of Disease: Syphilis and Racism in South Africa, 1880–1950*. Houndsmills, Basingstoke, Hampshire, U.K.: Palgrave, 2001.

John, Michael. "Das 'Haarabschneiderkommando' von Linz: Männlicher Chauvinismus oder nationalsozialistische Wiederbetätigung? Ein Fallbeispiel aus den Jahren 1945–1948." In *Historisches Jahrbuch der Stadt Linz, 1995: Entnazifizierung und Wiederaufbau in Linz*, ed. Fritz Mayrhofer and Walter Schuster, 335–59. Linz: Archiv der Stadt Linz, 1996.

Johnson, James Weldon, ed. *The Book of American Negro Spirituals*. 1925. Reprint, New York: Viking Press, 1947.

Jones, James H. *Bad Blood: The Tuskegee Syphilis Experiment*. New and expanded ed. New York: Free Press, 1993.

Jones, Larry Eugene, ed. *Crossing Boundaries: The Exclusion and Inclusion of Minorities in Germany and the United States*. New York: Berghahn Books, 2001.

"*Jonny spielt auf:* Between Jazz and New Music." Entartete Musik: Music Suppressed by the Third Reich. London: Decca, 1993.

Jordan, Winthrop D. *White over Black: American Attitudes towards the Negro, 1550–1812*. Chapel Hill: University of North Carolina Press, 1968.

Kaes, Anton. "What to Do with Germany? American Debates about the Future of Germany, 1942–1947." *German Politics and Society* 13 (Fall 1995): 130–41.

Kaplan, Alice. *The Interpreter*. New York: Free Press, 2005.

Kardiner, Abram, and Lionel Ovesey. *The Mark of Oppression: A Psychosocial Study of the American Negro*. New York: W. W. Norton & Co., 1951.

Kater, Michael H. *Composers of the Nazi Era: Eight Portraits*. New York: Oxford University Press, 2000.

———. *Different Drummers: Jazz in the Culture of Nazi Germany*. New York: Oxford University Press, 1992.

———. "The Jazz Experience in Weimar Germany." *German History* 6:2 (1988): 145–58.

———. *The Twisted Muse: Musicians and Their Music in the Third Reich*. New York: Oxford University Press, 1997.

Keiler, Allan. *Marian Anderson: A Singer's Journey*. New York: Scribner, 2000.

Kelly, Alfred. *The Descent of Darwin: The Popularization of Darwinism in Germany, 1860–1914*. Chapel Hill: University of North Carolina Press, 1981.

Kesting, Robert W. "Forgotten Victims: Blacks in the Holocaust." *Journal of Negro History* 77 (1992): 30–36.

Killingray, David. "Africans and African Americans in Enemy Hands." In *Prisoners of War and Their Captors in World War II*, ed. Bob Moore and Kent Fedorowich, 181–204. Oxford: Berg, 1996.

Kleinschmidt, Johannes. "Antwort auf Martin Meyer." *Amerikastudien* 41 (1996): 499–500.

———. "Besatzer und Deutsche: Schwarze GIs nach 1945." *Amerikastudien* 40 (1995): 647–65.

———. *"Do Not Fraternize": Die schwierigen Anfänge deutsch-amerikanischer Freundschaft, 1944–49*. Mosaic: Studien und Texte zur amerikanischen Kultur und Geschichte, Band 1. Trier: WVT Wissenschaftler Verlag, 1997.

Knauer, Wolfram. " 'Jazz, GI's und German Fräuleins': Einige Anmerkungen zur deutsch-amerikanischen Beziehung im musikalischen Nachkriegsdeutschland." In *Ekkehard Jost: Festschrift zum 65. Geburtstag*, ed. Bernd Hoffmann et al., *Jazzforschung Jazz Research* 34 (2002): 77–88.

Koeppen, Wolfgang. *Pigeons on the Grass*. Trans. David Ward. New York: Holmes & Meier, 1988.

———. *Tauben im Gras*. Stuttgart: Scherz & Goverts Verlag, 1951.

Koikari, Mire. "Rethinking Gender and Power in the U.S. Occupation of Japan, 1945–1952." *Gender & History* 11 (1999): 313–35.

Koonz, Claudia. *Mothers in the Fatherland: Women, the Family, and Nazi Politics*. New York: St. Martin's Press, 1987.

Krehbiel, Henry Edward. *Afro-American Folksongs: A Study in Racial and National Music*. 1914. Reprint, New York: Frederick Ungar Publishing, 1962.

Kreuzer, Margot Dominika. "Die Entwicklung der heterosexuellen Prostitution in Frankfurt am Main von 1945 bis zur Gegenwart unter besonderer Betrachtung des Einflusses von Syphilis und AIDS." Doktorgrades der Medizin diss., Johann Wolfgang Goethe-Universität, 1987.

Kryder, Daniel. *Divided Arsenal: Race and the American State during World War II*. Cambridge: Cambridge University Press, 2000.

Kühl, Stefan. *The Nazi Connection: Eugenics, American Racism, and German National Socialism*. New York: Oxford University Press, 1994.

Kuhn, Annette. "Die stille Kulturrevolution der Frau: Versuch einer Deutung der Frauenöffentlichkeit, 1945–1947." In *Kulturpolitik im besetzten Deutschland, 1945–1949*, ed. Gabriele Clemens, 83–101. Stuttgart: Franz Steiner Verlag, 1994.

———. "Power and Powerlessness: Women after 1945, or the Continuity of the Ideology of Femininity." *German History* 7 (1989): 35–46.

Lange, Horst H. *Jazz in Deutschland: Die Deutsche Jazz-Chronik bis 1960*. Hildesheim: Olms Presse, 1996.

Lareau, Alan. "Jonny's Jazz: From *Kabarett* to Krenek." In *Jazz and the Germans: Essays on the Influence of "Hot" American Idioms on 20th-Century German Music*, ed. Michael J. Budds. Monographs and Bibliographies in American Music no. 17, series ed. Michael J. Budds. 19–60. Hillsdale, N.Y.: Pendragon Press, 2002.

Lebzelter, Gisela. "Die 'Schwarze Schmach': Vorurteile, Propaganda Mythos." *Geschichte und Gesellschaft* 11 (1985): 37–58.

Leder, Harald Thomas Oskar. "Americans and German Youth in Nuremberg, 1945–1956: A Study in Politics and Culture." Ph.D. diss., Louisiana State University, 1997.

Lee, Ulysses. *The Employment of Negro Troops*. The United States Army in World War II: Special Studies. Washington, D.C.: U.S. Government Printing Office, 1966.

Lemke Muniz de Faria, Yara-Colette. *Zwischen Fürsorge und Ausgrenzung: Afrodeutsche "Besatzungskinder" im Nachkriegsdeutschland*. Reihe Dokumente, Texte, Materialien: Veröffentlicht vom Zentrum für Antisemitismusforschung, vol. 43. Berlin: Metropol Verlag, 2002.

Leonard, Neil. *Jazz and the White Americans: The Acceptance of a New Art Form*. Chicago: University of Chicago Press, 1962.

Lerner, Gerda. *The Creation of Patriarchy*. New York: Oxford University Press, 1986.

Lester, Rosemarie K. "Blacks in Germany and German Blacks: A Little-Known Aspect of Black History." In *Blacks and German Culture*, ed. Reinhold Grimm and Jost Hermand, 113–34. Madison: University of Wisconsin Press, 1986.

Levine, Lawrence W. "Jazz and American Culture." *Journal of American Folklore* 102 (1989): 6–22.

Levine, Philippa. *Prostitution, Race, and Politics: Policing Venereal Disease in the British Empire*. New York: Routledge, 2003.

Lewis, David Levering. *W.E.B. Du Bois: Biography of a Race*. New York: Henry Holt, 1993.

Libby, Brian Arthur. "Policing Germany: The United States Constabulary, 1946–1952." Ph.D. diss., Purdue University, 1977.

Linke, Uli. *Blood and Nation: The European Aesthetics of Race*. Contemporary Ethnography, ed., Dan Rose and Paul Stoler. Philadelphia: University of Pennsylvania Press, 1999.

———. *German Bodies: Race and Representation after Hitler*. New York: Routledge, 1999.

Little, Monroe H., Jr. "The Black Military Experience in Germany: From the First World War to the Present." In *Crosscurrents: African Americans, Africa, and Germany in the Modern World*, ed. David McBride, Leroy Hopkins, and C. Aisha Blackshire-Belay, 177–96. Columbia, S.C.: Camden House, 1998.

Locke, Alain, ed. *The New Negro*, with an introduction by Arnold Rampersad. 1925. Reprint, New York: Atheneum, 1992.

Logan, Rayford W., ed. *What the Negro Wants*. Chapel Hill: University of North Carolina Press, 1944.

Lott, Eric. *Love and Theft: Blackface Minstrelsy and the American Working Class*. New York: Oxford University Press, 1993.

Lotz, Rainer E. "Schwarze Entertainer in der Weimarer Republik." In *Zwischen Charleston und Stechschritt: Schwarze im Nationalsozialismus*, ed. Peter Martin and Christine Alonzo, 255–61. Hamburg: Dölling und Galitz Verlag, 2004.

Lüdtke, Alf, Inge Marßolik, and Adelheid von Saldern, eds. *Amerikanisierung: Traum und Alptraum im Deutschland des 20. Jahrhunderts*. Stuttgart: Franz Steiner Verlag, 1996.

Lusane, Clarence. *Hitler's Black Victims: The Historical Experiences of Afro-Germans, European Blacks, Africans, and African Americans in the Nazi Era*. Crosscurrents in African American History, ed. Graham Russell Hodges and Margaret Washington. New York: Routledge, 2003.

MacGregor, Morris J., Jr. *Integration of the Armed Forces, 1940–1965*. Defense Studies Series. Washington, D.C.: Center of Military History, United States Army, 1981.

MacGregor, Morris J., Jr., and Bernard C. Nalty, eds. *Blacks in the United States Armed Forces: Basic Documents*. Vol. 7, *Planning for the Postwar Employment of Black Personnel*. Wilmington, Del.: Scholarly Resources, 1977.

———. *Blacks in the United States Armed Forces: Basic Documents*. Vol. 8, *Segregation under Siege*. Wilmington, Del.: Scholarly Resources, 1977.

MacMaster, Neil. *Racism in Europe, 1870–2000*. European Culture and Society, ed. Jeremy Black. New York: Palgrave, 2001.

Malanowski, Wolfgang, ed. *1945: Deutschland in der Stunde Null*. Reinbek bei Hamburg: SPIEGEL Verlag, 1985.

Marger, Martin N. *Race and Ethnic Relations: American and Global Perspectives*. 5th ed. Stamford, Conn.: Wadsworth/Thomson Learning, 2000.

Marks, Jonathan. *Human Biodiversity: Genes, Race, and History*. Foundations of Human Behavior. New York: Aldine de Gruyter, 1995.

Marks, Sally. "Black Watch on the Rhine: A Study in Propaganda, Prejudice and Prurience." *European Studies Review* 13 (1983): 297–334.

Martin, Peter. ". . . Als wäre gar nichts geschehen." In *Zwischen Charleston und Stechschritt: Schwarze im Nationalsozialismus*, ed. Peter Martin and Christine Alonzo, 700–710. Hamburg: Dölling und Galitz Verlag, 2004.

———. *Schwarze Teufel, edle Mohren*. Hamburg: Junius Verlag, 1993.

Martin, Peter, and Christine Alonzo, eds. *Zwischen Charleston und Stechschritt: Schwarze im Nationalsozialismus*. Hamburg: Dölling und Galitz Verlag, 2004.

Massaquoi, Hans J. *Destined to Witness: Growing Up Black in Nazi Germany*. New York: William Morrow and Company, 1999.

Massin, Benoit. "From Virchow to Fischer: Physical Anthropology and 'Modern Race Theories' in Wilhelmine Germany." In *Volksgeist as Method and Ethic: Essays on Boasian Ethnography and the German Anthropological Tradition*, ed. George W. Stocking Jr., 79–154, History of Anthropology, vol. 8. Madison: University of Wisconsin Press, 1996.

Mauldin, William Henry. "The War Isn't Won." In *Responsibility of Victory: Report of the New York Herald Tribune Annual Forum on Current Problems*, 204–7. New York: New York Tribune, 1945.

Medical Department, United States Army. *Preventive Medicine in World War II*. Vol. 5, *Communicable Diseases Transmitted through Contact or by Unknown Means*, prepared and published under the direction of Lieutenant General Leonard D. Heaton, The Surgeon General, United States Army. Washington, D.C.: Office of the Surgeon General, Department of the Army, 1960.

Meinecke, Friedrich. *The German Catastrophe: Reflections and Recollections*, trans. Sidney B. Fay. Cambridge, Mass.: Harvard University Press, 1950.

Merritt, Anna J., and Richard L. Merritt, eds. *Public Opinion in Occupied Germany: The OMGUS Surveys, 1945–1949*. With a foreword by Frederick W. Williams. Urbana: University of Illinois Press, 1970.

Merritt, Richard L. *Democracy Imposed: U.S. Occupation Policy and the German Public, 1945–1949*. New Haven, Conn.: Yale University Press, 1995.

Mershon, Sherie, and Steven Schlossman. *Foxholes and Color Lines: Desegregating the U.S. Armed Forces*, A RAND Book. Baltimore: Johns Hopkins University Press, 1998.

Meyer, Martin. *Nachkriegsdeutschland im Spiegel amerikanischer Romane der Besatzungszeit, 1945–1955*. AAA, Buchreihe zu den Arbeiten aus Anglistik und Amerikanistik, no. 9. Tübingen: Gunter Narr Verlag, 1994.

————. Replik: "Schwarze GIs im Nachkriegsdeutschland." *Amerikastudien* 41 (1996): 497–99.

Meyers Lexikon. 8th ed. Vol. 8, *Muskete-Rakete.* Leipzig: Bibliographisches Institut, 1940.

Miller, James A., Susan D. Pennybacker, and Eve Rosenhaft. "Mother Ada Wright and the International Campaign to Free the Scottsboro Boys, 1931–1934." *AHR* 106 (2001): 387–430.

Mills, Charles W. *The Racial Contract.* Ithaca, N.Y.: Cornell University Press, 1997.

Mitchell, Maria. "Materialism and Secularism: CDU Politicians and National Socialism, 1945–1949." *The Journal of Modern History* 67 (1995): 278–308.

Mitchell, Michele. "'The Black Man's Burden': African Americans, Imperialism, and Notions of Racial Manhood, 1890–1910." In *Complicating Categories: Gender, Class, Race and Ethnicity,* ed. Eileen Boris and Angélique Janssens, *International Review of Social History,* Supplement 7, 77–99. Cambridge: Press Syndicate of the University of Cambridge, 1999.

Möding, Nori. "Die Stunde der Frauen? Frauen und Frauenorganisationen des bürgerlichen Lagers." In *Von Stalingrad zur Währungsreform: Zur Sozialgeschichte des Umbruchs in Deutschland,* ed. Martin Broszat, Klaus-Dietmar Henke, and Hans Woller, 619–47. Munich: R. Oldenbourg Verlag, 1990.

Moeller, Robert G. "Introduction: Writing the History of West Germany." In Robert Moeller, ed., *West Germany under Construction: Politics, Society, and Culture in the Adenauer Era,* 1–30. Ann Arbor: University of Michigan Press, 1997.

————. *Protecting Motherhood: Women and the Family in the Politics of Postwar West Germany.* Berkeley: University of California Press, 1993.

————, ed. *West Germany under Construction: Politics, Society, and Culture in the Adenauer Era.* Social History, Popular Culture, and Politics in Germany, ed. Geoff Eley. Ann Arbor: University of Michigan Press, 1997.

Monod, David. *Settling Scores: German Music, Denazification, and the Americans, 1945–1953.* Chapel Hill: University of North Carolina Press, 2005.

Moore, Bob, and Kent Fedorowich, eds. *Prisoners of War and Their Captors in World War II.* Oxford: Berg, 1996.

Morehouse, Maggie M. *Fighting in the Jim Crow Army: Black Men and Women Remember World War II.* Lanham, Md.: Rowman & Littlefield Publishers, 2000.

Moskowitz, Eva S. *In Therapy We Trust: America's Obsession with Self-Fulfillment.* Baltimore: Johns Hopkins University Press, 2001.

Mosse, George L. *Nationalism and Sexuality: Respectability and Abnormal Sexuality in Modern Europe.* New York: Fertig, 1985.

————. *Toward the Final Solution: A History of European Racism.* New York: Oxford University Press, 1978.

Motley, Mary Penick. *The Invisible Soldier: The Experience of the Black Soldier, World War II.* Detroit: Wayne State University Press, 1987.

Myrdal, Gunnar. *An American Dilemma: The Negro Problem and Modern Democracy.* 2 vols. New York: Harper & Brothers, 1944.

Naimark, Norman M. *The Russians in Germany: A History of the Soviet Zone of Occupation, 1945–1949.* Cambridge, Mass.: Belknap Press of Harvard University Press, 1995.

Nalty, Bernard C. *Strength for the Fight: A History of Black Americans in the Military.* New York: Free Press, 1986.

Naumann, Christine. "African American Performers and Culture in Weimar Germany." In *Crosscurrents: African Americans, Africa, and Germany in the Modern World*, ed. David McBride, Leroy Hopkins, and C. Aisha Blackshire-Belay, 96–112. Columbia, S.C.: Camden House, 1998.

Naumann, Klaus, ed. *Nachkrieg in Deutschland*. Hamburg: Hamburger Edition, 2001.

Nelson, Keith. "The 'Black Horror on the Rhine': Race as a Factor in Post–World War I Diplomacy." *Journal of Modern History* 42 (1970): 606–27.

Niethammer, Lutz, ed. *"Hinterher merkt man, daß es richtig war, daß es schiefgegangen ist": Nachkriegserfahrungen im Ruhrgebiet*. Vol. 2, *Lebensgeschichte und Sozialkultur im Ruhrgebiet, 1930 bis 1960*. Berlin: Verlag J.H.W. Dietz Nachf., 1983.

Noakes, Jeremy. "The Development of Nazi Policy towards the German-Jewish 'Mischlinge' 1933–1945." *Leo Baeck Yearbook* 34 (1989): 291–354.

Noakes, Jeremy, and Geoffrey Pridham, eds. *Nazism 1919–1945*. Vol. 3, *Foreign Policy, War and Racial Extermination: A Documentary Reader*. Exeter Studies in History No. 13. Exeter: Exeter University Publications, 1988.

Norrell, Robert J. *The House I Live In: Race in the American Century*. Oxford: Oxford University Press, 2005.

Oguntoye, Katharina. *Eine afro-deutsche Geschichte: Zur Lebenssituation von Afrikanern und Afro-Deutschen in Deutschland von 1884 bis 1950*. Berlin: Hoho Verlag, Christine Hoffmann, 1997.

Oguntoye, Katharina, May Opitz, and Dagmar Schultz, eds. *Farbe Bekennen: Afro-Deutsche Frauen auf den Spuren ihrer Geschichte*. Berlin: Orlanda Verlag, 1986.

Omi, Michael, and Howard Winant. *Racial Formation in the United States: From the 1960s to the 1980s*. Critical Social Thought, ed. Michael Apple. New York: Routledge & Kegan Paul, 1986.

Ottley, Roi. *No Green Pastures*. New York: Charles Scribner's Sons, 1951.

Overmans, Rüdiger. *Deutsche militärische Verluste im Zweiten Weltkrieg*, Beiträge zur Militärgeschichte, Bd. 46. Munich: R. Oldenbourg Verlag, 1999.

Padover, Saul K. *Experiment in Germany: The Story of an American Intelligence Officer*. New York: Duell, Sloan, and Pearce, 1946.

———. "How the Nazis Picture America." *The Public Opinion Quarterly* (October 1939): 663–69.

Panish, Jon. *The Color of Jazz: Race and Representation in Postwar American Culture*. Jackson: University Press of Mississippi, 1997.

Papers of the NAACP. Part 9, *Discrimination in the U.S. Armed Forces, 1918–1955*. Series A: *General Office Files on Armed Forces' Affairs, 1918–1955*. Frederick, Md.: University Publications of America, 1989.

———. Series C: *The Veterans' Affairs Committee, 1940–1950*. Frederick, Md.: University Publications of America, 1989.

Paul, Heike. *Kulturkontakt und Racial Presences: Afro-Amerikaner und die deutsche Amerika-Literatur, 1815–1914*, American Studies—a Monograph Series, vol. 126. Heidelberg: Universitätsverlag Winter, 2005.

Peery, Nelson. *Black Fire: The Making of an American Revolutionary*. New York: New Press, 1994.

Peiss, Kathy, and Christina Simmons. "Passion and Power: An Introduction." In *Passion and Power: Sexuality in History*, ed. Kathy Peiss and Christina Simmons, with Robert A. Padgug, 3–13. Philadelphia: Temple University Press, 1989.

Pence, Katherine. "The 'Fräuleins' Meet the 'Amis': Americanization of German Women in the Reconstruction of the West German State." *Michigan Feminist Studies* 7 (1992–93): 83–108.

Penny, H. Glenn, and Matti Bunzl, eds. *Worldly Provincialism: German Anthropology in the Age of Empire.* Social History, Popular Culture, and Politics in Germany, ed. Geoff Eley. Ann Arbor: University of Michigan Press, 2003.

Peterson, Edward N. *The American Occupation of Germany: Retreat to Victory.* Detroit: Wayne State University Press, 1977.

Peukert, Detlev J.K. *Inside Nazi Germany: Conformity, Opposition, and Racism in Everyday Life.* Trans. Richard Deveson. New Haven, Conn.: Yale University Press, 1987.

Philipson, Robert. *The Identity Question: Blacks and Jews in Europe and America.* Jackson: University Press of Mississippi, 2000.

Plummer, Brenda Gayle. "Brown Babies: Race, Gender, and Policy after World War II." In *Window on Freedom: Race, Civil Rights, and Foreign Affairs, 1945–1988,* ed. Brenda Gayle Plummer, 67–92. Chapel Hill: University of North Carolina Press, 2003.

———. *Rising Wind: Black Americans and U.S. Foreign Affairs, 1935–1960.* Chapel Hill: University of North Carolina Press, 1996.

Poiger, Uta G. *Jazz, Rock, and Rebels: Cold War Politics and American Culture in a Divided Germany.* Berkeley: University of California Press, 2000.

———. "A New, 'Western' Hero? Reconstructing German Masculinity in the 1950s." In *The Miracle Years: A Cultural History of West Germany, 1949–1968,* ed. Hanna Schissler, 412–27. Princeton, N.J.: Princeton University Press, 2001.

Pollock, James K., James H. Meisel, and Henry L. Bretton, eds. *Germany under Occupation: Illustrative Materials and Documents.* Ann Arbor, Mich.: George Wahr Publishing, 1949.

Pommerin, Reiner, ed. *Culture in the Federal Republic of Germany, 1945–1995.* German Historical Perspectives, ed. Gerhard A. Ritter and Anthony J. Nicholls, vol. 11. Oxford: Berg, 1996.

———. "The Fate of Mixed Blood Children in Germany." *German Studies Review* 5 (1982): 315–23.

———. *"Sterilisierung der Rheinlandbastarde": Das Schicksal einer farbigen deutschen Minderheit, 1918–1937.* Düsseldorf: Droste Verlag, 1979.

Posner, David Braden. "Afro-America in West German Perspective, 1945–1966." Ph.D. diss., Yale University, 1997.

Potter, Pamela M. *Most German of the Arts: Musicology and Society from the Weimar Republic to the End of Hitler's Reich.* New Haven, Conn.: Yale University Press, 1998.

Proctor, Robert. *Racial Hygiene: Medicine under the Nazis.* Cambridge, Mass.: Harvard University Press, 1988.

"Psychology for the Fighting Man: Prepared for the Fighting Man Himself by a Committee of the National Research Council with the Collaboration of Science Service as a Contribution to the War Effort." 2nd ed. Washington, D.C.: Infantry Journal, Penguin Books, 1944.

Puckett, Dan J. "Hitler, Race, and Democracy in the Heart of Dixie: Alabamian Attitudes and Responses to the Issues of Nazi and Southern Racism, 1933–1946." Ph.D. diss., Mississippi State University, 2005.

Purkis, Charlotte. *Jonny spielt auf* entry in *New Grove Dictionary of Music and Musicians.* 2nd ed., ed. Stanley Sadie. New York: Grove Dictionaries, 2001, www. e-grove.com.

Radano, Ronald. "Hot Fantasies: American Modernism and the Idea of Black Rhythm." In *Music and the Racial Imagination*, ed. Ronald Radano and Philip V. Bohlman, with a foreword by Houston A. Baker Jr. Chicago Studies in Ethnomusicology, ed. Philip V. Bohlman and Bruno Nettl, 459–80. Chicago: University of Chicago Press, 2000.

Radano, Ronald, and Philip V. Bohlman, eds. *Music and the Racial Imagination.* With a foreword by Houston A. Baker Jr. Chicago Studies in Ethnomusicology, ed. Philip V. Bohlman and Bruno Nettl. Chicago: University of Chicago Press, 2000.

Raphael-Hernandez, Heike, ed. *Blackening Europe: The African American Presence*, with a foreword by Paul Gilroy. New York: Routledge, 2004.

Rasmussen, Birgit Brander, Eric Klinenberg, Irene J. Nexica, and Matt Wray, eds. *The Making and Unmaking of Whiteness.* Durham, N.C.: Duke University Press, 2001.

Reinders, Robert C. "Racialism on the Left: E. D. Morel and the 'Black Horror on the Rhine.'" *International Review of Social History* 13 (1968): 1–28.

Reiß, Matthias. *"Die Schwarzen waren unsere Freunde": Deutsche Kriegsgefangene in der amerikanischen Gesellschaft, 1942–1946.* Krieg in der Geschichte, vol. 11, ed. Stig Förster, Bernhard R Kroener, and Bernd Wegner. Paderborn: Ferdinand Schöningh, 2002.

Ringer, Fritz K. *The Decline of the German Mandarins: The German Academic Community, 1890–1933.* Cambridge, Mass.: Harvard University Press, 1969; Hanover, N.H.: Wesleyan University Press, published by University Press of New England, 1990.

Rodnick, David. *Postwar Germans: An Anthropologist's Account.* New Haven, Conn.: Yale University Press, 1948.

Roediger, David, ed. *Black on White: Black Writers on What It Means to Be White.* New York: Schocken Books, 1998.

———. *The Wages of Whiteness: Race and the Making of the American Working Class.* New York: Verso, 1991.

Rogers, J. A. "Jazz at Home." In *The New Negro,* ed. Alain Locke, with an introduction by Arnold Rampersad. 1925. Reprint, New York: Atheneum, 1992.

Romano, Renee C. *Race Mixing: Black-White Marriage in Postwar America.* Cambridge, Mass.: Harvard University Press, 2003.

Rooy, Piet de. "Of Monkeys, Blacks, and Proles: Ernst Haeckel's Theory of Recapitulation." In *Imperial Monkey Business: Racial Supremacy in Social Darwinist Theory and Colonial Practice,* ed. Jan Breman, 7–34. Amsterdam: Vu University Press, 1990.

Rose, Sonya O. "Sex, Citizenship, and the Nation in World War II Britain." *AHR* 103 (1998): 1147–76.

Rosenberg, Alfred. *Race and Race History and Other Essays by Alfred Rosenberg.* Ed. and introduction by Robert Pois. Roots of the Right: Readings in Fascist, Racist and Elitist Ideology, ed. George Steiner. New York: Harper & Row, 1974.

Rosenberg, Jonathan. "'Sounds Suspiciously Like Miami': Nazism and the U.S. Civil Rights Movement, 1933–1941." In *The Cultural Turn: Essays in the History of U.S. Foreign Relations*, ed. Frank Ninkovich and Liping Bu. Chicago: Imprint Publications, 2001.

Ruffner, Kevin Conley. "The Black Market in Postwar Berlin: Colonel Miller and an Army Scandal." *Prologue* 34 (Fall 2002): 170–83.

Ruhl, Klaus-Jörg, ed. *Frauen in der Nachkriegszeit, 1945–1963*. Munich: Deutscher Taschenbuch Verlag, 1988.

Rupieper, Hermann-Josef. "Bringing Democracy to the Frauleins: Frauen als Zielgruppe der amerikanischen Demokratisierungspolitik in Deutschland, 1945–1952." *Geschichte und Gesellschaft* 17 (1991): 61–91.

———. *Die Wurzeln der westdeutschen Nachkriegsdemokratie: Der amerikanische Beitrag, 1945–1952*. Opladen: Westdeutscher Verlag, 1993.

Rupp, Leila. *Mobilizing Women for War: German and American Propaganda, 1939–1945*. Princeton, N.J.: Princeton University Press, 1978.

Sadji, Amadou Booker. *Das Bild des Negro-Afrikaners in der Deutschen Kolonialliteratur (1884–1945): Ein Beitrag zur literarischen Imagologie Schwarzafrikas*. Berlin: Dietrich Reimer Verlag, 1985.

Sauerteig, Lutz. *Krankheit, Sexualität, Gesellschaft: Geschlechtskrankheiten und Gesundheitspolitik in Deutschland im 19. und frühen 20. Jahrhundert*. Medizin, Gesellschaft und Geschichte, Jahrbuch des Instituts für Geschichte der Medizin der Robert Bosch Stiftung, ed. Robert Jütte, no. 12. Stuttgart: Franz Steiner Verlag, 1999.

Schaller, Karl Friedrich. "Polizei und Geschlechtskrankheitenbekämpfung." *Zeitschrift für Haut- und Geschlechtskrankheiten* 4 (1948): 296–99.

Scheck, Raffael. "'They Are Just Savages': German Massacres of Black Soldiers from the French Army in 1940." *The Journal of Modern History* 77 (2005): 325–44.

Schildt, Axel. "Die USA als 'Kulturnation': Zur Bedeutung der Amerikahäuser in den 1950er Jahren." In *Amerikanisierung: Traum und Alptraum im Deutschland des 20. Jahrhunderts*, ed. Alf Lüdtke, Inge Marßolek, and Adelheid von Saldern. Transatlantische historische Studien, ed. Detlef Junker, vol. 6, 256–69. Stuttgart: Steiner, 1996.

———. *Zwischen Abendland und Amerika: Studien zur westdeutschen Ideenlandschaft der 50er Jahre*. Ordnungssyteme: Studien zur Ideengeschichte der Neuzeit, ed. Dietrich Beyrau, Anselm Doering-Manteuffel, and Lutz Raphael, vol. 4. Munich: R. Oldenbourg Verlag, 1999.

Schissler, Hanna. "Introduction: Writing about 1950s West Germany." In *The Miracle Years: A Cultural History of West Germany, 1949–1968*, ed. Hanna Schissler, 3–15. Princeton, N.J.: Princeton University Press, 2001.

———, ed. *The Miracle Years: A Cultural History of West Germany, 1949–1968*. Princeton, N.J.: Princeton University Press, 2001.

———. "'Normalization' as Project: Some Thoughts on Gender Relations in West Germany during the 1950s." In *The Miracle Years: A Cultural History of West Germany, 1949–1968*, ed. Hanna Schissler, 359–75. Princeton, N.J.: Princeton University Press, 2001.

Schivelbusch, Wolfgang. *In a Cold Crater: Cultural and Intellectual Life in Berlin, 1945–1948*. Trans. Kelly Barry. Berkeley: University of California Press, 1998.

Schmidt, Uta C., Andreas Müller, and Richard Ortmann. *Jazz in Dortmund. Hot – Modern – Free – New*. Essen: Klartext Verlag, 2004.

Schmidt-Harzbach, Ingrid. "Eine Woche im April: Berlin 1945 — Vergewaltigung als Massenschicksal." *Feministische Studien* 2 (1984): 51–65.

Schmundt-Thomas, Georg. "America's Germany: National Self and Cultural Other after World War II." Ph.D. diss., Northwestern University, 1992.

———. "Hollywood's Romance of Foreign Policy: American GIs and the Conquest of the German Fraulein." *Journal of Popular Film and Television* 19 (1992): 187–97.

Schubert, Michael. *Der schwarze Fremde: Das Bild des Schwarzafrikaners in der parlamentarischen und publizistischen Kolonialdiskussion in Deutschland von den 1870er bis in die 1930er Jahre.* Beiträge zur Kolonial- und Überseegeschichte, no. 86. Stuttgart: Franz Steiner Verlag, 2003.

Schwab, Jürgen. *Der Frankfurt Sound: Eine Stadt und ihre Jazzgeschichte(n).* Frankfurt a.M.: Societäts-Verlag, 2004.

Shukert, Elfrieda Berthiaume, and Barbara Smith Scibetta. *War Brides of World War II.* Novato: Presidio Press, 1988.

Sieg, Katrin. *Ethnic Drag: Performing Race, Nation, Sexuality in West Germany.* Social History, Popular Culture, and Politics in Germany, ed. Geoff Eley. Ann Arbor: University of Michigan Press, 2002.

Simpson, David Michael. "The Moral Battlefield: Venereal Disease and the British Army during the First World War." Ph.D. diss., University of Iowa, 1999.

Simpson, J. A., and E.S.C. Weiner. *The Oxford English Dictionary.* 2nd ed. Vol. 6, *Follow–Haswed.* Oxford: Clarendon Press, 1989.

Sitkoff, Harvard. "Racial Militancy and Interracial Violence in the Second World War." *Journal of American History* 58 (December 1971): 661–81.

Smith, Graham. *When Jim Crow Met John Bull: Black American Soldiers in World War II Britain.* London: I. B. Tauris & Co., 1987.

Smith, Helmut Walser. "The Talk of Genocide, the Rhetoric of Miscegenation: Notes on Debates in the German Reichstag Concerning Southwest Africa, 1904–14." In *The Imperialist Imagination: German Colonialism and Its Legacy,* ed. Sara Friedrichsmeyer, Sara Lennox, and Susanne Zantop, 107–23. Ann Arbor: University of Michigan Press, 1998.

Smith, Jean Edward. *Lucius D. Clay: An American Life.* New York: Henry Holt, 1990.

———, ed. *The Papers of General Lucius D. Clay: Germany, 1945–1949.* 2 vols. Bloomington: Indiana University Press, 1974.

Smith, William Gardner. *Last of the Conquerors.* New York: Farrar, Straus and Co., 1948.

Smith, Woodruff D. *The German Colonial Empire.* Chapel Hill: University of North Carolina Press, 1978.

Snowball, David. "Controlling Degenerate Music: Jazz in the Third Reich." In *Jazz and the Germans: Essays on the Influence of "Hot" American Idioms on 20th-Century German Music,* ed. Michael J. Budds. Monographs and Bibliographies in American Music no. 17, series ed. Michael J. Budds, 149–66. Hillsdale, N.Y.: Pendragon Press, 2002.

Standifer, Leon C. *Binding up the Wounds: An American Soldier in Occupied Germany, 1945–1946.* Baton Rouge: Louisiana State University Press, 1997.

Steiert, Thomas. "Zur Musik- und Theaterpolitik in Stuttgart während der amerikanischen Besatzungszeit." In *Kulturpolitik im besetzten Deutschland, 1945–1949,* ed. Gabriele Clemens, 55–68. Stuttgart: Franz Steiner Verlag, 1994.

Steiner, John M., and Jobst Freiherr von Cornberg. "Willkür in der Willkür: Befreiungen von den antisemitischen Nürnberger Gesetzen." *VfZ* 46 (1998): 143–87.

Steinert, Johannes-Dieter. "Flüchtlinge und Vertriebene." In *Deutschland unter alliierter Besatzung, 1945–1949/55*, ed. Wolfgang Benz, 123–29. Berlin: Akademie Verlag, 1999.

Steininger, Rolf. *Deutsche Geschichte seit 1945: Darstellung und Dokumente in vier Bänden.* Vol. 1, *1945–1947.* Frankfurt a.M.: Fischer Taschenbuch Verlag, 1996.

Stephenson, Jill. *The Nazi Organization of Women.* London: Croom Helm, 1981.

———. *Women in Nazi Society.* London: Croom Helm, 1975.

Stern, Frank. "The Historic Triangle: Occupiers, Germans and Jews in Postwar Germany." In *West Germany under Construction: Politics, Society, and Culture in the Adenauer Era*, ed. Robert Moeller, 199–229. Ann Arbor: University of Michigan Press, 1997.

———. *The Whitewashing of the Yellow Badge: Antisemitism and Philosemitism in Postwar Germany.* Trans. William Templer. New York: Pergamon Press, published for the Vidal Sassoon International Center for the Study of Antisemitism, the Hebrew University of Jerusalem, 1992.

Stewart, John L. *Ernst Krenek: The Man and His Music.* Berkeley: University of California Press, 1991.

Stewart, Rex. *Boy Meets Horn,* ed. Claire P. Gordon. Michigan American Music Series, ed. Richard Crawford. Ann Arbor: University of Michigan Press, 1991.

Stocking, George, Jr. *Race, Culture, and Evolution: Essays in the History of Anthropology.* New York: Free Press, 1968.

———. *Victorian Anthropology.* New York: Free Press, 1987.

———, ed. *Volksgeist as Method and Ethic: Essays on Boasian Ethnography and the German Anthropological Tradition.* History of Anthropology, vol. 8. Madison: University of Wisconsin Press, 1996.

Stoler, Ann Laura. *Race and the Education of Desire: Foucault's History of Sexuality and the Colonial Order of Things.* Durham, N.C.: Duke University Press, 1995.

Stoll, Ulrike. *Kulturpolitik als Beruf: Dieter Sattler (1906–1968) in München, Bonn und Rom.* Veröffentlichungen der Kommission für Zeitgeschichte, Reihe B: Forschungen, Bd. 98. Paderborn: Ferdinand Schöningh, 2005.

Stoltzfus, Nathan. "The Limits of Policy: Social Protection of Intermarried German Jews in Nazi Germany." In *Social Outsiders in Nazi Germany*, ed. Robert Gellately and Nathan Stoltzfus, 117–44. Princeton, N.J.: Princeton University Press, 2001.

Stone, Vernon W. "German Baby Crop Left by Negro GI's." *The Survey* (November 1949): 579–83.

Sundquist, Eric J., ed. *The Oxford W.E.B. Du Bois Reader.* New York: Oxford University Press, 1996.

"Symposium: African Americans and U.S. Foreign Relations." *Diplomatic History* 20 (1996): 531–650.

Tapper, Melbourne. *In the Blood: Sickle Cell Anemia and the Politics of Race.* Critical Histories, ed. David Ludden. Philadelphia: University of Pennsylvania Press, 1999.

Tent, James F. *Mission on the Rhine: Reeducation and Denazification in American-Occupied Germany.* Chicago: University of Chicago Press, 1982.

Theweleit, Klaus. *Male Fantasies.* Trans. Stephen Conway, vol. 2. Minneapolis: University of Minnesota Press, 1987.

Timm, Annette F. "The Ambivalent Outsider: Prostitution, Promiscuity, and VD Control in Nazi Berlin." In *Social Outsiders in Nazi Germany*, ed. Robert Gellately and Nathan Stoltzfus, 192–211. Princeton, N.J.: Princeton University Press, 2001.

———. "The Legacy of *Bevölkerungspolitik*: Venereal Disease Control and Marriage Counselling in Post–WW II Berlin." *Canadian Journal of History* 33 (1998): 174–214.

Trial of the Major War Criminals before the International Military Tribunal, Nuremberg, 14 November 1945–1 October 1946. Washington, D.C.: U.S. Government Printing Office, 1951.

Trittel, Günter J. "Ernährung." In *Deutschland unter allierter Besatzung, 1945–1949/55*, ed. Wolfgang Benz, 117–23. Berlin: Akademie Verlag, 1999.

Tröger, Annemarie. "Between Rape and Prostitution: Survival Strategies and Chances of Emancipation for Berlin Women after World War II." Trans. Joan Reutershan. In *Women in Culture and Politics: A Century of Change*, ed. Judith Friedlander, Blanche Wiesen Cook, Alice Kessler-Harris, and Carroll Smith-Rosenberg, 97–117. Bloomington: Indiana University Press, 1986.

U.S. Congress. Senate. Special Committee Investigating the National Defense Program. *Investigation of the National Defense Program*. Part 42. 80th Cong., 1st sess., 1948. Washington, D.C.: U.S. Government Printing Office, 1948.

U.S. Department of State. *Germany, 1947–1949: The Story in Documents*. Washington, D.C.: U.S. Government Printing Office, 1950.

U.S. Office of Military Government. *Monthly Report of the Military Governor, 1945–49*. Office of Military Government, 1949. Wilmington, Del.: Scholarly Resources Inc., 1983.

Usborne, Cornelie. *The Politics of the Body in Weimar Germany: Women's Reproductive Rights and Duties*. Social History, Popular Culture, and Politics in Germany, ed. Geoff Eley. Ann Arbor: University of Michigan Press, 1992.

Vent, Helmut. *Verwahrlosung Minderjähriger: Die Verdeutlichung eines unbestimmten Rechtsbegriffes unter Berücksichtigung pädagogischer und soziologischer Kriterien*. Frankfurt a.M.: Haag Herchen Verlag, 1979.

Volk, Ludwig, ed. *Akten deutscher Bischöfe über die Lage der Kirche 1933–1945*. Vol. 6, *1943–1945*. Veröffentlichungen der Kommission für Zeitgeschichte, Bd. 38. Mainz: Matthias-Grünewald-Verlag, 1985.

Von Eschen, Penny M. *Satchmo Blows up the World: Jazz Ambassadors Play the Cold War*. Cambridge, Mass.: Harvard University Press, 2004.

von Hornbostel, Erich M. "American Negro Songs." *The International Review of Missions* 15 (1926): 748–53.

von Salomon, Ernst. *Der Fragebogen*. Hamburg: Rowohlt Verlag, 1951.

Wachendorfer, Ursula. "Weiß-Sein in Deutschland: Zur Unsichtbarkeit einer herrschenden Normalität." In *AfrikaBilder: Studien zu Rassismus in Deutschland*, ed. Susan Arndt, 87–101. Münster: Unrast, 2001.

Waegner, Cathy Covell. "Rap, Rebounds, and Rocawear: The 'Darkening' of German Youth Culture." In *Blackening Europe: The African American Presence*, ed. Heike Raphael-Hernandez, with a foreword by Paul Gilroy, 171–86. New York: Routledge, 2004.

Wagnleitner, Reinhold. *Coca-Colonization and the Cold War: The Cultural Mission of the United States in Austria after the Second World War*. Trans. Diana Wolf. Chapel Hill: University of North Carolina Press, 1994.

Waldmann, Guido, ed. *Rasse und Musik*. Musikalische Volksforschung: Eine Schriftenreihe, vol. 3. Berlin-Lichterfelde: C. F. Vieweg, 1939.

Ward, Brian. *Just My Soul Responding: Rhythm and Blues, Black Consciousness and Race Relations*. London: UCL Press, 1998.

Wehler, Hans-Ulrich. *Deutsche Gesellschaftsgeschichte*. Vol. 4, *Vom Beginn des Ersten Weltkriegs bis zur Gründung der beiden deutschen Staaten, 1914–1949*. Munich: Verlag C. H. Beck, 2003.

Weindling, Paul. *Health, Race and German Politics between National Unification and Nazism, 1870–1945*. Cambridge History of Medicine. Cambridge: Cambridge University Press, 1989.

Weingart, Peter, Jürgen Kroll, and Kurt Bayertz. *Rasse, Blut und Gene: Geschichte der Eugenik und Rassenhygiene in Deutschland*. Frankfurt a.M.: Suhrkamp, 1988.

Wertheim, Wim F. "Netherlands-Indian Colonial Racism and Dutch Home Racism." In *Imperial Monkey Business: Racial Supremacy in Social Darwinist Theory and Colonial Practice*, ed. Jan Breman, 71–88. Amsterdam: Vu University Press, 1990.

White, Osmar. *Conquerors' Road*. Cambridge: Cambridge University Press, 1996.

White, Shane, and Graham White. *Stylin': African American Expressive Culture from Its Beginnings to the Zoot Suit*. Ithaca, N.Y.: Cornell University Press, 1998.

White, Walter. *A Man Called White*. New York: Arno Press and the New York Times, 1969.

Wildenthal, Lora. *German Women for Empire, 1884–1945*. Durham, N.C.: Duke University Press, 2001.

———. "Race, Gender, and Citizenship in the German Colonial Empire." In *Tensions of Empire: Colonial Cultures in a Bourgeois World*, ed. Frederick Cooper and Ann Laura Stoler, 263–83. Berkeley: University of California Press, 1997.

Willenbacher, Barbara. "Zerrüttung und Bewährung der Nachkriegs-Familie." In *Von Stalingrad zur Währungsreform: Zur Sozialgeschichte des Umbruchs in Deutschland*, ed. Martin Broszat, Klaus-Dietmar Henke, and Hans Woller, 595–618. Munich: R. Oldenbourg Verlag, 1989.

Willis, F. Roy. *The French in Germany, 1945–1949*. Stanford, Calif.: Stanford University Press, 1962.

Willoughby, John. *Remaking the Conquering Heroes: The Social and Geopolitical Impact of the Post-War American Occupation of Germany*. New York: Palgrave, 2001.

———. "The Sexual Behavior of American GIs during the Early Years of the Occupation of Germany." *The Journal of Military History* 62 (1998): 155–74.

Woller, Hans. *Gesellschaft und Politik in der amerikanischen Besatzungszone: Die Region Ansbach und Fürth*. Munich: Oldenbourg, 1986.

Wright, Richard. "The American Problem—Its Negro Phase." In *Richard Wright: Impressions and Perspectives*, ed. David Ray and Robert M. Farnsworth, 9–16. Ann Arbor: University of Michigan Press, 1971.

Wynn, Neil A. *The Afro-American and the Second World War*. New York: Holmes & Meier, 1975.

———. "The Impact of the Second World War on the American Negro." *Journal of Contemporary History* 6 (1971): 42–53.

Zantop, Susanne. *Colonial Fantasies: Conquest, Family, and Nation in Precolonial Germany, 1770–1870*. Post-Contemporary Interventions. Durham, N.C.: Duke University Press, 1997.

Zeitler, Peter. *Neubeginn in Oberfranken, 1945–1949: Die Landkreise Kronach und Kulmbach*. Kronach: 1000 Jahre Kronach e.V., 1997.

Ziegler, Hans Severus. "Entartete Musik: Eine Abrechnung." In *Entartete Musik: Dokumentation und Kommentar zur Düsseldorfer Ausstellung von 1938*, revised and expanded edition, ed. Albrecht Dümling and Peter Girth, 174–90. Düsseldorf: dkv, der kleine Verlag, 1993.

Ziemke, Earl F. *The U.S. Army in the Occupation of Germany, 1944–1946*. Army Historical Series. Washington, D.C.: Center of Military History, United States Army, 1990.

Zimmermann, Heinz Werner. "The Influence of American Music on a German Composer." In *Jazz and the Germans: Essays on the Influence of "Hot" American Idioms on 20th-Century German Music*, ed. Michael J. Budds. Monographs and Bibliographies in American Music no. 17, series ed. Michael J. Budds, 179–201. Hillsdale, N.Y.: Pendragon Press, 2002.

Zink, Harold. *The United States in Germany 1944–1955*. Princeton, N.J.: Van Nostrand, 1957.

Index